THE GIST OF THE BIBLE

A Complete Handbook for Class
and Home Study

By

CHARLES A. SHOOK

Author of "Cumorah Revisited,"
"The True Origin of Mormon
Polygamy," "The True
Origin of the Book
of Mormon."

"Search the Scriptures"—JESUS

Wipf and Stock Publishers
EUGENE, OREGON

Wipf and Stock Publishers
199 West 8th Avenue, Suite 3
Eugene, Oregon 97401

The Gist of the Bible
A Complete Handbook for Class and Home Study
By Shook, Charles A.
Copyright©1916 by Shook, Charles A.
ISBN: 1-59244-329-X
Publication date 9/4/2003
Previously published by The Standard Publishing Company, 1916

PREFACE

This book is the result of systematic study prosecuted by the author, first, to better inform himself on Biblical history, and, secondly, to equip himself more fully for Bible-class work. It is intended to be just what its title states—the gist of the Bible. Not every Scriptural event is given. Those that are, have been described as briefly and tersely as possible, the main thought being to fix in the student's mind the systematic unfolding of sacred history as it has come down to us.

With this end in view, the author has followed the natural divisions of the Bible: first, giving the periods; then their subdivisions, and, lastly, the events themselves, each with its proper reference. The text of King James' Version has been made use of and Usher's chronology has been adopted, though, in a number of instances, new chronological data appear in the footnotes. A few points of interest and importance have also been elucidated in the footnotes. At the close of each study, questions covering the subject-matter discussed are given.

The divisions of the book are termed "studies" in the place of "lessons," because, in some instances, they are too lengthy to be considered at one time. The suggestion is made, therefore, that if this treatise should be used as a text-book for Bible classes, the lengthy studies be considered at two, or even at

PREFACE

three, different times instead of during one class hour.

The author wishes here to acknowledge the helpfulness of many authors whom he has consulted in the preparation of this work, especially Dr. C. I. Scofield's "Reference Bible" and Dr. J. A. Broadus' "Harmony of the Gospels."

If this book should lead some to a better understanding of God's word, so that in Bible-school work they might be better prepared to instruct others to Him be all the praise. THE AUTHOR.

ANSLEY, Neb.

CONTENTS

STUDY		PAGE
I	THE BIBLE	11
II	BIBLICAL INSPIRATION	18
III	BIBLICAL GEOGRAPHY	25
IV	BIBLICAL ETHNOLOGY	31
V	THE HOLY LAND	37
VI	JEWISH INSTITUTIONS	42
VII	THE CREATION	51
VIII	THE FALL	59
IX	THE ANTEDILUVIAN WORLD	64
X	THE FLOOD	71
XI	THE DISPERSION	76
XII	THE AGE OF THE PATRIARCHS—ABRAHAM	81
XIII	THE AGE OF THE PATRIARCHS—ISAAC	91
XIV	THE AGE OF THE PATRIARCHS—JACOB	97
XV	THE EGYPTIAN BONDAGE—JOSEPH	106
XVI	THE EXODUS—MOSES	118
XVII	THE CONQUEST OF CANAAN—JOSHUA	135
XVIII	THE PERIOD OF THE JUDGES	150
XIX	THE UNDIVIDED KINGDOM—SAUL	170
XX	THE UNDIVIDED KINGDOM—DAVID	184
XXI	THE UNDIVIDED KINGDOM—SOLOMON	211
XXII	THE DIVIDED KINGDOM—ISRAEL	223
XXIII	THE DIVIDED KINGDOM—JUDAH	251
XXIV	THE CAPTIVITIES	272
XXV	THE RETURN	289

CONTENTS

STUDY		PAGE
XXVI	THE PROPHETS	302
XXVII	THE PERSIAN PERIOD	317
XXVIII	THE GRECIAN PERIOD	331
XXIX	THE MACCABEAN PERIOD	343
XXX	THE ROMAN PERIOD	359
XXXI	THE PERIOD OF PREPARATION	375
XXXII	THE BEGINNINGS OF CHRIST'S MINISTRY	387
XXXIII	THE GREAT GALILEAN MINISTRY	393
XXXIV	THE PERIOD OF RETIREMENT	407
XXXV	THE CLOSING OF CHRIST'S MINISTRY	417
XXXVI	THE LAST WEEK	428
XXXVII	THE RESURRECTION DAYS	444
XXXVIII	THE BEGINNINGS OF THE CHURCH	451
XXXIX	THE LIFE OF PAUL	465
XL	THE NEW TESTAMENT WRITINGS	488

LIST OF MAPS

		PAGE
1	Map of Bible Lands	27
2	Map of Biblical Ethnology	33
3	Map of the Natural Divisions of Palestine	39
4	Map of the Dispersion of Noah's Posterity	77
5	Map of Palestine in the Time of the Patriarchs	83
6	Map of the Exodus	119
7	Map of Canaan at the Time of the Conquest	137
8	Map of the Division of Canaan	145
9	Map of Canaan in the Time of the Judges	151
10	Map of the Kingdom of Saul	171
11	Map of the Davidic Kingdom	185
12	Map of the Divided Kingdom	225
13	Map of the Captivities	273
14	Map of the Babylonian Empire	279
15	Map of the Persian Empire	319
16	Map of the Grecian Empire	333
17	Map of the Roman Empire	361
18	Map of Palestine in the Time of Christ	377
19	Map of Paul's Missionary Journeys	467

PART I. BIBLICAL INTRODUCTION

Study I. The Bible.
Study II. Biblical Inspiration.
Study III. Biblical Geography.
Study IV. Biblical Ethnology.
Study V. The Holy Land.
Study VI. Jewish Institutions.

STUDY I. THE BIBLE

I. MEANING OF THE TERM

Our word "Bible" is from the Greek *biblos*, which means "book."

II. THE NAMES WHICH THE BIBLE GIVES ITSELF

The Bible designates itself by various names, as follows: "The word of God" (Heb. 4:12); "the scriptures" (John 5:39); "the law and the prophets" (Luke 16:16), and "the oracles of God" (1 Pet. 4:11).

III. DIVISIONS OF THE BIBLE

The Bible is composed of sixty-six books, and is divided into two grand divisions known as the Old Testament and the New Testament, there being thirty-nine books in the former and twenty-seven in the latter.

I. THE OLD TESTAMENT

The Old Testament is divided into five divisions, which, with their designations and the names of their books, are as follows:

1. **Law** (five books): Genesis, Exodus, Leviticus, Numbers and Deuteronomy.
2. **History** (twelve books): Joshua, Judges, Ruth,

THE GIST OF THE BIBLE

1 Samuel, 2 Samuel, 1 Kings, 2 Kings, 1 Chronicles, 2 Chronicles, Ezra, Nehemiah and Esther.

3. **Devotion** (five books): Job, Psalms, Proverbs, Ecclesiastes and Song of Solomon.

4. **Major Prophets** (five books): Isaiah, Jeremiah, Lamentations, Ezekiel and Daniel.

5. **Minor Prophets** (twelve books): Hosea, Joel, Amos, Obadiah, Jonah, Micah, Nahum, Habakkuk, Zephaniah, Haggai, Zechariah and Malachi.

II. THE NEW TESTAMENT

The New Testament is also divided into five divisions, which, with their designations and the names of their books, are:

1. **Biography** (four books): Matthew, Mark, Luke and John.

2. **History** (one book): Acts.

3. **Special Letters** (fourteen books): Romans, 1 Corinthians, 2 Corinthians, Galatians, Ephesians, Philippians, Colossians, 1 Thessalonians, 2 Thessalonians, 1 Timothy, 2 Timothy, Titus, Philemon and Hebrews.

4. **General Letters** (seven books): James, 1 Peter, 2 Peter, 1 John, 2 John, 3 John and Jude.

5. **Prophecy** (one book): Revelation.

IV. THE ORIGINAL LANGUAGES OF THE BIBLE

The Bible was originally written in three languages—the Hebrew, Chaldee or Aramaic, and the Greek.

1. **The Old Testament.** The language of the entire Old Testament is Hebrew, excepting those pas-

THE BIBLE

sages in Dan. 2:4-7:28; Ezra 4:8-6:18; 7:12-26 and Jer. 10:11, which are in the closely related Chaldee or Aramaic.

2. The New Testament. The language of the New Testament is a simplified form of the Greek.

V. THE PRESERVATION OF THE BIBLE

The Bible has been preserved to us in its manuscripts, the versions made from these manuscripts and the quotations from it which appear in the writings of the early Church Fathers.

1. The manuscripts. The manuscripts of the Bible are those copies of it which were made in the same languages in which it was originally written. The oldest manuscript of the Old Testament (which we possess) dates from a little before the time of William the Conqueror. Of the New Testament, we have 2,080, eighty-three of which are *uncials; i. e.*, those written in capitals, and which date from before the tenth century of the Christian era; and 1,997 are *cursives; i. e.*, those written in a running hand, and which are of later date.[1] These manuscripts are written either upon parchment or vellum. The most important of the *uncial* manuscripts are:

(1) *The Codex Sinaiticus.* This manuscript was discovered by Tischendorf in the Convent of St. Catherine, at the foot of Mt. Sinai, in 1859, and is now preserved in the Royal Library at Petrograd. It contains all of the New Testament and the greater part of the Greek version of the Old, with the apocryphal Epistle of Barnabas and a portion of the

---
[1] Between the tenth and the fifteenth century, when the art of printing was invented.

Shepherd of Hermas. It dates from the first half of the fourth century.

(2) *The Codex Alexandrinus.* This codex was sent as a present to Charles I. of England, in 1628, by Cyril Lucar, the Greek Patriarch of Constantinople, who had brought it from Alexandria. It contains the Septuagint version of the Old Testament nearly complete and also most of the New. It dates from the close of the fourth, or the beginning of the fifth, century A. D.

(3) *The Codex Vaticanus.* This manuscript has been preserved since 1448 in the Vatican at Rome, where it is now jealously guarded by the Catholic Church. It contains most of both Testaments and is the rival of the Sinaiticus in point of antiquity.

(4) *The Codex Ephraemi.* This is a *palimpsest,* or a *codex rescriptus;* that is, a copy on which another work has been written over the faded letters of the original writing. About the twelfth century, the ancient Greek Scriptures of this manuscript were written over with the writings of a Syrian Christian of the fourth century by the name of St. Ephraem, hence its name. It is of about the same age as the Codex Alexandrinus, but it is supposed by some to be more accurate. It was brought from some unknown library in the East to Florence in 1535.

2. The versions. These are the translations of the Scriptures from their original languages into other tongues. The most important of the ancient versions are:

(1) *The Peshito Syriac.* This is a translation of both Testaments into the Syriac, or Aramean, the

THE BIBLE

language of northern Syria and upper Mesopotamia. It was made in the second century A. D.

(2) *The Old Latin.* This is a translation of the Bible made into Latin in the second century.

(3) *The Latin Vulgate.* A Latin version made by Jerome about 385 A. D., under the orders of Damasus, Bishop of Rome.

(4) *The Coptic.* This translation was made for the benefit of the Copts, or Egyptian Christians, before the close of the second century.

(5) *The Ethiopic.* A vernacular translation for the inhabitants of Abyssinia, made about the end of the fourth century A. D.

(6) *The Gothic.* The production of a Cappadocian monk, Ulphilas, about the year 375 A. D. It was made for the Goths who had lately crossed the northern borders of the Roman Empire.

(7) *The Armenian.* A translation into the Armenian language by Miesrob about the fifth century.

3. **The quotations.** So great is the number of Scriptural quotations in the writings of the early Church Fathers that it is said the Bible can nearly be reproduced from them alone.[1]

---

[1] A few examples will illustrate this: *Theophilus*, a writer of the second century, evidently refers to Matt. 6:4 in the following: "Thus he teaches those that do good not to boast, that they be not pleasers of men. 'Let not thy left hand know what thy right hand doeth.'" *Tatian:* "All things were made by him, and without him was not anything made" (John 1:3). *Clement of Alexandria:* "'Behold,' says Paul, 'the goodness and severity of God'" (Rom. 11:32). *Tertullian:* "Paul himself writes to the Philippians, 'If by any means I may attain to the resurrection of the dead'" (Phil. 3:11). *Irenaeus:* "And on this account the apostle, in the first Epistle to the Thessalonians, speaking thus, 'May the God of peace sanctify you wholly; and may your whole spirit, soul and body be preserved unto the coming of the Lord Jesus Christ'" (1 Thess. 5:23).

VI. ENGLISH TRANSLATIONS OF THE BIBLE

1. *Wycliffe's Translation.* This version appeared in the year 1380, and was immediately put under the ban by the Archbishop of Canterbury, who threatened excommunication to any one who should read it.

2. *Tyndale's Translation.* The work of William Tyndale, which was published at Worms in 1525. Its author was burned at the stake, October 5, 1536.

3. *Coverdale's Bible.* This version, the work of Miles Coverdale, appeared in 1535 and was prefaced with a fulsome dedication to King Henry VIII.

4. *Genevan Version.* The work, principally, of William Whittingham, Calvin's brother-in-law. It appeared in 1560 and became at once the people's book in both England and Scotland.

5. *Bishops' Bible.* The work of fifteen scholars appointed by Archbishop Parker in 1563-64. As eight of these were bishops, it was called "The Bishops' Bible." It was completed in the year 1568.

6. *King James' Version.* This translation was the work of forty-seven scholars appointed by King James II. in 1604. The work was completed in 1611.

7. *Revised Version.* The Revised Version was produced between the years 1870 and 1884 by eighty-two scholars, fifty-two of whom were from England and thirty from America. Fourteen years of labor were expended upon the Old Testament, but only ten upon the New, which was completed in 1880.

8. *The Emphasized Bible.* The work of the renowned scholar, J. B. Rotherham, of London, England, and published by The Standard Publishing Company,

THE BIBLE

QUESTIONS

What is the meaning of the term "Bible"? What names does the Bible give itself? How many books are there in the Bible? How many in the Old Testament? How many in the New Testament? Give the divisions of the Old Testament and the number and names of the books in each. Give the divisions of the New Testament and the number and names of the books in each. Name the books of the Old Testament. Name the books of the New Testament. Name the books of the entire Bible. In what languages was the Old Testament originally written? In what language was the New Testament originally written? By what means have the Scriptures been preserved to us? What is the difference between a manuscript and a version? What is an *uncial* manuscript? From before what century do the *uncial* manuscripts date? Name the four most important of the *uncial* manuscripts. Name seven of the ancient versions. What can you say about the Scriptural quotations in the writings of the early Church Fathers? Give the date of Wycliffe's translation. The date of Tyndale's. The date of Coverdale's. The date of the Genevan Version. The date of the Bishops' Bible. Give the date of the King James' translation. How many scholars were employed upon it? Give the date of the Revised Version. How many scholars were employed upon it? How long did they work upon the Old Testament? How long upon the New?

STUDY II. BIBLICAL INSPIRATION

The Bible is unlike all other books in that it is inspired of God. Paul declares:

"All scripture is given by inspiration of God, and is profitable for doctrine, for reproof, for correction, for instruction in righteousness: that the man of God may be perfect, throughly furnished unto all good works" (2 Tim. 3:16, 17).

In just what way the Bible has been inspired, is a much-discussed question, but two elements, a human and a divine, must be conceded. The divine element may be divided into two processes: first, *divine impulsion,* by which the Bible writers were impelled to write; secondly, *divine preservation,* by which in writing they were preserved from error.

But, while it is true that the Bible writers wrote through divine impulsion and under divine preservation, it is also true that each wrote in his own style and manner of expression, by which his writings may be distinguished from the writings of the others. As Christ possessed both a human and a divine side, so, also, the Bible possesses both a human and a divine side, and any theory of inspiration that does not recognize both can not be the true one. The blending of the human and divine elements in the Bible is forcibly brought out in the following Scripture:

"Holy men of God *spake*"—the human element: "as they were *moved by the Holy Ghost*"—the divine element (2 Pet. 1:21).

BIBLICAL INSPIRATION

Let us now pass to certain reasons that may be assigned for believing the Bible to be the inspired word of God.

I. THE BIBLE IS PROVED INSPIRED BY ITS WONDERFUL UNITY

Although the books of the Bible were written in different ages, in different countries, under different conditions and by different men, they constitute *one* book. These books may be compared to sixty-six links of a great chain, any one of which is essential to its integrity. How are we, then, to account for this remarkable book, the parts of which were written in different climes, in different ages and by different men, except upon the hypothesis that there was *one* great Mind operating through them all?

II. THE BIBLE IS PROVED INSPIRED BY THE WONDERFUL EFFECT IT HAS HAD UPON THE WORLD

No other book has exerted the influence for good upon the world that the Bible has. To this book, more than to any other agency, is due the world's progress in civilization, philanthropy and religion. It has transformed both individuals and nations; it has been the world's greatest standard in determining right from wrong; it has inspired those who love it with a desire to help their fellow-men, and it has given man hope in the hour of death. A book that has produced such an effect upon the world could only have emanated from the mind of God Himself.

III. THE BIBLE IS PROVED INSPIRED BY THE CORROBORATORY TESTIMONY OF SCIENTIFIC RESEARCH

A credible book may not be inspired, but an inspired book must be credible. So, if the Bible is what it claims to be, its historical statements must agree with the *established* facts of profane history. The opponents of the Bible, knowing the force of this argument, have ever sought zealously to show that it clashes with these established facts. They have declared that many of its kings are mere myths; that many of its descriptions of life and custom are overdrawn, and that many of its accounts are purely legendary. Most of these objections were raised before the inscriptions on the monuments were deciphered, and some of them have been so completely refuted since that they are no longer even referred to. As for the rest, it is the hope and expectation that, as the pick and shovel of the archeologist continue to turn up the records of the past, these, too, will be refuted, leaving the Bible to stand as a miracle of historical accuracy, which, when we consider the natural limitations and fallibility of the men who wrote it, could only be if it has emanated from the divine Mind.

First, the geographical descriptions of the Bible have been demonstrated to be in perfect agreement with the land. Major Condor declares that of the 840 places noticed in the Bible, fully three-fourths have already been discovered and marked on maps, and the geographical accuracy of the account given in the four Gospels is even conceded by skeptics

BIBLICAL INSPIRATION

themselves. Renan, the celebrated French doubter, says:

"I have traversed in all directions the country of the Gospels. I have visited Jerusalem, Hebron and Samaria; scarcely an important locality of the history of Jesus has escaped me. All this history, which at a distance seems to float in the clouds of an unreal world, thus took a form, a solidity which astonished me. The striking agreement of the texts with the places, the marvellous harmony of the Gospel ideal with the country which served it as a framework, were like a revelation to me. I had before my eyes a fifth Gospel, torn, but still legible."—*Life of Jesus*, pp. 30, 31.

Secondly, many of the historical accounts, which, for years, were either questioned or denied, have been fully corroborated by later research. It was long denied that the kings of Gen. 14:9—Chedorlaomer, Tidal, Amraphel and Arioch—were historical characters; but more recent investigations have fully identified them with Kudur Lagomer, Tugdula, Hammurabi and Ariaku of profane history. Many of the accounts in the history of Israel have also been fully substantiated by the Assyrio-Babylonian inscriptions. Such kings are mentioned as Omri, Ahab, Jehu, Menahem, Pekah and Hoshea, of Israel; Azariah, Ahaz, Hezekiah and Manasseh, of Judah; Hiram, of Tyre, and Ben-hadad, Hazael and Rezin, of Damascus. The Books of Esther and Daniel, which specially have been attacked by the critics, have likewise been wonderfully confirmed by archæological research, and many of the most serious objections have been refuted. For a long time it was denied that such a king as Belshazzar ever reigned upon a Babylonian throne; but, in 1854, his name was found on a brick

THE GIST OF THE BIBLE

at Mugheir, Ur of the Chaldees, by Rawlinson, and since then other facts have been brought to light which establish his claim to being an historical character.

Thirdly, if due respect is paid to figures of speech and the language of phenomena, the account of creation, as given in the first chapter of Genesis, is perfectly consistent with the origin of things as demonstrated by science. The beginning of the universe in a state in which all things were without form and void, the ascending scale of living things and the introduction of man as the climax of creation, are facts as basically scientific as they are basically Biblical.

IV. THE BIBLE IS PROVED INSPIRED BY THE TESTIMONY OF JESUS CHRIST

Most of those, even, who question the inspiration of the Bible, acknowledge Christ as the supreme Teacher. Yet our Lord bore testimony both to the inspiration of certain portions of the Old Testament and also of the New.

First, with Him the Old Testament was the infallible court of final appeal. He called the Fifth Commandment "the word of God" (Mark 7:10-13); He also applied the same expression to Ps. 82:6 (John 10:35); He frequently referred to "the law and the prophets" (Matt. 11:13), and He declared that the "scripture cannot be broken" (John 10:35).

Secondly, He spoke of some of the Old Testament writers as having been inspired of God. He declared that David called Him Lord by the Spirit (Matt. 22:43); He referred to Daniel as a prophet

BIBLICAL INSPIRATION

(Matt. 24:15), and He asserted that the words of Moses were the words of God (Mark 7:10-13).

Thirdly, He referred to the occurrences mentioned in the Old Testament as though there were no doubt as to their truthfulness. He referred to the creation of man, male and female, as a fact (Matt. 19:4, 5); He incidentally mentioned the feeding of the Israelites with manna (John 6:31); He called the attention of Nicodemus to the lifting up of the brazen serpent (John 3:14); He cited the destruction of Sodom as an illustration of the coming judgment (Luke 17:28, 29); He referred to the visit of the queen of Sheba (Matt. 12:42), and He spoke of the experience of Jonah as though it were an unquestioned fact (Matt. 12:40).

Fourthly, in respect to the New Testament, He taught His apostles that He would pray the Father and He would send them another Comforter, who would abide with them, teach them all things, bring all things to their remembrance and guide them into all truth (see John, chapters 14, 15, 16).

V. THE BIBLE IS PROVED INSPIRED BY THE FULFILLMENT OF ITS PROPHECIES

Peter declares that "holy men of God spake as they were moved by the Holy Ghost," and Paul says that God "at sundry times and in divers manners spake in time past unto the fathers by the prophets." That these assertions are true is proved by the fulfillment of the predictions in both the Old Testament and the New. Many of the prophecies concerning Israel, the neighboring nations, the birth and work of

THE GIST OF THE BIBLE

Christ, the church, the apostasy, and even conditions to prevail in the last days, have plainly come to pass. The second, seventh, eighth, ninth and eleventh chapters of Daniel, with that remarkable prophecy of our Lord in Matthew 24, Mark 13 and Luke 21, read almost like history, so perfectly have their predictions been met in the experiences of nations.

QUESTIONS

In what way is the Bible unlike all other books? Give the two elements in Biblical inspiration. Give the two processes of the divine element. What passage blends the two elements? Give five reasons for believing the Bible to be the inspired word of God. What can you say of the unity of the Bible? Of its effects upon the world? Of its agreement with history? What does Renan say of the agreement of the land and the book? What accounts in Bible history have been verified by the monuments? For what must we make allowance in the Biblical account of creation? Making this allowance, does the Bible disagree with what has been established by scientific research? How did Christ speak of the Old Testament? How did He speak of Moses, David and Daniel? What accounts in the Old Testament did Christ accept as historical? What did He teach the apostles as to their own inspiration? What can you say of the Bible prophecies?

STUDY III. BIBLICAL GEOGRAPHY

The lands of the Bible comprise adjacent portions of Asia, Africa and Europe, a territory that may be estimated at three thousand miles east and west by twenty-eight hundred north and south.

I. THE LANDS OF THE BIBLE

1. **Canaan.** The land of Canaan was that portion of territory which lay between the river Jordan and the Mediterranean Sea.
2. **Egypt.** The land of Egypt comprised that portion of northeastern Africa included in the northern Nile Valley and contiguous territory.
3. **Cush.** The Biblical Cush, or Ethiopia, lay south of Egypt, and took in what is now comprised in Nubia, Abyssinia, Kordofan and Senaar.
4. **Libya.** This country was in northern Africa, bordering on the Mediterranean Sea and west of Egypt.
5. **Arabia.** The country of Arabia lay southeast of Canaan.
6. **Phœnicia.** This country was north of Canaan and bordered on the Mediterranean Sea.
7. **Syria.** Syria was just east of Phœnicia.
8. **Asia Minor.** Asia Minor lay north of Phœnicia and the Mediterranean Sea.
9. **Armenia.** Armenia joined Asia Minor on the east.

THE GIST OF THE BIBLE

10. **Mesopotamia.** The land of Mesopotamia lay between the Tigris and Euphrates Rivers.
11. **Assyria.** The country of Assyria bordered Mesopotamia on the east.
12. **Babylonia.** Babylonia, or Chaldea, generally speaking, lay south of Assyria.
13. **Media.** Media lay east of Assyria.
14. **Elam.** Elam was south of Media.
15. **Persia.** Persia lay south of Elam and southeast of Babylonia.
16. **Greece.** This country is a peninsula projecting out from the European continent into the Mediterranean Sea.
17. **Macedon.** This country joined Greece on the north.
18. **Italy.** Italy is a peninsula projecting out from Europe into the Mediterranean Sea, west of Greece.

II. THE SEAS OF THE BIBLE

1. **Mediterranean.** The Mediterranean, the "great sea" of Bible history, lies south of Europe, west of Asia and north of Africa.
2. **Red.** The Red Sea is found between the continent of Africa and the peninsula of Arabia.
3. **Dead.** The Dead Sea is the name of that body of water which borders Canaan on the southeast.
4. **Galilee.** Galilee, or Tiberias, is the name of that fresh-water lake which lies directly east of Galilee in Palestine.
5. **Waters of Merom.** The "Waters of Merom," or Huleh, are a small fresh-water lake which lies north of the Sea of Galilee.
6. **Black.** The Black Sea lies north of Asia Minor.

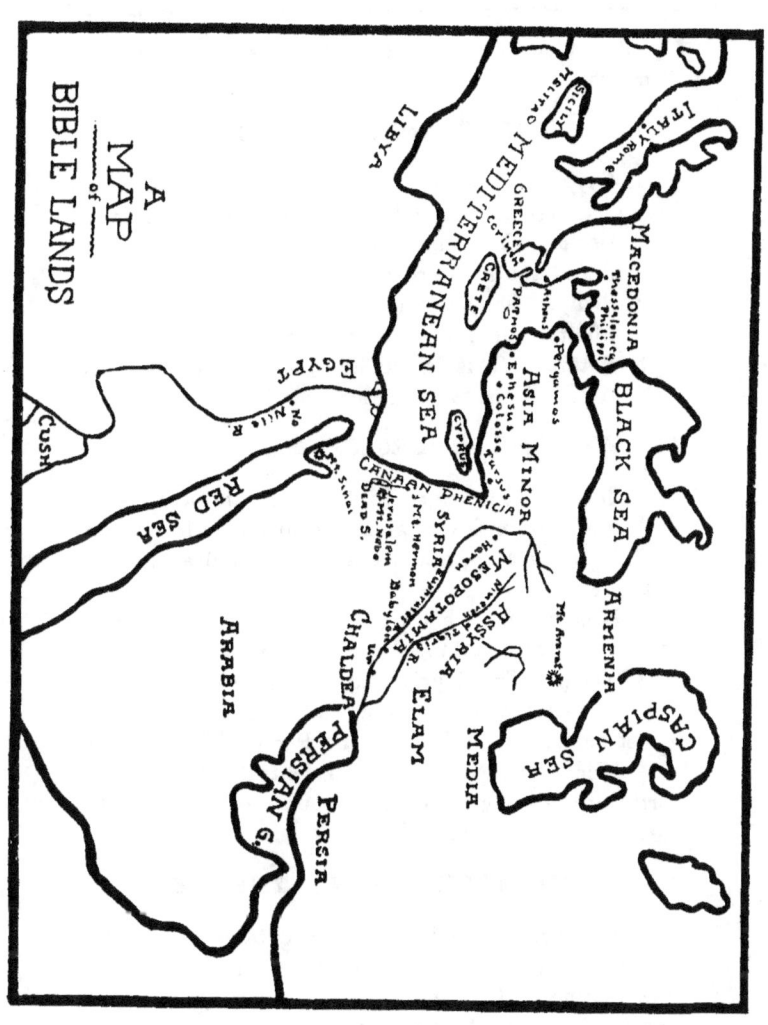

7. **Caspian.** The Caspian Sea lies northeast of Armenia.

III. THE ISLANDS OF THE BIBLE

1. **Cyprus.** This island is in the Mediterranean Sea, just west of Phœnicia and south of Asia Minor.
2. **Crete.** Crete lies in the same sea, west of Cyprus and southeast of Greece.
3. **Sicily.** Sicily lies just south of Italy.
4. **Melita.** Melita is south of Sicily.
5. **Patmos.** This island lies just off the coast of Asia Minor in the Ægean Sea.

IV. THE RIVERS OF THE BIBLE

1. **Jordan.** The river Jordan rises at the base of the Anti-Lebanon Mountains and flows south through the Waters of Merom and the Sea of Galilee into the Dead Sea.
2. **Euphrates.** This river rises in Armenia and flows southeast into the Persian Gulf.
3. **Tigris.** The Tigris also rises in Armenia, and, flowing eastward of the Euphrates, becomes one with it just before it empties into the Persian Gulf.
4. **Nile.** The Nile, rising in central Africa, flows northward, through the eastern part of Africa, into the Mediterranean Sea.

V. THE MOUNTAINS OF THE BIBLE

1. **Lebanon.** The Lebanon Mountains lie on the northern border of the land of Palestine.
2. **Carmel.** This is the name of the range that formed the natural boundary between Samaria and

BIBLICAL GEOGRAPHY

Galilee, and, running in a northwesterly direction, juts out into the Mediterranean Sea.

3. **Hermon.** This mountain is located in the northern part of Galilee.

4. **Tabor.** Tabor is located a short distance southwest of the Sea of Galilee.

5. **Calvary.** Calvary lies just north of Jerusalem.

6. **Olives.** The Mount of Olives lies just east of Jerusalem.

7. **Nebo.** This mountain, sometimes called Pisgah, lies just east of the northern extremity of the Dead Sea.

8. **Sinai.** Sinai is situated on the point of land known as the Sinaitic Peninsula, which extends southward into the Red Sea.

VI. THE CITIES OF THE BIBLE

1. **Jerusalem.** Jerusalem, the capital of the Jews, lies nearly midway between the northern extremity of the Dead Sea and the Mediterranean.

2. **Bethlehem.** This town was six miles south of Jerusalem.

3. **Nazareth.** Nazareth was located a few miles west of the Sea of Galilee in the country of the same name.

4. **Capernaum.** This city, which was the headquarters of our Lord during His Galilean ministry, stood on the northern shore of the Sea of Galilee.

5. **Cæsarea.** This city lay on the shore of the Mediterranean Sea, in a southwesterly direction from the Sea of Galilee and a northwesterly direction from Jerusalem.

THE GIST OF THE BIBLE

6. **Damascus.** This city lay a little northeast of Mount Hermon.

7. **Antioch.** Antioch lay almost due north of Damascus and just east of the Mediterranean Sea.

8. **Corinth.** This city was located in the central part of Greece.

9. **Athens.** Athens lay directly east of Corinth.

10. **Thessalonica.** This city was in Macedonia, on the shore of the Ægean Sea.

11. **Philippi.** Philippi lay nearly east of Thessalonica.

12. **Pergamos, Thyatira, Sardis, Philadelphia, Ephesus, Colosse, Troas, Miletus** and **Laodicea.** These cities, or towns, were in the province of Asia, Asia Minor.

13. **Babylon.** Babylon was located on the Euphrates River, almost directly east of Jerusalem.

14. **Nineveh.** The city of Nineveh lay almost directly north of Babylon, on the Tigris River.

15. **Noph.** This city was the same as Memphis, and was located on the Nile a few miles below where Cairo now stands.

QUESTIONS

Let the student be able to locate on the map each country, sea, island, river and city mentioned

STUDY IV. BIBLICAL ETHNOLOGY

In order properly to understand the history of God's chosen people, it is necessary for the student to have some knowledge of those nations by whom they were surrounded and with whom they maintained commercial and warlike relations during that period of time in which they occupied the Holy Land.[1]

I. THE CANAANITES

The Canaanites were the descendants of Canaan, the youngest son of Ham, and were the original possessors of the land of Canaan. Among their tribes may be mentioned the Amorites, Hittites, Jebusites, Girgashites, Perizzites and Hivites. Most of these tribes were small bodies, comprising, in some instances, only a single city. The Hittites, however, are known to have been a very strong and enterprising people.

II. THE PHILISTINES

The Philistines were a part of the posterity of Mizraim, the second son of Ham. In an early day they left Caphtor, in Egypt, and settled a small strip of Mediterranean seacoast in southwestern Canaan. They were the inveterate enemies of Israel, and long maintained five fortified cities—Gaza, Ashkelon, Ash-

---

[1] See "The Self-Interpreting Bible," Vol. I., p. 81, for a somewhat full account of the nations and peoples mentioned.

dod, Ekron and Gath. After suffering reverses under the Persians and Greeks, they were finally subdued by the Jews under Janneus, the grandnephew of Judas Maccabeus, about 88 B. C., with which they lost their national existence.

III. THE EGYPTIANS

The Egyptians were the descendants of Ham through Mizraim, and occupied the valley of the Nile and contiguous territory. They were among the most enlightened of the peoples of antiquity, and their history may be divided into three periods: The period of the Old Empire, from the earliest times to about 1900 B. C.; the period of the Hyksos, or Shepherd Kings, from 1900 to 1525 B. C., and the third period of the New Empire, from 1525 to 525 B. C., when the country passed under the rule of the Persians. In 332 B. C., Egypt passed into the hands of Alexander the Great, and, upon his death, was ruled for nearly three centuries by his successors, the Ptolemies, when, in B. C. 30, it passed under the dominion of Rome.

IV. THE CUSHITES

These people were the descendants of the eldest son of Ham. Originally they inhabited the country which lies southeast of Babylon and west of Persia, and which was known as Susiana or Chusistan; *i. e.,* "the country of Cush." Later they moved westward into Arabia, but finally settled in Africa, south of Egypt, in the country which is known as Abyssinia. In the Old Testament prophecies they are frequently spoken of in connection with the Egyptians.

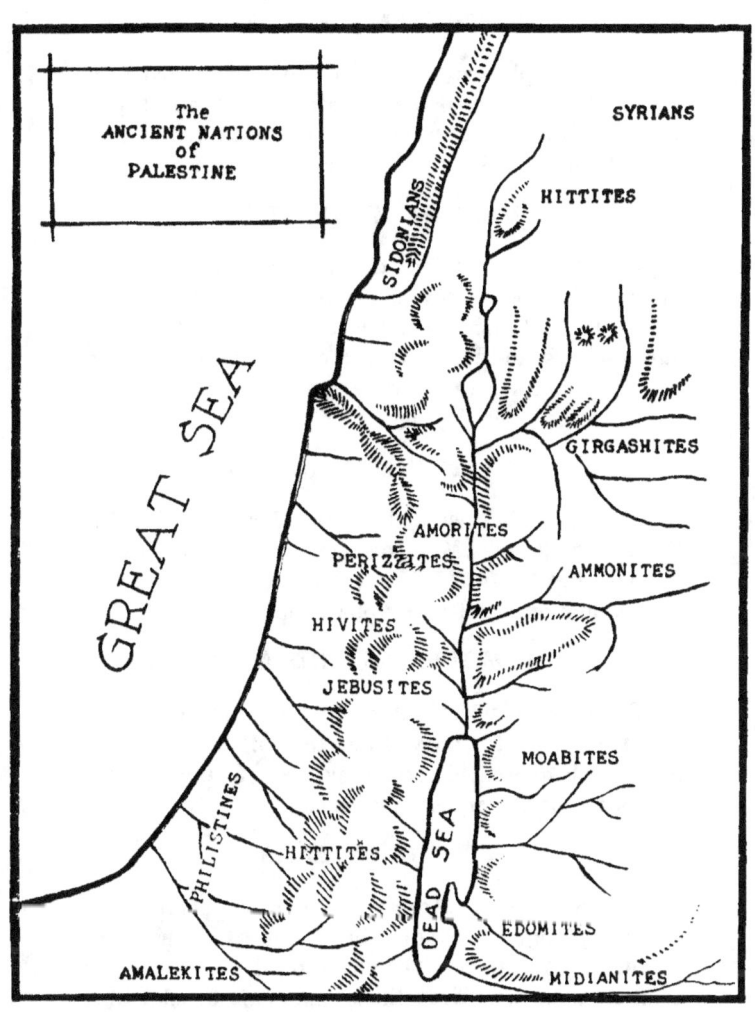

V. THE AMALEKITES

These people are thought to have descended from Ham. They occupied that territory south and southwest of Canaan and extending almost from the west gulf of the Red Sea to the Euphrates.

VI. THE EDOMITES

The Edomites were the descendants of Esau, brother of Jacob. They inhabited that territory which lay south of Judah. They were a nation of hunters and warriors, and were often in conflict with the Jews, with whom their remnant was at last forced to incorporate by John Hyrcanus.

VII. THE MIDIANITES

The Midianites were the descendants of Abraham through Keturah. Most of them dwelt southeast of Canaan, but eastward of the Edomites. They were a very immoral and idolatrous people.

VIII. THE MOABITES AND AMMONITES

These were closely allied and related tribes, descendants of Lot. They dwelt east of the Dead Sea. After a chequered history, they were finally reduced to a state of slavery by Janneus.

IX. THE SYRIANS

The Syrians, or Aramites, were the descendants of the youngest son of Shem and of Nahor, the brother of Abraham. Their country lay northeast of Canaan, and, in ancient times, extended considerably

BIBLICAL ETHNOLOGY

beyond the Euphrates. During the reign of David they came under the scepter of Israel, but afterwards revolted.

X. THE ASSYRIANS

This people was one of the most accomplished races of antiquity. They were the descendants of Shem through Ashur, and inhabited the valley of the Tigris, where they built Nineveh. For a long time they held supreme sway throughout that region, but in 625 B. C. their capital was taken by the combined forces of the Medes and Babylonians, when they passed under the scepter of the latter.

XI. THE BABYLONIANS

The Babylonians, or Chaldeans, were the descendants of Shem through Arphaxad. They inhabited the valley of the Euphrates, where it is claimed they erected Babylon upon the ruins of the Tower of Babel. At first they were a very accomplished race, and were the inventors of the cuneiform, or wedge-shape, style of writing, but, during the supremacy of Assyria, they degenerated and became little better than bands of thieving banditti. About 750 B. C., however, under Pul, they were again consolidated into a regular nation. In 625 B. C. they conquered Nineveh, and, later, extended their invasions throughout the west, even to Egypt. Under Nebuchadnezzar, they subjugated the Jews and led them away to Babylon between the years 606 and 585 B. C. They continued the strongest empire in the Orient from about 625 to 538 B. C., when Belshazzar, their last ruler, was overthrown by Cyrus.

XII. THE MEDO-PERSIANS

The Medes and the Persians were closely allied nations who lived eastward of Assyria and Babylonia. Under Cyrus, they extended their conquests until they were practically masters of the whole civilized world. After continuing as such for about two centuries, they fell before the power of Alexander the Great in 331 B. C.

XIII. THE GRECIANS

The Greeks were the descendants of Javan, a son of Japheth. They inhabited the peninsula of Greece and adjacent territory, and were divided into a number of petty nations; as, the Spartans, Athenians, Ionians, Æolians and Dorians. They were a race of sculptors, artists and poets. Under Alexander, they became the conquerors of the civilized world and spread their culture throughout both Asia and Africa.

XIV. THE ROMANS

The inhabitants of Italy were called Romans. They were the descendants of Japheth, either through Javan or Gomer. The kingdom of Rome was founded in 753 B. C., but it was not until about 60 B. C. that they attained the zenith of their glory and became the supreme power among the nations of the earth. It was under their reign that Christ was born.

QUESTIONS

Let the student give a description of each of the nations mentioned and described in the foregoing lesson.

STUDY V. THE HOLY LAND

The Holy Land proper extended from Mount Hermon on the north to Kadesh-barnea on the south, a distance of 180 miles. Its extreme breadth was one hundred miles and its average breadth, sixty-five miles. Within this territory occurred most of those events described in the Old and New Testaments.

I. NAMES OF THE HOLY LAND

1. **Canaan.** This was the original name and was given because its first inhabitants were the descendants of Canaan.

2. **Land of Promise.** The Holy Land was called the "Land of Promise" because of the promise that the Lord made to Abraham that it should be given to him and his seed after him for an everlasting possession.

3. **Land of Israel.** This name was applied to the Holy Land after its division among the twelve tribes.

4. **Judea.** Judea, or Judah, was the name first applied to the territory of the southern kingdom, but, after the Babylonian captivity, it was, in a rather loose way, applied to the whole territory.

5. **Palestine.** This is the designation by which the Holy Land has been known mainly since the time of Christ. It is derived from "Philistine," the name of the people who formerly inhabited its southwestern borders.

THE GIST OF THE BIBLE

II. NATURAL DIVISIONS OF THE HOLY LAND

The Holy Land is divided into seven natural divisions, as follows:

1. The Maritime Plain. This is the name of that lowland section which skirts the Mediterranean Sea and extends from Philistia on the south nearly to Asia Minor on the north. Below Carmel it is divided, about equally, into two divisions, the plain of Philistia and the plain of Sharon.

2. The Shephelah. This term is applied by our later geographers to that irregular mass of foothills which lies between the Philistine Plain and the mountains of Judah.

3. The Mountains of Judah. This is the name given to those mountains which extend nearly from the Carmel range on the north to Beer-sheba on the south.

4. The Valley of the Jordan. This is that very low and narrow valley through which flows the Jordan River.

5. The Plain of Esdraelon. This plain is a very narrow strip of lowland extending in a northwesterly direction from the valley of the Jordan to the Mediterranean Sea, just north of the Carmel range. It is one of the most fertile districts in Palestine.

6. The Mountains of Galilee. The mountains of Galilee lie north of the Carmel range and between the Mediterranean Sea and the river Jordan.

7. The Trans-Jordanic Highlands. These highlands comprise that part of the Holy Land which lies eastward of the valley of the Jordan.

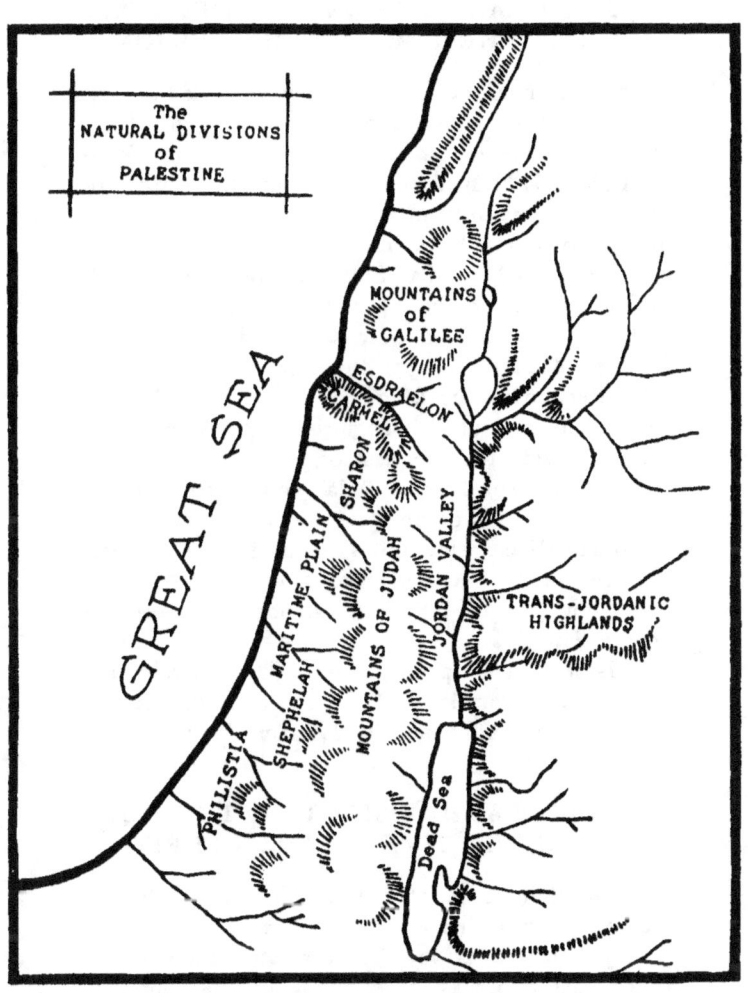

III. POLITICAL DIVISIONS OF THE HOLY LAND AT THE TIME OF THE DIVISION

Under Joshua, the Holy Land was divided among the twelve tribes, nine and one-half being given territory west of the Jordan and two and one-half (Reuben, Gad and the half-tribe of Manasseh) being provided with territory in the trans-Jordanic region. Under David, the boundaries of the kingdom were greatly extended, so that Solomon "reigned over all kingdoms from the river [Euphrates] unto the land of the Philistines, and unto the border of Egypt" (1 Kings 4:21). But, at the time of the division under Rehoboam, the kingdom had considerably diminished its size, until it comprised only about what it did following the conquest of Joshua.

1. **Judah.** The land of Judah comprised that territory lying south of an irregular line drawn from the Jordan River, a few miles north of the Dead Sea, to a point on the Mediterranean seacoast a short distance above where Jaffa now stands, and north of the Arabian Desert.

2. **Israel.** The land of Israel lay between the northern boundary-line of Judah and the Arnon River on the south, and the Lebanon Mountains on the north.

IV. POLITICAL DIVISIONS OF THE HOLY LAND IN THE TIME OF JESUS CHRIST

In the time of Christ, the Holy Land was divided into five political divisions, as follows:

1. **Judea.** Judea lay between an irregular line drawn east and west through about the center of

THE HOLY LAND

Palestine on the north, and the Arabian Desert on the south; the Dead Sea and the Jordan on the east, and the Mediterranean on the west.

2. **Samaria.** Samaria lay between the northern boundary of Judah on the south, and the Carmel Mountains and the city of Scythapolis on the north; the Jordan River on the east, and the Mediterranean Sea on the west.

3. **Galilee.** Galilee lay between the Carmel Mountains and the city of Scythapolis on the south, and the Lebanon Mountains on the north; the Jordan River and the Sea of Galilee on the east, and the Mediterranean on the west.

4. **Perea.** Perea was bounded on the north by the Yarmuk River, on the south by the river Arnon, on the east by the Arabian Desert, and on the west by the Dead Sea and the Jordan.

5. **Bashan.** Bashan was bounded on the north by Syria, on the east by the Arabian Desert, on the south by the Yarmuk, and on the west by the Sea of Galilee and the Jordan.

QUESTIONS

Give the length and breadth of the Holy Land. Give the different names of the Holy Land. Give the seven natural divisions of the Holy Land and locate each. Give the extent of the land of Israel in the days of Joshua. At the accession of Solomon. Give the extent of the territory of Judah. Of Israel. Name the political divisions in the time of Christ. Locate each.

STUDY VI. JEWISH INSTITUTIONS

The Jews were an intensely religious people, and, as such, had their places of worship, their religious observances, and, later in their history, were divided into a number of sects or religio-political parties.

I. JEWISH PLACES OF WORSHIP

1. The Tabernacle. The Tabernacle was the worshiping-place of the children of Israel during their wanderings in the wilderness, and was built according to the minute directions of God. It was a rectangular structure, 45 feet long, 15 feet wide and 15 feet high, made of acacia wood, the roof being composed of four curtains laid one upon another. The inside of the Tabernacle was separated into two apartments by a veil. The smaller of these apartments, which was 15x15 feet, was called the Holy of Holies and contained the ark of the covenant. The larger, which was 15x30 feet, was called the Holy Place and contained the table of showbread, the golden candlestick and the altar of incense. Around the Tabernacle was a wall made of wooden pillars, upon which was hung a linen curtain. The inclosed area was called the court, and was 150 feet long by seventy-five feet wide. In this court were found the brazen altar and the brazen laver.

2. The Temple. After Israel had become permanently settled in the Holy Land, they began to

JEWISH INSTITUTIONS

lay plans to build a permanent place of worship. This was accomplished during the reign of Solomon, when **Solomon's Temple** was built. This structure was erected upon the plan of the Tabernacle, with the exception that it was built of stable materials and that a number of courts were added. Solomon's Temple being destroyed by Nebuchadnezzar, **Zerubbabel's Temple** was erected upon the return from captivity. After some centuries, this temple was desecrated by Antiochus Epiphanes, and was later sacked by the Romans and was left in a dilapidated condition, but was afterwards rebuilt by Herod the Great, following which it was known as **Herod's Temple**. It was this temple that was standing in the time of Christ and was the one which was finally destroyed by Titus in 70 A. D.

3. **The Synagogue.** The Synagogue was an invention of the Jews after the Babylonian captivity. Meeting together for public worship, the places of such worship were designated "synagogues," from the Greek *sun*, "together," and *ago*, "to lead." The space within the synagogue, says Bissell, "was divided much on the same principle and in the same manner as that of the tabernacle and temple."—*Biblical Antiquities*, p. 313.

II. JEWISH SABBATHS

The Jews were required by their law to observe certain days, or periods, of rest. These days, or periods, were called sabbaths, or "rests," and were strictly observed by the Jews.

1. **The weekly sabbath.** This sabbath was observed on the seventh day of the week, and was a

requirement of the Fourth Commandment of the Decalogue.

2. **The lunar sabbath.** This sabbath was observed on the first day of the lunar month.

3. **The sabbatical month.** Tisri, the seventh month of the sacred year, was, in a sense, a sabbatical month.

4. **The sabbatical year.** During the seventh year, the land of Israel was supposed to rest. It was not to be sown; the vineyards were not to be dressed, and no fruit or produce was to be gathered.

5. **The year of jubilee.** Every fiftieth year was a year of jubilee. It began on the tenth day of the seventh month. Sacrifice being offered and the trumpet being blown, liberty was proclaimed to the captives and all alienated possessions were returned to their original owners.

III. JEWISH FEASTS

1. **The Passover.** This was a solemn festival observed during the week between the 14th and the 21st of Nisan (April), the first month of the sacred year, in commemoration of the deliverance of the first-born of Israel from the tenth plague that fell upon the Egyptians, when the angel of death smote their first-born.

2. **Pentecost.** This feast is also known as the "feast of weeks" or "harvest feast." It occurred fifty days after the 16th of Nisan, about the end of our May, and lasted one day.

3. **Tabernacles.** This feast was held in the autumn (October) upon the completion of the harvest. It lasted one week, during which Israel dwelt in

JEWISH INSTITUTIONS

booths in commemoration of their experiences in the wilderness. The three feasts just named are known as the greater feasts of Israel.

4. **Trumpets.** This feast announced the beginning of the new civil year and was observed in our month of October. It lasted just one day.

5. **Dedication.** The feast of dedication commemorated the purging of the temple, after its defilement by Antiochus Epiphanes, by Judas Maccabeus. It lasted eight days and was held in the month of December.

6. **Purim.** This feast was observed in March, lasted two days, and commemorated the deliverance of the Jews from the plot of Haman. The last three feasts were known as the lesser feasts of Israel.

IV. JEWISH OFFERINGS

1. **The Burnt-offering.** For this offering an unblemished male—bullock, ram or goat—was necessary. In the case of poor Jews, turtle-doves or tame pigeons were accepted. This offering was an atonement for sin.

2. **The Peace-offering.** Animals of various kinds were accepted for this offering, but doves were excluded as not sufficient for a common meal. This offering signified communion with God.

3. **The Sin-offering.** The sin-offering for the high priest was invariably a bullock; for the congregation, either a bullock or a male goat; for the ruler, a male goat, and for the private individual, a female goat, a female kid or a lamb. This offering signified reconciliation with God.

4. **The Trespass-offering.** For this offering a ram

or a male lamb was required. It was for those who sinned unwittingly in holy things and for other minor offenses and conditions. It signified forgiveness for actual transgression.

5. **The Meal-offering.** This was an offering of fruit or grain and was an expression of thanksgiving.

V. JEWISH SECTS AND PARTIES

1. **The Pharisees.** The term "Pharisees" means "separated ones," and was applied for the first time, about 200 B. C., to that body of Jews who professed an advanced degree of sanctity. The Pharisees held to the doctrines of the existence of angels, the terrestrial kingdom of the Messiah, the resurrection of the good and a mild form of fatalism.

2. **The Sadducees.** The Sadducees derived their name from one Sadok, about 260 years before Christ. They denied any future life, taught the free will of the individual and rejected all tradition, confining themselves mainly to the books of Moses. While comparatively few in numbers, they constituted the opulent and elevated class in the time of our Saviour.

3. **The Samaritans.** The Samaritans dwelt in Samaria between Judea and Galilee, and were the descendants of the heathen colonists who settled that country, under the direction of Esar-haddon, after the deportation of the ten tribes. Their religion was an admixture of Judaism and heathen superstitions.

4. **The Essenes.** Just when this sect arose is unknown. They were very plain in their dress and food, lived in societies, had their goods in common, observed a rigid morality, were strict in their observance

JEWISH INSTITUTIONS

of the sabbath, believed in the immortality of the soul, but denied the resurrection of the body, and held to a future state of rewards and punishments.

5. **The Herodians.** This sect, or party, favored the policies of Herod. They were not opposed to idolatrous worship, were in favor of instituting pagan games and denied any future life.

QUESTIONS

Describe the Tabernacle. Give the number and names of the Jewish temples and the circumstances under which each was erected. Give the origin of the synagogue. How many sabbatical days or periods did the Jews observe? Describe the weekly sabbath. The lunar sabbath. The sabbatical month. The sabbatical year. The year of jubilee. Give the names of the Jewish feasts. Describe the Passover. Pentecost. Tabernacles. Trumpets. Dedication. Purim. Name the Jewish offerings. Describe each. Who were the Pharisees? The Sadducees? The Samaritans? The Essenes? The Herodians?

PART II. OLD TESTAMENT HISTORY

Study VII.	The Creation.
Study VIII.	The Fall.
Study IX.	The Antediluvian World.
Study X.	The Flood.
Study XI.	The Dispersion.
Study XII.	The Age of the Patriarchs—Abraham.
Study XIII.	The Age of the Patriarchs—Isaac.
Study XIV.	The Age of the Patriarchs—Jacob.
Study XV.	The Egyptian Bondage—Joseph.
Study XVI.	The Exodus—Moses.
Study XVII.	The Conquest of Canaan—Joshua.
Study XVIII.	The Period of the Judges.
Study XIX.	The Undivided Kingdom—Saul.
Study XX.	The Undivided Kingdom—David.
Study XXI.	The Undivided Kingdom—Solomon.
Study XXII.	The Divided Kingdom—Israel.
Study XXIII.	The Divided Kingdom—Judah.
Study XXIV.	The Captivities.
Study XXV.	The Return.
Study XXVI.	The Prophets.

STUDY VII. THE CREATION

(Gen. 1:1-2:7)

INTRODUCTION

1. **The scope of Genesis 1.** The account of creation, as recorded in Genesis 1, undoubtedly covers vast epochs of time. It begins when God by His fiat first spoke order out of chaos, and closes when He formed man from the dust of the ground into His own image and likeness. It has been estimated that not fewer than one hundred million years have elapsed since the earliest life-forms appeared, which, being true, the account of the first chapter of Genesis must comprehend vast and incomprehensible ages.

2. **The significance of the term "day."** It has long been a mooted question whether the term "day," as employed in this chapter, must of necessity be understood literally or whether it may be understood representatively. The latter is now the prevailing opinion. It is probable that God revealed the stages of his great creative work to Moses in six consecutive visions, or tableaux,[1] each of which, being gradually introduced and gradually fading out, appeared to the prophet as an ordinary day, while they stood in the divine mind, with whom "one day is as a thousand years and a thousand years as

---

[1] Dr. E. Nisbet, in his "Science of the Day and Genesis," explains this view.

THE GIST OF THE BIBLE

one day," as representatives of great epochs of time.

3. **The purpose of the account.** It was certainly not the divine purpose in inspiring Moses to write the account of creation, to teach geology, or any other of the sciences. The great spiritual truth that God wished to impress was that the entire universe, and man, had their origin in Himself. Therefore, the account is brief and is stated in simple and popular, not scientifically—technical, language.

4. **The harmony between science and Genesis.** If the fact just stated is fully recognized, it will readily be seen that there is no vital inharmony between science and Genesis. In fact, the two agree in a number of important respects:

(1) Although a few scientists, as Spencer and Haeckel, have tried to dispense with the need of a sensient Creator by supposing that matter and motion, operating together, produced the first form, or forms, of life, the hypothesis of spontaneous generation is now rejected by most scientists as utterly incapable of proof and wholly unscientific.[1] It may be said, therefore, that science and the Bible agree in declaring that before all things there existed an almighty, sensient, creative power, whom we call God.

---

[1] "This doctrine [spontaneous generation] is equally at variance with science, revelation and common sense, and destitute of any foundation in fact."—*Sir J. W. Dawson, celebrated Canadian geologist.*

"The fact is that at the present moment there is not a shadow of trustworthy, direct evidence that abiogenesis [spontaneous generation] does take place, or has taken place, within the period during which the existence of life on the globe is recorded."—*Prof. T. H. Huxley.*

"Of this [spontaneous generation] we do not possess any actual proof. No one has ever seen a *generatio equivoca* really effected; and whoever supposes that it has occurred, is contradicted by the naturalist, and not merely by the theologian."—*Dr. Rudolph Virchow, the distinguished anatomist of Vienna.*

THE CREATION

(2) The Bible and science agree in the establishment of certain gradations of life by which we ascend from the lower to the higher forms.

(3) The Bible and science also seem to agree in fixing certain definite lines of demarkation between the species. In other words, "connecting links" are not found either in the Bible or in the rocks. So far as we can ascertain, laying aside certain mere evolutionary hypotheses or guesses, there has been no difference in character between the species at the time of their introduction and at the time of their passing out of existence.

5. **The date of man's creation.** The date of man's creation is wholly unknown and wholly unknowable. Archbishop Usher fixed upon 4004 B. C., but Origen gave 4830; Hales, 5411; Crawford, 12500, and Bunsen, 20000 B. C., as the correct date. This broad diversity among different scholars should teach us caution in attempting to fix the exact time when man first appeared upon the earth.

These few introductory remarks bring us to consider the great creative work of God as that work is revealed in the first and second chapters of Genesis.

I. THE FIRST DAY

At the opening of the first creative day, all was chaos, the earth being "without form and void." This description fully agrees with what is now known as the nebular hypothesis, according to which, at first, all things were in a nebulous state.[1] The first great

---
[1] See Chapter I., "The Story of the Earth and Man," by Sir J. W. Dawson, for an explanation of this theory from the viewpoint of the Christian scientist.

act of God was to create *light*, and to divide the light from the darkness, calling the light day and the darkness night.

"And the earth was without form, and void; and darkness was upon the face of the deep. And the Spirit of God moved upon the face of the waters. And God said, Let there be light: and there was light. And God saw the light, that it was good: and God divided the light from the darkness. And God called the light Day, and the darkness he called Night. And the evening and the morning were the first day" (Gen. 1:2-5).

II. THE SECOND DAY

On the second day the great Creator separated the *heaven* from the *earth* and divided "the waters which were under the firmament from the waters which were above the firmament," or the vapor in the aerial heavens above from the waters of the earth below.

"And God said, Let there be a firmament in the midst of the waters, and let it divide the waters from the waters. And God made the firmament, and divided the waters which were under the firmament from the waters which were above the firmament: and it was so. And God called the firmament Heaven. And the evening and the morning were the second day" (Gen. 1:6-8).

III. THE THIRD DAY

On the third day God separated the *land* from the *sea* and began the creation of *plant life*.

"And God said, Let the waters under the heaven be gathered together unto one place, and let the dry land appear: and it was so. And God called the dry land Earth; and the gathering together of the waters called he Seas: and God saw that it was good. And God said, Let the earth bring forth grass, the herb yielding seed, and the fruit tree yielding fruit after his kind, whose seed is in itself, upon the earth: and it was so. And the earth brought forth grass, and herb yielding seed after his

THE CREATION

kind, and the tree yielding fruit, whose seed was in itself, after his kind: and God saw that it was good. And the evening and the morning were the third day" (Gen. 1:9-13).

IV. THE FOURTH DAY

On the fourth day the *heavenly bodies became visible*. Prior to this time, the light had been diffused through nebulous clouds, but now these clouds were removed, and the sun, moon and stars became visible as distinct bodies. The word "made" of verse 16 does not imply a creative act; verses 14-18 are declarative of function merely.[1]

"And God said, Let there be lights in the firmament of the heaven to divide the day from the night; and let them be for signs, and for seasons, and for days, and years; and let them be for lights in the firmament of the heaven to give light upon the earth: and it was so. And God made two great lights; the greater light to rule the day, and the lesser light to rule the night: he made the stars also. And God set them in the firmament of the heaven to give light upon the earth, and to rule over the day and over the night, and to divide the light from the darkness: and God saw that it was good. And the evening and the morning were the fourth day" (Gen. 1:14-19).

V. THE FIFTH DAY

On the fifth day *fishes* and *birds* of every kind were introduced.

"And God said, Let the waters bring forth abundantly the moving creature that hath life, and fowl that may fly above the earth in the open firmament of heaven. And God created great whales, and every living creature that moveth, which the waters brought forth abundantly, after their kind, and every winged fowl after his kind: and God saw that it was good. And God

---

[1] For this explanation, see Dr. C. I. Schofield's "Reference Bible" at this place.

blessed them, saying, Be fruitful, and multiply, and fill the waters in the seas, and let fowl multiply in the earth. And the evening and the morning were the fifth day" (Gen. 1:20-23).

VI. THE SIXTH DAY

The first act of the sixth day was the creation of *cattle, creeping things* and *beasts of the earth*. The second act was the *creation of man*. Some have supposed that the accounts of the creation of man, as given in chap. 1:26, 27 and chap. 2:7, are not accounts of the same creative act, but that the first refers to the creation of the spirit and the second to the formation of the body. This position is incorrect, the first being the *general,* and the second the *particular,* account.

"And God said, Let the earth bring forth the living creature after his kind, cattle, and creeping thing, and beast of the earth after his kind: and it was so. And God made the beast of the earth after his kind, the cattle after their kind, and every thing that creepeth upon the earth after his kind: and God saw that it was good. And God said, Let us make man in our image, after our likeness: and let them have dominion over the fish of the sea, and over the fowl of the air, and over the cattle, and over all the earth, and over every creeping thing that creepeth upon the earth. So God created man in his own image, in the image of God created he him; male and female created he them" (Gen. 1:24-27)

"And the Lord God formed man of the dust of the ground, and breathed into his nostrils the breath of life; and man became a living soul" (Gen. 2:7).

From these accounts we draw three important truths:

1. *God* created man. He has not always existed; he has not been produced by spontaneous generation; he is the work of God.

2. God *created* man. He was not evolved from the

THE CREATION

brutes, independent of divine power; he was the creation of God. If we take this view, it is not necessary, as has been charged, that we adopt the unscientific theory of creation independent of law. The creation of man may be reasonably assumed to have been consistent with that law of which God was the great Lawgiver. Creation without law is as erroneous as creation without God.[1]

3. God created *man*. Not men—many pairs—but a single pair from whom all races have sprung. During the past century the theory of *polygenism,* or the diverse origin of the human race, was held by such scholars as Morton, Agassiz, Nott and Gliddon. Agassiz claimed that the Almighty created seven distinct sources from whence the seven great divisions of humanity sprang. But this theory is now generally considered untenable, and scientists, both creationists and evolutionists, have pretty generally settled down to the conclusion that all men have sprung from one source, whatever that source may have been.[2] This is called the theory of *monogenism.*

VII. THE SEVENTH DAY

Completing His creative work, God *rested* on the seventh day.

"Thus the heavens and the earth were finished and all the host of them. And on the seventh day God ended his work which he had made; and he rested on the seventh day from all his work which he had made. And God blessed the seventh day, and

---
[1] See "The Story of the Earth and Man," pp. 340-42.
[2] "The theory of 'monogenism,' or the specific unity of man, is now adopted by most anthropologists."—*Dr. D. G. Brinton, in his "Myths of the New World," p. 63.*

sanctified it: because that in it he had rested from all his work which God created and made" (Gen. 2:1-3).

Two things are to be noticed:

1. **The seventh day was God's great rest-day.** On it He rested from all His creative work. This day has not yet had an end, for, while we read of the beginning and ending of the other six days, no limit is placed to this, by which we know that God is still resting.[1] The word "rested" does not imply that God was fatigued with his labor, but it is used simply in the sense of ended or completed. God completed His work and ceased to create.

2. **Not given to man.** While God rested on the seventh day, there is not a hint that it was *then* given to man. God hallowed and blessed it at creation, but it was not "made known" to man until the law was given on Mount Sinai (Neh. 9:14).

QUESTIONS

What can you say as to the scope of the account of creation as given in Genesis 1? Give the significance of the term "day." What is the purpose of the account? Give three points of agreement between science and Genesis. What can you say as to the date of man's creation? Give what occurred on the first day. On the second day. On the third day. On the fourth day. On the fifth day. On the sixth day. Who created man? Was man created or evolved from the lower forms of life? What can you say about the relation of law to creation? What is the theory of polygenism? Of monogenism? In what sense did God rest? Was the sabbath given to man at creation? If not, when was it given to him?

---

[1] God is simply resting from his *creative*, not his *redemptive*, **work**.

STUDY VIII. THE FALL

(Gen. 2:8-3:24)

INTRODUCTION

1. **The location of Eden** (Gen. 2:8). The Bible declares that after man had been created, he was placed in a garden eastward in Eden. The location of Eden has ever been a mooted question. The most reasonable hypotheses are that it either lay in the highlands of Armenia or else was in the valley of the Euphrates.

2. **The formation of Eve** (Gen. 2:21-25). After man had been placed in the garden, the Lord reasoned that "it is not good that man should be alone." He, therefore, caused a deep sleep to fall upon Adam and from one of his ribs formed Eve. Some one has said that woman was not taken from man's head that she might rule over him, nor from his feet that he might rule over her, but from his side that she might be his equal.

I. MAN'S ORIGINAL CONDITION

1. **It was one of innocence.** As originally created, man was as pure from defilement as a new-born babe. He was created morally upright:

> "Lo, this only have I found, that God hath made man upright; but they have sought out many inventions" (Eccl. 7:29).

2. It was one of dominion over the lower creatures.

"And out of the ground the Lord God formed every beast of the field, and every fowl of the air; and brought them unto Adam to see what he would call them: and whatsoever Adam called every living creature, that was the name thereof" (Gen. 2:19).

This was in agreement with the original promise, which was:

"Let them have dominion over the fish of the sea, and over the fowl of the air, and over the cattle, and over all the earth, and over every creeping thing that creepeth upon the earth" (Gen. 1:26).

3. It was one of labor.

"And the Lord God took the man, and put him into the garden of Eden to dress it and to keep it" (Gen. 2:15).

4. It was, evidently, one of exemption from death. Death is the consequence of sin, and, as sin had not yet been committed, death had not yet passed upon the race.

II. THE TEMPTER

1. The tempter was, without doubt, a personality. Notwithstanding some have made the devil a simple personification of sin, the general teaching of the Bible seems to prove that he is a *being* morally antithetical to God. He is called "the devil" (Matt. 4:1), "Satan" (Job 1:6), "father of lies" (John 8:44), "enemy" (Matt. 13:39), "prince of this world" (John 12:31), "prince of the power of the air" (Eph. 2:2), etc.

2. The tempter operated through a serpent (Gen. 3:1-15). We are not to suppose from the account

THE FALL

that a literal serpent became the devil. The serpent was simply the agent through which the devil operated in the deception. It seems probable from the account that originally this beast walked upright, and that as a result of the curse (Gen. 3:14) his species crawl upon the ground.

III. THE TEMPTATION

1. **The tree of the knowledge of good and evil** (Gen. 2:9). Among the trees of the garden, there were two sufficiently important to be mentioned, the "tree of life" and the "tree of the knowledge of good and evil." The latter was the test-tree of the temptation.

2. **The divine prohibition.** The Lord laid the following prohibition upon the tree of the knowledge of good and evil:

"Of every tree of the garden thou mayest freely eat: but of the tree of the knowledge of good and evil, thou shalt not eat of it: for in the day that thou eatest thereof thou shalt surely die" (Gen. 2:16, 17).

3. **The deception of the serpent** (Gen. 3:4, 5). Following the placing of the prohibition upon the tree of the knowledge of good and evil, the serpent appeared to the woman, both with a lie and a truth. The *lie* was: "Ye shall not surely die;" the *truth* was: "Ye shall be as gods, knowing good and evil."

4. **The fall of Eve and Adam** (Gen. 3:6). Flattered and deceived, the woman partook of the forbidden fruit, and gave it unto her husband also, and he did eat. Their eyes being then opened, they saw their nakedness and attempted to cover the same with aprons of fig leaves.

IV. THE CONSEQUENCES OF THE FALL

1. **Man was driven from the garden of Eden** (Gen. 3:23, 24). In other words, he lost Paradise, that beautiful home which God had specially prepared for him.

2. **The ground was cursed** (Gen. 3:17, 18). Thorns and thistles sprang up in place of the fruits which had grown spontaneously in Eden.

3. **Man was condemned to toil** (Gen. 3:19). He was to eat his bread in the sweat of his face until he returned to his dust.

4. **Sorrow and pain were introduced.**

"Unto the woman he said, I will greatly multiply thy sorrow and thy conception; in sorrow thou shalt bring forth children; and thy desire shall be to thy husband, and he shall rule over thee" (Gen. 3:16).

5. **Man became a sinner.**

"Wherefore, as by one man sin entered into the world, and death by sin; and so death passed upon all men, for that all have sinned" (Rom. 5:12).

6. **He became a mortal, dieable creature.** The clause of the prohibition, "Thou shalt surely die," evidently refers to physical death and means no more than "thou shalt become dieable."[1] That physical death is a consequence of the fall is made certain from the following declaration of Paul:

"For as in Adam all die, even so in Christ shall all be made alive" (1 Cor. 15:22).

---

[1] "From that moment thou shalt become mortal, and shall continue in a dying state till thou die."—*Paraphrase of Dr. Adam Clarke.* "Thou shalt be mortal."—*Greek of Symmachus.* "Thou shalt be subject to death."—*Targum of Jonathan.*

THE FALL

QUESTIONS

Give two hypotheses as to the location of Eden. Why was Eve created? Why was she taken from Adam's side? What was man's original state? What was the character of the tempter? Was the tempter a real serpent? What two trees of the garden are specially mentioned? Give the divine prohibition. How did the serpent deceive Eve? Give six consequences of the fall.

STUDY IX. THE ANTEDILUVIAN WORLD

(Gen. 4:1-6-12)

INTRODUCTION

The antediluvian epoch was that period of time which lay between the fall of man and the flood. The length of this period can not be determined, although many attempts have been made to do so.[1] The leading characters of the antediluvian world were Adam, Cain, Abel, Seth, Jared, Enoch, Methuselah, Lamech and Noah. During this period, the people progressed considerably in civilization, but also delved deeply into sin and corruption.

I. THE FIRST MURDER

(Gen. 4:1-15)

Immediately after the fall, men began to offer sacrifices unto the Lord. These sacrifices, no doubt, were enjoined of the Lord, and were for the purpose of keeping before man the fact of his fall and also the fact of the coming Sacrifice through the

---

[1] "The Hebrew chronology may be computed with accuracy to the era of the building of the Temple, or at least to the division of the tribes—tenth century B. C. In the interval between that date and the arrival of Abraham in Palestine, Hebrew chronology can not be ascertained with exactness, but may be computed with near approximation to the truth. Beyond Abraham, we can never know how many centuries, nor even how many chiliads of years, may have elapsed since the first man of clay received the image of God and the breath of life."—*Dr. Charles Pritchard, quoted in "Science of the Day and Genesis," p. 101.*

shedding of whose blood he should be redeemed from sin and death. The two sons of Adam, Cain and Abel, brought sacrifices unto the Lord. Cain's consisted of the "fruit of the ground," while Abel brought of the "firstlings of his flock." The offering of Abel was accepted, while that of Cain was rejected, evidently because it was not typical of the bleeding Sacrifice that was afterwards offered on Mount Calvary. Because of this, Cain was jealous of Abel, and in his wrath slew him. The Lord then asked Cain where his brother was, to which Cain replied: "Am I my brother's keeper?" The Lord answered: "What hast thou done? the voice of thy brother's blood crieth unto me from the ground." Cain was then cursed, and was told that he should be a fugitive and a vagabond in the earth.

II. LONGEVITY

(Gen. 5:1-32)

The record tells us that the people of the antediluvian world lived to great ages. Adam was 930 years old when he died. Seth was 912. Enos was 905. And Methuselah was 969. The great age that has been attributed to the antediluvians has been objected to by the enemies of the Bible as impossible, and this part of the account has been relegated to the realms of mythology. The defenders of the Bible have met this objection in two ways: First, some have contended that such names as Abel, Seth, Methuselah and Jared were mere tribal designations. Thus, one has suggested that Abel was the name of a tribe of shepherds who were extirpated by the predatory clan of Cain; that Jared, which means "ruling," was the name of a dominant clan or tribe which exercised supreme authority, etc. Others have contended that the account is to be taken literally, but that the age of the antediluvians was *miraculously* prolonged, or was due to the character of the lives they lived and the fact that sin and death had not become so virulent as in after years. If we take the account literally, we must attribute the great age of the antediluvians wholly to the miraculous intervention of God, and then it will not be necessary to understand that all men attained to such extreme lengths of life, but only those whose names are mentioned. On this point, Jamieson, Fausset and Brown, in their "Commentary," say:

"The most striking feature in this catalogue is the longevity of Adam and his immediate descendants. . . . It is useless to inquire whether and what secondary causes may have contributed to this protracted longevity—vigorous constitutions, the nature of their diet, the temperature and salubrity of the climate; or, finally, as this list comprises only the true worshippers of God, whether their great age might be owing to the better government of their passions, and the quiet, even tenor of their lives. Since we can not obtain satisfactory evidence upon these points, it is wise to resolve the fact into the sovereign will of God."

III. ANTEDILUVIAN CIVILIZATION.

The Bible teaches that the people of the antediluvian world were not mere savages, but that they had attained to a considerable degree of civilization.

1. **Herdsmen.** Some of the descendants of Lamech were herdsmen:

THE ANTEDILUVIAN WORLD

"And Adah bare Jabal: he was the father of such as dwell in tents, and of such as have cattle" (Gen. 4:20).

2. **Musicians.** Others of the descendants of Lamech were musicians:

"And his brother's name was Jubal: he was the father of all such as handle the harp and organ" (Gen. 4:21).

3 **Metallurgists.** Still others of the descendants of Lamech worked in the metals:

"And Zillah, she also bare Tubal-cain, an instructor of every artificer in brass and iron: and the sister of Tubal-cain was Naamah" (Gen. 4:22).

4. **Builders.** The art of building seems to have made progress in the days before the flood:

"And Cain knew his wife; and she conceived and bare Enoch: and he builded a city, and called the name of the city, after the name of his son, Enoch" (Gen. 4:17).

IV. THE SINS OF THE ANTEDILUVIAN WORLD

The antediluvian world was exceedingly sinful. Sins that beggar description were practiced and evil was rampant.

1. **Forgetfulness of God.** Notwithstanding their high degree of culture and the blessings of the Lord, the antediluvians were very forgetful of God. In fact, in no age since has there been so much spiritual carelessness as in that age just preceding the flood. This is shown by the great proportion of evil against the small proportion of good.

2. **Immorality.** It seems that in this age, so soon after God had created *one* woman for *one* man,

polygamy was introduced. Of Lamech, the account says:

"And Lamech took unto him two wives: the name of the one was Adah, and the name of the other Zillah" (Gen. 4:19).

The social sin was also rampant:

"And it came to pass, when men began to multiply on the face of the earth, and daughters were born unto them, that the sons of God saw the daughters of men that they were fair; and they took them wives of all which they chose" (Gen. 6:1, 2).

Some, as the Rabbins, most of the Church Fathers, Luther, Stier, Alford, Kurtz and Delitszch, have thought that "the sons of God" were angels who consorted with the daughters of men, and the *Codex Alexandrinus* renders the phrase "the angels of God," but most modern Bible students are of the opinion that "the sons of God" were the godly descendants of Seth who became enamored and consorted with the godless descendants of Cain, thereby wrecking their faith and plunging themselves into wickedness.

3. Violence. It seems, also, that deeds of violence were practiced by the antediluvians.

"The earth also was corrupt before God, and the earth was filled with violence" (Gen. 6:11).

4. Sinful imaginations. So exceedingly sinful were the antediluvians that their every thought was evil:

"And God saw that the wickedness of man was great in the earth, and that every imagination of the thoughts of his heart was only evil continually" (Gen. 6:5).

THE ANTEDILUVIAN WORLD

5. **But all of those who lived before the flood were not evil.** Of Enoch we read:

"And Enoch walked with God: and he was not; for God took him" (Gen. 5:24).

Again, of Noah it is said:

"But Noah found grace in the eyes of the Lord" (Gen. 6:8).

V. THE WARNING TO THE ANTEDILUVIANS

But, notwithstanding the exceeding sinfulness of the people of the antediluvian world, God did not inflict punishment upon them without first giving them an adequate warning and an opportunity to repent.

1. **The preacher.** The one who was divinely called to warn the antediluvian world of the impending judgment was Noah, the son of Lamech.

2. **The message.** The message that Noah delivered, according to Peter (2 Pet. 2:5), was a message of "righteousness," from which we infer that its burden was the immorality and corruption of those days, as well as the emphasizing of the thought of judgment.

3. **The length of Noah's ministry.** Although the length of time in which Noah preached righteousness to the antediluvians is not given, the account is that the Lord said:

"My spirit shall not always strive with man, for that he also is flesh: yet his days shall be an hundred and twenty years" (Gen. 6:3).

This was the time of the "longsuffering of God,"

which makes it probable that the length of Noah's ministry was 120 years, if not longer.

4. **The results of Noah's ministry.** (1) The world was made responsible before God for its own condition and end. (2) Eight souls, including Noah, were saved from destruction in the flood.

QUESTIONS

Define the expression "antediluvian epoch." Name the leading characters of this epoch. Give two reasons for the sacrifices that were offered. Who was the first murderer? Who was the first man murdered? How old was Adam? How old was Methuselah? What objection is made to the longevity of the antediluvians? Give the two theories of those who accept the Bible account. If we accept the account as literal, how may the great age of these men be explained? If we accept the account literally, is it necessary for us to understand that all of the antediluvians attained to such great ages? Give four occupations that were followed in antediluvian times. Were all who lived before the flood wicked people? Mention nine who were not. Through whom did God warn the antediluvians? What was the character of his message? Give the length of God's longsuffering. Give the results of Noah's ministry.

STUDY X. THE FLOOD

(Gen. 6:13-8:22)

INTRODUCTION

1. **The flood a divinely-sent judgment.** Unlike most similar occurrences, the flood was not simply a natural cataclysm, due to natural causes, but was a divinely-sent judgment upon the antediluvian world on account of its sins.

2. **Traditions of the flood.** Traditions of the flood are widely extant. They are found among nations in all parts of the world, both enlightened and unenlightened. Lenormant, the great Oriental scholar, says: "Among all the traditions which concern the history of primitive humanity, the most universal is that of the flood." These traditions have been found among the Chaldeans, Hindoos, Chinese, Persians, Greeks and many other peoples.

I. THE BUILDING OF THE ARK

(Gen. 6:13-22)

The ark was a vessel made of gopherwood, 450 feet long, 75 feet wide and 45 feet high.[1] It contained a window, a door in the side, and was built

---

[1] A cubit, originally, was the distance from the elbow to the extremity of the middle finger, or about eighteen inches in length. The sacred cubit was nearly twenty-two inches in length. Whether or not the above dimensions are correct, depends upon the cubit meant.

with three stories. It was pitched both within and without. Into this vessel, with Noah and his family, were received animals of various kinds: those that were unclean in pairs, male and female, and those that were clean in sevens. With these was also gathered "all food that is eaten," both for man and beast.

II. THE CAUSES OF THE FLOOD

(Gen. 7:11, 12)

We have already mentioned the fact that the purpose of God to inflict punishment upon the ungodly was the primal cause of the flood; but there were also two secondary causes: (1) *Rain*. For forty days and forty nights it rained incessantly, but this was not sufficient to inundate the earth. So (2) *the fountains of the great deep were broken up*. This, undoubtedly, was the main secondary cause of the flood. The ground probably sank, and the water, gushing up from its bowels, covered the entire land. That such an occurrence is possible is proved by the geological record.

III. THE EXTENT OF THE FLOOD

(Gen. 7:19-24)

Because the Book of Genesis speaks of "all the high hills, that were under the whole heaven," as being covered with water, some have inferred that the flood covered the entire earth. But this supposition is now no longer considered tenable. Similar expressions are employed elsewhere in the Bible with undoubtedly restricted senses; for instance, in

THE FLOOD

Gen. 41:56 a famine is said to have been "over all the face of the earth," whereas it affected the land of Egypt and adjacent countries only. Again, in Deut. 2:25, it is said that the fear of Israel should be put "upon the nations that are under the whole heaven," which was true only of a limited area in the Old World. On the extent of the flood, Delitzsch says: "The Scripture demands the universality of the flood only for the earth as inhabited, not for the earth as such." Such a view can not be objected to as unscientific.

IV. THE DURATION OF THE FLOOD
(Gen. 7:11-8:14)

The period of time in which the waters prevailed upon the earth is said to have been 150 days (Gen. 7:24), but from the time that "the foundations of the great deep were broken up, and the windows of heavens were opened" (Gen. 7:11), to the time when the earth was dried (Gen. 8:14), was just one year and ten days.

V. THE BIRDS SENT OUT
(Gen. 8:6-12)

After the waters had prevailed upon the earth for 150 days, God remembered Noah and those that were with him in the ark, and made a wind to pass over the earth so that the waters were assuaged. The ark then rested upon the summit of Mount Ararat, and when the tops of the mountains began to appear, Noah opened the window of the ark and sent out a *raven*, which flew hither and thither until the waters were dried up. He also sent forth a *dove*, but as it found no rest for the soles of its feet, it returned. After seven days, the dove was sent out again and returned with an olive leaf, by which Noah knew that the waters had begun to go down. Seven days later, the dove was sent out again, but did not return.

VI. NOAH LEAVES THE ARK

When the waters were fully abated, Noah and his family, with the beasts that were in the ark, went forth upon the dry land.

1. **Noah builds an altar** (Gen. 8:20). No sooner did Noah reach the dry ground than he erected an altar and offered thereon burnt-offerings of every clean beast and clean fowl.

2. **The promise of Jehovah** (Gen. 8:21, 22). Probably in recognition of this act of worship, Jehovah made the following promise:

> "And the Lord smelled a sweet savour; and the Lord said in his heart, I will not again curse the ground any more for man's sake; for the imagination of man's heart is evil from his youth; neither will I again smite any more everything living, as I have done. While the earth remaineth, seedtime and harvest, and cold and heat, and summer and winter, and day and night shall not cease."

3. **The covenant of Jehovah** (Gen. 9:1-19). The Lord then enjoined upon man the duty of multiplying and replenishing the earth; declared the sacredness of human life (Gen. 9:5, 6), and established his covenant not only with man, but also with all of the beasts of the earth, that there should not "any more be a flood to destroy the earth" (Gen. 9:11).

THE FLOOD

The *token* of this covenant was the rainbow, which the Lord promised He would set in the clouds.

4. **Noah's drunkenness** (Gen. 9:20-27). After this, Noah became an husbandman and planted a vineyard. Making wine from the fruit of the vine, he became drunken in his tent. His son Ham, seeing his nude condition, told his brethren, Shem and Japheth, who, going backward, covered him with a garment. When Noah awoke from his drunkenness and discovered that Ham had informed his brethren of his condition, he said: "Cursed be Canaan; a servant of servants shall he be unto his brethren."

5. **Noah's death** (Gen. 9:28, 29). Noah lived 950 years, or about 350 years after the flood, when he died.

QUESTIONS

Was the flood simply a natural occurrence? What can you say about the traditions of the flood? Give a description of the ark. How did the animals go into the ark? Give two secondary causes of the flood. Why have some supposed that the waters of the flood covered the whole earth? How do you know that this was not necessarily so? What is the theory of the extent of the flood generally accepted at the present time? How long did the waters prevail upon the earth? Give the entire length of the period of the flood. How many birds were sent out and what were they? Why did Noah build an altar? What kind of beasts and fowls did he offer upon it? What was the promise of Jehovah? What was the token of the covenant? What sin did Noah commit? What curse did he pronounce upon Canaan? How old was Noah when he died? How long was it after the flood that his death occurred?

STUDY XI. THE DISPERSION
(Gen. 10:1-11:9)

INTRODUCTION

1. **The tower of Babel** (Gen. 11:1-9). Following the flood, the whole earth was of one speech, and, as they journeyed eastward, they came to the land of Shinar and dwelt there. Here they determined to build an enormous tower, whose top was to reach unto heaven, which was to be a memorial unto them so that they might not be scattered abroad. This tower is known to us as the "Tower of Babel," and is supposed to have been erected where the city of Babylon afterwards stood. When the Lord saw what the people were doing, He came down and confounded their language, so that they left off to build the city and were scattered upon the face of all the earth.

2. **The historical value of the table of nations.** The table of nations who are said to have sprung from Noah's sons, as that table is given in Genesis 10, is declared to possess historical value and to be both accurate and reliable. Says Rawlinson: "When we examine the groups which the author of the tenth chapter of Genesis has thrown together, we find, to say the least, a most remarkable agreement between the actual arrangement which he has made, and the conclusions to which ethnological inquirers

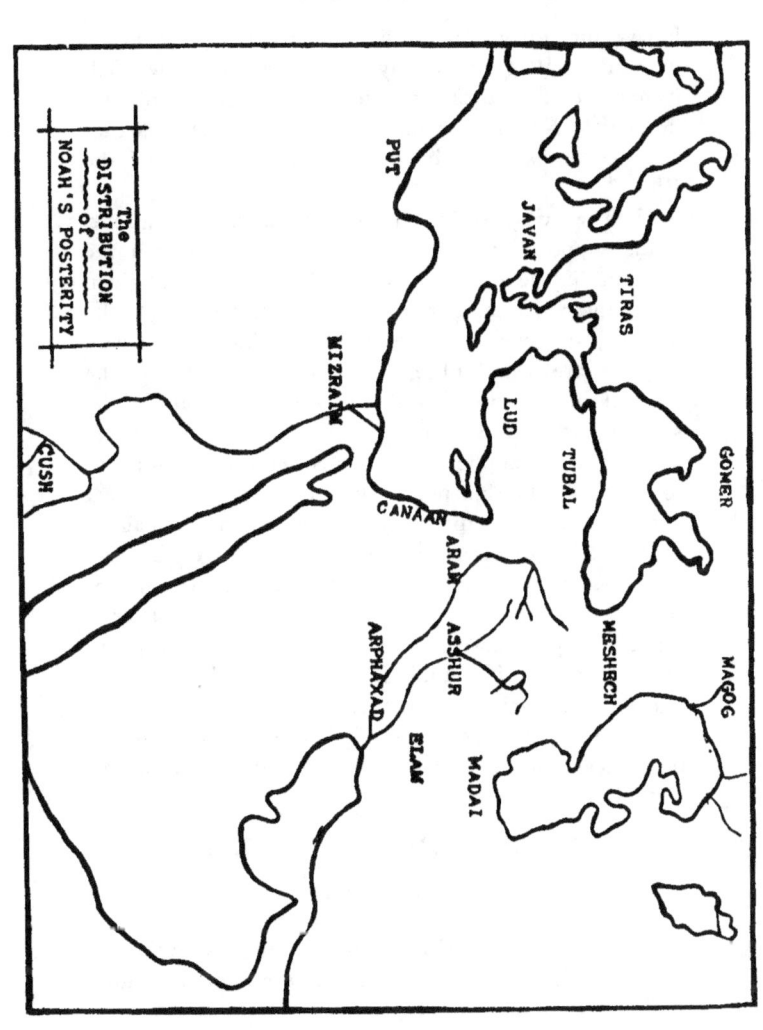

have come from a consideration of the facts of human language and physical type." While Delitzsch, in the latest edition of his "Commentary," declares: "Nowhere is found a survey of nations that can be compared with the ethnological table of the Bible."

3. **The outspreading and scattering of the nations.** Some suppose that there is a difference between the account of the *outspreading* of the nations, as given in chapter 10, and that of the *scattering* of the nations, as given in chap. 11:1-9. The first is said to antedate the building of the tower and to be general in its application; the second is said to be subsequent to the building of Babel, and to be restricted in its application to those countries adjacent to Shinar. On this point, the "Popular and Critical Biblical Encyclopedia" says: "An unbiased reading of the text appears most plainly to mark the distinctness, in time and character, of the two narratives. The first was universal, regulated, orderly, quiet and progressive; the second, local, embracing only a part of mankind, sudden, turbulent and attended with marks of the divine displeasure."

Let us now pass to establish the identification of the descendants of Noah with the nations known to history.

I. THE SONS OF JAPHETH

(Gen. 10:1-4)

1. **Gomer.** The Gomerites settled northwest of the Black Sea, and from them have come the Gauls, Britons, Russians and Germans.

THE DISPERSION

2. Magog. Magog settled north of the Caspian Sea, and from him sprang the Scythians.
3. Madai. Madai settled Media, south of the Caspian Sea, and from him came the Medes.
4. Javan. Javan settled Greece, and from him sprang the Greeks and Romans.
5. Tubal. Tubal settled between the Black and Caspian Seas, and from him have come the Iberians.
6. Meshech. Meshech settled between the Black Sea and the country of Armenia, and the Moschi have come from him.
7. Tiras. Tiras settled in the vicinity of Constantinople, and from him sprang the Thracians.

II. THE SONS OF HAM

(Gen. 10:6-20)

1. Cush. Cush journeyed southward from Babel and settled Ethiopia, or Cush, south of Egypt.
2. Mizraim. Mizraim settled Egypt, and from him sprang the Egyptians.
3. Phut. This son of Ham settled northern Africa, west of Egypt, and from him came the Libyans.
4. Canaan. Canaan settled in Palestine, and from him sprang the Canaanites.

III. THE SONS OF SHEM

(Gen. 10:21-31)

1. Elam. The descendants of Elam settled that country which lay east of Babylon. They were known as the Elamites.
2. Ashur. Ashur settled on the east bank of the river Tigris, and from him came the Assyrians.

THE GIST OF THE BIBLE

3. **Arphaxad.** Arphaxad settled on the Euphrates, and from him came the Babylonians or Chaldeans.

4. **Lud.** The children of Lud inhabited Asia Minor, and from them came the Lydians, from whom the country of Lydia was named.

5. **Aram.** Aram settled what is known as Syria, and from him came the Syrians.

QUESTIONS

Linguistically speaking, what were the inhabitants of the world immediately after the flood? What did they build? Where did they build it? What did they build in connection with the tower? What did God do? What can you say of the historical value of the table of nations as given in Genesis 10? Do Bible students agree that all the nations were scattered from Babel? What difference do they assume between the outspreading and the scattering of nations? Generally speaking, what continent did each of the sons of Noah colonize? How many sons did Japheth have? What nation, or nations, sprang from each? How many sons did Ham have? What nation, or nations, sprang from each? How many sons did Shem have? What nation, or nations, sprang from each?

STUDY XII. THE AGE OF THE PATRIARCHS—ABRAHAM

(Gen. 11:26-25:10)

INTRODUCTION

1. **The name "Abram."** This name, which was the first to be applied to that character about whom we are to study in this lesson, means "high father" "father of elevation." It was subsequently changed to "Abraham," which means "father of a multitude."

2. **The times in which Abraham lived.** Abraham lived in the twentieth and nineteenth centuries before Christ. At this time, Egypt was probably the strongest and most accomplished nation of the Old World, although Chaldea was not far behind. While he was born during the existence of the old Egyptian Empire, Abraham lived long after the Hyksos, or Shepherd Kings, had overthrown that power and had established a Semitic line upon the throne of Egypt. Chaldea was also basking in the smiles of fortune, and, in both countries, commerce, education and art flourished.

3. **Commercial intercourse.** The great nations of the time of Abraham carried on commerce with one another. The Nile, Mediterranean and Euphrates were great waterways of commerce, and carried the traffic of the civilized nations back and forth upon their bosoms. Great caravans, also, passing up the

Euphrates Valley, crossed over into Phœnicia and down through Canaan into Egypt, laden with the wares of Babylon, and returned, bringing with them the products of Egypt and Ethiopia. At this time the Chaldean writing, called the *cuneiform,* was the written language of trade and letters, and great libraries of cylinders and tablets of baked clay, bearing its peculiar wedge-shape characters, have been unearthed at Tel-el-Amarna, Egypt, and at other points in Oriental lands, which reveal the high degree of civilization that was enjoyed during those early times.

I. THE LIFE OF ABRAM BEFORE ENTERING CANAAN

1. **Abram at Ur** (Gen. 11:26-30). Abram was born in the city of Ur in the land of Chaldea, a short distance below the city of Babylon. This town is now known as Mugheir. His father's name was Terah, and the names of his two brothers were Nahor and Haran, the latter being the father of Lot. Haran died before they left Ur. It was at Ur that Abram obtained his beloved Sarah, and it was here (Acts 7:2-4) that the Lord made to him the promise that, if he would leave his kindred and his father's house, He would make him a great nation and that in him should all the families of the earth be blessed. Abram lived in idolatrous surroundings, and it is even said that his father was a manufacturer of idols.

2. **Abram at Haran** (Gen. 11:31-12:4). After the death of Haran and the marriage of Abram, Terah, taking his family and starting for Canaan,

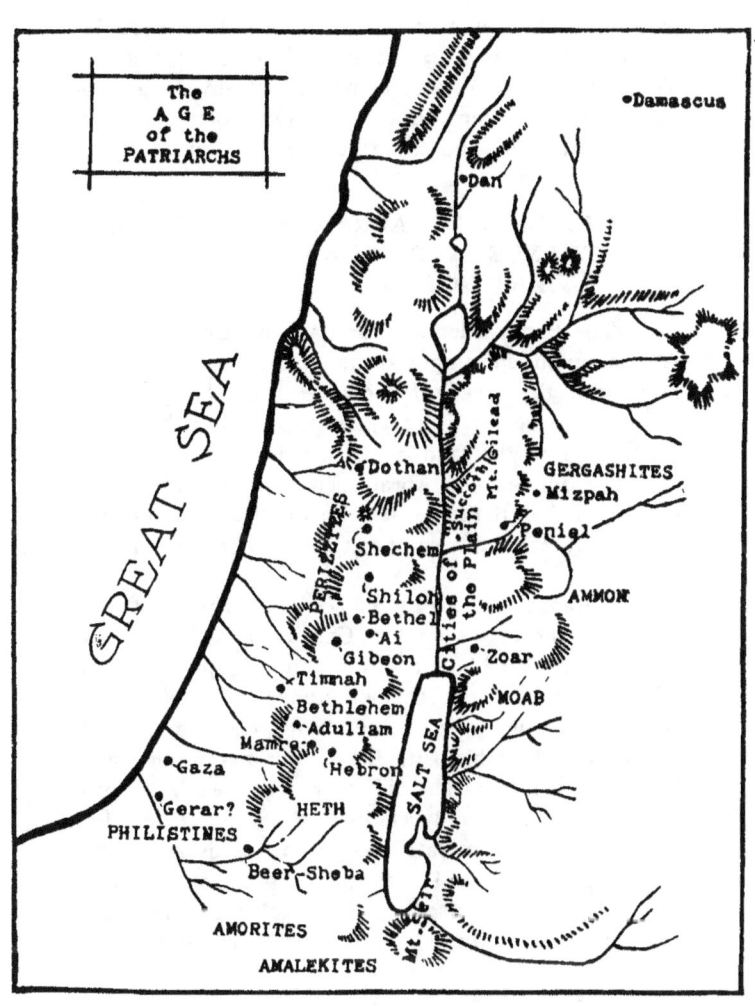

passed up the Euphrates Valley in a northwesterly direction and came to Haran. Here, after a time, Terah died, and Abram, being seventy-five years of age, took his nephew Lot, and "went forth into the land of Canaan; and into the land of Canaan they came."

II. THE LIFE OF ABRAM FROM HIS ENTRANCE INTO CANAAN TO THE BIRTH OF HIS SON ISAAC

1. **The first settlements in Canaan** (Gen. 12:5-9). Abram, upon entering Canaan, "passed through the land unto the place of Sichem,¹ unto the plain of Moreh." Here the Lord again appeared to him and promised him the land, upon which Abram built an altar. From Sichem, Abram removed to a mountain on the east of Bethel, where he pitched his tent and built another altar, calling upon the name of the Lord.

2. **Abram goes into Egypt** (Gen. 12:10-20). There was a famine in the land of Canaan, and Abram left that country and went down into Egypt. As his wife, Sarah, was fair to look upon, he charged her that she should pose as his sister, fearing that if she appeared as his wife the Egyptians would take his life. This Sarah did and was received into Pharaoh's house, and Abram was well treated for her sake and accumulated flocks and herds and servants. But the Lord was displeased and plagued Pharaoh and his house, whereupon Pharaoh, learning that Sarah was Abram's wife, sent them both away.

---
¹ The same as Shechem.

THE AGE OF THE PATRIARCHS—ABRAHAM

3. Abram separates from Lot (Gen. 13: 1-13). Leaving Egypt, Abram returned to Bethel, where trouble arose between the herdsmen of his cattle and the herdsmen of Lot's cattle. He then proposed to Lot that he should choose the portion of the land that he desired and that the two should separate. This Lot did, and selected the valley of the Jordan, which included the cities of Sodom and Gomorrah.

4. Jehovah renews his covenant with Abram (Gen. 13: 14-18). After Abram and Lot had separated, the Lord again appeared to Abram and told him to look northward and southward, eastward and westward, promising him all the land that he should see as an everlasting inheritance, and also promising him a seed as numerous as the dust of the earth. Abram then removed to Mamre, where he built an altar unto the Lord.

5. Abram delivers Lot (Gen. 14: 1-24). Sometime after Abram had removed to Mamre, the kings, Amraphel of Shinar, Arioch of Ellasar, Chedorlaomer of Elam, and Tidal, king of nations, made war upon the kings of Sodom and Gomorrah and neighboring kingdoms, because they had revolted against Chedorlaomer, and, coming to the cities of Sodom and Gomorrah, sacked them and carried Lot and his goods away with them. When Abram heard that Lot had been taken captive, he pursued his captors to Dan, in the northern part of Palestine, and rescued him and his goods. On his return, Melchizedek, priest of the most high God, met him and blessed him, and to Melchizedek Abram paid tithes of all.

6. The covenant renewed and Abram's vision (Gen. 15: 1-21). The Lord again appeared to Abram and promised him an innumerable seed. As confirmation of this covenant, Abram was told to take a heifer, a she-goat and a ram, each three years old, and a turtle-dove and a young pigeon, and to divide them, excepting the birds, laying one piece against the other.[1] When night came, a deep sleep fell upon Abram, and in a vision he saw a smoking furnace, and a burning lamp pass between the pieces. Following this, the Lord promised him and his seed all the land from the river of Egypt to the river Euphrates.

7. **The birth of Ishmael** (Gen. 16:1-16). As Sarah was childless, she gave to Abram her bondmaid, Hagar, as a concubine, who, when she had conceived, was despised in the eyes of her mistress and was driven from her face. Fleeing into the wilderness, Hagar came to a fountain in the way of Shur, where the angel of the Lord found her. Here she was commanded to return to her mistress and was promised a numerous seed through the son who was to be born to her. When the son was born, she gave to him the name of "Ishmael," which means "God hears."

8. **Abram's name changed and circumcision instituted** (Gen. 17:1-19). When Ishmael was born, the Almighty appeared to Abram, renewed the covenant, changed Abram's name to Abraham, instituted circumcision as a sign of the covenant and promised an heir through Sarah.

9. **The destruction of Sodom** (Gen. 18:1-19:38). As Abraham sat in the door of his tent at Mamre at

---

[1] This formality is still practiced by the Oriental nations in making contracts.

THE AGE OF THE PATRIARCHS—ABRAHAM

noon; three men[1] appeared to him. After receiving the courtesies of his house, one of them, the Lord, revealed to Abraham his purpose to destroy Sodom. Hearing this, Abraham began to intercede for the city. He asked the Lord if He would spare it if fifty just ones could be found in it. The Lord replied that He would. The number was then reduced to forty-five, then to forty, then to thirty, then to twenty and then to ten, with the same answer. The Lord then went His way, and at evening two angels appeared to Lot as he sat in the gate of Sodom. Lot took them into his house and fed them, whereupon the men of Sodom, hearing that he was entertaining strangers, encompassed the house and threatened him with violence if the men were not given up. The angels then reached forth their hands, drew Lot into the house and smote those without with blindness. Lot was then commanded to take his family and flee from the city, which he did, going to Zoar. On the way, his wife looked back and was turned into a pillar of salt. Then the Lord rained fire and brimstone upon Sodom and Gomorrah and destroyed them. Lot shortly left Zoar and dwelt in a cave, where he committed a great sin by which he became the father of Moab and Ammon.

10. **Abraham's lapse at Gerar** (Gen. 20: 1-18). After the destruction of Sodom, Abraham left Mamre and sojourned at Gerar. Abimelech, king of Gerar, upon being told by Abraham that Sarah was his sister, took her to wife. But the Lord told Abimelech in a dream that Sarah was Abraham's wife, and

---
[1] The "three men" are supposed to have been a theophany of the Father, Son and Holy Spirit.

he called Abraham and rebuked him for his deception, restored Sarah to him and made him a present of sheep, oxen and servants. Strictly speaking, Abraham did not lie either to Pharaoh or Abimelech, for Sarah was his half-sister (Gen. 20:12), yet he was guilty of practicing deception.

III. THE LIFE OF ABRAHAM FROM THE BIRTH OF ISAAC TO HIS OWN DEATH

1. **The birth of Isaac** (Gen. 21:1-8). When Abraham became one hundred years old, the Lord fulfilled the promise which He had made him, and Sarah bore him a son whom he called Isaac. The child was circumcised when eight days old, and his birth was made the occasion of great rejoicing to Abraham and his friends.

2. **Hagar and Ishmael cast out** (Gen. 21:9-21). After the birth of Isaac, Sarah saw Ishmael mocking, and, going to Abraham, she demanded that Hagar and her son be cast out. This grieved Abraham, but the Lord appeared and told him to hearken to the voice of Sarah, promising him that Ishmael should become a great nation. Abraham then complied with this demand, and, rising up early and taking bread and a bottle of water, he sent Hagar and her son into the wilderness of Beer-sheba. When the water was all drunken, Hagar cast the child under a shrub and went a good way off that she might not see him die. But the Lord heard her cry and opened her eyes so that she saw a well of water, and, filling her bottle, she gave the child drink. Ishmael grew, became an archer and dwelt in the wilderness of Paran. When he reached a marriage-

THE AGE OF THE PATRIARCHS—ABRAHAM

able age, his mother took for him a wife out of the land of Egypt.

3. **The offering of Isaac** (Gen. 22: 1-24). The Lord tempted Abraham and commanded him to take Isaac upon one of the mountains in the land of Moriah and offer him there for a burnt-offering. Abraham, making all necessary preparations, started. When they neared the appointed place, Isaac said "Behold the fire and the wood: but where is the lamb for a burnt-offering?" Abraham then erected the altar and, placing the wood in order upon it, bound Isaac and laid him upon the wood. He then reached forth his hand to slay his son, when an angel of the Lord called to him out of heaven and commanded him not to slay Isaac. As Abraham lifted up his eyes, he saw behind him a ram caught in a thicket by his horns. Slaying the ram, he offered it as a burnt-offering in place[1] of his son, and called the place Jehovah-jireh. Then the angel reconfirmed the covenant with Abraham and he returned to Beer-sheba.

4. **The death and burial of Sarah** (Gen. 23: 1-20). Sarah died at the age of 127 years and was buried in a cave in Machpelah, near Mamre, which Abraham purchased of the sons of Heth.

5. **Seeking a bride for Isaac** (Gen. 24: 1-25: 23). Abraham dispatched his chief servant, Eliezer, to Haran to secure a wife for his son from among his own kindred. Eliezer returned with Rebekah, who became the wife of Isaac.

6. **Abraham weds Keturah** (Gen. 25: 1-4). After

---

[1] This was typical of the vicarious atonement of Jesus Christ.

THE GIST OF THE BIBLE

the death of his beloved Sarah, Abraham took to wife Keturah, by whom he had Zimran, Jokshan, Medan, Midian, Ishbak and Shuah.

7. The death of Abraham (Gen. 25:7-10). Abraham, having made Isaac his sole heir, died at the age of 175 years and was buried by his sons, Isaac and Ishmael, in the cave of Machpelah by the side of his wife Sarah.

QUESTIONS

Give the general outline of this study. What is the meaning of the names "Abram" and "Abraham"? What can you say about the times in which Abraham lived? Tell about the commercial intercourse of the nations in the time of Abraham. Where was Abram born? Who was his father? Where did Abram go from Ur? How old was he when he left Haran? Name the two points at which he first stopped in Canaan. Where did Abram go from Bethel? What happened in Egypt? Why did Abram and Lot separate? What covenant did God make with Abram? Tell about Abram delivering Lot. Who was Ishmael? Tell about the destruction of Sodom. Who was Abimelech? How old was Abraham when Isaac was born? Tell about the casting out of Hagar and Ishmael. Tell about the offering of Isaac. Where was Sarah buried? Who was Abraham's chief servant? Where was he sent to find a wife for Isaac? Whom did Abraham marry after Sarah's death? How old was Abraham when he died and where was he buried?

STUDY XIII. THE AGE OF THE PATRIARCHS—ISAAC

(Gen. 21:1-35:29)

INTRODUCTION

1. **The name "Isaac."** The name "Isaac" means "laughter" and was given by Abraham to his son by Sarah because of his great joy over his birth.

2. **The date of his birth.** The date of Isaac's birth, as given by Usher, is 1897 B. C.

I. THE EARLY LIFE OF ISAAC

1. **The birth of Isaac** (Gen. 21:1-8). Isaac was the son of Abraham by his legitimate wife, Sarah, and was born at Gerar. When eight days of age, he was circumcised by his father, who also made a great feast on the day that he was weaned.

2. **The offering of Isaac** (Gen. 22:1-14). Sometime after Isaac had arrived at boyhood, he was taken by his father, by divine command, out upon Mount Moriah to be offered as a burnt-offering. This was simply to test Abraham's faith, and Isaac's life was spared by divine intervention, a ram being provided as an offering in his place.

II. SEEKING A BRIDE FOR ISAAC

1. **Abraham's instructions to Eliezer** (Gen. 24:1-9). As Abraham grew in years, he became solicitous in regard to Isaac's welfare and, calling his

eldest servant, Eliezer, he made him place his hand under his thigh and swear that he would not take for his son a wife from among the Canaanites, but that he would go to his own country and kindred and there find a wife for him.

2. **Eliezer starts for Mesopotamia** (Gen. 24:10-14). Following the instructions of Abraham, Eliezer departed for the city of Nahor in Mesopotamia, with ten camels laden with the goods of his master. When he reached the city, he made his camels kneel without by a well of water, and there he prayed that the Lord might show favor to his master's house and that, when the women of the city came to draw water, the one who, when asked for a drink, should say, "Drink, and I will give thy camels drink also," should be the one divinely chosen to be the wife of Isaac.

3. **Eliezer meets Rebekah** (Gen. 24:15-28). While Eliezer was tarrying at the well, there came, among the women to draw water, Rebekah, the daughter of Bethuel, who was a son of Nahor, Abraham's brother. As she came to the well, Abraham's servant ran to meet her and said: "Let me, I pray thee, drink a little water of thy pitcher." To which she replied: "Drink, my lord." She also filled the trough for the camels. Eliezer then took a golden earring and two bracelets of gold, and, giving them to her, inquired whose daughter she was and if there was room in her father's house for him to lodge. The damsel replied that she was the daughter of Bethuel son of Nahor, and that her father had both straw and provender and room to lodge in. She then ran ahead and told her brother Laban who Eliezer was.

THE AGE OF THE PATRIARCHS—ISAAC

4. Eliezer meets Laban and Bethuel (Gen. 24: 29-61). When Laban saw the earring and the bracelets which Eliezer had given to Rebekah, and heard her words, he exclaimed to Abraham's servant: "Come in, thou blessed of the Lord; wherefore standest thou without?" Entering the house and ungirding and feeding his camels, Eliezer proceeded to state the object of his mission. He told of the greatness of Abraham and of his wealth; how a son had been given him through Sarah to whom he had given all that he possessed; how his master had made him swear that he would not take a wife for Isaac from among the Canaanites, but from among his own kindred; how he had prayed that the Lord might direct him, and how Rebekah had come to the well in fulfillment of his petition. When Bethuel and Laban heard the story of Eliezer, they exclaimed: "The thing proceedeth from the Lord: we cannot speak unto thee bad or good. Behold, Rebekah is before thee, take her, and go, and let her be thy master's son's wife." At these words, Eliezer bowed himself to the earth and worshiped God, and, bringing forth his precious things of gold and silver and raiment, he gave them to Rebekah and also presents to her mother and brother.

5. Rebekah is brought to Isaac (Gen. 24:62-67). The necessary preparations having been made, Eliezer, Rebekah and their attendants started on their journey to Canaan. As Isaac came from the way of the well Lahai-roi, he went out at eventide into a field to meditate, and, lifting up his eyes, he saw the camels of Eliezer coming. When Rebekah saw him, she lighted from her camel, covered her face with a veil, and Isaac took her into his mother's tent and she became his wife.

III. THE LATTER DAYS OF ISAAC

1. **The birth of Esau and Jacob** (Gen. 25:24-26). The first important event in the life of Isaac, after taking Rebekah to wife, was the birth of the twin brothers, Esau and Jacob. Isaac was sixty years of age when Esau and Jacob were born.

2. **The Abrahamic covenant confirmed to Isaac** (Gen 26:1-5). There was a famine in the land, like the famine in the days of Abraham, and Isaac went down to Abimelech, king of Gerar. Here the Lord said to him: "Sojourn in this land, and I will be with thee, and will bless thee; for unto thee, and unto thy seed, I will give all these countries, and I will perform the oath which I sware unto Abraham thy father; and I will make thy seed to multiply as the stars of heaven, and will give unto thy seed all these countries; and in thy seed shall all the nations of the earth be blessed."

3. **Isaac's lapse at Gerar** (Gen. 26:6-16). Isaac, like his father Abraham, lapsed at Gerar. When he was asked by the men of that place if Rebekah was his wife, he answered that she was his sister. But this deception was exposed, and Isaac was asked to leave the country, Abimelech saying: "Go from us; for thou art much mightier than we."

4. **Isaac, the well-digger** (Gen. 26:17-33). Isaac then departed from Gerar and dwelt in the valley of Gerar. Here he reopened the wells which had been dug in the days of Abraham, but which had been closed by the Philistines after Abraham's

THE AGE OF THE PATRIARCHS—ISAAC

death. This created strife between his herdsmen and those of Gerar, the latter declaring that the water was theirs. Following this, the Lord again appeared to Isaac in Beer-sheba and reconfirmed His covenant, upon which Isaac erected an altar. After this, Abimelech came to Isaac for the purpose of renewing their friendship. But Isaac replied to him and his servants: "Wherefore come ye to me, seeing ye hate me, and have sent me away from you?" To which Abimelech answered: "We saw certainly that the Lord was with thee." A covenant was then made and confirmed between the two.

5. **Esau weds Hittites** (Gen. 26:34, 35). When Esau was forty years of age, he married Judith, the daughter of Beeri the Hittite, and also Bashemath, the daughter of Elon the Hittite, which was very displeasing to Isaac and Rebekah.

6. **The deception of Jacob** (Gen. 27:1-33). Isaac became old, and Jacob, his son, deceived him into placing upon his head the blessing which rightfully belonged upon the head of Esau. As this will be considered in the next study, we will let it pass with the mere mention here.

7. **The death of Isaac** (Gen. 35:27-29). Isaac died in Mamre, where his father Abraham had lived, when 180 years old, and was buried by his sons, Esau and Jacob.

QUESTIONS

Give the general outline of this study. What does the name "Isaac" mean? When was Isaac born? What was the name of his mother? Where was he taken to be offered as a burnt-offering? What was the name of Abraham's chief servant? What did Abraham instruct Eliezer to do? Where did Eliezer

THE GIST OF THE BIBLE

go? Where did he meet Rebekah? Tell about his meeting with Bethuel and Laban. Tell about the meeting of Isaac and Rebekah. What was the first important event in the life of Isaac after his marriage to Rebekah? Where did Isaac go after the birth of Esau and Jacob? What did the Lord promise him there? What was the name of the king of Gerar? What trouble did Isaac have with him? What did Isaac do after he left Gerar? Whom did Esau wed? How did Isaac and Rebekah feel about it? Where did Isaac die? How old was he?

STUDY XIV. THE AGE OF THE PATRIARCHS—JACOB

(Gen. 25:24-50:14)

INTRODUCTION

1. **The name "Jacob."** The name "Jacob" means "supplanter" and was given to its bearer by his father Isaac, because of him having supplanted his brother Esau, both in his birthright and his blessing.

2. **The date of Jacob's birth.** According to Usher, Jacob was born in the year 1836 B. C.

I. THE EARLY LIFE OF JACOB

1. **The birth of Jacob** (Gen. 25:24-26). Jacob was the son of Isaac and Rebekah and the twin brother of Esau.

2. **Jacob buys Esau's birthright** (Gen. 25:27-34). The brothers grew and developed different dispositions. Esau was a cunning hunter and a man of the field, while Jacob was a plain man, dwelling in tents. The first was the favorite of his father, the second of his mother. Jacob sod pottage, and, as Esau came in faint from the field and asked for food, he said: "Sell me this day thy birthright." To which Esau replied: "Behold, I am at the point to die: and what profit shall this birthright do to me?" Jacob then made him confirm the sale with an oath, in return

for which he gave him bread and a pottage of lentiles.¹

3. **Jacob steals Esau's blessing** (Gen. 27:1-41). When Isaac became old, he called Esau to him and requested him to take his bow and quiver and go into the field and procure for him some venison. Esau departed, and his mother, who had overheard Isaac's request, went to Jacob, told him of the same and charged him to go to the flock, slay two kids, bring them to her and she would make of them savory meat for his father. Jacob with some reluctance departed, slew the kids and brought them to Rebekah, who prepared them as she had suggested. Then, clothing Jacob in Esau's garments and giving the food into his hands, she sent him to Isaac. As Jacob entered into the presence of his father, Isaac demanded that he come near, and, when he had felt of his son, for he was blind and could not see, he said: "The voice is Jacob's voice, but the hands are the hands of Esau." He then demanded: "Art thou my very son Esau?" Jacob replied in the affirmative, and Isaac ate the food and blessed him. After Jacob had received the blessing and had gone out, Esau came in with his savory dish and offered it to his father. Isaac trembled exceedingly and exclaimed: "Where is he that hath taken venison, and brought it me, and I have eaten of all before thou camest, and have blessed him? yea, and he shall be blessed." When Esau heard these words, he cried out in the deepest anguish: "Bless me, even me also, O my father." But Isaac replied: "Thy brother came with

---

¹ A plant belonging to the same family as the common garden pea.

subtilty, and hath taken away thy blessing." To which Esau exclaimed: "Is not he rightly named Jacob? for he hath supplanted me these two times: he took away my birthright; and, behold, now he hath taken away my blessing." When Isaac heard this, he blessed Esau also, and promised him that his dwelling should be the fatness of the earth and of the dew of heaven from above, and that, when he should obtain dominion, he should break his brother's yoke from off his neck. Upon receiving this blessing, Esau said in his heart: "The days of mourning for my father are at hand; then will I slay my brother Jacob."

II. JACOB'S FLIGHT TO HARAN

1. **Rebekah plans Jacob's flight** (Gen. 27:42-28:9). Esau's purpose to slay Jacob was told Rebekah, and she sent for Jacob and charged him to flee to her brother Laban in Haran, and dwell there until his brother's anger should subside. She then went to Isaac and complained to him that she was weary of her life because of the daughters of Heth, for fear Jacob would take one of them to wife. Isaac then called Jacob and commanded him to go to Padan-aram and there take a wife from the daughters of Laban.

2. **Jacob at Bethel** (Gen. 28:10-22). As Jacob journeyed toward Haran, he came to a certain spot where he tarried for the night, resting his head upon a pillow of stones. During the night he dreamed that a great ladder was set up into heaven and that the angels of God descended and ascended upon it. The Lord also appeared to him, standing at its

head, and confirmed the covenant which He had made with Abraham and Isaac, promised him the land upon which he lay, and also that he should have a seed as numerous as the dust of the earth, through whom the families of the earth should be blessed. In the morning Jacob took the stones which had served him as a pillow and erected of them a pillar which he anointed with oil. He then called the place Bethel and departed.

3. Jacob at Haran (Gen. 29:1-30:24). As Jacob neared Haran, he came to a well in the midst of a field. Around this well were lying three flocks of sheep. Jacob inquired of the shepherds whence they had come, and they replied: "Of Haran are we." They also told him that Rachel, Laban's daughter, would come with her sheep for the purpose of giving them water. Rachel came to the well as the shepherds had said, and Jacob rolled away the stone from the well's mouth and watered her sheep, telling her, at the same time, that he was the son of her father's sister. Upon hearing this, Rachel ran and told her father, who came out to meet Jacob and to welcome him into his house. Laban had two daughters: Leah, the elder, who was tender-eyed, and Rachel, who was beautiful and well favored. Jacob loved Rachel and promised Laban that he would serve him seven years if he would give her to him for his wife. To this Laban assented, and for seven years Jacob served him. But, at the expiration of this time, Laban deceived Jacob and gave him Leah instead. When Jacob discovered the deception, he reproached Laban, but the latter replied that it was not the custom of his country to give the younger

THE AGE OF THE PATRIARCHS—JACOB

before the firstborn. He then told Jacob that if he would serve him another seven years, he would give him Rachel. This Jacob consented to do and, at the expiration of that time, received Rachel to wife. Eleven of Jacob's sons were born to him at Haran: Reuben, Simeon, Levi, Judah, Issachar and Zebulun by Leah; Gad and Asher by Zilpah, Leah's maid; Dan and Naphtali by Bilhah, the maid of Rachel, and Joseph by Rachel.

4. Jacob's settlement with Laban (Gen. 30:25-31:55). After the birth of Joseph, Jacob went to Laban and demanded a settlement that he might return to his own country. Laban at first insisted upon Jacob tarrying with him, but, upon his refusal, he consented to the proposition. According to the agreement of settlement, Jacob was to have the speckled and spotted cattle and goats and the brown sheep from Laban's flocks and herds, as his hire. These were separated from the rest, but when it was ascertained that Jacob's flocks and herds were far in excess of those of Laban, the latter was wroth, and by divine direction Jacob fled out of the land. But Rachel had carried off certain images which belonged to her father, and, when Laban discovered that these were gone, he pursued Jacob and overtook him at Mount Gilead. He reproached Jacob for leaving him so abruptly and at unawares, and accused him of stealing his gods. Upon hearing this accusation, Jacob permitted Laban to search his goods, but, as Rachel had hidden the images among the camels' furniture and had sat upon them, they were not found, and the search ended with a covenant between Laban and Jacob, made at Mizpah, after which Laban returned to Haran and Jacob continued on his journey to Canaan.

III. THE RECONCILIATION BETWEEN JACOB AND ESAU

1. Jacob prepares to meet Esau (Gen. 32:1-32). As Jacob went on his way, he sent messengers to his brother Esau, asking for a peaceful settlement of their difficulty. The messengers returned with the word that Esau and four hundred men were on their way to meet him. Jacob was greatly troubled at this information, and divided his possessions into two bands so that if one was attacked by Esau the other might escape. He then besought the Lord for deliverance, and, selecting 220 goats, 220 sheep, 30 camels with their colts, 50 cattle and 30 asses, he sent them on ahead as a present to Esau. Having done this, he arose and took his family over the ford Jabbok, after which he went away by himself and wrestled with a man[1] until the breaking of the day. As the man could not prevail against him, he touched Jacob's thigh so that it slipped out of joint, and yet he wrestled on, saying: "I will not let thee go, except thou bless me." As a reward for his persistency, the man changed his name from "Jacob" to "Israel," which means "a prince with God."

2. Jacob meets Esau (Gen. 33:1-20). On the morrow Jacob lifted up his eyes and saw Esau coming in the distance. Putting himself in the front of his family, he went out to meet his brother, and, drawing near to him, bowed before him seven

---
[1] This "man" was none other than the Angel of the Covenant, He who afterwards became the Christ.

THE AGE OF THE PATRIARCHS—JACOB

times. At this Esau embraced him, fell on his neck and kissed him, and they wept. Esau then inquired who the women and children were, and Jacob replied that they were those whom the Lord had given him. Esau also asked in regard to the drove which Jacob had sent on before him. Jacob replied that they were intended as a present from him, upon which Esau, with some objections, received them. The brothers then parted, Esau returning to Mount Seir and Jacob following to Succoth. From Succoth he came to Shalem in Shechem, where he purchased a parcel of a field from the children of Hamor.

IV. THE LATTER DAYS OF JACOB

1. **Jacob's difficulty with Shechem** (Gen. 34: 1-31). Shechem, the son of Hamor, loved Dinah, the daughter of Jacob, and asked his father to get her for him that she might become his wife. As Hamor was considering the matter with Jacob, the sons of Jacob came in from the field, and, hearing of the folly that had been wrought in Israel, they were very wroth, and two of them, Simeon and Levi, taking their swords, went into the city and slew Hamor and Shechem and carried away their possessions. This rash act greatly grieved Jacob, for fear that it might raise the enmity of the inhabitants of Canaan against him.

2. **Jacob returns to Bethel** (Gen. 35: 1-15). Jacob now returned by divine command to Bethel. He first charged his household to put away their strange gods and to change their apparel, after which they set out for that place. When they came to Bethel, Jacob erected an altar and called the name of the

place El-Bethel. Here the Lord renewed His covenant with Jacob.

3. The birth of Benjamin and death of Rachel (Gen. 35:16-20). Leaving Bethel, Jacob came to Ephrath, where Benjamin was born and where Rachel died. Ephrath is the same as Bethlehem.

4. Death of Isaac (Gen. 35:27-29). Leaving Ephrath, Jacob spread his tent beyond the tower of Edar. He then removed to Mamre, where his father, Isaac, dwelt. Soon after this, Isaac died and was buried by Jacob and Esau.

5. Jacob goes into Egypt (Gen. 37:1-47:26). After Isaac's death, Joseph, the son of Jacob, being sold into Egypt, Jacob and his sons went down into that land under divine direction and promise. Here they were exalted by the reigning Pharaoh, who, learning that they were shepherds, permitted them to settle in the land of Goshen, where they grew in numbers, wealth and affluence under the paternal reign of the Shepherd Kings.

6. Death of Jacob (Gen. 47:27-50:14). Jacob died at the age of 147 years, after dwelling in Egypt for seventeen years. As his end drew near, he called Joseph to him and requested that he might be carried back to the land of his fathers for burial. He then blessed Joseph's sons, Manasseh and Ephraim, placing his right hand upon the head of Ephraim, the younger. Then, calling his twelve sons to him and blessing each, he "gathered up his feet into the bed, yielded up the ghost, and was gathered unto his people." Jacob was afterwards embalmed, according to the custom of Egypt, and, when seventy days of mourning had expired, he was taken by his

THE AGE OF THE PATRIARCHS—JACOB

sons back to the land of Canaan and buried in the cave of Machpelah.

QUESTIONS

Give the general outline of this study. What does the name "Jacob" mean? When was Jacob born? Give the names of his father and mother. Give the difference in character between Esau and Jacob. What did Jacob give Esau for his birthright? Tell how Jacob stole Esau's blessing. Why did Jacob flee to Haran? How did Rebekah plan his flight? What did Jacob see at Bethel? Where did Jacob first meet Rachel? How was he received by Laban? How many years did he first serve Laban for Rachel? How did Laban deceive him? How many more years did he serve before Rachel was given him? How many sons were born to Jacob in Haran? Tell about Jacob's settlement with Laban. What preparations did Jacob make to meet Esau? Tell about the meeting of Jacob and Esau. Give the name of Jacob's daughter. Whom did Simeon and Levi slay at Shechem? Where did Jacob go from Shechem, and what did he do there? Where was Benjamin born? What happened at the time of his birth? Why did Jacob go into Egypt? Where did he die? How old was he when he died? How long had he been in Egypt? Give the names of Joseph's sons. What did Jacob do just before his death? Where was he buried?

STUDY XV. THE EGYPTIAN BONDAGE—JOSEPH

(Gen. 37:1-Ex. 12:36)

INTRODUCTION

1. **The name "Joseph."** The name "Joseph" signifies "increaser" or "adding."

2. **The date of Joseph's birth.** Joseph was the son of Jacob and Rachel, and was born in Haran in the year 1746 B. C., Usher's chronology.

3. **The Shepherd Kings.** The rulers, or Pharaohs, of Egypt, at the time that Joseph was sold into that country, were the Shepherd Kings, or Hyksos. They were of the Semitic race and overthrew the old Egyptian empire about 1900 B. C. They were an enterprising dynasty and completely changed the conservative policy of the old empire. Under them, foreign conquests were undertaken, a canal was dug from the Nile at Bubastis to the Red Sea at Suez, the continent of Africa was circumnavigated, and navigators were dispatched to determine the source of the Nile. Shepherds were also welcomed into the country from Asia, and this accounts for the warm reception given Jacob and his sons.

4. **The Pharaoh of the oppression.** The Pharaoh of the oppression is supposed to have been Rameses II., a warlike prince who was also noted for his great architectural projects.

THE EGYPTIAN BONDAGE—JOSEPH

I. THE EGYPTIAN BONDAGE BEFORE THE DEATH OF JOSEPH

1. Joseph sold (Gen. 37: 1-36). Joseph was the special favorite of his father and was accordingly hated by his brothers. Three things conspired to arouse and intensify their jealousy: his complaint to Jacob of the evil deeds of the sons of Bilhah and Zilpah; a coat of many colors which his father had given him, and two dreams which he told his brethren, in one of which the sheaves which they bound made obeisance to the sheaves which he bound, and, in the other, the sun, moon and eleven stars made obeisance to him. As his brethren were feeding the flocks of their father at Shechem, Joseph was sent to them. When they saw him coming, they conspired against him and, taking from him his coat of many colors, threw him into a pit. But, as they ate their bread, a caravan of Ishmaelites passed by who were on their way to Egypt with spices and perfumes, so, drawing Joseph up from the pit, they sold him to the Ishmaelites for twenty pieces of silver. They then slew a kid, and, dipping the coat of many colors into its blood, they took it to Jacob, who was thus led to believe that his son had been devoured by a wild beast. The Ishmaelites, in turn, sold Joseph to Potiphar, the captain of Pharaoh's guard.

2. Joseph tried (Gen. 39: 1-23). After Joseph had been sold to Potiphar, he became overseer in his house, and the Lord blessed the Egyptian's house for his sake. But, as Joseph was a goodly person and well favored, Potiphar's wife loved him. As day after day he rejected her blandishments, she became intensely jealous and laid a plan to ruin him in the eyes of his master. So, as he was with her one day, she caught his garment and carried it to Potiphar with the story that Joseph had greatly offended her. For this Potiphar thrust him into the prison where the king's prisoners were bound. But so favorable did he become in the eyes of the keeper, that he was given charge over all the other prisoners.

3. **Joseph interprets dreams** (Gen. 40:1-41:38). After these things, the butler and baker of Pharaoh offended their lord and he thrust them into the prison with Joseph. While there they each dreamed a dream which made them very sad. Joseph, observing their sadness, inquired the cause of the same. He was told that each had dreamed a dream, but that there was no interpreter at hand. Joseph then commanded each to tell his dream, which he did and Joseph interpreted it. The butler dreamed that there was a vine of three branches with clusters of ripe grapes, that he had Pharaoh's cup in his hand, and that he pressed the juice of the clusters into the cup and Pharaoh did drink. This Joseph interpreted to mean that in three days the butler would be reinstated by Pharaoh. The baker dreamed that he had three white baskets on his head, the uppermost filled with bake-meats for Pharaoh, and that the birds came and ate the food out of the basket. This Joseph interpreted to mean that in three days Pharaoh would take the baker and hang him to a tree. Both of these interpretations were fulfilled. At the expiration of two years, Pharaoh dreamed that, as he stood by the river, seven well-favored and fat-fleshed kine came up out of the river and fed in a meadow. These were

THE EGYPTIAN BONDAGE—JOSEPH

followed by seven others, ill-favored and lean-fleshed, which devoured the seven that went before. The same night he dreamed another dream, in which seven ears of corn, rank and good, grew upon one stalk. After these, seven ears blasted with the east wind sprang up and devoured them. When Pharaoh awoke, he was deeply troubled, and, calling the wise men of Egypt, he told them his dreams, but not one was able to interpret them. His butler then told him of Joseph, and he was sent for. Being told the dreams, he replied that they signified that there were to come seven years of plenty, followed by seven years of famine.

4. **Joseph exalted** (Gen. 41: 39-57). When Pharaoh heard the interpretation of his dreams by Joseph, he was deeply impressed that the Spirit of God was in him, and he made Joseph the second ruler in the kingdom and gave him authority to prepare for the coming famine. This Joseph did, gathering up in the seven plenteous years the surplus food throughout the land and laying it up in the cities, so that, when the seven years of famine came and the people were famishing, they came to Joseph and he opened the storehouses and sold them food. Joseph was thirty years of age when he became Pharaoh's governor, and Pharaoh changed his name to Zaphnath-paaneah and gave him Asenath, daughter of Potipherah, priest of On, to wife. By her he had two sons, Manasseh and Ephraim.

5. **Joseph meets his brethren** (Gen. 42: 1-26). The famine affected other lands besides Egypt, and Jacob sent his ten eldest sons down into Egypt to buy corn. When the brethren came to Joseph, he inquired of

them their country, and when they replied that it was Canaan, he accused them of being spies who had come to spy out the nakedness of the land. This they vehemently denied and told Joseph that originally there were twelve brothers, one of whom was with their father and the other was not. Joseph then accused them a second time of being spies and told them that they would not be permitted to return to Canaan until he had seen their brother. He then put them into prison, but, at the expiration of three days, they were released, their sacks were filled with corn and they were permitted to return to their father, excepting Simeon, who was retained as a hostage until Benjamin should be brought down to Joseph.

6. **Joseph's brethren return to Canaan** (Gen. 42: 27-43:14). After they had departed, one of them, on opening his sack for corn to feed his beast, espied the money which he had paid for it. When he called the attention of his brethren to it, they were sore afraid and exclaimed: "What is this that God hath done unto us?" Arriving in Canaan, they told their father all that had been done to them and the demand that Joseph had made. As Jacob heard it, he was overcome with grief and exclaimed: "Me have ye bereaved of my children: Joseph is not, and Simeon is not, and ye will take Benjamin away." Then Reuben spoke to his father and said: "Slay my two sons, if I bring him not to thee again." But Jacob at first refused to let Benjamin go, and it was only after the famine had become more severe, and they began to want for food, that he gave his consent.

7. **Joseph's brethren go into Egypt a second time**

THE EGYPTIAN BONDAGE—JOSEPH

(Gen. 43: 15-34). The brethren then, taking the money which they had found in their sacks and the same amount besides, with Benjamin, went down into Egypt and stood before Joseph. When Joseph saw Benjamin, he gave orders to the ruler of his house to prepare for them a feast. This made the brethren fearful, for they thought that he was laying a plan to entrap them and make them bondsmen. So they went to the steward of Joseph and explained how that they had found the money which they had paid for their corn in their sacks and that they had brought it to him again. The steward of Joseph declared that God had given their treasures into their hands, and, bringing out Simeon, he presented him to them. When the feast was prepared, Joseph sent out to his brethren messes from his own table, but to Benjamin he sent out five times as much as to the rest, and they drank and were merry with him.

8. Joseph reveals his identity to his brethren (Gen. 44: 1-45: 24). As the brethren were about to return to their father, Joseph commanded his steward to fill their sacks with food, put their money in their sacks and, in addition, Joseph's silver cup in the sack of Benjamin. When this was done and the brethren had departed, Joseph sent his steward after them, who accused them of returning evil for good. This they emphatically denied, but when the silver cup was found in the sack of Benjamin, he brought them back with him. Coming into Joseph's presence, they fell down before him with protestations of innocence, but Joseph dismissed them with the exception of Benjamin, who, he declared, should be his servant. But the sons of Jacob refused to depart, further protested their innocence, told him of the great sorrow it would bring to their father if Benjamin did not return, and importunated him for Benjamin's release. With this, Joseph could not restrain himself, and, dismissing his servants, he wept aloud and made himself known to his brethren. He told them not to be grieved that they had sold him into Egypt, quieted their fears, and commanded them to hasten to their father and bring him and their families down into the land of Goshen. Then, giving them provisions, raiment and wagons, he sent them away.

9. **Jacob is brought into Egypt** (Gen. 45:25-49:33). When the brethren came to their father and told him that they had seen Joseph, he at first doubted, but when he had seen the wagons which Joseph had sent to convey him and his family into Egypt, his spirit revived and he believed and consented to go. Upon entering Egypt, Joseph told Pharaoh that they were shepherds, and they were permitted to settle in the land of Goshen.

10. **Joseph's death** (Gen. 50:22-26). Joseph died in Egypt at the age of 110 years, having seen Ephraim's children of the third generation. After his death, he was embalmed and put in a coffin, and subsequently his bones were carried back to Canaan, where they found a resting-place at Shechem.

II. THE EGYPTIAN BONDAGE AFTER THE DEATH OF JOSEPH

1. **The oppression** (Ex. 1:1-22). After the death of Joseph, the children of Israel increased rapidly and filled the land of Goshen under the paternal reign of the Hyksos kings. But, about 1525 B. C., these

THE EGYPTIAN BONDAGE—JOSEPH

rulers were overthrown by the Theban prince Amosis, who headed a new dynasty, which was hostile to the descendants of Jacob. This hostility was probably due to their loyalty to the preceding dynasty. Among the edicts which were issued by the new Pharaoh against the Israelites was one that the Hebrew midwives should kill the male children of Hebrew parents at the time of their birth. Furthermore, taskmasters were set over the children of Israel, and they were compelled to build the treasure-cities of Pithom and Raamses and perform other bitter and rigorous labors.

2. **The birth of Moses** (Ex. 2:1-10). Although Pharaoh ordered the Hebrew midwives to kill the male children of Israel, they feared God and saved them alive, whereupon the king commanded that the males should be thrown into the river. Among the Hebrews were a man and his wife by the names of Amram and Jochebed, of the tribe of Levi. The woman bore a son and hid him for three months, but, being unable to conceal him longer, she made an ark of bulrushes, slime and pitch, and, putting the child in this ark, she laid it among the flags by the river's brink, leaving her daughter, Miriam, near at hand to watch what was done with the babe. The daughter of Pharaoh, coming down to the river to bathe and finding the ark, had compassion on the child, and when his sister, who was near at hand, inquired if she should go and call a nurse from among the Hebrew women, she was told to do so, and, running, she brought the child's mother. The child grew and was brought to Pharaoh's daughter, who adopted him and gave him the name of "Moses," which means "drawn out of the water."

3. **Moses flees to Midian** (Ex. 2:11-25). Moses grew to manhood, and one day, espying an Egyptian beating one of his countrymen, slew him. The next day he saw two of his own brethren striving together, and when he asked the aggressor why he smote his brother, he retorted: "Who made thee a prince and a judge over us? intendest thou to kill me, as thou killedst the Egyptian?" Hearing this, Moses knew that his deed was known, and feared greatly. When the deed came to the ears of Pharaoh, he sought to slay Moses, but he fled into the land of Midian and dwelt with Reuel,[1] a priest of that land, who gave him his daughter, Zipporah, to be his wife. By her he had a son, Gershom.

4. **The call of Moses** (Ex. 3:1-4:18). Moses tended the flocks of his father-in-law and came to Mount Horeb. Here the angel of the Lord appeared to him in a flaming bush and commanded him to remove his shoes from off his feet, telling him that the place whereon he stood was holy ground. The Lord also told him that He had seen the affliction of his people; that He purposed to bring them into their own land, and that Moses should return and perform this work. To this, Moses made two objections: First, the unbelief of the people, and, second, his own lack of eloquence. To the first the Lord replied with two miracles, changing Moses' rod into a serpent and back again into a rod, and striking his hand with leprosy and cleansing it again. To the second objection the Lord replied by promising him Aaron as a spokesman.

---
[1] Another name for the man Jethro.

THE EGYPTIAN BONDAGE—JOSEPH

5. **Moses' return** (Ex. 4:19-7:19). After this interview with the Lord, Moses returned to the house of Jethro, his father-in-law, and demanded that he release him so that he might go to his brethren. This was granted, and Moses, taking his family, returned into the land of Egypt. The Lord also revealed himself to Aaron and commanded him to go into the wilderness to meet his brother. This Aaron did, and Moses revealed to him all that the Lord had said. The two then went to Pharaoh and demanded that he let the children of Israel go a three days' journey into the wilderness that they might hold a feast. This Pharaoh refused, and gave orders to his taskmasters to withdraw the straw with which the Israelites made bricks, but not to reduce the tale of bricks each day. Failing in their interview with Pharaoh, Moses and Aaron were addressed by the Lord, who said: "Now shalt thou see what I will do to Pharaoh: for with a strong hand shall he drive them out of his land." The two then went into Pharaoh's presence again, and, when he demanded a sign, Aaron threw down his rod, which became a serpent. Then Pharaoh called in the sorcerers of Egypt, and when they threw down their rods, they, too, became serpents, but Aaron's rod swallowed them up.

6. **The ten plagues** (Ex. 7:20-12:36). Following this, the Lord sent ten plagues upon the land. With each plague, except the last, Pharaoh's heart was hardened[1] and he would not permit Israel to depart

---

[1] In Ex. 4:21, and elsewhere, God is said to harden Pharaoh's heart, and in Ex. 8:15, and elsewhere, Pharaoh is said to harden his own heart. The discrepancy is only apparent, however, for God was only the *occasion* of this condition, while Pharaoh was the *cause* of it.

out of the land. The ten plagues were as follows: (1) The waters of Egypt were turned into *blood;* (2) *frogs* covered the land; (3) the dust of the land became *lice;* (4) a grievous swarm of *flies;* (5) a grievous *murrain* upon the flocks and herds; (6) *blains* upon man and beast; (7) *hail* sent upon the entire land; (8) a scourge of *locusts;* (9) *darkness* upon the land; (10) the *smiting of the firstborn.*

QUESTIONS

Give the general outline of this study. Give the meaning of the name "Joseph." Give the date of Joseph's birth. Who were the Shepherd Kings? Who was the Pharaoh of the oppression? Give three reasons for Joseph not being on good terms with his brethren. To whom was Joseph first sold? What did Jacob believe had happened to him? To whom did the Ishmaelites sell Joseph? What difficulty did Joseph have with Potiphar's wife? What did Potiphar do? What two servants of Pharaoh were imprisoned with Joseph? Give the dream of each and its significance. How did Joseph come to the attention of Pharaoh? Give Pharaoh's dreams and their significance. What position was Joseph called to fill in Egypt? What did Joseph do after his exaltation? Give the name of Joseph's wife. Name his two sons. How did Joseph's brethren happen to go down into Egypt? What did Joseph first accuse them of being? Whom did Joseph demand that they should bring down to him? Whom did he hold as a hostage? What did his brethren find in their sacks besides the grain? How did Jacob feel in regard to letting Benjamin return with them? Why did he let him go at last? What did Joseph prepare for them upon their return? When they had departed, what was found in Benjamin's sack? What did Joseph say should be done with Benjamin? What was the feeling manifested when Joseph revealed his identity? What did his brethren do after this? How old was Joseph when he died? What was done with him after his death? Where was he finally buried? What happened to the Hyksos after the death of Joseph? Why were the new Pharaohs hostile to the children of Israel? What were the

THE EGYPTIAN BONDAGE—JOSEPH

Hebrew midwives commanded to do? Give the name of one child that escaped. Give the circumstances of his deliverance. Give the meaning of his name. Give the names of his father, mother and sister. Whom did Moses kill, and why? Where did Moses flee? What man did Moses meet in Midian? Give the names of Moses' wife and son. Where did the Lord appear to Moses? What two objections did Moses make to the divine call? How did God answer these objections? What did Moses and Aaron demand of Pharaoh? What did Pharaoh do? What did the Lord say? Name, in their order, the ten plagues.

STUDY XVI. THE EXODUS—MOSES

(Ex. 12:29-Deut. 34:12)

INTRODUCTION

1. **Moses.** The life of Moses may be divided into three periods of forty years each: forty years in Egypt, forty years in Midian and forty years in the wilderness. We have already considered the events that occurred during the first two periods; we shall now take up those that occurred during his last forty years.

2. **The Pharaoh of the exodus.** The Pharaoh of the exodus was Menephthah, the son and successor of Rameses II.

3. **The date of the exodus.** The exodus from Egypt occurred in the year 1491, and the wanderings in the wilderness continued for forty years, or till 1451 B. C., Usher's chronology.

4. **The number of the Israelites.** Of the people who went out of Egypt, there were six hundred thousand men, besides children and a mixed multitude.

I. FROM EGYPT TO MOUNT SINAI

1. **Preparations for the exodus** (Ex. 12:29-36). The children of Israel were at Raamses in Egypt, and, when the tenth plague occurred, Pharaoh and the Egyptians urged Moses and his people to leave the land. The people took their dough before it was

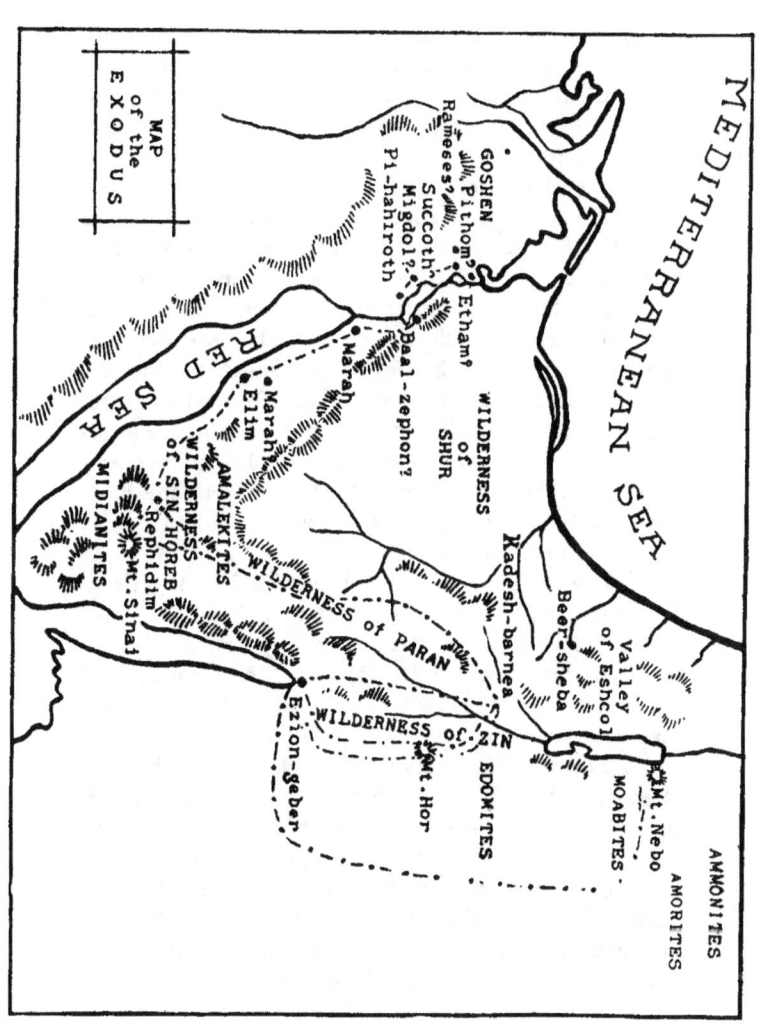

leavened and their kneading-troughs upon their shoulders, and with jewels of silver and gold and raiment, which they borrowed from the Egyptians, they, with their flocks and herds, left Raamses and went to Succoth.

2. **The Passover instituted** (Ex. 12:37-13:19). When the Lord was about to send the tenth plague upon the Egyptians, the children of Israel were commanded to take a bunch of hyssop, dip it into the blood of a lamb and smear the blood upon the lintels and side-posts of each house, with the promise that, if such were done, the destroying angel would pass over and spare their firstborn. Therefore, when Israel had left Raamses and had come to Succoth, the ordinance of the Passover was instituted in commemoration of this event, and from that time forth the firstborn of both man and beast were required to be sanctified unto the Lord.

3. **The pillar and cloud** (Ex. 13:20-22). From Succoth the Israelites journeyed to Etham, the Lord going before them in a cloud by day and a pillar of fire by night. These tokens of the divine presence and leadership continued with Israel throughout the entire wilderness journey.

4. **The Egyptian pursuit** (Ex. 14:1-14). The children of Israel had hardly left the land of their bondage before Pharaoh's heart was hardened and he repented of letting them go. Gathering together a force of six hundred chariots, with an army of horsemen and foot soldiers, he began pursuit. When the children of Israel saw the Egyptians coming, they were greatly frightened, and complained against Moses. But Moses replied: "Fear ye not, stand still,

THE EXODUS—MOSES

and see the salvation of the Lord, which he will show to you to-day."

5. **Israel crosses the Red Sea** (Ex. 14:15-22). Israel was encamped at this time at Pi-hahiroth, between Migdol and the sea, and the Lord said to Moses: "Wherefore criest thou unto me? speak unto the children of Israel, that they go forward." Moses was then commanded to lift up his rod over the sea, with the promise that the waters should divide so that Israel might go over dry-shod. Moses obeyed, and the sea was made to go back by a strong east wind, and the angel of the Lord, with the cloud, went from before them and stood between them and the Egyptians, and so Israel crossed the Red Sea.

6. **The destruction of the Egyptians** (Ex. 14:23-31). The Egyptians attempted to follow the Israelites, but the Lord took off their chariot-wheels so that the chariots pulled heavily, which greatly affrighted them and they declared that the Lord fought with Israel. Moses was then commanded to lift his rod again over the sea, and the waters came together and the Egyptians were drowned.

7. **Israel sings a song of deliverance** (Ex. 15:1-21). Upon the destruction of their enemies, Israel sang a song of triumph, and Miriam, the prophetess, sister of Moses and Aaron, with the women, took timbrels and danced for joy.

8. **The waters of Marah made sweet** (Ex. 15:22-26). From the Red Sea, Moses led the children of Israel on a three days' journey into the wilderness of Shur, but found no water. When they came to Marah, they found water, but it was bitter, so the Lord commanded Moses to take a branch from a cer-

tain tree and throw it into the water, which he did and the water became sweet. Then Moses declared to Israel that if they would observe the commandments of God, none of the diseases that came upon the Egyptians would fall upon them.

9. **Israel at Elim** (Ex. 15:27). From Marah, Israel journeyed to Elim, where there were twelve wells and seventy palm-trees, and encamped there.

10. **The giving of the manna** (Ex. 16:1-22). From Elim, Israel went into the wilderness of Sin, where they murmured against Moses, complaining that it would have been better for them to have remained in Egypt than to perish in the wilderness from hunger. Then the Lord told Moses that He would rain bread from heaven six days out of the week, that Israel should gather it each day, and that on the sixth she should gather sufficient to last over the seventh. This bread was called "manna" and came down with the dew, and when the dew was gone, it lay upon the ground like hoarfrost. The Lord also sent quails into the camp that Israel might have meat.

11. **The test sabbath** (Ex. 16:23-36).[1] In connection with the giving of manna, the Lord instituted a test sabbath and required that the people should refrain from gathering manna on the seventh day that He might "prove them, whether they would walk in my [His] law or no" (Ex. 16:4). Moses also commanded Aaron to gather a pot of this food to preserve it for future generations. This was afterwards placed in the ark of the covenant.

---

[1] This sabbath was not the sabbath of the Decalogue, but a test sabbath to prove Israel, to ascertain whether or not they would walk in the law when that was given.

THE EXODUS—MOSES

12. The rock of Horeb smitten (Ex. 17:1-7). From the wilderness of Sin the Lord led the people to Rephidim, but there was no water there and they complained against Moses. Moses then besought the Lord, who commanded him to take his rod and smite the rock of Horeb. This Moses did and the water gushed out.

13. Israel's conflict with Amalek (Ex. 17:8-16). The children of Israel found enemies in the Amalekites at Rephidim. So Moses commanded Joshua to take a force and go out and fight them. Joshua did this, and, while the battle was in progress, Moses took Aaron and Hur and went to the summit of a hill, where he lifted up his rod and Israel prevailed, but, when he let down his rod, Amalek prevailed. So Aaron and Hur took a stone, and, seating Moses thereon, held up his hands until the going down of the sun, when Amalek was discomfited. In remembrance of this victory, Moses erected an altar which he called Jehovah-nissi.

14. The visit of Jethro (Ex. 18:1-27). When Jethro, the priest of Midian, heard all that the Lord had done for Israel, he came down to Horeb to visit Moses. Here, out of thankfulness for what had occurred, he took a burnt-offering and offered it before the Lord, after which Aaron and the elders of Israel came and ate bread with him. As Moses sat to judge Israel, Jethro complained that the task was too arduous for him and advised that he select able men to be rulers of thousands, hundreds, fifties and tens. Moses did this, deciding only the most difficult cases himself. Jethro then returned to his own land.

THE GIST OF THE BIBLE

II. FROM MOUNT SINAI TO KADESH-BARNEA

1. **Preparations for the law** (Ex. 19:1-20). From Rephidim the children of Israel came into the wilderness of Sinai. Here the Lord promised them that if they would obey His voice and keep His covenant, they should be a kingdom of priests. To this the people agreed. Then the Lord commanded Moses to sanctify them for two days, with the promise that upon the third He would come down in a cloud upon Mount Sinai. The Lord also prescribed that Moses should set bounds round about Sinai, and that no one should go into the mount or touch the border of it under penalty of death. On the morning of the third day there were thundering and lightning, and a dark cloud rested upon the mountain out of which came the voice of a trumpet exceedingly loud. At this the children of Israel assembled around the base of the mount, and Moses was commanded to ascend to its summit.

2. **Moses receives the law** (Ex. 19:21-34:35). To be brief, there was a threefold giving of the law:

(1) *Orally.* When Moses first went into Mount Sinai, he received from the lips of the Lord, Himself, the Ten Commandments,[1] certain "judgments"

---

[1] The Ten Commandments were never given to the Gentiles, but to a race of people who had been in the land of Egypt and the house of bondage (**Ex.** 20:2; Deut. 5:6). They constituted the covenant (Deut. 4:13) that was made with that people, and that people alone (Deut. 5:2, 3), and as this was afterwards abolished (2 Cor. 3:7-11; Eph. 2:14-18; Col. 2:14-17), and the new covenant substituted in its place (Jer. 31:31-34; Gal. 4:22-31; Heb. 8:7-13), we are under no obligations to observe it, only so far as its requirements have been adopted into the latter. As the Sabbath has nowhere been so incorporated, Christians are in no sense obligated to keep it.

THE EXODUS—MOSES

which related to the relations between Hebrew and Hebrew, directions for keeping the three annual feasts and instructions for the conquest of Canaan. Moses went down and communicated these to Israel, and they answered with one voice: "All the words which the Lord hath said will we do."

(2) *The first tables of stone.* Moses then went into the mount a second time and received the Ten Commandments written on two tables of stone by the finger of God, with certain instructions concerning the building of the Tabernacle, the institution of the priesthood, the offering of sacrifices, etc. But, as he was in the mount for forty days and forty nights, the Israelites supposed him dead and, at the command of Aaron, took off their golden ornaments and out of them fashioned a golden calf, which they fell down before and worshiped. As Moses came down from the mount, he heard the shouting, and, ascertaining the cause, became very angry, and, throwing the tables down, broke them.

(3) *The second tables of stone.* When Moses had condemned the people for their sins and had interceded with God in their behalf, he was commanded to hew out other tables of stone and bring them into the mount. The Lord then rewrote[1] on these tables the words of the covenant, even the Ten Commandments. At this time, Moses was in the mount for forty days and forty nights, with neither food nor drink, and, when he returned to the people, his face

---

[1] Compare Ex. 34: 27, 28 with Deut. 10: 1-4. This seeming discrepancy is explained by the fact that Moses wrote in the book of the law the ceremonial and judicial parts, while God wrote upon the tablets the moral part contained in the Ten Commandments.

shone so that it was necessary to cover it with a veil.

3. **The erection of the Tabernacle** (Ex. 35:4-40:
38). While he was in the mount, Moses received full
instructions from Jehovah regarding the construction
of the Tabernacle and the institution of divine worship. Then, having received the law, he set himself
immediately to the task. The materials, which consisted of cloths of various kinds, skins, gold, silver,
brass, oil, etc., were provided by the offerings of the
people. The builder of the Tabernacle was Bezaleel,
of the tribe of Judah, who was assisted by Aholiab,
of the tribe of Dan. The priests, who were to offi-
ciate in the Tabernacle, were Aaron, the high priest,
assisted by his sons, Nadab, Abihu, Eleazar and Ithamar.

4. **The destruction of Nadab and Abihu** (Lev. 10:
1-7). After the Tabernacle worship had been established, Nadab and Abihu, two of the sons of Aaron,
came before the Lord with strange fire in their censers of incense, for which they were immediately
destroyed by fire that went out from the Lord's
presence.

5. **The numbering of Israel** (Num. 1:1-2:34).
While the children of Israel were yet in the wilderness of Sinai, the Lord commanded Moses to take
a census of all the males over twenty years of age.
He was assisted in this work by the heads of the
twelve tribes. According to this census, there were
603,550 men able to bear arms, omitting those of the
tribe of Levi, whose exclusive duty was the service of
the sanctuary. The Lord also commanded Moses to
arrange the tribes so that they would encamp around
the Tabernacle in the following order: On the *east*,

THE EXODUS—MOSES

Judah, Issachar and Zebulun; on the *south*, Reuben, Simeon and Gad; on the *west*, Ephraim, Manasseh and Benjamin, and on the *north*, Dan, Asher and Naphtali.

6. The march to Kadesh-barnea (Num. 10:11-12:16). The children of Israel journeyed from Sinai to Kadesh-barnea. On the way a number of events occurred which it will be necessary to mention only briefly:

After leaving Sinai, the cloud rested, first, at Paran. Here Moses gave an urgent invitation to Hobab, the son of Raguel the Midianite, his father-in-law, to join the host of Israel, but this invitation was refused (Num. 10:29, 30).

At Taberah the people complained, and the Lord sent fire among them which consumed those in the uttermost parts of the camp. Moses, at the solicitation of the people, prayed to the Lord and the fire was quenched (Num. 11:1-3).

The children of Israel began to lust for the fish and vegetables of Egypt and to complain of the manna. Moses, hearing these murmurings, went to the Lord with the complaint that He had laid the whole burden upon him and had not provided meat for the people, and demanded that if He intended to continue to deal so with him to kill him outright. The Lord then told him to select seventy of the elders and bring them to the Tabernacle of the congregation, and He would put the Spirit upon them and they should help bear the burden (Num. 11:4-25).

The Lord then sent forth a wind from the sea which brought quails into the camp. These flew two cubits above the ground¹ and for two days were gathered up. But, as the children of Israel feasted upon them, the Lord smote them with a great plague so that many died (Num. 11:31-35).

The anger of the Lord was kindled against Aaron and Miriam because they spoke against Moses for marrying an Ethiopian woman, and Miriam was stricken with leprosy, but when Aaron petitioned Moses and he interceded for her, the Lord commanded that she should be compelled to remain without the camp for seven days, at the expiration of which she was to be received again (Num. 12:1-16).

III. FROM KADESH-BARNEA TO NEBO

1. **The spies sent out** (Num. 13:1-33). The children of Israel now came to Kadesh-barnea, and Moses was commanded to select from each of the tribes a ruler who was to go and spy out the land of Canaan. The spies thus chosen went through the land from south to north, and returned, after forty days, with a large cluster of grapes from Eshcol, besides pomegranates and figs. All of the spies brought back a glowing report of the richness of the land, but ten of them declared that it was invincible. Only two, Caleb and Joshua, thought that the land could be conquered and the inhabitants driven out.

2. **The unbelief of Israel** (Num. 14:1-45). When the people heard the report, they murmured against Moses and Aaron and said: "Would God that we had died in the land of Egypt! or would God we had died

---

¹ This does not mean that the quails were three feet thick upon the ground, as infidels have sometimes tried to make out, but that they flew no more than three feet above the ground.

THE EXODUS—MOSES

in this wilderness!" Hearing this, Joshua and Caleb rent their clothes and charged their brethren not to rebel against the Lord or fear the inhabitants of the land. But the people cried for them to be stoned, and the Lord said to Moses: "I will smite them with the pestilence, and disinherit them, and will make of thee a greater nation and mightier than they." But, upon Moses' intercession, the Lord pardoned their complaints, but declared that not one of those who had murmured would be permitted to enter the land.

3. The destruction of Korah, Dathan and Abiram (Num. 16: 1-50). Korah, Dathan and Abiram, with a company of princes, revolted against Moses and Aaron, charging them with assuming too much authority, and insisting that the entire congregation possessed the prerogatives of the priesthood.[1] The day following, Moses put their claim to the test, and they were commanded to appear with fire in their censers before the door of the Tabernacle. The Lord then commanded Moses to separate the people from the rebels, after which He caused the earth to open and to swallow them alive, with all of their possessions.

4. The budding of Aaron's rod (Num. 17: 1-13). Each of the tribes was then commanded to take a rod and to lay it up in the Tabernacle of the congregation, the Lord saying that the rod which He would choose should blossom. On the morrow, when Moses

---

[1] It was God's original intention that all the tribes should constitute a kingdom of priests (Ex. 19: 5, 6). But this intention was thwarted by the disobedience of Israel, and the sacerdotal office was confined wholly to the tribe of Levi. But, under the new covenant, God's purpose is fulfilled, and the entire church, not a part of it, constitutes the priesthood (1 Pet. 2: 5, 9).

went into the Tabernacle, he found that Aaron's rod, for the tribe of Levi, had budded, blossomed and brought forth almonds. The Lord then told Moses that this rod was to be preserved as a witness against the rebels. When the people saw this, they exclaimed: "Behold, we die, we perish, we all perish." Aaron's rod was afterwards put in the ark of the covenant.

5. **The death of Miriam** (Num. 20:1). Miriam died and was buried in the wilderness of Zin.

6. **The sin of Moses** (Num. 20:2-13). The people thirsted in the wilderness of Zin and murmured against Moses and Aaron. The Lord then commanded Moses to speak to a certain rock and the water would gush out. But, instead of speaking to the rock, Moses smote it twice, for which sin the Lord told him that he and Aaron should not enter the promised land.

7. **The Edomites refuse a passage to Israel** (Num. 20:14-22). Moses sent messengers from Kadesh to the king of Edom, asking permission to pass through his land on their way to Canaan. This the king of Edom refused, and the children of Israel journeyed to Mount Hor.

8. **The death of Aaron** (Num. 20:23-29). By the command of the Lord, Moses took Aaron, with his son Eleazar, into Mount Hor, where, in the sight of the congregation, he stripped him of his priestly garments, which he put upon Eleazar, and there Aaron died.

9. **The victory over the Canaanites** (Num. 21:1-3). Arad the Canaanite, hearing that Israel came by the way of the spies, went out to fight them and took

THE EXODUS—MOSES

some of them prisoners. But the Israelites vowed a vow that if the Lord would deliver the Canaanites into their hands, they would utterly destroy them. So, turning upon them, they defeated and exterminated them and destroyed their cities. The name of the place was called Hormah.

10. **The brazen serpent** (Num. 21:4-9). As the children of Israel journeyed from Mount Hor by the way of the Red Sea to compass the land of Edom, they became discouraged and again murmured against God. Because of their murmurings, the Lord sent fiery serpents among them and many were bitten and died. The people then repented, and Moses was directed to make a serpent of brass and erect it upon a pole in the camp, with the promise that whosoever looked upon it should live.

11. **The defeat of the Amorites** (Num. 21:21-32). As the Israelites continued their journey around Edom, they requested permission of Sihon, king of the Amorites, to pass through his land. This was not only refused, but Sihon, gathering his forces together, went out and fought Israel at Jahaz, where he was decisively defeated.

12. **The defeat of Og, king of Bashan** (Num. 21:33-35). Og, king of Bashan, also went out against Israel, and met them in battle at Edrei. But the Lord told Moses to fear him not, and the children of Israel smote him and his host until they were all utterly destroyed.

13. **The opposition of Balak, king of the Moabites** (Num. 22:1-24:25). Israel now came into the country of the Moabites and encamped in the plains of Moab. This greatly troubled Balak, the Moabite

king, and he sent messengers to Balaam, the son of Beor, at Pethor in Mesopotamia, requesting him to come and curse Israel. Balaam consulted the Lord, and He told him not to return with them to curse Israel, for they were a blessed people. The messengers then returned to Balak, but when they reported to him what Balaam had said, he was not satisfied, and sent more honorable messengers, who insisted that he return with them and offered him an honorable position. Balaam again consulted the Lord, who, in anger, told him to go with the messengers, but to speak the word which He should say unto him. On the way, the ass upon which he rode, meeting an angel, turned aside and, when smitten by Balaam, miraculously spoke to him. Coming to Balak, Balaam was brought out to curse Israel, but, instead, he blessed them in prophecies spoken from the high places of Baal, the summit of Mount Pisgah, and from Peor.

14. The immoral and idolatrous relations of the Israelites with the Moabites and Midianites (Num. 25:1-18). The children of Israel now dwelt at Shittim and began to enter into immoral and idolatrous relations with their Moabite and Midianite neighbors. Because of this, the Lord's anger was kindled against Israel, and He commanded Moses to slay those who were guilty of sin. The number that fell by the sword and the plague were twenty-four thousand. Afterwards (Num. 31:1-54) the children of Israel, by divine command, smote Midian, slew her kings, took her women and children captive, burned her cities and despoiled her possessions.

15. The renumbering of Israel (Num. 26:1-65).

THE EXODUS—MOSES

After this, the Lord ordered Moses to take a new census of Israel, by which it was ascertained that there were 601,730 men over twenty years of age, who were able to bear arms.

16. The call of Joshua (Num. 27:15-23). Moses went to the Lord and asked Him to appoint his successor. He was commanded to lay his hands upon Joshua, the son of Nun, and to bring him before Eleazar, the high priest, and was told that Joshua should go in and out before the children of Israel as his successor.

17. Preparations for entering the land of Canaan (Num. 28:1-Deut. 33:29). The preparations for entering the land of Canaan consisted in a restatement of the law, counsels to the priests, appointment of the cities of refuge, etc.

18. The vision and death of Moses (Deut. 34:1-8). The last act of Moses' life was his going up to the summit of Mount Nebo, where the Lord showed him the promised land, after which he died, at the age of 120 years. The children of Israel mourned for him thirty days.

QUESTIONS

Give the general outline of this study. Give the three periods of Moses' life. Who was the Pharaoh of the exodus? Give the date of the exodus. How many Israelites went out of Egypt? Give the preparations that were made for the exodus. Where was the Passover instituted? What did it commemorate? What did the pillar and the cloud signify? How many chariots did Pharaoh have when he pursued Israel? Tell about Israel crossing the Red Sea. How were the waters of Marah made sweet? Tell about the falling of the manna. Why was the test sabbath instituted? How did Moses get water out of the rock at Horeb?

THE GIST OF THE BIBLE

Describe Israel's conflict with Amalek at Rephidim. Tell about the visit of Jethro. What preparations was Moses commanded to make for the reception of the law? How many times did the Lord give the Ten Commandments to Moses and give the circumstances of each? Who were constituted priests? Who offered strange fire before the Lord and what happened to them? At the second numbering of Israel, how many fighting men were there found to be? How were the tribes to encamp around the Tabernacle? What did the Lord do to Miriam, and why? How many spies were sent out at Kadesh-barnea? Give their diverse reports. How did Israel receive their reports? What happened to Korah, Dathan and Abiram, and why? Tell about the budding of Aaron's rod. Where did Miriam die? What sin did Moses commit in the wilderness of Zin? What request did Moses make of the Edomites? What Canaanite king did Israel defeat? Where did Aaron die? Give the circumstances of the erection of the brazen serpent in the camp of Israel. What Amoritish king did Israel defeat? What other king did they defeat? Tell about the opposition of Balak. What two relations did Israel have with the Moabites? Give the number of fighting men at the time of the third census of Israel. Who was chosen as Moses' successor? What preparations were made for entering the land of Canaan? Where did Moses die and how old was he?

STUDY XVII. THE CONQUEST OF CANAAN—JOSHUA

(Book of Joshua)

INTRODUCTION

1. **Joshua.** Joshua was the son of Nun and of the tribe of Ephraim. His name signifies "savior," and he was one of the faithful companions of Moses during the exodus. He first came into notice as the commander of the Israelites in their battle with the Amalekites at Rephidim, and was afterwards one of the spies sent out at Kadesh-barnea. He was eighty-four years of age at the time that he entered Canaan.

2. **The date of the conquest.** The conquest of Canaan lay between 1451 and 1427 B. C., a period of twenty-four years.

3. **The inhabitants of Canaan.** The inhabitants of the land of Canaan at this time were known as Canaanites, and were divided into a number of tribes; as, the Hittites, Hivites, Perizzites, Girgashites, Amorites and Jebusites.

I. SPECIAL PREPARATIONS FOR THE CONQUEST

1 **Joshua commissioned** (Josh. 1:1-9). We have already seen that Joshua was appointed successor of Moses by Jehovah at the suggestion of that leader that such a successor be appointed. Now that Moses is dead, the Lord commissions him to lead his

people, promising him victory if he is courageous and observes the law.

2. **Joshua takes command** (Josh. 1:10-18). Following the reception of his commission, Joshua took command of the host of Israel. He first gave orders to the officers to pass through the army and instruct the people to prepare food, telling them that in three days they would cross the Jordan. He then told the Reubenites, Gadites and the half-tribe of Manasseh, that, although land had been allotted to them on the east of Jordan, they would be expected to cross the river and assist their brethren in driving out the inhabitants of the land.

3. **The two spies sent out** (Josh. 2:1-24). Joshua next sent two spies to view the land in the vicinity of Jericho. These men crossed the Jordan and lodged at the house of a woman by the name of Rahab. It was told the king of Jericho that these men were spies, and he sent to Rahab and demanded that they be given up. But this Rahab did not do, telling those who made the demand that they had gone out about the time of the shutting of the gate. She then took the spies to the roof of her house and hid them with the stalks of flax that were on the roof. When their pursuers were gone, she told them of the fears of the people, and exacted a promise from them that, when Jericho was taken, she and her father's house should be spared. This promise was made and confirmed with an oath, and she then let them down from the window with a scarlet cord to the outside of the city wall, the understanding being that this cord bound in the window should be the sign by which the Israelites

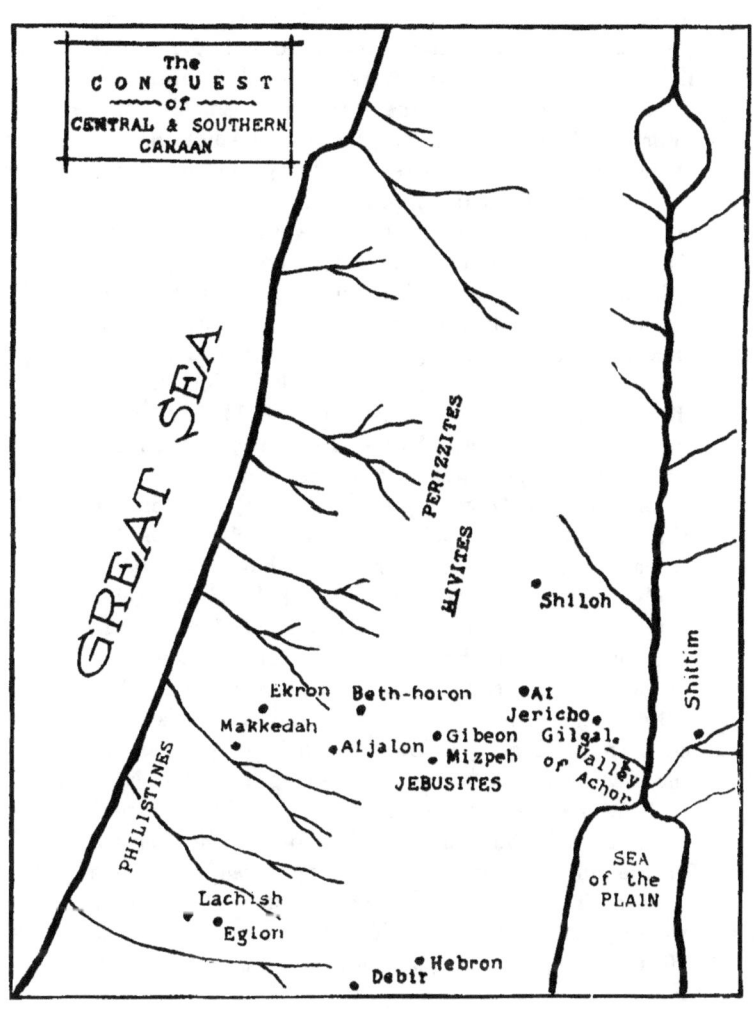

might know where she dwelt. The spies then made their way to Joshua and revealed to him the weakness of the place and the fears of its inhabitants.

4. **The passage of the Jordan** (Josh. 3:1-17). When Joshua heard the report of the spies, he led Israel from Shittim, where they had been encamped, to the east bank of the Jordan, and commanded them to sanctify themselves for the work before them. The following day Israel began to cross the Jordan. The priests were in the lead, bearing the ark of the covenant, and when their feet touched the waters, they divided and, the priests stepping aside, Israel went over dry-shod and encamped at Gilgal. By this Israel was to know that God would drive their enemies, the Hittites, Hivites, Perizzites, Girgashites, Amorites and Jebusites, out of the land.

5. **Israel at Gilgal** (Josh. 4:1-5:15). After the children of Israel had come up safely from the Jordan, the Lord commanded Joshua to appoint twelve men to take from the bed of the river twelve stones and to erect them as a memorial at Gilgal, and also to take twelve other stones and set them up for a memorial in the midst of Jordan. The Lord then commanded Joshua to circumcise the children of Israel, following which they observed the Passover and ate of the old corn of the land, with which the manna ceased to fall from heaven. Here, also, Joshua had revealed to him the Captain of the host of the Lord, who appeared as a man with a drawn sword. When Joshua fell down to worship him, the angel said: "Loose thy shoe from off thy foot; for the place whereon thou standest is holy."

THE CONQUEST OF CANAAN—JOSHUA

II. THE CONQUEST OF CANAAN

1. **The conquest of Jericho** (Josh. 6:1-27). When the inhabitants of Jericho saw that Israel had crossed the Jordan, they shut the gates of the city so that no one was allowed to go out or come in. Then the Lord commanded Joshua to arrange his host with a company of armed men and seven priests with trumpets at its head, followed by the ark. Thus arranged, the host was to march round the city once each day for six days, the priests blowing the trumpets. On the seventh day Israel was to march round the city seven times, and on the seventh round the trumpets were to be blown and the people were to shout, and the walls of the city were to fall. This was done, and Jericho fell before Joshua, who put the inhabitants to the sword, sparing only Rahab and her house. Among the things that, by divine command, were devoted to the Lord were the gold, silver and vessels of brass and iron, which were to come into the treasury of the Lord's house.

2. **The sin of Achan** (Josh. 7:1-26). After the fall of Jericho, Joshua sent spies to Ai, who returned and reported that the whole host of Israel would not be required to take that city—only two or three thousand men. So Joshua dispatched the latter number, but they were defeated by the inhabitants of the place. When Joshua went to the Lord, He replied that Israel had been defeated because it had sinned and had taken of the spoils of Jericho, which belonged to the Lord, and had appropriated them to its own private use. Joshua was then commanded to sanctify the people, and was assured that there

was an accursed thing in their midst which would have to be removed before they could be victorious over their enemies. He was told to bring the people before the Lord, and from them He selected the tribe of Judah as the guilty tribe, the family of Zarhites as the guilty family, the house of Zabdi as the guilty house, and from this He took Achan, the son of Carmi, as the guilty individual. When Achan was accused of his guilt, he admitted that he had taken "a goodly Babylonish garment, and two hundred shekels of silver, and a wedge of gold," and that they were hid in the earth in his tent. Joshua sent messengers to his tent, and, when the stolen articles were found, Achan was taken, and with him his family, into the valley of Achor, where all Israel stoned him to death and burned his body with fire. They then raised over him a great pile of stones.

3. **The conquest of Ai** (Josh. 8:1-29). Following the stoning of Achan, Joshua was commanded to take his entire host and proceed against Ai. He was told that he should do unto this city and its king as he had done unto Jericho and its king, but that the spoils were to be kept by the children of Israel for themselves. Ai was taken by stratagem. Joshua made a feint upon it with a part of his force while another part lay in ambush between it and Bethel. Seeing Joshua's depleted force, the king of Ai attacked him and Joshua fell back, upon which the Lord commanded him to stretch out his spear against the city. Joshua did as he was commanded, and the force in ambush rushed into the city and set it on fire, while the force that was with him turned on their pursuers, who were thus crushed between the

THE CONQUEST OF CANAAN—JOSHUA

two divisions. In all, twelve thousand men, women and children perished, excepting the king, who was spared alive, but who was afterwards hanged to a tree. The cattle and the spoils of the city Joshua and the Israelites took for a prey.

4. The league with the Gibeonites (Josh. 9:1-27). When the inhabitants of Canaan heard of the victories of Joshua, they leagued together for common defense. But the inhabitants of Gibeon, who were Hivites, dressed themselves in tattered garments, and, taking dry and mouldy bread and old and rent wine-bottles, came to Joshua and offered to be his servants, saying that they had heard what the Lord had done for Israel in Egypt and in the wilderness. Joshua made a league with them and confirmed it with an oath. But, three days afterwards, the children of Israel heard that the Gibeonites were their neighbors, and, calling them, Joshua inquired why they had deceived him. They replied that they had heard of the promise that the Lord had made to Moses concerning the land and that the inhabitants were to be destroyed, and that they had resorted to this stratagem in order to save themselves. Upon hearing this, Joshua promised them that he would not destroy them for his oath's sake, but declared that they should be "hewers of wood and drawers of water."

5. The victory at Gibeon (Josh. 10:1-27). Adonizedec was the king of Jerusalem, and when he heard of the fall of Ai and the league of the Israelites and Gibeonites, he greatly feared, for Gibeon was a very strong city. So, sending to the surrounding kings, he made a league with them, saying: "Come up unto me, and help me, that we may smite Gibeon: for it hath made peace with Joshua and with the children of Israel." The league was formed, and when these kings came against Gibeon, the Gibeonites sent to Joshua, who was at Gilgal, for help. Joshua gathered his army, and, with the promise of the Lord that he should be victorious, he came against the enemies of Gibeon, defeated them, slew many and pursued the remainder through Beth-horon as far as Azekah and Makkedah. As the allies fled before Israel, the Lord rained great hailstones upon them, so that more died from the hail than by the sword of Israel. At Beth-horon, Joshua commanded the sun and moon to stand still, which they did until Israel had avenged themselves upon their enemies. After the victory was won, Joshua and all Israel returned to Gilgal. But when it was told him that the five kings of the allies were hidden in a cave at Makkedah, he commanded that great stones should be rolled against the mouth of the cave and that a guard should be left to defend it, while the rest pursued the remnant of the Amorites and smote them until they were consumed. When this force returned, Joshua commanded the five kings to be brought before him, and, after his captains had put their feet upon their necks, he slew them and hung their bodies to trees until evening, when they were flung into the cave where they had hid.

6. **Further conquests in southern Canaan** (Josh. 10:28-43). Joshua now turned his attention to Makkedah, Libnah, Lachish, Eglon, Hebron and Debir, all of which cities he conquered, putting their

THE CONQUEST OF CANAAN—JOSHUA

kings and inhabitants to the sword. After these conquests, he returned to Gilgal.

7. The conquest of northern Canaan (Josh. 11: 1-23). Jabin, king of Hazor, being told how Joshua had conquered the cities of southern Canaan, enlisted in a league a large number of the neighboring kings, with a multitude of men, horses and chariots, and pitched at the waters of Merom to fight against Israel. Joshua, hearing this, led his army against Jabin, defeated him and followed the remnant of his force northward into Phœnicia. On his way back, he took Hazor, slew its king and burned the city to the ground. In course of time, all the cities in that part of the land fell before him, and he slew their kings, though he spared the cities themselves and the cattle.

8. Recapitulation (Josh. 12:1-24). At the close of the conquest, the children of Israel had conquered, in all, thirty-one kings. Yet the land was not entirely subdued, for there yet remained the country of the Philistines on the southwest, and other territory on the south, east and north which was still in the possession of the original inhabitants.

III. THE DIVISION OF THE LAND

After Joshua had conquered the land, the Lord commanded him to divide it among the tribes. The inheritance of each tribe was as follows:

1. The portion of Reuben (Josh. 13:23). The portion of the land that was allotted to Reuben lay directly east of the northern half of the Dead Sea.

2. The portion of Gad (Josh. 13:24-28). The tribe of Gad was given the territory east of the

Jordan and north of the territory of Reuben. Its southern limit would be a line drawn directly east from the northern extremity of the Dead Sea, and its northern limit would be a line drawn directly east from the Jordan about midway between the two seas, although the valley of the Jordan, eastward of that river and as far north as the Sea of Galilee, was also included in the territory belonging to this tribe.

3. **The portion of the half-tribe of Manasseh east of the Jordan** (Josh. 13:29-31). The portion of land given to the half-tribe of Manasseh east of the Jordan lay north of the territory of Gad and east of the territory of Gad, the Sea of Galilee and the Jordan River.

4. **The portion of Simeon** (Josh. 19:1-9). The portion of land allotted to the tribe of Simeon was the most southerly of any west of the Jordan. It lay between, and south of, the portion given to Judah and the land of Philistia.

5. **The portion of Judah** (Josh. 15:1-63). Judah's inheritance skirted the entire west coast of the Dead Sea and extended westward to a point about midway between that sea and the Mediterranean.

6. **The portion of Benjamin** (Josh. 18:11-28). The land of the Benjamites lay just west of the Jordan River, north of the portion of Judah and east of a point midway between the Jordan and the Mediterranean.

7. **The portion of Dan** (Josh. 19:47-51). The tribe of Dan had territory allotted to it which lay north of Judah and Philistia, west of Benjamin and Ephraim and east of the Mediterranean.

8. **The portion of Ephraim** (Josh. 16:5-10). The

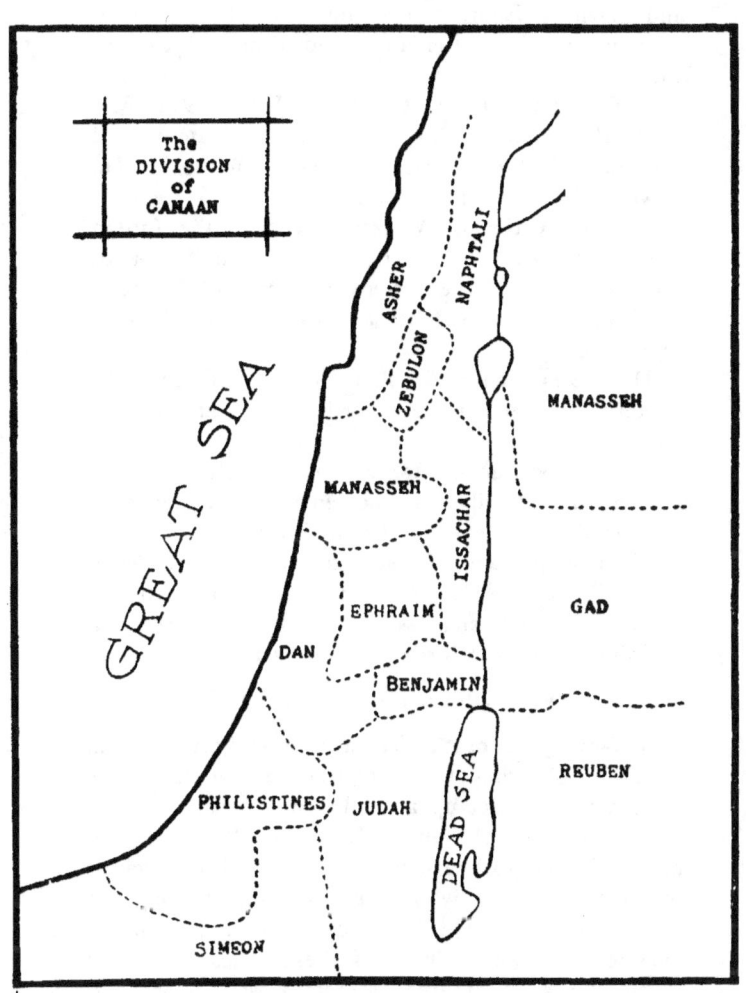

land given to Ephraim lay almost in the center of Palestine, north of Benjamin and Dan and east of Dan.

9. **The portion of Issachar** (Josh. 19:17-23). Issachar's territory lay north of Benjamin and Ephraim and skirted nearly the whole of the Jordan, between the seas, on the west.

10. **The portion of Manasseh west of the Jordan** (Josh. 17:1-18). The territory of the half-tribe of Manasseh west of the Jordan lay north of Ephraim and Dan, west of Issachar and east of the Mediterranean Sea.

11. **The portion of Zebulun** (Josh. 19:10-16). The territory of Zebulun lay north of Manasseh and Issachar.

12. **The portion of Asher** (Josh. 19:24-31). The territory of this tribe was located north of Manasseh and Zebulun and east of the Mediterranean.

13. **The portion of Naphtali** (Josh. 19:32-46). Naphtali's portion lay east of Asher and Zebulun, north of Zebulun and Issachar and west of the Sea of Galilee, the river Jordan and the waters of Merom.

IV. CONCLUDING EVENTS

1. **Setting up of the Tabernacle at Shiloh** (Josh. 18:1). Following the conquest of the land, the Tabernacle was set up at Shiloh in Ephraim.

2. **The cities of refuge** (Josh. 20:1-9). By command of God, Joshua established six cities of refuge to which a person who killed another, at unawares or unwittingly, might flee and find refuge from the avenger of blood. Three of these cities were east of the Jordan and three of them west. Those east

THE CONQUEST OF CANAAN—JOSHUA

of the Jordan were: Bezer, in the territory of Reuben; Ramoth, in Gad, and Golan, in Manasseh. Those west were: Kirjath-arba, or Hebron, in Judah; Shechem, in Ephraim, and Kedesh, in Naphtali.

3. **The allotments of the Levites** (Josh. 21:1-45). When the land was divided, no territory was allotted to the tribe of Levi, as they were a tribe of priests. But, after the other tribes had received their portions, the fathers of the Levites came to Joshua and Eleazar and the fathers of Israel, and demanded that cities with their suburbs be given them according to the divine command through Moses. This was acceded to, and forty-eight cities were allotted to them, scattered throughout the land of Canaan.

4. **The schism of Reuben, Gad and Manasseh** (Josh. 22:1-34). Joshua now called the Reubenites, Gadites and Manassehites, whose territory lay beyond Jordan, and instructed them to return to the lands which had been allotted them. These instructions they obeyed, and built a great altar by the Jordan. The other tribes, when they heard this, were greatly incensed and gathered together at Shiloh to prepare for war. They sent messengers to the Reubenites, Gadites and Manassehites, one from each of the ten remaining tribes, who charged them with having rebelled against the Lord. This charge the Reubenites, Gadites and Manassehites denied, and replied that they had built the altar, not for burnt-offering or sacrifice, but to be a witness between them and the other tribes and their generations after them that they had part and lot in the common worship of Israel. When the messengers of the ten tribes

heard this, they were greatly pleased and returned to their own land and war was averted.

5. **The last counsels of Joshua** (Josh. 23:1-24:28). Joshua was now very old, and, calling before him the leaders of the people, he recounted their victories and the ways in which the Lord had delivered them, and admonished them to be true and faithful to their God. He then put the test in the following words: "And if it seem evil unto you to serve the Lord, choose you this day whom ye will serve; whether the gods which your fathers served that were on the other side of the flood, or the gods of the Amorites, in whose land ye dwell: but as for me and my house, we will serve the Lord." At this, Israel cried: "God forbid that we should forsake the Lord, to serve other gods." Then Joshua made a covenant with the people and set up a stone in Shechem as a memorial of it.

6. **The death of Joshua** (Josh. 24:29-33). Joshua died and was buried in Timnath-serah in Mount Ephraim. Eleazar, son of Aaron, also died, and his son, Phinehas, took his place as high priest.

QUESTIONS

Give the general outline of this study. Give a brief account of the early history of Joshua. How many years were spent in the conquest of Canaan? When did the conquest begin? Name the tribes that inhabited Canaan before the conquest. Tell about the commission of Joshua. What was the first thing that he did when he took command of the armies of Israel? Tell about the visit of the spies to Jericho. Describe the passage of the Jordan. Where was Israel's first stopping-place in Canaan? What four things occurred there? Tell about the fall of Jericho. What was the sin of Achan and what penalty befell him? Describe the conquest of Ai. Tell about the league with the Gibeonites. De-

THE CONQUEST OF CANAAN—JOSHUA

scribe the victory at Gibeon. Mention the names of other cities which Joshua conquered. Let each student draw a map of Canaan and locate the portion of each tribe. After the conquest, where was the Tabernacle set up? How many cities of refuge were there? Name and locate them. How many cities were allotted to the Levites? Why were the Levites not given a portion with the other tribes? Tell about the schism of Reuben, Gad and Manasseh. What were the last counsels of Joshua? What did Joshua erect at Shechem? Where was Joshua buried? Who died about the same time? Who succeeded Eleazar?

STUDY XVIII. THE PERIOD OF THE JUDGES

(Judg. 1:1-1 Sam. 25:1)

INTRODUCTION

1. **The judges.** The judges were the fifteen patriots and religious reformers who were raised up by the Lord to be leaders of His people during that period of time which lay between the death of Joshua (1425 B. C.) and the accession of Saul (1095 B. C.).

2. **The condition of the people.** During this period, each tribe was a law unto itself, although they confederated together in time of common danger. The existing conditions are well expressed in chap. 17:6: "Every man did that which was right in his own eyes." The spiritual condition was one of vacillation—apostasy and reform.

3. **The incomplete victories of the tribes** (Judg. 1:1-3:4). As has before been stated, the conquest of Canaan was not complete at the death of Joshua. In some parts of the land, the original nations had strongholds either on the outskirts of or among the tribes. Judah went out against the Canaanites and drove out the inhabitants of the mountain, but could not drive out the inhabitants of the valley, because they had chariots of iron. The Benjamites also failed to drive out the Jebusites who inhabited Jeru-

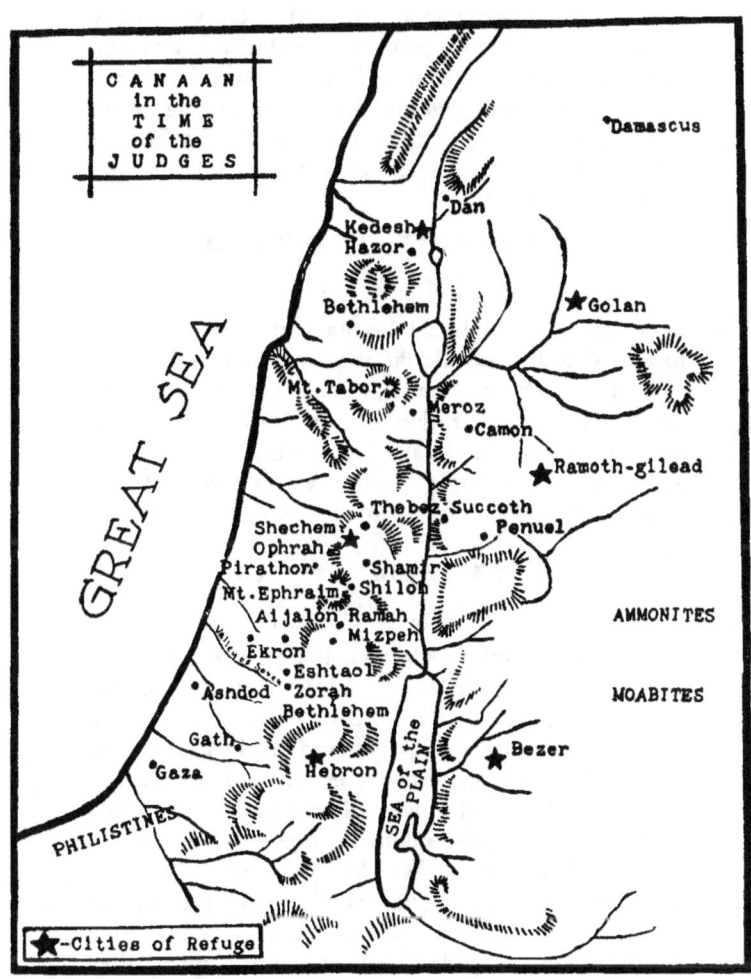

salem, and the Manassehites the inhabitants of many towns within their borders. Ephraim, Zebulun, Asher, Naphtali and Dan also made partial failures, and the Canaanites continued to dwell among them. It was the mingling of these nations with Israel that caused the latter so often to forsake Jehovah and worship Baalim.

I. THE RULE OF OTHNIEL
(Judg. 3:5-11)

So corrupt did Israel become after the death of Joshua that the Lord sold them to Chushanrishathaim, king of Mesopotamia, whom they served eight years. At the expiration of this period, the Lord heard their cries and raised up Othniel, the son of Kenaz, Caleb's younger brother, who delivered them. The land then had rest for forty years, when Othniel died.

II. THE RULE OF EHUD
(Judg. 3:12-30)

After the death of Othniel, the children of Israel apostatized, and the Lord delivered them into the hands of Eglon, king of Moab, whom they served for eighteen years. But the Lord again heard their cries and raised up Ehud, the left-handed son of Gera, the Benjamite, who delivered them. Ehud made a dagger and, taking a present, went in to Eglon and requested to see him in secret. After the attendants had gone out, Ehud thrust the dagger into his body and fled, locking the door behind him. When Eglon's attendants re-entered the room, they found their lord dead upon the ground. Fleeing to

THE PERIOD OF THE JUDGES

Mount Ephraim, Ehud blew a trumpet, and, gathering Israel around his standard, he went against Moab and slew ten thousand men. Following this, the land had rest for eighty years.

III. THE RULE OF SHAMGAR

(Judg. 3:31)

But little is known of this judge. He was probably of the tribe of Judah. The only historical fact that is recorded concerning him is that he slew six hundred Philistines with an ox-goad.

IV. THE RULE OF DEBORAH AND BARAK

(Judg. 4:1-5:31)

The children of Israel again apostatized, and were delivered into the hands of Jabin, king of Hazor, who mightily oppressed them for twenty years, being very strong, having nine hundred chariots of iron. Deborah, a prophetess of Ephraim, judged Israel at this time. Her associate was Barak, of the tribe of Naphtali, whom she ordered to take ten thousand men of Naphtali and Zebulun and proceed to Mount Tabor, where she would draw Sisera, captain of Jabin's host, to him. But Barak refused to go unless Deborah would go with him, which she readily consented to do. Heber the Kenite, who was a descendant of Hobab, Moses' father-in-law, when he saw that Barak had gone up to Tabor, went and told Sisera, who gathered his force together and went against Barak, who came down from the mountain with his ten thousand men to meet him. In this conflict, Sisera's army was defeated and fled, pursued by Barak. Sisera himself fled on foot to the tent of Jael, wife of Heber the Kenite, where, when he had quenched his thirst, he lay down and fell fast asleep. When Jael saw that he was asleep, she took one of the nails of the tent and, with a hammer, drove it through his temple. As Barak pursued, Jael went out to meet him and told him to follow her and she would show him the man that he sought. When he entered the tent, Sisera lay there dead before him. The children of Israel followed up their victory until finally Jabin himself was slain. Then Deborah and Barak sang a song of praise, glorifying God, praising the people, especially Jael, and pronounced a curse upon Meroz because the inhabitants of that place did not come up to the help of the Lord against the mighty.

V. THE RULE OF GIDEON

For the fourth time Israel apostatized, and the Lord delivered them into the hands of the Midianites, whom they served for seven years. The Midianites oppressed them so sorely that the children of Israel fled to the dens and caves of the mountains, while their enemies destroyed their crops and plundered their land.

1. **The call of Gideon** (Judg. 6:11-23). The children of Israel cried to the Lord, and He raised up Gideon, of the tribe of Manasseh, to lead them against their enemies. Gideon was threshing wheat when an angel appeared to him and said: "Go in this thy might, and thou shalt save Israel from the hand of the Midianites." Gideon replied that his family was poor in Manasseh and that he was the

THE PERIOD OF THE JUDGES

least in his father's house. But the Lord answered: "Surely I will be with thee, and thou shalt smite the Midianites as one man." In proof of this, Gideon asked a sign, and, begging the angel to tarry, he went into his house, and, preparing a kid and unleavened cakes, he put the meat in a basket and the broth in a pot and carried it out to the angel. The angel told Gideon to lay the flesh and cakes on a rock and to pour out the broth, which he did. The angel then touched the cakes and the flesh with his staff, and there rose up fire out of the rock and consumed them. This was the sign by which Gideon was to know that his visitor was an angel of the Lord.

2. **Gideon reforms his father's house** (Judg. 6: 24-32). That same night the Lord appeared to Gideon and commanded him to slay his father's bullock, seven years old, tear down his father's altar to Baal,[1] cut down the grove, and erect on the stone above mentioned an altar to Jehovah. So, taking ten servants, he did as he was commanded. The next morning, when the people of the place saw that Baal's altar and grove were destroyed, they inquired who had done it, and when it was told them that it was Gideon, the son of Joash, they demanded of his father that he be brought out that they might slay him. His father replied that if Baal was God, he was able to defend his own cause.

3. **Gideon prepares for battle** (Judg. 6:33-7:6). The Spirit of the Lord now rested upon Gideon, and he blew a trumpet and gathered around his standard

---
[1] Baal (pl. Baalim). The supreme male divinity of the Phœnician and Canaanitish nations, as Ashtoreth was their supreme female divinity.

the inhabitants of his own town, Abiezer. Then messengers were sent throughout Manasseh, Asher, Zebulun and Naphtali, and they, too, came. Having done this, Gideon demanded of the Lord that if he would deliver Israel, a fleece of wool put upon the floor might be covered with dew, while the ground should remain dry. The fleece was placed upon the floor, and while the ground remained dry, the wool was wet. Then Gideon asked the Lord, as a further sign, that the wool might be dry and the floor wet. Again the Lord answered as Gideon had requested. By these signs Gideon knew that the Lord would save Israel. Gideon then pitched at the well Harod, while the Midianites pitched by the hill Moreh in the valley. The Lord then told Gideon that Israel's number was too great to deliver the Midianites into their hands, lest they vaunt themselves, so he was commanded to permit all who were fearful to return. There returned twenty-two thousand men, leaving only ten thousand. But the Lord again told him that the number was too great, and he was commanded to take them down to the water, and was told that all who lapped as a dog should be kept, while the remainder should be sent home. By those who lapped, three hundred in all, the Lord told Gideon that he would deliver the Midianites into his hands.

4. **The overthrow of Midian** (Judg. 7:7-25). The same night, by divine command, Gideon and his servant Phurah went down into the host of Midian, which lay in the valley like grasshoppers for multitude. Entering the camp, Gideon heard one Midianite telling his fellow a dream, in which he had seen a

THE PERIOD OF THE JUDGES

cake of barley tumble into the host of Midian and overturn a tent. His fellow replied that this was nothing else than the sword of Gideon, to whom the Lord had delivered Midian. Gideon worshiped God, and, returning to Israel, divided his three hundred men into three companies, and gave each man a trumpet, an empty pitcher and a lamp, the latter to be put within the pitcher. Having done this, he commanded that, when he blew his trumpet, the others were to blow their trumpets and shout, "The sword of the Lord and Gideon." Gideon then led his army down to the camp of Midian, and, when he blew his trumpet, the three hundred blew their trumpets, broke their pitchers, held their lamps in their hands and shouted their battle-cry. This caused consternation in the Midianite camp, every man's hand being against his brother, and the Midianites fled, pursued by Manasseh, Asher, Naphtali and Ephraim. Among the Midianites slain were the two princes, Oreb and Zeeb, whose heads were brought to Gideon.

5. **The complaint of Ephraim** (Judg. 8:1-3). But the Ephraimites complained because they had not been called to share in the struggle with the Midianites, and Gideon said: "God hath delivered into your hands the princes of Midian, Oreb and Zeeb: and what was I able to do in comparison of you?" Their anger was then abated.

6. **Gideon pursues the kings of Midian** (Judg. 8:4-21). Gideon pursued the fleeing kings of Midian, Zebah and Zalmunnah, and passed through Succoth and Penuel. He demanded bread of the inhabitants of these cities, but, as this was refused, on his way

back he tore the flesh of the elders of Succoth with the thorns and briars of the wilderness and beat down the tower of Penuel and slew its inhabitants. Capturing the kings, Gideon asked them whom they had slain at Tabor. They replied that each one resembled the child of a king. Whereupon, Gideon ordered his son, Jether, to slay them. But, Jether being afraid because of his youth, Gideon took the sword and slew them and took away their ornaments.

7. **Gideon offered the crown** (Judg. 8:22-27). After the defeat of the Midianites, the children of Israel demanded that Gideon should rule over them. But this he refused to do, replying: "I will not rule over you, neither shall my son rule over you: the Lord will rule over you." He requested, however, that all the earrings taken from the Midianites should be given him, and out of them he made an ephod, which he put in his own city, but which became a snare to him and his house.

8. **The death of Gideon** (Judg. 8:28-32). Gideon ruled Israel for forty years and, dying in a good old age, was buried in Ophrah, having had seventy sons by his wives and one son, Abimelech, by a concubine at Shechem.

VI. THE RULE OF ABIMELECH
(Judg. 8:33-9:57)

After the death of Gideon, the children of Israel returned to the worship of Baal. The successor of Gideon was Abimelech, who began his rule by slaying his father's sons on one stone in Ophrah, but one of them, Jotham, escaping. The men of Shechem then made Abimelech king. When this was told

Jotham, he went to the summit of Mount Gerizim and there rebuked them in his fable of the trees meeting together to anoint a king. Abimelech ruled at Shechem three years, when the Shechemites revolted against his cruelty and laid an ambuscade for him. But, being told of this by Zebul, the ruler of the city, he escaped, defeated the Shechemites, destroyed their city and sowed it with salt. He met his death in an attack upon Thebez, where a certain woman cast a piece of millstone upon his head from the top of a tower, breaking his skull. Seeing that he was mortally wounded, he said to his armor-bearer: "Draw thy sword, and slay me, that men say not of me, A woman slew him."

VII. THE RULE OF TOLA
(Judg. 10:1, 2)

The next judge was Tola, the son of Puah, a man of Issachar. He dwelt at Shamir, where he died and was buried after ruling Israel twenty-three years.

VIII. THE RULE OF JAIR
(Judg. 10:3-5)

Tola was followed by Jair, a Gileadite, who judged Israel twenty-two years. He had thirty sons who rode thirty ass colts and had thirty cities. When he died he was buried at Camon.

IX. THE RULE OF JEPHTHAH

After the death of Jair, the children of Israel again lapsed into idolatry, and the Lord, in anger, sold them into the hands of the Philistines and the children of Ammon, who invaded their land and oppressed them eighteen years. But, at the expiration of this time, the children of Israel repented and assembled at Mizpeh, saying: "What man is he that will begin to fight against the children of Ammon? he shall be head over all the inhabitants of Gilead" (Judg. 10:6-18).

    1. **The birth and parentage of Jephthah** (Judg. 11:1-3). Jephthah was the son of Gilead by a harlot and was born in Gilead. He was a mighty man of valor, but was thrust out of his father's house by his half-brothers on account of his illegitimacy, and dwelt in the land of Tob.

    2. **Jephthah called to lead Israel** (Judg. 11:4-29). But when the Ammonites came against Israel, the elders of Gilead came to Tob and urged him to take command of their forces. This, at first, Jephthah refused to do, on account of their ill treatment, but finally consented. Having been chosen to lead the forces of Israel in Mizpeh, he sent messengers to the king of the Ammonites asking him why he had come against him. The Ammonite replied that it was because Israel had taken away a part of his land. This, Jephthah denied and called God to witness between Israel and Ammon.

    3. **Jephthah's awful vow** (Judg. 11:30-40). When the Ammonites refused to pass out of the land, Jephthah made a vow that, if the Lord would deliver them into his hands, upon his return whatsoever he met coming forth from the doors of his house should surely be the Lord's and (or) he would offer it as a burnt-offering. The Ammonites were severely defeated and were smitten from Aroer to Minnith,

THE PERIOD OF THE JUDGES

and Jephthah returned in peace. The first thing that he met coming from his house upon his return was his only daughter. When he saw her he rent his clothes, exclaiming: "Alas, my daughter! thou hast brought me very low, and thou art one of them that trouble me: for I have opened my mouth unto the Lord, and I cannot go back." His daughter replied that he should do as he had vowed. And he sent her away for two months upon the mountains to bewail her virginity with her friends, at the expiration of which time she returned and he did with her according as he had promised the Lord.[1]

4. **The second jealousy of Ephraim** (Judg. 12:1-6). The men of Ephraim were jealous because they had not been invited to share in the conflict with and victory over the Ammonites, and threatened to burn Jephthah's house with fire. Jephthah gathered the men of Gilead, defeated them and took the passages of the Jordan. And, whenever one passed over, he was required to say "Shibboleth," but, if he pronounced it "Sibboleth," it was known that he was an Ephraimite and he was accordingly slain. There

---

[1] This account of Jephthah's offering his daughter has long been a favorite argument against the inspiration of the Bible with skeptics. But, if Jephthah really did, in accordance with his vow, make his daughter a burnt-offering, God was in nowise responsible for it, for human sacrifices were condemned in the law (Lev. 18:21; 20:2; Deut. 12:31). If Jephthah really sacrificed his daughter, he followed, not a custom of his own people, but one derived from the heathen nations with whom his tribe (Gad) came continually in contact. Some expositors, however, render the Hebrew of Judg. 11:31 to read: 'Then it shall be, that whatsoever cometh forth of the doors of my house to meet me, when I return in peace from the children of Ammon, shall surely be the Lord's, *or* I will offer it up for a burnt-offering." Meaning that if a person came to meet him, that person was to be specially dedicated to the Lord; while if a clean beast came out, it was to be offered as a burnt-offering.

fell at this time forty-two thousand of the children of Ephraim.

5. **The death of Jephthah** (Judg. 12:7). Jephthah judged Israel six years, when he died and was buried in one of the cities of Gilead.

X. THE RULE OF IBZAN

(Judg. 12:8-10)

The tenth judge was Ibzan, who judged Israel seven years. He had thirty sons and thirty daughters, and, upon his death, was buried at Bethlehem.

XI. THE RULE OF ELON

(Judg. 12:11, 12)

Elon, a Zebulunite, next judged Israel. He ruled for ten years and was buried at Aijalon.

XII. THE RULE OF ABDON

(Judg. 12:13-15)

After Elon came Abdon, the son of Hillel, a Pirathonite, who judged Israel eight years. He had forty sons and thirty nephews, and, upon his death, was buried at Pirathon in the land of Ephraim.

XIII. THE RULE OF SAMSON

The children of Israel again apostatized, and the Lord delivered them into the hands of the Philistines, who afflicted them forty years.

1. **The birth and parentage of Samson** (Judg. 13: 2-25). This judge was born at Zorah in the territory of Dan, and was the son of Manoah. He was a

THE PERIOD OF THE JUDGES

Nazarite from his birth, drinking neither wine nor strong drink, nor eating any unclean thing.

2. **Samson desires a Philistine wife** (Judg. 14:1-4). Samson went down to Timnath, and, seeing a certain woman of the Philistines, he returned to his parents and requested them to get her for him to wife. At first they objected because of her nationality, but afterwards consented, not knowing that it was of the Lord.

3. **Samson's riddle** (Judg. 14:8-20). As Samson went down to Timnath to see his wife, he slew a lion. Returning to take her, he discovered that the carcass was full of bees and honey. At the marriage feast he propounded the following riddle to thirty Philistines: "Out of the eater came forth meat, and out of the strong came forth sweetness." The seven days of the feast were allotted for its answer, and the forfeit, put up by each side, was thirty sheets and thirty changes of garments. The Philistines, not guessing the riddle by the seventh day, went to Samson's wife and by threats induced her to endeavor to obtain the answer from him. This she did, and the Philistines claimed the wager, which Samson paid with the garments of thirty men whom he slew at Ashkelon. His wife was then given to his companion.

4. **The foxes and the firebrands** (Judg. 15:3-8). In the time of the wheat harvest, Samson, taking a kid, went down to Philistia to visit his wife. Her father refused to permit him to see her, offering her younger sister to him instead, and in wrath he caught three hundred foxes and, tying them together in pairs and attaching a firebrand to each pair, let

them loose in their grainfields, with the result that not only the grain, but the vineyards and olive groves, also, were destroyed. For this the Philistines burned Samson's wife and her father with fire. Samson smote them with great slaughter for this and went to dwell on the top of the rock Etam.

5. **Samson slays a thousand Philistines** (Judg. 15: 9-20). This judge was next delivered into the hands of the Philistines by the men of Judah and taken to Lehi. But when they shouted against him, the Spirit of the Lord came upon him, he burst his bands asunder, and slew a thousand of them with the jawbone of an ass. Thirsting, he called upon the Lord, who "clave a hollow place that was in the jaw," water gushed out, and he drank and was refreshed.

6. **Samson at Gaza** (Judg. 16:1-3). Samson went down to Gaza, and when it was told the Philistines that he was in the city, they locked its gates, intending to kill him in the morning. But he escaped by carrying off the city gate with its posts and bar.

7. **Samson and Delilah** (Judg. 16:4-22). In the valley of Sorek there was a woman by the name of Delilah, whom Samson loved. The lords of the Philistines came to her and offered her a large reward if she would discover the source of Samson's strength, that they might prevail against him. At first he told her that if he were bound with seven *green withes*, he would be as weak as other men. But when he was bound and the Philistines came upon him, he broke the withes as though they were tow touched with fire. He then told her that if he were bound with *new ropes*, his strength would de-

THE PERIOD OF THE JUDGES

part from him. But these, too, he broke like thread. The third time he told her that if the *seven locks* of his head were *woven in a web,* his power would depart. But, when this was done and the Philistines had come upon him, he went away with the pin of the beam and the web. But the fourth time Samson told Delilah the truth, that, as a Nazarite, his strength was in his hair. The woman went and told the lords of the Philistines, and, while Samson slept upon her knees, they came in, shaved off his seven locks, and, when he awoke, put out his eyes and carried him captive to Gaza, where they bound him with fetters of brass and made him grind in the prison-house.

8. **The death of Samson** (Judg. 16:23-31). At Gaza the Philistines offered a great sacrifice to their fish-god, Dagon,[1] and Samson was brought in and set between two pillars to make sport for them. But he said to the lad who led him by the hand: "Suffer me that I may feel the pillars whereupon the house standeth, that I may lean upon them." This was permitted him, and, calling upon the Lord, he bowed himself and pushed with all his might, and the house fell, killing his enemies and himself. He was buried in the sepulchre of his fathers between Zorah and Eshtaol, having judged Israel twenty years.

XIV. THE RULE OF ELI

Following the death of Samson there were apostasy, confusion and civil strife among the tribes (Judg. 17:1-21:25). The next judge, unless he

---
[1] The name of the national god of the Philistines at Gaza and Ashdod. He was represented with the face and hands of a man and the tail of a fish.

ruled part of the time contemporaneously with Samson, was Eli.

1. **The lineage and character of Eli.** Eli was a descendant of Ithamar, and was a pious but indolent man who was blinded by paternal affection to the degree that he lost the government over his children.

2. **The evil sons of Eli** (1 Sam. 1:3; 2:12-17, 22-25). The two sons of Eli, Hophni and Phinehas, were sons of Belial, notorious for their sacrilegious and immoral conduct. When their father reproved them for their evil lives, they hearkened not unto him.

3. **The warning to Eli** (1 Sam. 2:18-36). The parents of Samuel, Elkanah and Hannah, brought him to the Tabernacle and left him in charge of Eli, where he ministered before the Lord in a linen ephod. Then there came a man of God to Eli, telling him that his house should be cast out, that Hophni and Phinehas should die in one day, and that God would raise up unto Himself a faithful priest.

4. **The Philistines capture the ark** (1 Sam. 4:1-11). The children of Israel went out against the Philistines and pitched at Ebenezer, where they were defeated. Then the elders sent to Shiloh for the ark of the covenant, supposing that by this means they could win the victory over their foes. When the ark was brought into the camp, the children of Israel shouted and the Philistines were sore afraid. But in the battle which ensued, Israel was defeated, the ark was taken, and thirty thousand men, including Hophni and Phinehas, were slain.

5. **The death of Eli** (1 Sam. 4:12-18). The tidings of the loss of the ark and the death of his sons came to Eli as he was sitting upon a seat by the

THE PERIOD OF THE JUDGES

wayside, and so overcome was he that he fell backward off his seat and broke his neck. At the time of his death he was ninety-eight years of age and had ruled Israel forty years.

XV. THE RULE OF SAMUEL

1. **The parentage of Samuel** (1 Sam. 1:1-23). Samuel was the son of Elkanah and Hannah and of the tribe of Levi, and was promised to the Lord before his birth. He was born at Ramah.

2. **Samuel in the Tabernacle** (1 Sam. 1:24-2:36). When Samuel was weaned, his mother took him, with three bullocks, an ephah of flour and a bottle of wine, to the house of the Lord at Shiloh. Here, year by year, his parents came to offer the yearly sacrifice, and at each visit his mother brought him a little coat.

3. **The call of Samuel** (1 Sam. 3:1-21). In the days of Eli, there was no open vision, because of which the word of the Lord was precious. As Eli lay down in his place and his eyes became dim with sleep, and before the lamp went out in the Tabernacle, the voice of the Lord called, "Samuel." Samuel answered, "Here am I," and ran to Eli to ask if he had called him. Eli replied that he had not, and told Samuel to lie down. Twice was this repeated, and the second time Eli perceived that it was the voice of the Lord, and commanded Samuel to lie down again, saying that, if the Lord spoke as before, he was to reply: "Speak, Lord; for thy servant heareth." The Lord spoke the fourth time, and Samuel answered as he was bidden by Eli. Then the Lord told him that the house of Eli was rejected on ac-

count of its sins. Samuel told Eli this, and all Israel knew that the lad had been called to the prophetship.

4. The ark recovered from the Philistines (1 Sam. 5:1-7:1). When the Philistines carried away the ark from Ebenezer to Ashdod, they placed it in the house of their god, Dagon. But on the morrow, when the men of Ashdod went into the temple, they found that their god had fallen upon his face to the earth before the ark. They set him in his place again, but the same thing was repeated and the palms of both hands were broken off. The men of Ashdod were also smitten with emerods. The ark was then taken to Gath, with the same results, and then to Ekron, where the same affliction came upon the people. The Philistines then clamored for it to be returned to Israel, which was done, and, along with it, five golden emerods and five golden mice were sent as a trespass-offering. Upon its return to Israel, it was first placed in charge of Joshua, the Bethshemite, but was afterwards removed to the house of Abinadab at Kirjath-jearim, where Abinadab's son, Eleazar, was sanctified to keep it.

5. The revival at Mizpeh (1 Sam. 7:2-14). Following the restoration of the ark, Samuel commanded the people to put away their strange gods. The people did this, and served the Lord only. He then gathered them at Mizpeh, where they made an acknowledgment of all their sins before the Lord. When the Philistines heard that Israel had gathered at Mizpeh, they went up against them to battle. At this the Israelites feared greatly, but Samuel took a sucking lamb and offered it as a burnt-offering, at

THE PERIOD OF THE JUDGES

which the Philistines were defeated and were driven back to their own land.

6. **The latter years of Samuel** (1 Sam. 7:15-25:1). The remainder of Samuel's life is so interwoven with the lives of Saul and David that it will be considered in the following two lessons. Briefly, however, the events were as follows: The anointing of Saul as king; the announcement of the kingdom; the announcement of Saul's failure; the anointing of David; the death of Samuel at Ramah after having ruled Israel for forty years.

QUESTIONS

How many judges were there? Who were the judges? What was the condition of the people under their rule? Mention some of the incomplete victories of the tribes. Who was Othniel and how long did he rule? What nation of people were the enemies of Israel during Othniel's rule? Who was Ehud and who were the enemies of Israel under his rule? Who was Shamgar and what nation of people were enemies of Israel under his rule? Tell about Deborah and Barak. Who was Gideon? How was he called? What did he do first? What nation did he fight? How was the victory won? Give some of the events in the latter part of Gideon's life. Tell something about Abimelech. Tell about the rule of Tola. Of Jair. Who was Jephthah? Who were the enemies of Israel during his rule? What awful vow did he make? Tell about Ibzan. Tell about Elon. Tell about Abdon. Who was Samson? Tell about him taking a Philistine wife. Give the story of the foxes. Tell about the relations of Samson and Delilah. How did Samson die? Who was Eli? What was his character? What kind of sons did he have? How did the ark happen to fall into the hands of the Philistines? What effect did this have upon Eli? Give the names of Samuel's father and mother. How did he happen to be placed in the Tabernacle? Tell about his call. Tell about the recovery of the ark. Tell about the revival at Mizpeh. Give the important events of the latter years of Samuel's life. Where did he die? How long did he rule?

STUDY XIX. THE UNDIVIDED KINGDOM —SAUL

(1 Sam. 9:1-31:13)

INTRODUCTION

1. **The meaning of the name "Saul."** The name "Saul" means "asked for."

2. **The condition of the times.** The corrupt administration of justice by Eli's sons furnished an occasion for the desire for a king on the part of the children of Israel. This desire was further strengthened by the example of the nations around them who were ruled by kings. Samuel had prepared the people for the kingdom by influencing them to renounce their idolatry and sin and by bringing the tribes more together into one body, yet he protested against the kingdom to the last.

3. **The time of Saul's reign.** Saul reigned between the years 1095 and 1055 B. C., Usher's chronology.

I. THE EARLY LIFE OF SAUL

1. **The parentage of Saul** (1 Sam. 9:1, 2). Saul was of the tribe of Benjamin, and the son of Kish, a mighty man of power.

2. **Saul meets Samuel** (1 Sam. 9:3-27). The asses of Kish were lost, and Saul and a servant were dispatched to find them. Passing through Mount Ephraim, Shalisha, Shalim and the land of the Benjamites,

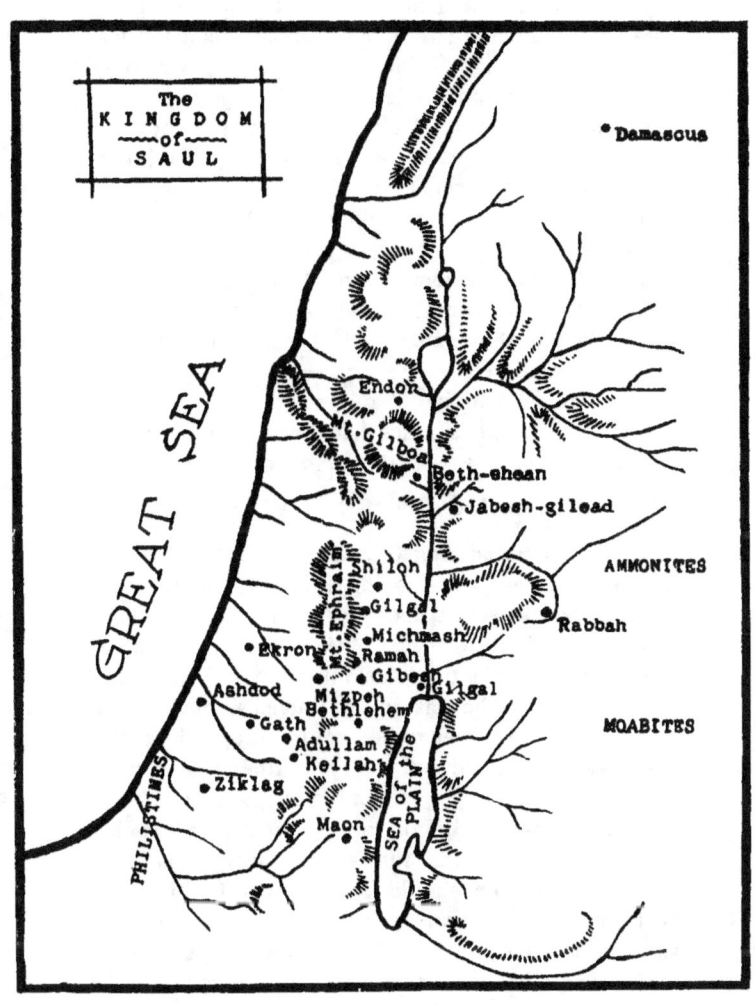

they came to the land of Zulph, but, not finding the asses, Saul suggested that they return home for fear that his father might think that they, too, were lost. To this the servant objected, and suggested that they visit Samuel at Ramah, who might be able to show them the way they should go. Saul consented, and they went into the city in search of Samuel. Now, the day before, the Lord had told Samuel that he would send to him a man out of the land of Benjamin whom he should anoint king over Israel. So, when Samuel beheld Saul, the Lord said to him: "Behold the man whom I spake to thee of! this same shall reign over my people." Upon hearing this, Samuel invited Saul to eat with him, told him that his father's asses had been found, and informed him that he was the desire of Israel.

II. KING SAUL UNDER DIVINE FAVOR

1. Saul anointed king (1 Sam. 10:1-16). The next morning, as Saul was leaving the city, Samuel took a vial of oil, poured it upon his head and kissed him, exclaiming: "Is it not because the Lord hath anointed thee to be captain over his inheritance?" He then told him that as he passed by Rachel's sepulchre he should meet two men who would inform him that the asses were found and that his father was sorrowing for him as lost. Samuel also gave him other signs by which he might know that he had spoken the truth, telling him, further, to tarry seven days at Gilgal until he should come down to him with burnt-offerings, sacrifices and peace-offerings and show him what to do. When they parted, Saul's heart was changed, and, meeting a company of

THE UNDIVIDED KINGDOM—SAUL

prophets, he prophesied unto them. All the signs predicted came to pass.

2. **Saul chosen king** (1 Sam. 10:17-27). Samuel then called all Israel together at Mizpeh. When all the tribes came near, he selected the tribe of Benjamin. Then, out of the tribe of Benjamin he selected the family of Matri. And then, out of the family of Matri, he chose Saul, the son of Kish. When inquiry was made as to the whereabouts of Saul, the Lord told those who sought him that he was hiding among the stuff. They then ran and brought him before the people, and he stood head and shoulders above them all. Then Samuel introduced him as the chosen of the Lord, and the people shouted: "God save the king!"

3. **Saul's victory over the Ammonites** (1 Sam. 11: 1-11). Nahash, the king of the Ammonites, came against Jabesh-gilead, and the men of that city said: "Make a covenant with us, and we will serve thee." But Nahash replied: "On this condition will I make a covenant with you, that I may thrust out all your right eyes, and lay it for a reproach upon all Israel." When the elders of Jabesh heard this, they requested seven days in which to consider the matter, which was granted. During this time they sent messengers to Gibeah of Saul, who told the inhabitants of that place of the demands of the Ammonites. When Saul heard the tidings, the Spirit of the Lord came upon him, and, in his anger, he hewed a yoke of oxen in pieces and sent the pieces throughout the land of Israel by messengers, with these words: "Whosoever cometh not forth after Saul and after Samuel, so shall it be done unto his oxen." Upon hearing this threat, fear came upon the people, and they assembled to-

gether with one consent, and on the following morning, 330,000 strong, they fell upon the Ammonites, slew part of them and scattered the rest.

4. **The renewal of the kingdom at Gilgal** (1 Sam. 11:12-15). So delighted were the people with the victory that they said to Samuel: "Who is he that said, Shall Saul reign over us? bring the men, that we may put them to death." But Saul replied: "There shall not a man be put to death this day: for to-day the Lord hath wrought salvation in Israel." Samuel then commanded them to assemble at Gilgal, where the kingdom was renewed and where sacrifices and peace-offerings were made amidst great rejoicing.

5. **The proclamation of the kingdom** (1 Sam. 12: 1-25). Samuel then called all Israel to witness before God that he had not defrauded nor oppressed them, nor taken their possessions, nor received bribes. He also recounted the deliverances of Jehovah from the hands of Pharaoh, Sisera, the Philistines, the Moabites and the Ammonites, and declared that, whereas God had given them a king, if they followed Him, they should be blessed, but if they did not follow Him, His hand should be against them as it was against their fathers. As a sign that Israel had sinned against God, Samuel prayed and the Lord sent a storm of thunder and rain because of which the people feared greatly.

III. KING SAUL UNDER DIVINE DISFAVOR

1. **Saul's rejection announced** (1 Sam. 13:1-14). Saul had reigned two years, and chose for himself a body-guard of two thousand men at Michmash and

THE UNDIVIDED KINGDOM—SAUL

also a body-guard for Jonathan of one thousand men at Gibeah. Jonathan smote the garrison of the Philistines at Geba, and, when the tidings of this reached Philistia, the Philistines gathered together an army of thirty thousand chariots, six thousand horsemen and a multitude besides, and came and pitched in Michmash. While the Philistines were making these preparations, Saul blew a trumpet throughout the land and assembled all Israel together at Gilgal. But, when they saw the multitude of the Philistines, they hid themselves in caves, thickets, rocks, high places and pits. Then Saul, after waiting seven days according to the command of Samuel, offered a burnt-offering himself. After he had done this, Samuel came and inquired why he had offered the burnt-offering. Saul replied that he had not come at the time appointed, and, as the Philistines were about to come against him, he forced himself to offer it. Samuel rebuked him for this, and told him that the kingdom should be taken from him.

2. **Jonathan's great victory over the Philistines** (1 Sam. 13:15-14:23). Following this, the Philistines went out in three companies against Israel. On a certain day, Jonathan, with his armor-bearer, secretly left the camp of Israel and went up to the Philistine garrison at Michmash. When the Philistines saw them coming, they derisively cried: "Behold, the Hebrews come forth out of the holes where they had hid themselves." And again: "Come up to us, and we will show you a thing." Upon hearing these taunts, Jonathan and his armor-bearer, confident that the Lord had given the Philistines into their hands, fell upon them and slew twenty. The remainder

trembled with fear and fell upon one another. Saul's watchmen saw the Philistines melting away and reported the same to Saul, who commanded that Israel should be numbered that he might ascertain who was missing. When this was done, it was ascertained that Jonathan and his armor-bearer were the missing ones. Then Saul gathered his army, fell upon the Philistines and they fled.

3. **Saul angry with Jonathan** (1 Sam. 14:24-45). In the morning of this day, Saul had adjured the people, saying: "Cursed be the man that eateth any food until evening, that I may be avenged on mine enemies." At the time that this adjuration was made, Jonathan and his armor-bearer were without the camp on their way to the Philistine garrison. Following the battle, the people came to a wood and there was honey upon the ground, but none of them dared to partake of it. Jonathan, not knowing the vow of his father, dipped his rod into the honey and tasted it. When Saul became aware of Jonathan's transgression, although it had been committed in ignorance, he was about to slay him in conformity with his vow, but the people flew to his defense and exclaimed: "Shall Jonathan die, who hath wrought this great salvation in Israel? God forbid: as the Lord liveth, there shall not one hair of his head fall to the ground; for he hath wrought with God this day."

4. **A resume of Saul's wars** (1 Sam. 14:46-52). After Saul had taken the kingdom, he fought and overcame the Moabites, Ammonites, Edomites, Philistines and Amalekites. In these wars, Saul's captain was Abner, the son of Ner, Saul's uncle.

5. **Saul's incomplete obedience** (1 Sam. 15:1-35).

THE UNDIVIDED KINGDOM—SAUL

Samuel the prophet came to Saul and commanded him to smite Amalek, charging him to "utterly destroy all that they have, and spare them not; but slay both man and woman, infant and suckling, ox and sheep, camel and ass." So Saul went and smote Amalek from Havilah to Shur, but saved Agag, the king, and the best of the flocks alive. When Samuel came to Saul, the latter said: "Blessed be thou of the Lord: I have performed the commandment of the Lord." But Samuel replied: "What meaneth then this bleating of the sheep in mine ears, and the lowing of the oxen which I hear?" Samuel then condemned Saul for his sin, and declared again that the Lord had rejected him from being king. At this, Saul bitterly repented, but Samuel refused to give heed and demanded that Agag be brought before him. When this was done, Samuel hewed Agag in pieces before the Lord in Gilgal. Then Samuel returned to Ramah and Saul to Gibeah.

6. **Saul troubled with an evil spirit** (1 Sam. 16:1-23). By divine command, Samuel now anointed David king, and the Spirit of the Lord departed from Saul and an evil spirit from the Lord troubled him.[1] Saul's servants suggested that they be authorized to find a man who was a cunning player upon the harp, who would be able thereby to drive the evil spirit away. This they were commanded to do, and they found David and brought him to the court. Whenever Saul was afflicted, David played upon his harp and refreshed him.

7. **Saul becomes jealous of David** (1 Sam. 17:1-

---
[1] This was not a spirit of *moral*, but of *mental*, evil which the Lord sent upon Saul as a judgment for his sins.

18:19). After this, David slew Goliath and, on account of the applause of the people, Saul became jealous of him. So, when David came into his presence to play, after his return from the battlefield, Saul, being afflicted with the evil spirit, threw his javelin at him two times, but David escaped unharmed. Saul also promised Merab, his daughter, to David to be his wife, but, when the time came, she was given to Adriel the Meholathite.

8. Saul gives Michal to David (1 Sam. 18:20-30). Michal, the daughter of Saul, loved David, and, when this was told the king, he said: "I will give him her, that she may be a snare to him, and that the hand of the Philistines may be against him." The servants of Saul told this to David and he exclaimed: "Seemeth it to you a light thing to be a king's son in law, seeing that I am a poor man, and lightly esteemed?" Saul required of David as a dowry the death of one hundred Philistines, and David and his men went forth and slew two hundred. Then Saul gave Michal to David to wife.

9. Saul attempts to kill David again (1 Sam. 19: 1-17). After this, Saul commanded Jonathan and all his servants to kill David. But Jonathan loved him and warned him of his father's orders. Then he went before his father and pleaded for David. At this Saul relented and swore that, as the Lord lived, David should not be slain. David was then recalled into his presence and was sent to fight the Philistines. After he had defeated them, he returned and played the harp in Saul's presence. But Saul, being again afflicted with the evil spirit, became enraged and sought to smite David to the wall with his javelin, but he

THE UNDIVIDED KINGDOM—SAUL

escaped and fled. That night the king set watchers around David's house that they might slay him in the morning, but Michal let him down through a window and he escaped. She then placed an image in his bed with a pillow of goat's hair for a bolster and reported to the guard that David was sick. When the messengers were come in and had discovered the deception, they reported the same to the king, who censured Michal for letting her husband escape, telling her that he was her enemy. David fled to Samuel at Ramah.

10. **David shows mercy to Saul** (1 Sam. 19: 18-24: 22). From Ramah David fled to Ahimelech, the priest, at Nob, and from there to Achish, king of Gath. But, fearing the Philistines, he escaped to the cave of Adullam, where he gathered about him a company of four hundred men. After this, David went to Mizpeh in Moab, and from there, by the command of the prophet Gad, he departed to the forest of Hareth in Judah. But Saul discovered where David was and laid his plans to kill him. He slew Ahimelech and his house of priests, who had befriended David, but David escaped and fled to the mountain of Ziph. Here Jonathan found him and the two renewed their covenant, but the Ziphites revealed David's hiding-place to Saul and offered to deliver him up, upon which he fled to the wilderness of Maon in the plain on the south of Jeshimon. Later, David dwelt in En-gedi, and when this was told the king, he went down to capture him. Coming to a cave, Saul went in to rest, not knowing that David was concealed within. When the men of David saw his opportunity to kill Saul, they said to

their leader: "Behold the day of which the Lord said unto thee, Behold, I will deliver thine enemy into thine hand, that thou mayest do to him as it shall seem good unto thee." But David refused to slay Saul, being content simply to cut off the skirt of his robe. Saul departed from the cave and David, following him, cried: "My lord the king." Upon hearing this, Saul stopped, and David, bowing himself, came to him and inquired why he had opened his ears to the idle tales of men, declaring that he meant him no harm, showing him the piece of his garment and telling him how he had spared his life. When the king heard David's words and saw the evidence of his mercy, he relented, and declared that David was better than he and that he knew that he would yet possess the kingdom. He also made David swear that he would not cut off his seed after his death. They then parted, Saul going home and David to his stronghold.

11. David shows Saul mercy a second time (1 Sam. 26:1-25). But Saul's good intentions were short-lived, and when the Ziphites told him that David was in the hill of Hachilah, he took three thousand chosen men and sought him. David, hearing through his spies where Saul had pitched, took a servant (Abishai) and went to his camp. Saul lay in the midst of the camp with his spear thrust into the ground at his head and a cruse of water by his side. David took these with him, and when he reached the summit of a near-by hill, he cried out to Abner, who was with Saul, and accused him of not diligently protecting the king. He then told him to see where Saul's spear and cruse of water were.

THE UNDIVIDED KINGDOM—SAUL

Then David showed the spear and told him to send young men to bring it, chiding him at the same time for seeking to slay him. Hearing this, the king confessed his sin and returned to Gibeah. David then went into Philistia, where he allied himself with Achish, king of Gath, to fight against Israel, but was providentially saved from this mistake by the disfavor of the lords of the Philistines.

12. Saul consults the witch of Endor (1 Sam. 28: 7-25). Saul saw the host of the Philistines advancing and inquired of the Lord, but received no answer, "neither by dreams, nor by Urim, nor by prophets," so he consulted the witch of Endor. Taking two of his companions and disguising himself, he went to her by night, and requested that she bring up the one whom he should name. But the woman was afraid, for Saul had cut off from the land those who had familiar spirits. Saul quieted her fears, and told her that no punishment should come upon her, and requested her to bring up Samuel. When Samuel appeared, the woman knew that her interviewer was Saul. As she described the form of the appearance which she saw coming up out of the earth, Saul knew that it was Samuel and bowed himself to the ground. Then Samuel asked Saul why he had disquieted him, and Saul replied that he was sore distressed because of the Philistines; that the Lord had refused to answer him, and that he had called him up in order that he might know what to do. Samuel then told him that the kingdom had been rent from him and given to David, and that on the morrow he and his sons should be with him. At these words, Saul was prostrated, and the woman killed a calf and made bread, and brought it before him and his servants, and they did eat.

13. **The death of Saul** (1 Sam. 31:1-13; 1 Chron. 10:1-14). On the morrow, Saul fought the Philistines at Mount Gilboa, and Israel was defeated. Among the slain were Saul's sons, Jonathan, Abinadab and Melchi-shua, Saul himself being wounded. Seeing his condition, Saul called his armor-bearer and commanded him to take a sword and thrust him through lest the Philistines come and abuse him. The armor-bearer refused to do this, and Saul fell upon a sword himself and so died. His armor-bearer then followed his example and died with his master. On the morrow, when the Philistines found the bodies of Saul and his sons, they sent the tidings of their death back to the land of Philistia, and, stripping off Saul's armor, they placed it in the house of Ashtaroth and fastened his body to the wall of Beth-shan. The inhabitants of Jabesh-gilead, hearing what the Philistines had done, came by night and took the bodies of Saul and his sons and burned them at Jabesh, afterwards burying their bones at the same place under a tree. They then fasted seven days.

QUESTIONS

What does the name "Saul" mean? Give the conditions under which Saul took the throne. Who was Saul's father? To what tribe did he belong? How did Saul come to meet Samuel? Tell about Saul's anointing. Tell about the public announcement of Saul as king. Describe Saul's victory over the Ammonites. Following this victory, what occurred at Gilgal? Tell about the defeat of the Philistines at Michmash. In what respect did Saul sin in connection with this last battle? Tell about Saul's attempt to slay Jonathan. Against what nations did Saul fight? Tell

THE UNDIVIDED KINGDOM—SAUL

about Saul's incomplete obedience. How was Saul afflicted? Whom did his servants secure as a harper to drive away the evil spirit? Why did Saul become jealous of David? Who was Michal? Tell about Saul's second attempt to kill David. How many times did David show mercy to Saul? Tell about the first. The second. Why did Saul consult the witch of Endor? What did Samuel tell him? Describe the death of Saul.

STUDY XX. THE UNDIVIDED KINGDOM— DAVID

(1 Sam. 16:1-1 Kings 2:11; 1 Chron. 11:1-29:30)

INTRODUCTION

1. **The meaning of the name "David."** The name "David" probably means "beloved."

2. **The condition of the times.** Under David, the kingdom reached the zenith of its power, and, at his death, he reigned over that territory which extended "from the river of Egypt to the Euphrates: from Gaza on the west to Thapsacus on the east." From all the tribes in this vast territory a yearly tribute was exacted. Conditions were particularly auspicious for the establishment of a broad empire. Egypt, through internal troubles, was in no condition to prosecute foreign conquests; Assyria had nearly sunken out of sight as a dominating power; the Hittites were practically helpless.

3. **The time of David's reign.** David reigned between the years 1055 and 1015 B. C., Usher's chronology.[1]

I. DAVID THE YOUTH

1. **David's parentage** (1 Sam. 16:1). David was of the tribe of Judah and was the son of Jesse the Bethlehemite. His early occupation was the care of

---
[1] As this study is too lengthy for one lesson, it might be divided into two, the first four divisions being taken in the first and the fifth division in the second.

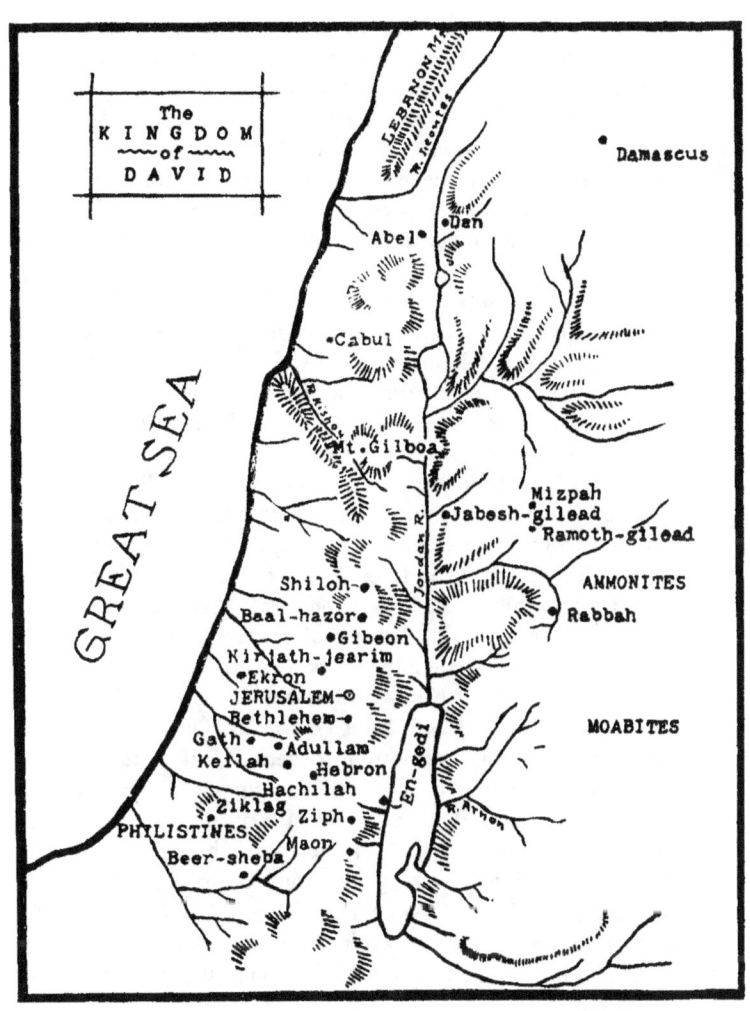

his father's flocks. During his shepherd life, he composed some of the most beautiful of his Psalms, which he sang to the accompaniment of his harp. As a shepherd he was also renowned for his strength and courage. Once, when a lion came and took a lamb out of the flock, David slew the lion and rescued the lamb. In personal appearance he is described as of a ruddy countenance and beautiful to look upon.

2. David anointed king (1 Sam. 16:2-13). When the Lord rejected Saul, he sent Samuel to the house of Jesse, at Bethlehem, to anoint one of his sons to be king over Israel. Samuel at first objected, saying that if Saul heard of it he would kill him. But the Lord told him to take an heifer and to pretend that he was going to Bethlehem to sacrifice. The Bethlehemites saw him coming, and trembled, inquiring if he were coming peaceably. He replied that he was coming to sacrifice, and for them to sanctify themselves. He then called the house of Jesse, and, as they passed before him, he said of the first son, Eliab: "Surely the Lord's anointed is before him." But the Lord told him that Eliab was rejected. Then Abinadab passed by without being chosen. Then Shammah, and, in their turn, four others. But none of these was Samuel commanded to anoint. Samuel then asked Jesse if these were all of his children. Jesse replied that he had another son, the youngest, who was keeping the sheep. Samuel commanded him to send for him, and, when David came in, the Lord said to Samuel: "Arise, anoint him: for this is he." Then Samuel arose and anointed David, and returned to Ramah.

THE UNDIVIDED KINGDOM—DAVID

II. DAVID THE COURTIER

1. **David brought before Saul** (1 Sam. 16:14-23). We have already seen, in the preceding lesson, how David was brought before Saul to play the harp and drive away the evil spirit that possessed him. It will not, therefore, be necessary more than to mention this and other events already touched upon.

2. **David slays Goliath** (1 Sam. 17:1-58). During the time that David's relations with Saul existed, there was war between the Philistines and Israel, and the Philistines pitched at Ephes-dammim, between Shochoh and Azekah, while Saul and his army pitched in the valley of Elah. While these armies were in battle array against each other, there came out of the camp of the Philistines a giant, Goliath by name, an inhabitant of Gath, who defied the armies of Israel forty days, and challenged a champion of the same to come out and meet him in mortal combat, saying that the victory should rest with the side of the one who slew the other. When Israel heard these words, they were greatly dismayed, and there was found no man who dared to meet him. But David had been sent down to Saul's army with food for his three eldest brethren, who were soldiers, and, when he heard the taunts of the Philistines, he inquired what the king would do to the man who slew the giant. He was told that Saul would enrich him, make his father's house free, and give his daughter to him to wife. Saul, hearing of the inquiries of David, sent for him, and, when he had entered his presence, David said: "Let no man's heart fail because of him; thy servant will go and fight with this Philistine." At

first Saul objected because of David's youth, but, as he was persistent, the king bade him go. Saul put his armor on David and his sword in his hand, but, as the lad had not proved them, he put them off, and, taking his staff, he went to the brook, from the bed of which he selected five smooth stones, and, with his sling in his hand, he went forth to meet the giant. When Goliath saw David coming, he exclaimed: "Am I a dog, that thou comest to me with staves?" David replied: "Thou comest to me with a sword, and with a spear, and with a shield: but I come to thee in the name of the Lord of hosts, the God of the armies of Israel, whom thou hast defied." The Philistine then drew near, and David ran out to meet him. Taking one of the stones from his bag, he threw it, and it struck the giant in the forehead, and he fell on his face to the earth. Then David ran, and, taking Goliath's sword, he cut off his head. When the Philistines saw that their champion was slain, they fled, pursued by Israel even to the gates of Ekron. David brought the head of Goliath to Jerusalem and put his armor in his tent.

3. **Jonathan makes a covenant with David** (1 Sam. 18:1-7). From this time forth, Jonathan, the son of Saul, loved David. He made a covenant with him, placed his own robe upon him, and gave him his garments, sword, bow and girdle. Saul, also honored David by making him the commander of his army.

4. **Saul becomes jealous of David** (1 Sam. 18:8-19). David returned from the slaughter of the Philistines and the women sang: "Saul hath slain his thousands, and David his ten thousands." This provoked Saul's jealousy, and, as has already been stated,

THE UNDIVIDED KINGDOM—DAVID

he tried at two different times to slay him. He also removed him from the command of his army and made him commander of only one thousand men.

5. **Saul gives Michal to David** (1 Sam. 18:20-30). Saul promised his elder daughter, Merab, to David, but, instead, gave her to Adriel. His younger daughter, Michal, loved David, and, when Saul heard this, he was greatly pleased and readily consented that she should be his wife, supposing that she would become a snare to him so that the Philistines would prevail against him. But, instead, she proved true to her husband and helped him to escape out of her father's hands.

6. **David flees the court** (1 Sam. 19:1-17). Saul's third and last attempt to kill David being unsuccessful, he fled to Samuel at Ramah. From this time to his selection as king over Judah at Hebron, he was an outlaw fleeing from the vengeance of King Saul.

III. DAVID THE OUTLAW

1. **Jonathan warns David** (1 Sam. 20:1-42). From Ramah, David fled to Jonathan and inquired of him why his father sought to slay him. To this inquiry Jonathan replied that David should not die, as he would discover his father's intention and reveal it unto him. So it was arranged that on the next day Jonathan should go to the feast of the new moon, and, when Saul should inquire after David, he should reply that he gave him permission to go to Bethlehem to the yearly sacrifice of his family. If Saul said, "Thy servant shall have peace," it was to be taken that David's life was in no imminent danger, but if he became wroth, it was to be taken as evidence that

it would be best for David to flee. It was also arranged that David should hide behind a certain rock at Ezel, and that, after the feast, Jonathan should come out into the field and should shoot three arrows as though he were shooting at a mark, and if he should say to the lad whom he should send for the arrows, "Behold, the arrows are on this side of thee," David would know that his life was safe; but if he said, "Behold, the arrows are beyond thee," he was to know that his life was in danger and that he must flee. Saul inquired of his son the whereabouts of David, and Jonathan replied that David had gone to Bethlehem with his permission. At this Saul became very angry and threw his javelin at Jonathan, but it missed its mark. Rising from his father's table in anger, Jonathan went into the field and warned David as it was agreed upon. When the lad who gathered up the arrows had returned into the city, David arose from his hiding-place, saluted and kissed Jonathan, and renewed the covenant with him that had previously been made.

2. **David's flight** (1 Sam. 21:1-24:22). David fled to Nob, to Ahimelech the priest, from whom he received showbread to satisfy his hunger. Ahimelech also turned over to him the sword of Goliath. From Ahimelech, David fled to Achish, king of Gath. But some of the servants of Achish revealed David's identity, and, out of fear for his life, he was forced to feign madness, and "scrabbled on the doors of the gate, and let his spittle fall down upon his beard." From Achish, David fled to the cave of Adullam, where he gathered about him an army of four hundred choice men. From Adullam he fled to Mizpeh

THE UNDIVIDED KINGDOM—DAVID

in Moab; from Mizpeh to Keilah, where he defeated the Philistines; from Keilah to the wilderness of Ziph; from the wilderness of Ziph to the wilderness of Maon, and from the wilderness of Maon to the strongholds of En-gedi, where he had mercy on Saul and spared his life.

3. **The death of Samuel** (1 Sam. 25:1). At this point in the life of David, Samuel died and was buried, after which David arose and went down to the wilderness of Paran.

4. **David and Nabal** (1 Sam. 25:2-44). There was a man in Maon by the name of Nabal, whose possessions were in Carmel, where his servants were shearing his sheep. This man was of a churlish and evil disposition, but his wife, Abigail, was "a woman of good understanding, and of a beautiful countenance." David's men had performed many good services for Nabal, and, when David heard that he was shearing his sheep, he sent two of his young men to ask him for a present. But Nabal refused this, and the young men returned to David. When David was told of Nabal's refusal, he was very angry, and commanded his men to gird on their swords, and, putting himself at the head of four hundred of them, two hundred remaining "by the stuff," he started out to be avenged on Nabal. But one of the servants had told Abigail of the treatment that David's men had received at the hands of her husband, and of the kindness of David and of the vengeance that would surely follow. So, preparing a large quantity of food, she went out to meet David. When she came near to him, she alighted from her beast, and, bowing to the earth, confessed her husband's insult, and pleaded

for his life and the lives of those that were his. At this David's passion cooled, and he sent her to her house, assuring her that Nabal and those that were his should be spared. Upon Abigail's return, she found Nabal intoxicated, and so she told him nothing until the following morning, when she informed him of what she had done. When he heard her words, "his heart died within him, and he became as a stone." Ten days afterward he was smitten of the Lord and died, following which Abigail became the wife of David, as did also Ahinoam, the Jezreelitess, Michal having been taken from him by Saul and given to Phalti, the son of Laish.

5. **David's flight continued** (1 Sam. 26: 1-30: 31). From En-gedi, David fled to the hill of Hachilah, where he spared Saul's life a second time. From the hill of Hachilah he went again into Philistia and joined himself with the Philistines to fight against Israel, but was providentially saved from such a course. From Philistia he went to Ziklag, where he found that the Amalekites had burned the city and taken his wives and children captives. David immediately began pursuit, by the direction of the Lord through the Urim and Thummim, and, though two hundred of his six hundred men fell exhausted at the brook Besor, he continued to follow them, and finally, being directed by the Egyptian servant of one of the Amalekites, he overtook them, attacked them, slew all but four hundred who escaped on camels, and rescued his wives and children. The spoils of the Amalekites he divided among his men, also sending a portion of them as a present to the elders of Judah.

6. **David mourns for Saul** (2 Sam. 1: 1-27). David

THE UNDIVIDED KINGDOM—DAVID

had been in Ziklag, after his return from the defeat of the Amalekites, but two days when the tidings of Saul's death at Mount Gilboa came to him. On the third day a man came from Saul's camp with his clothes rent and dirt upon his head, and fell in obeisance upon the ground before David. David inquired from whence he had come, and he exclaimed: "Out of the camp of Israel am I escaped." Being pressed further, he told of the defeat of Saul and how, at Saul's request, he had stood upon him and slain him. He then delivered to David the crown which he had taken from Saul's head and the bracelet which he had taken from his arm. Pressing him still further, David learned that he was an Amalekite, whereupon he ordered him slain because he had dared to stretch forth his hand to destroy the Lord's anointed. Then David mourned for Saul and Jonathan.

IV. DAVID KING OVER JUDAH

1. **David received as king by Judah** (2 Sam. 2: 1-4). David now inquired of the Lord if he should go into any of the cities of Judah, and was told to go to Hebron. Here he was anointed king over the house of Judah.

2. **David blesses the men of Jabesh-gilead** (2 Sam. 2: 5-7). It was told David that the men of Jabesh-gilead had buried Saul, and he sent messengers to them, who said: "Blessed be ye of the Lord, that ye have shewed this kindness unto your lord, even unto Saul, and have buried him. And now the Lord show kindness and truth unto you: and I also will requite you this kindness, because ye have done this thing.

Therefore now let your hands be strengthened, and be ye valiant: for your master Saul is dead, and also the house of Judah have anointed me king over them."

3. **War between Judah and Israel** (2 Sam. 2:8-32). Following the death of Saul, Abner, the captain of his host, took Ish-bosheth, Saul's son, and brought him to Mahanaim, where he was made king over the eleven tribes. Soon after his accession, war was declared between the two rival kingdoms, and the army of Ish-bosheth, under Abner, and the army of David, under Joab, met in deadly conflict at the pool of Gibeon. In this battle Abner was defeated and his army routed. Abner attempted to escape, but was followed by Asahel, Joab's brother. Abner charged Asahel to turn aside lest he slay him, but this he refused to do, upon which Abner, turning round, thrust him through with his spear. Joab finally blew the trumpet and recalled his pursuing warriors, and the battle ended. The body of Asahel was buried in the sepulchre of his father at Bethlehem.

4. **Abner's desertion and death** (2 Sam. 3:7-39). Ish-bosheth accused Abner of intimacy with his father's concubine, Rizpah, which made him very wroth, and he sent messengers to David offering to deliver the eleven tribes into his hands. David agreed to consider the proposition under the condition that Abner deliver into his hands Michal, the daughter of Saul. David also sent messengers to Ish-bosheth demanding that he deliver Michal up. This Ish-bosheth did, taking her from her husband, Phaltiel, to whom she had been given by Saul after

THE UNDIVIDED KINGDOM—DAVID

David had been driven from the court. Abner then spoke favorably to the elders of Israel of David, and, taking twenty men, he went down to Hebron to see him. After conferring with him, Abner started to return, but on the way was captured by Joab's messengers and was brought back to Hebron, where he was slain by Joab and his brother Abishai, for having killed Asahel. When David heard of Abner's death, he was greatly grieved and pronounced a curse upon the house of Joab's father. Abner's body was then buried amid the lamentations of David and all Israel.

5. **The murder of Ish-bosheth** (2 Sam. 4: 1-12). When Ish-bosheth and all Israel heard of the murder of Abner, they were sorely troubled. Ish-bosheth had two captains, Baanah and Rechab, of the tribe of Benjamin, who conspired against him and slew him as he lay in his bed, cut off his head, and, escaping, carried it to David. At this treachery David was greatly incensed, and ordered Baanah and Rechab slain.

V. DAVID KING OVER ALL ISRAEL

1. **David made king over all Israel** (2 Sam. 5: 1-16; 1 Chron. 11: 1-9). With the death of Ish-bosheth, the elders of Israel came to David at Hebron and invited him to become their king. David consented to this, and a league was made and David was anointed king over all Israel. He made Jerusalem[1] his capital, and employed Phœnician carpenters and masons to build him an house. He also took more wives and concubines.

---

[1] Prior to this time, Jerusalem had been a city of the Jebusites.

2. **War with the Philistines** (2 Sam. 5:17-25; 1 Chron. 14:8-17). No sooner did the Philistines hear that David had been anointed king over all Israel than they invaded the land. David went out to meet them and gained a decisive victory over them at Baal-perazim.

3. **The ark brought up** (2 Sam. 6:1-23; 1 Chron. 15:25-16:3). Gathering together thirty thousand chosen men of Israel, David went down to Kirjath-jearim, or Baale, to bring up the ark of the covenant. The ark was placed on a new cart, driven by Ahio and Uzzah, sons of Abinadab, and was followed by David and the children of Israel playing upon all manner of musical instruments. When they reached Nachon's threshing-floor, Uzzah reached forth his hand to steady the ark, and was smitten by the Lord so that he died. This made David afraid to bring the ark into Jerusalem, and he left it in the house of Obed-edom, where it remained for three months. But, at the expiration of that time, it was told David that the Lord had blessed the house of Obed-edom, and he went and brought the ark to Jerusalem, and placed it in the Tabernacle which had been pitched for it, amid the shouting, the sacrificing and the feasting of all Israel. As the ark was being brought into the city, David danced before it, which caused him to be despised in the eyes of Michal, the daughter of Saul. When he returned to bless his family, Michal reproached him for his unseemly behavior, for which she was rendered barren and had no children unto the day of her death.

4. **David desires to build an house for the Lord** (2 Sam. 7:1-29; 1 Chron. 17:1-27). As the king sat

THE UNDIVIDED KINGDOM—DAVID

in his house, being at peace with all his enemies, he conceived the purpose of building an house for the Lord. To Nathan the prophet he said: "See now, I dwell in an house of cedar, but the ark of God dwelleth within curtains." That night the word of the Lord came to Nathan telling him to inform David that he should not build Him an house, but that his seed would be established after him and that he should build the house. When this was told David, he praised the Lord for what He had done, and interceded Him that his seed might continue forever before Him.

5. **The full extent of the Davidic kingdom** (2 Sam. 8.1-18; 1 Chron. 18:1-17). Under David the kingdom of Israel reached the zenith of its power and glory. He subdued the Philistines, the Moabites, Hadadezer, king of Zobah, the Syrians, the Ammonites, the Amalekites and the Edomites. Joab was the commander-in-chief of his army, Jehoshaphat was the recorder, Zadok and Ahimelech were the priests, and Seraiah was the scribe.

6. **David's kind treatment of Mephibosheth** (2 Sam. 9:1-13). David inquired if there yet remained any of the seed of Saul to whom he might show kindness for Jonathan's sake, and was told by Ziba, one of Saul's servants, that Jonathan yet had a son, Mephibosheth by name, who was lame in his feet. When David heard this, he ordered that Mephibosheth be brought before him, and restored to him all of his father's lands and told him that he should eat bread continually at his table.

7. **The Ammonite-Syrian war** (2 Sam. 10:1-19; 1 Chron. 19:1-19). Nahash, king of the Ammonites,

died, and Hanun, his son, reigned in his stead. When David heard of the death of Nahash, he sent servants to his son to comfort him. But the princes of the land told Hanun that David's servants had not come to console him, but to spy out the city that he might overthrow it. So Hanun took David's servants and shaved one-half of their heads, cut off their garments in the middle and sent them back. When this was told David, he ordered his servants to remain in Jericho until their beards were grown out. The Ammonites, seeing that this act had rendered them odious in the sight of David, made a league with the Syrians and hired thirty-three thousand men to assist them in their defense. David, hearing of this alliance, sent out Joab against them, who divided his army into two divisions, he commanding one and his brother, Abishai, the other. The first was to fight the Syrians, the second the Ammonites. In the battle which ensued, the allies were defeated and Joab returned to Jerusalem. Hearing of the defeat, Hadarezer, king of the Syrians, gathered together a new force and came against David, who had encamped at Helam. But here they were again overwhelmingly defeated and sued for peace.

8. **David's great sin** (2 Sam. 11:1-12:23). David became deeply infatuated with Bath-sheba, the wife of Uriah the Hittite, and sent her husband to Joab, who was carrying on the war with the Ammonites, with the instructions that Uriah should be placed in the forefront of the battle so that he might be slain. In the besiegement of Rabbah, Uriah was given a conspicuous and dangerous position with the valiant men, and, in the sally of the defenders

THE UNDIVIDED KINGDOM—DAVID

of that city, he lost his life. When the news of Uriah's death came to David, he took Bath-sheba, after her mourning was ended, into his house, and she became his wife and bore him a son. But the Lord was displeased with David for this sin and sent the prophet Nathan to him, who spoke the following parable: There were two men in one city, one of whom was rich and had many flocks and herds; the other was poor and had just one little ewe lamb. A traveler came to the home of the rich man, but, instead of killing one of his own flock and dressing it for his guest, he slew the lamb of his poor neighbor and served it. Hearing this, David was greatly incensed, not discerning the parabolic character of Nathan's language, and declared that the man who did this should restore the lamb fourfold and should also be put to death. Then Nathan said: "Thou art the man." The prophet also told David that the sword should not depart from his house and that his child by Bath-sheba should die. At this, David was greatly troubled and confessed that he had sinned against the Lord, upon which Nathan told him that the Lord had put away his sin and that he should not die, but that the child should surely die. On the seventh day the child died according to the prediction of Nathan.

9. **The birth of Solomon** (2 Sam. 12:24, 25). David comforted Bath-sheba, and she bore him a son whom he called Solomon, but Nathan called him Jedidiah because of the Lord.

10. **Rabbah taken** (2 Sam. 12:26-31; 1 Chron. 20:1-3). Rabbah, the city of waters and capital of the Ammonites, was taken by Joab and David. The

crown of the king was placed upon David's head; the spoils of the city were taken in great abundance, and the people were made to pass under saws, harrows and axes of iron and through the brick-kiln.

11. **Amnon's awful crime and death** (2 Sam. 13: 1-39). Amnon, one of the sons of David, fell deeply in love with his sister Tamar, and wronged her. Absalom, her brother, heard of this and took her into his house and hated Amnon for his deed. After two full years, Absalom invited the king's sons to his sheep-shearing at Baal-hazor, beside Ephraim. At first David refused to let them go, but after much importunity he consented. At the feast, when Amnon was intoxicated, Absalom's servants, by Absalom's command, fell upon him and slew him. At this his brethren fled, and the word was carried to David that all of them had been slain, upon which the king rent his clothes in great sorrow. But Jonadab, David's nephew, corrected this false report, and when his sons appeared there was great rejoicing, both among them and with David. After this crime, Absalom fled to Geshur, where he remained three years. Yet, notwithstanding Absalom's crime, David's heart went out to him.

12. **Absalom recalled through Joab's craft** (2 Sam. 14: 1-33). At the expiration of three years, through Joab's craft, he was commanded to go to Geshur and bring up Absalom to Jerusalem, but he was forbidden to bring him into the king's presence. This Joab did, and Absalom dwelt in the city for two years without seeing the face of his father. At the expiration of this period, Absalom sent for Joab two times, but, as he refused to come, he commanded

THE UNDIVIDED KINGDOM—DAVID

his servants to set Joab's field of barley on fire, and when Joab came to inquire why his servants had done this, Absalom replied that he should go before the king and demand that he be permitted to see his face, and that, if he had done iniquity, the king should slay him. This plan was effective, and Absalom was admitted into David's presence.

13. **Absalom's revolt** (2 Sam. 15:1-16:14). After Absalom had been restored to David's favor, he set about by flattery to steal the hearts of the ten tribes from his father. Going to the king, he received permission to go to Hebron, there to pay the vow that he had made to the Lord. Taking with him two hundred men from Jerusalem, who were ignorant of his intentions, he departed. From Hebron he sent spies throughout Israel who told the people that, when the trumpet sounded, they were to say: "Absalom reigneth in Hebron." Absalom was popular and his power increased. When this was told David, he and his household fled into the wilderness, accompanied by the priests and Ittai the Gittite. David sent back the priests, Zadok and Abiathar, with the ark, into the city, and also Hushai the Archite, who came out to meet him in his flight. The latter was commissioned to play the spy and to offset the counsels of Ahithophel, who had revolted with Absalom. As David was fleeing, Ziba, the servant of Mephibosheth, met him with two beasts upon which were two hundred loaves, an hundred bunches of raisins, summer fruit and a bottle of wine. He told David that his master had also revolted against him, believing that the children of Israel would restore to him his father's kingdom. In this flight, also, David

was cursed by Shimei, of the house of Saul, who accused him of being a bloody man. David's servants would have beheaded Shimei had it not been for the king's intercession in his behalf.

14. **Absalom enters Jerusalem** (2 Sam. 16: 15-23). After David had fled from the city of Jerusalem, Absalom and Ahithophel, with the men of Israel, entered and took possession of it. Here Hushai, by flattery, ingratiated himself into Absalom's favor as he had been commanded of David.

15. **Hushai defeats the counsels of Ahithophel** (2 Sam. 17: 1-29). Once in possession of the city, Ahithophel counseled Absalom to permit him to choose twelve thousand men and pursue David while he was weak and weary, scatter the people that were with him, and slay him. This plan pleased Absalom, but he decided first to consult Hushai. But, when Hushai was called, he discouraged the plan, telling Absalom that David was a mighty man of war; that he would not lodge with his people, and that he was, undoubtedly, hid in some pit, advising Absalom to gather Israel together from Dan to Beer-sheba that he might fall upon his father and his followers as the dew fell from heaven, so that there might be left not so much as one. This advice pleased Absalom, and, when Ahithophel saw it, he got on his beast, rode home and hanged himself. Then Hushai told the priests, Zadok and Abiathar, to send word to David not to abide in the wilderness, but to pass over Jordan and be lost to sight. This message the priests sent by a wench to Jonathan and Ahimaaz, who were without the city, to deliver to the king. A lad, seeing them, reported the same to Absalom,

THE UNDIVIDED KINGDOM—DAVID

who sent his servants after them, but they fled to Bahurim, where they concealed themselves in a well. The woman of the house covered the mouth of the well with a covering, upon which she spread ground corn, and, when Absalom's servants came down, they could not find them and returned to Jerusalem, after which Jonathan and Ahimaaz went on their way and told David all that they had been commanded. Heeding the instructions, David and his followers passed over Jordan, where they were befriended by the inhabitants of the country.

16. **The defeat and death of Absalom** (2 Sam. 18: 1-18). David now reorganized his army and divided it into three divisions, under Joab, Abishai and Ittai the Gittite. David himself desired to go out at the head of his forces, but to this his men objected, and, leaving him behind, they marched out against the army of Absalom under Amasa, and defeated it with great slaughter in the wood of Ephraim. As Absalom was fleeing from the battlefield, the mule that he rode passed under a great oak and his hair caught in one of the boughs, while his mule passed on from under him. This was told Joab, and, in spite of the request of David that Absalom's life should be spared, he took three darts and thrust them through his heart. He then blew the trumpet, and, when his army was collected, the lifeless body of Absalom was taken and was thrown into a pit and a pile of stones was placed upon it.

17. **David's grief for Absalom** (2 Sam. 18; 19-19: 8). Then Ahimaaz, son of Zadok the priest, requested permission to run and tell David of the fate of Absalom, but this Joab refused, and Cushi was

sent in his stead. But, being importunate, Ahimaaz was permitted to follow, and, on the way, outstripped Cushi and reached David with the tidings first. David was sitting between the two gates, and, when Ahimaaz came up to him, he inquired: "Is the young man Absalom safe?" To which Ahimaaz replied: "When Joab sent the king's servant, and me thy servant, I saw a great tumult, but I knew not what it was." As Ahimaaz was speaking, Cushi came up and was asked the same question. He replied: "The enemies of my lord the king, and all that rise against thee to do thee hurt, be as that young man is." Upon hearing these words, David was greatly moved and, going to his chamber, he wept and exclaimed: "O my son Absalom, my son, my son Absalom! would God I had died for thee, O Absalom, my son, my son!" The people heard that David was weeping for Absalom and were greatly affected, so Joab, going to the king, reproached him for his unseemly grief, and told him that, if he did not appear before them, the people would all desert him. Then David went down and appeared before the people at the gate.

18. **David returns to Jerusalem** (2 Sam. 19:9-43). The children of Israel now began to inquire for the return of David to Jerusalem, but the men of Judah did not seem to show so much interest. So David sent to the elders of Judah, inquiring why there had not been more anxiety for his return on their part. He also deposed Joab, making Amasa commander in his place. This had the desired effect in humiliating Judah, and they sent a request for David's return. So he came to Gilgal, where he was met by

THE UNDIVIDED KINGDOM—DAVID

Judah; Shimei, who came to ask forgiveness for his bad treatment of David; Mephibosheth, who told David that he had been misrepresented by his servant Ziba, and a multitude of Israel, by all of whom David was conducted to Jerusalem.

19. **The revolt under Sheba** (2 Sam. 20:1-26). But, as the ten tribes had not received invitation to take part in the bringing back of the king, they were sorely displeased, and joined the standard of Sheba, a Benjamite, in a second revolt. David told Amasa to gather his army, pursue and defeat them. On the way, Joab took Amasa by the beard as if to kiss him, and thrust his sword into his bowels. Then, with his brother Abishai, he pursued Sheba and besieged him in the city of Abel, where his followers cut off his head and threw it over the wall to Joab, upon which Joab blew the trumpet and his army retired.

20. **The three years' famine** (2 Sam. 21:1-14). There was a three years' famine in the land, and when David inquired of the Lord the cause, He replied that it was a judgment upon Israel because Saul had slain the Gibeonites. So, calling the Gibeonites, David requested them to tell him what he should do for them that they might be requited. They replied that as an atonement seven sons of the house of Saul should be delivered to them. This was complied with, and the Gibeonites hanged them to a tree, whereupon David disinterred the bones of Saul and Jonathan which had been buried at Jabesh-gilead, and deposited them, with the bodies of those hanged, in the sepulchre of Kish in Benjamin.

21. **The war with the Philistines** (2 Sam. 21:15-

22:51). There was war between Israel and the Philistines, and David went out at the head of his army. In the battle that ensued, he waxed faint and would have been slain by Ishi-benob, a son of Goliath, had it not been for Abishai, brother of Joab, who smote the Philistine and killed him. After this narrow escape, the men of Israel would not permit David to go to battle lest he be killed and the light of Israel be quenched. The children of Israel and the Philistines then met in battle at Gob, where Sibbechai the Hushathite slew Saph, another of Goliath's sons. In a second battle at the same place, Elhanan, a Bethlehemite, slew the brother of the giant. And, in still another battle in Gath, another son of Goliath, who had six fingers on each hand and six toes on each foot, was slain by Jonathan, a nephew of David. Following these victories, David sang his celebrated song of deliverance.

22. **David commits sin in numbering Israel** (2 Sam. 23:8-24:25; 1 Chron. 21:1-30). In all, David had thirty-seven mighty men who fought in his wars and shared in his victories. The Lord became angry with Israel and moved David to order them numbered. The command was given to Joab, who, with his captains, passed through the entire host from Dan to Beer-sheba and returned to Jerusalem at the end of nine months and twenty days, and reported that there were in all eight hundred thousand valiant men in Israel and five hundred thousand in Judah.[1]

---

[1] These are the figures given in 2 Samuel; in 1 Chronicles the military strength of Israel is placed at 1,100,000 and of Judah at 470,000. The total military strength of Israel was probably 1,100,000, and that of Judah, 500,000, while 800,000 and 470,000 were probably the number actually set in battle array.

THE UNDIVIDED KINGDOM—DAVID

After this, David's heart smote him and he said to the Lord: "I have sinned greatly in that I have done: and now, I beseech thee, O Lord, take away the iniquity of thy servant: for I have done very foolishly." Then the word of the Lord came to the prophet Gad, seer of David, and he was commanded to appear before the king and to tell him that the Lord offered him three things, one of which he was to choose: seven years of famine, three months of flight before his enemies or three days of pestilence throughout the land. To this David exclaimed: "I am in a great strait: let us fall now into the hand of the Lord; for his mercies are great: and let me not fall into the hand of man." Then the Lord sent a pestilence upon Israel, and there fell seventy thousand men from Dan to Beer-sheba. David then purchased the threshing-floor of Araunah (Ornan) the Jebusite, with oxen for burnt-offerings, and erected an altar, upon which he offered sacrifices, and interceded God, and the plague was stayed.

23. **Adonijah's plot** (1 Kings 1:1-9). David was now very old and in failing strength, and Adonijah, son of Haggith and brother of Absalom, sought to take the kingdom. In this he was assisted by both Joab, the commander of David's army, and Abiathar, one of the priests, but was opposed by Zadok, one of the priests; Nathan the prophet; Benaiah, son of Jehoiada, and Shimei and Rei, all of whom supported Solomon. Adonijah made a feast and slew sheep, oxen and fat cattle by the stone of Zoheleth by En-rogel, but to this he did not invite those who supported Solomon. Then Nathan told Bath-sheba, Solomon's mother, to go before the king, remind him

of his promise that Solomon should succeed him, and tell him of the attempted usurpation of Adonijah. This Bath-sheba did, and, while she was speaking, Nathan came in and confirmed what she said. Then David swore to Bath-sheba that Solomon should be his successor, and he commanded Zadok and Nathan to take him to Gihon, where they were to anoint him king over all Israel, blow the trumpet and say: "God save king Solomon."

24. **Solomon anointed** (1 Kings 1:10-40; 1 Chron. 29:22). Zadok and Nathan complied with this command and, with those who were loyal to Solomon, took him down to Gihon, where Zadok took a horn of oil out of the Tabernacle and anointed him king over Israel. When they blew the trumpet, all the people shouted, "God save King Solomon," and piped with pipes and rejoiced with great joy.

25. **Adonijah submits** (1 Kings 1:41-53). Hearing what had been done, Jonathan, son of Abiathar, went and told Adonijah, who, with those who were with him, was terribly afraid, and he went and caught hold of the horns of the altar. When Solomon heard what Adonijah had done, he said: "If he will show himself a worthy man, there shall not an hair of him fall to the earth: but if wickedness shall be found in him, he shall die." He then sent for Adonijah, who came bowing before him and who was commanded by the king to return to his own house.

26. **The death of David** (1 Kings 2:1-11; 1 Chron. 29:26-30). The day of David's death drew nigh, and, charging Solomon to remember Joab for having slain Abner and Amasa, his captains, Shimei, son of Gera, for having cursed him, and Barzillai the Gileadite, for

THE UNDIVIDED KINGDOM—DAVID

his kindness to him, he slept with his fathers and was buried in Jerusalem.

QUESTIONS

Give the general outline of this study. What the meaning of the name "David"? Give the condition of the time which David lived. Give the name of David's father. What was David's youthful occupation? Give the circumstances of his anointing. How did he happen to be admitted to Saul's court? Tell about him slaying Goliath. Who was Jonathan? What kind of a covenant did he make with David? Why did Saul become jealous of David? Give the name of Saul's daughter who became David's wife. Why did Saul give her to David? Did she prove true to her husband? When David fled from Saul, what did he first do? Who warned him of Saul's wrath, and how? Who was the king of the Philistines at this time? In what cave did David find refuge? How many men did he have with him there? Tell about David's difficulty with Nabal. Give the name of Nabal's wife. Whose wife did she become after Nabal's death? How many times did David spare Saul's life? Give the circumstances of each. Over what tribe did he reign at first? Where? Why did David bless the men of Jabesh-gilead? Tell about the war between Judah and Israel. Tell about Abner's desertion and death. Who was Ish-bosheth? By whom was he murdered? Tell about David assuming the throne of all Israel. Tell about the bringing up of the ark to Jerusalem. What did David desire to build? What nations did David subdue during his reign? Tell about David's treatment of Mephibosheth. Tell about the Ammonite-Syrian war. What was David's great sin? Who was the mother of Solomon? Name the capital of the Ammonites. Who was Amnon? What awful sin did he commit? Who slew him? Where did Absalom flee? How was he recalled? Tell about Absalom's ungratefulness. Tell about David's flight. How was the counsel of Ahithophel defeated and what did Ahithophel do? Tell about the death of Absalom. How did David take Absalom's death? Tell about David's return to Jerusalem. Who led a second revolt against David, and why? What was the cause of the three years' famine? Tell about

THE GIST OF THE BIBLE

David's last war with the Philistines. What sin did David commit just before his death? What son of David tried to subvert the kingdom? What relation did he bear to Absalom? Tell about Solomon's anointing. What did Adonijah do? What did David do just before he died? Where was David buried?

STUDY XXI. THE UNDIVIDED KINGDOM —SOLOMON

(2 Sam. 12:24-1 Kings 11:43; 1 Chron. 22:5- 2 Chron. 9:31)

INTRODUCTION

1. **The meaning of the name "Solomon."** The name "Solomon" means "pacific."

2. **The condition of the times.** Under David the kingdom of Israel had greatly widened its bounds, and when Solomon took the throne, it was at the zenith of its greatness and glory. But, during his reign, the seeds of disintegration and decay were sown which sprang up and caused the disruption which immediately followed his death. While Solomon was a wise man, he is not to be compared with his father as a monarch. The nations outside of Israel were very corrupt and immoral, and their religious ceremonies almost beggar description. These corruptions Solomon fell into, and they were the means of the breaking up of the kingdom.

3. **The time of Solomon's reign.** Solomon reigned between the years 1015 and 975 B. C.

I. THE EARLY LIFE OF SOLOMON

1. **The birth of Solomon** (2 Sam. 12:24, 25). Solomon was the son of David and Bath-sheba, and was born at Jerusalem. To him the prophet Nathan gave the name of Jedidiah.

2. **The plot of Adonijah** (1 Kings 1:5-38). In the preceding study we saw how Adonijah, another son of David by Haggith, sought to take the kingdom. This was prevented by Zadok, Nathan and other supporters of Solomon.

3. **Solomon anointed king** (1 Kings 1:39, 40). Following this, by command of David, Solomon was anointed king by Zadok and, when this was announced by the blowing of the trumpet, all the people shouted: "God save king Solomon."

4. **The submission of Adonijah** (1 Kings 1:41-53). When Adonijah heard that Solomon had been anointed king, he went and caught hold of the horns of the altar. This being told Solomon, he said that if Adonijah would prove himself a man, he would spare his life. Hearing this, Adonijah went in where Solomon was and bowed himself before him.

5. **David's charge to Solomon** (1 Kings 2:1-9). David charged Solomon that he should be strong and show himself a man, that he should observe the law of the Lord, and that he should take vengeance on certain of his father's enemies and show mercy to certain of his friends.

6. **The death of David** (1 Kings 2:10, 11; 1 Chron. 29:26-30). Then David slept with his fathers and was buried in Jerusalem.

II. SOLOMON'S ACCESSION AND EARLY REIGN

1. **Solomon takes the throne** (1 Kings 2:12; 1 Chron. 29:23-25). Immediately following the death of David, Solomon took the throne and "his kingdom was greatly established."

THE UNDIVIDED KINGDOM—SOLOMON

2. **The execution of Adonijah** (1 Kings 2:13-25). Adonijah went to Bath-sheba and petitioned her to intercede with Solomon to give to him Abishag, the Shunammite, to wife. Bath-sheba told this to the king, who became very wroth and sent Benaiah to slay Adonijah.

3. **Abiathar deposed** (1 Kings 2:26, 27). Solomon also commanded Abiathar the priest to depart to his own fields, telling him that he was worthy of death, but promising him that he would not slay him because he bore the ark of the Lord.

4. **The death of Joab** (1 Kings 2:28-34). When Joab heard of these things, he fled to the Tabernacle of the Lord and caught hold of the horns of the altar. But this did not save him, and Solomon commanded Benaiah to fall upon him and slay him. Benaiah went to the Tabernacle and commanded Joab to come forth, but he replied that he would die there. So, in obedience to Solomon's orders, Benaiah fell upon him and slew him, and he was buried in his own house in the wilderness.

5. **The elevation of Benaiah and Zadok** (1 Kings 2:35). Benaiah was then made commander-in-chief of the armies of Israel in the place of Joab, and Zadok priest in the place of Abiathar.

6. **The execution of Shimei** (1 Kings 2:36-46). After this, Solomon called Shimei to him and commanded him to build himself a house in the city of Jerusalem, and forbade him leaving the city, telling him that whenever he passed over the brook Kidron he should be put to death. Shimei assented to this, but, after three years, when two of his servants fled to Achish, king of Gath, he followed them. Upon his

return, it was told Solomon that he had been out of the city, which so enraged the king that he commanded Benaiah to slay him.

7. **Solomon makes an alliance with Pharaoh** (1 Kings 3:1-3). Solomon made an alliance with the king of Egypt and married his daughter, whom he brought into the city of Jerusalem.

8. **Solomon sacrifices at Gibeon** (1 Kings 3:4; 2 Chron. 1:2-6). The account is that Solomon loved the Lord and walked in the statutes of his father David, only he offered sacrifices and burnt incense in high places. For this purpose he went down to Gibeon, where he made a thousand burnt-offerings.

9. **Solomon prays for wisdom** (1 Kings 3:5-15; 2 Chron. 1:7-16). At Gibeon the Lord appeared unto Solomon in a dream and said: "Ask what I shall give thee." To which Solomon replied: "Give therefore thy servant an understanding heart to judge thy people, that I may discern between good and bad: for who is able to judge this thy so great a people?" This speech pleased the Lord and he gave Solomon an understanding heart. When Solomon awoke, he returned to Jerusalem and stood before the ark of the covenant, where he offered burnt-offerings and peace-offerings and made a feast unto all his servants.

10. **Solomon decides a question of mothership** (1 Kings 3:16-28). Two women came to Solomon with a babe which each claimed as her own. They lived in the same house and to each a child had been born, the birth being three days apart. The complaint of one was that the child of the other had died and that, while they slept, the mother of the dead child had exchanged it for the living. This the other emphatically

THE UNDIVIDED KINGDOM—SOLOMON

denied. When Solomon heard their stories, he ordered a sword to be brought and commanded that the living child should be divided. At this command, the heart of the one woman who made the complaint yearned, and she exclaimed: "O my lord, give her the living child, and in no wise slay it." But the other said: "Let it be neither mine nor thine, but divide it." Solomon, upon discerning this exhibition of the mother instinct on the part of the first, said: "Give her the living child, and in no wise slay it: she is the mother thereof."

11. **Solomon's official cabinet** (1 Kings 4:1-28). The officials under Solomon were Azariah, son of Zadok, the chief prince; Elihoreph and Ahiah, scribes; Jehoshaphat, recorder; Benaiah, commander of the host; Zadok and Abiathar, priests; Azariah, son of Nathan, chief of the officers; Zabud, principal officer and king's friend; Ahishar, who looked after the household; Adoniram, collector of the tribute, and twelve commissaries who provided victuals for the king's house.

12. **Solomon's wisdom** (1 Kings 4:29-34). Solomon's wisdom excelled that of all the children of the east country and even that of Egypt. He spake three thousand proverbs and composed a thousand and five songs. His fame was so great that representatives from all the nations of the earth came to visit him at Jerusalem.

III. SOLOMON BUILDS THE TEMPLE

1. **Preparations for the building of the Temple** (1 Kings 5:1-18; 2 Chron. 2:1-18). Hiram, king of Tyre, heard that Solomon had ascended the throne

and sent to him a deputation of his servants with his congratulations. Solomon replied to him by saying that he intended to build a house to the name of his God, and requested him to furnish Sidonian artisans, who were more skillful than the workmen of Israel, to hew for this purpose the cedars of Lebanon, offering at the same time to raise a force of his own servants to assist them and to pay Hiram adequate wages for their services. Hiram was greatly pleased when he received this information, and made arrangements with Solomon to raise the required force of men. Solomon then raised a force of thirty thousand men in Israel whom he divided into three courses of ten thousand each, each course being required to work every third month in Lebanon. Besides these, Solomon had seventy thousand others who bore burdens, and eighty thousand hewers in the mountains. Adoniram was over the levy, while thirty-three hundred officers were over those who wrought in the mountains. Along with the preparation of the cedars, Solomon commanded that great stones be brought, which were cut for the foundation by his servants and those of Tyre.

2. **The Temple built** (1 Kings 6:1-38; 2 Chron. 3:1-4:22). In the 480th year after the children of Israel had come out of Egypt, and in the fourth year of Solomon's reign, he began to build the house of the Lord upon Mount Moriah. It was ninety feet long, thirty feet wide and forty-five feet high, and was built of stone, prepared before it was brought upon the ground, and was provided with windows and with chambers built around the walls without. The porch before the Temple was thirty feet long by fifteen

THE UNDIVIDED KINGDOM—SOLOMON

wide. On the inside, the floors were of cypress wood, and the sides and ceilings were of cedar, all of which were covered with gold. The Holy Place and the Holy of Holies were separated from each other by boards of cedar, which were, doubtless, also covered with the precious metal. This cedar partition was pierced with an opening over which hung a veil. The furniture of the Temple proper was overlaid with gold and was of larger dimensions than the furniture of the Tabernacle. The Temple, like the Tabernacle, was inclosed with a court, which, in the Book of Kings, is called the "inner court," and which was built of three rows of hewn stones and a row of cedar beams. This court was inclosed within another court, the walls of which were also made of stone. At the expiration of seven years the Temple was completed.

3. **Solomon erects other buildings** (1 Kings 7:1-51). In addition to the temple, Solomon erected other buildings. The first mentioned was his own house, which was 150 feet long, seventy-five broad and forty-five high, and which was constructed of the same costly materials as those employed in building the Temple. Thirteen years were expended in the building of this house. The second structure mentioned was the house of the forest of Lebanon, and the third was the house for Pharaoh's daughter. Some suppose, however, that these were not separate buildings, but only parts of one great building. In all of these operations Solomon was assisted by Hiram, king of Tyre, who was brought to Jerusalem specially to oversee the work.

4. **The ark brought into the Temple** (1 Kings 8:

1-11; 2 Chron. 5:2-14). When the Temple was completed, Solomon gathered together the chief men of Israel that they might bring the ark of the covenant from Mount Zion and place it in the Temple on Mount Moriah. This gathering occurred in the seventh month of the Jewish year on the date of the Feast of the Tabernacles. Those selected took up the ark, with the Tabernacle and all the vessels that were in the Tabernacle, and brought them to Moriah, where the ark was placed within the oracle. While this was being done, Solomon and the congregation offered sacrifices, and, when once the ark rested in its sacred place, the glory of the Lord filled the house.

5. **The dedicatory sermon** (1 Kings 8:12-21; 2 Chron. 6:1-11). Solomon then delivered his dedicatory sermon, in which he recounted the blessings of the Lord and explained how the house came to be built.

6. **The dedicatory prayer** (1 Kings 8:22-53; 2 Chron. 6:12-42). Solomon's sermon was followed by his dedicatory prayer. This was delivered with his hands spread out toward heaven, while he stood before the altar. In this prayer he thanked the Lord for his mercies in permitting the Temple to be erected, and petitioned him to forgive Israel's sins and to guide them in the future.

7. **The dedicatory blessing** (1 Kings 8:54-61). After the dedicatory prayer, Solomon arose and pronounced a blessing upon himself and his people, enjoining them to walk in the statutes and to keep the commandments of the Lord.

8. **The dedicatory sacrifices** (1 Kings 8:62-66). During the dedicatory services, Solomon offered a

THE UNDIVIDED KINGDOM—SOLOMON

peace-offering of twenty-two thousand oxen and one hundred and twenty thousand sheep. Also burnt-offerings and meat-offerings in the middle of the court, the brazen altar being too small for the occasion. At this same time, all Israel, from the entering in at Hamath to the river of Egypt, observed a feast for fourteen days, and there was great rejoicing throughout the land.

IV. THE LAST YEARS OF SOLOMON'S REIGN

1. **Jehovah appears again to Solomon** (1 Kings 9: 1-9; 2 Chron. 7: 12-22). The Lord appeared again to Solomon as He he had appeared to him at Gibeon. He told him that He had heard his supplications, that He had hallowed the house which he had built, and that, if Solomon would keep His statutes and judgments, He would establish his throne forever. But, if he failed to keep His commandments and if Israel went after other gods, He would cut Israel off from the land which He had given her, and she should be a proverb and a byword among the people.

2. **Solomon's unsatisfactory gift to Hiram** (1 Kings 9: 10-14). At the end of twenty years, during which time he had built the house of the Lord and his own house, Solomon gave to Hiram, king of Tyre, twenty cities in Galilee in return for the cedar, fir and gold which he had furnished the Temple. But this gift displeased Hiram, and he called the cities Cabul, "displeasing."

3. **Further enterprises of Solomon** (1 Kings 9: 15-28; 2 Chron. 8: 1-18). Among the other enterprises in which Solomon engaged, was the building of

Millo, the wall of Jerusalem, Hazor, Megiddo, Gezer, Beth-horon, Baalath and Tadmor in the wilderness.

4. **The visit of the queen of Sheba** (1 Kings 10: 1-13; 2 Chron. 9:1-12). The queen of Sheba, in southern Arabia, having heard of the wisdom of Solomon, came to Jerusalem in all her pomp and glory to see him. When Solomon had answered all her questions, and when she had seen the house which he had built for the glory of his kingdom, "there was no more spirit in her," and she confessed that, though she had doubted the stories which had been told her, the half had not been told. After exchanging gifts with Solomon, she returned to her own country.

5. **The resources of Solomon** (1 Kings 10: 14-29; 2 Chron. 9:13-28). In one year there came to Solomon 666 talents of gold, besides what came into his treasury for mercantile enterprises, and as tribute from the surrounding nations and as taxes from his own country. He made two hundred targets of beaten gold, six hundred shekels of gold to each, and three hundred shields of beaten gold, three pounds of gold to each shield. He also made a throne of ivory which was covered with beaten gold, and all the vessels of his house were of the same metal. He had a navy upon the sea which, once in three years, brought from Tarshish gold, silver, ivory, apes and peacocks. He also had fourteen hundred chariots and twelve thousand horsemen.

6. **Solomon turns away from the Lord** (1 Kings 11:1-8). In his old age Solomon loved many strange women. Of these, besides the daughter of Pharaoh, there were women of the Moabites, Ammonites, Edomites, Zidonians and Hittites. He had, in all,

THE UNDIVIDED KINGDOM—SOLOMON

seven hundred wives and three hundred concubines, and these turned his heart away from the Lord unto other gods, and he worshiped Ashtoreth, the goddess of the Zidonians, and Milcom, the abomination of the Ammonites, and he built a high place to Chemosh, the abomination of Moab, and another to Molech, a god of Ammon. To all of these gods he burned incense and sacrificed.

7. **The Lord's anger toward Solomon** (1 Kings 11: 9-25). The Lord became angry with Solomon because his heart had departed from Him, and He told him that as he had failed to keep His commandments, He would rend his kingdom from him and give it unto his servant, though not in his day because of his promise to David, but after his death, when it should be taken from his son, only one tribe remaining faithful to him. The Lord also raised up against Solomon Hadad the Edomite and Rezon the Syrian, who hampered him all his days.

8. **The rise of Jeroboam** (1 Kings 11:26-40). But these foes without were not the only enemies that Solomon had, for Jeroboam, son of Nebat, an Ephraimite and servant of Solomon, also lifted up his hand against him. As Jeroboam was going out of the city, clad in a new garment, he met Ahijah the prophet, who caught hold of his garment and rent it into twelve pieces, saying, at the same time, to Jeroboam: "Take thee ten pieces." The prophet then explained that the Lord would rend the kingdom from the house of Solomon and give ten tribes to him, promising him that, if he would keep the commandments of the Lord, He would establish his house as He had that of David. When Solomon had heard

THE GIST OF THE BIBLE

what Ahijah had said, he sought to slay Jeroboam, but he fled to Shishak, king of Egypt, and remained there until after Solomon's death.

9. **The death of Solomon** (1 Kings 11:41-43; 2 Chron. 9:29-31). After reigning over Israel for forty years, Solomon died and was buried in the city of David, and Rehoboam, his son, took the throne.

QUESTIONS

Give the general outline of this study. What is the meaning of the name "Solomon"? Give the conditions of his times. When did he reign? Give the name of his mother. Who conspired to take the throne? Who anointed Solomon king? What did the people say? What did Adonijah do? Give the substance of David's charge to Solomon. What the condition of the kingdom when Solomon took it? Why was Adonijah executed? Why was Abiathar deposed and why was he not slain? Tell about the death of Joab. Who took the places of Abiathar and Joab? Tell about the execution of Shimei. How did Solomon confirm an alliance with the king of Egypt? What did Solomon do at Gibeon? What request did he make of the Lord? How did Solomon decide a question of motherhood? Name Solomon's official cabinet. What ruler did Solomon engage to assist him in building the Temple? Tell about the arrangements. In what year of Solomon's reign was the Temple begun? Where was it built? Of what was it made? Give its dimensions. How long was Solomon in building it? What other buildings did Solomon erect? Tell about the bringing of the ark into the Temple. Tell about the dedicatory services. What promise did the Lord make to Solomon after the building of the Temple? Tell about Solomon's unsatisfactory gift to Hiram. Tell about the visit of the queen of Sheba. How many wives and concubines did Solomon have? What did they cause him to do? To what nations did they belong? Name some of their gods. How did the Lord feel toward Solomon because of this? Who was Jeroboam? What prophecy did Ahijah deliver to him? What did Solomon attempt to do? Where did Jeroboam flee? How long did Solomon reign?

STUDY XXII. THE DIVIDED KINGDOM—ISRAEL

(1 Kings 12:1-2 Kings 17:41; 2 Chron. 10:1-2 Chron. 28:15)

INTRODUCTION

1. **The causes of the division.** The causes of the division between Israel and Judah may be said to have been two: the idolatrous practices of the people during the last years of Solomon's reign, and the arbitrary measures of his son and successor, Rehoboam.

2. **The advantages of the northern kingdom.** The kingdom of Israel had many advantages over the kingdom of Judah. It was composed of ten, out of the original twelve, tribes, excepting the Levites and individuals out of the ten who remained loyal to the standard of David and the religion of their fathers. It outnumbered Judah nearly three to one in population and was superior in military power. It also possessed a more fertile soil.

3. **The kings of Israel.** Israel was ruled over by nineteen kings, constituting nine dynasties. These kings were all bad men, although two of them, Jehoash and Hoshea, were better than the rest.

4. **The period of the kingdom.** The period of the northern kingdom lay between the years 975 and 721 B. C., Usher's chronology.

THE GIST OF THE BIBLE

I. THE REIGN OF JEROBOAM

1. **The return of Jeroboam** (1 Kings 12:1-15; 2 Chron. 10:1-11). When Jeroboam heard that Solomon was dead and that his son was to be made king, he returned from Egypt, and with the children of Israel went to Shechem, where Rehoboam was, and demanded that he lighten the burdens of his people. Rehoboam refused to do this.

2. **The accession of Jeroboam**[1] (1 Kings 12:16-24; 2 Chron. 10:12-11:4). When the children of Israel heard Rehoboam's refusal, they cried: "What portion have we in David? neither have we inheritance in the son of Jesse: to your tents, O Israel: now see to thine own house, David." They then called Jeroboam and made him king over Israel.

3. **Jeroboam institutes idolatrous worship** (1 Kings 12:25-33). After this, Jeroboam built Shechem in Mount Ephraim and dwelt therein. He reasoned that if the children of Israel went up to Jerusalem to sacrifice, their hearts would be turned against him and unto Rehoboam, so he made two calves of gold and said: "Behold thy gods, O Israel, which brought thee up out of the land of Egypt." One of these calves he set up in Bethel and the other in Dan, and he appointed priests of the lowest of the people, who were not of the tribe of Levi, and built high places and instituted a feast on the fifteenth day of the eighth month, similar to the Feast of Tabernacles that was observed in Judah.

4. **Destruction of the altar foretold** (1 Kings 13:1-10). As Jeroboam stood by the altar of burnt in-

---
[1] Usher: 975-954 B. C. Kamphausen: 937-916 B. C.

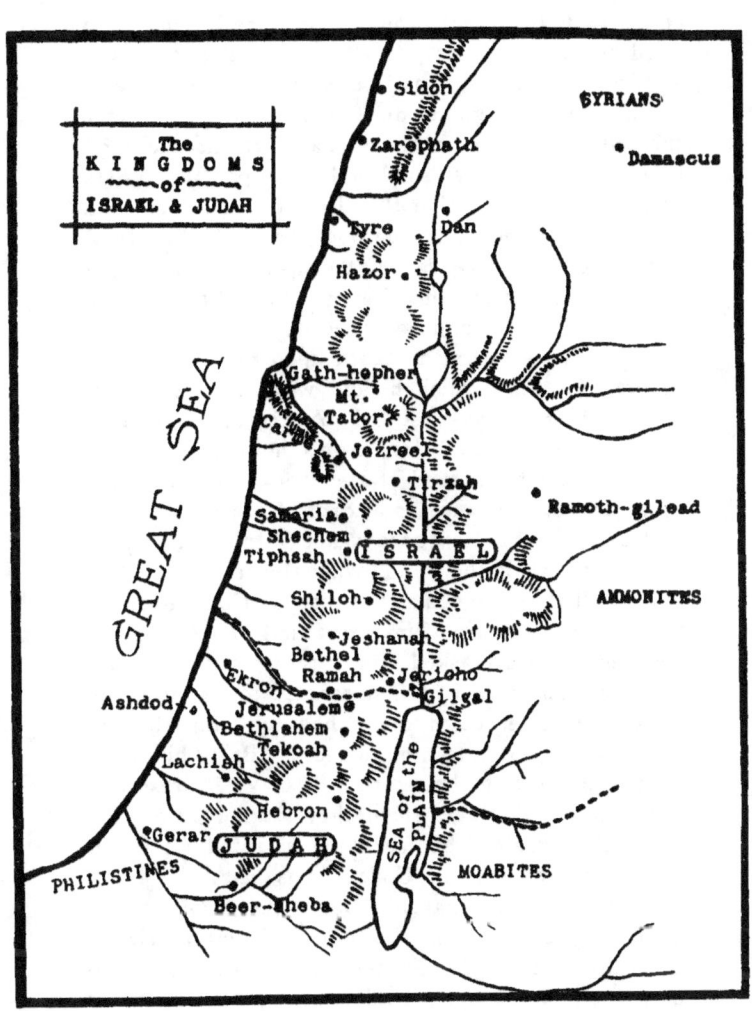

cense at Bethel, there came a man out of Judah who cried against the altar: "O altar, altar, thus saith the Lord; Behold a child shall be born unto the house of David, Josiah by name; and upon thee shall he offer the priests of the high places that burn incense upon thee, and men's bones shall be burnt upon thee." He then gave as a sign that the altar should be rent and the ashes thereon should be poured out. When Jeroboam heard these sayings of the man of God, he put forth his hand from the altar, saying: "Lay hold on him." At this his hand was dried up and the altar was rent. Then, in terror, he called upon the man of God to pray for him, which he did with the result that Jeroboam's hand was restored. After this, the man of God was invited into Jeroboam's house, but he refused the invitation and started back toward Judah.

5. **The disobedience and death of the man of God** (1 Kings 13:11-32). There was a certain old prophet who dwelt at Bethel, and, when his sons had told him of all the things that the man of God had done, he went in haste after him and found him sitting beneath an oak. He asked him to return with him, but this the man of God at first refused to do, although he acceded after the prophet had told him that an angel had appeared to him and said: "Bring him back with thee into thine house, that he may eat bread and drink water." But, when they had reached the prophet's house and had sat down to eat, the prophet cried unto the man of God: "Thus saith the Lord, Forasmuch as thou hast disobeyed the mouth of the Lord, and hast not kept the commandment which the Lord thy God commanded thee, but camest back, and hast eaten bread and drunk water in the place of

THE DIVIDED KINGDOM—ISRAEL

which the Lord did say to thee, Eat no bread, and drink no water, thy carcase shall not come unto the sepulchre of thy fathers." This prophecy was soon fulfilled, for, as the man of God was returning, a lion met him and slew him and stood by his carcass. The prophet, hearing that he was dead, went and brought his body to Bethel and laid it in his own grave with much mourning, saying, "Alas, my brother!" He then said to his sons: "When I am dead, then bury me in the sepulchre wherein the man of God is buried; lay my bones beside his bones."

6. **A prophecy against Jeroboam** (1 Kings 13:33-14:18). Notwithstanding his experience, Jeroboam persisted in his idolatrous practice, yet there remained in him confidence in the prophet Ahijah, at Shiloh, and when his son Abijah fell sick, he disguised his wife and sent her to the prophet to discover what would become of the child. Now, Ahijah was old and could not see, but the Lord warned him of the deception, and when Jeroboam's wife came to his door, he said: "Come in, thou wife of Jeroboam; why feignest thou thyself to be another? for I am sent to thee with heavy tidings." He then told her that whereas the Lord had rent the kingdom from the house of David and had given it to Jeroboam, but he had not walked after His commandments, but had gone after other gods and had made molten images, He would cut off his seed, and that eventually Israel herself would be scattered. He then sent the woman away and, when she reached the door of her house, Abijah died.

7. **The war between Abijam and Jeroboam** (1 Kings 15:7; 2 Chron. 13:3-19). When Abijam ascended the throne of Judah, war was begun between

him and Jeroboam. In this conflict, Jeroboam was defeated and lost five hundred thousand chosen men, and was forced to relinquish Bethel, Jeshanah and Ephrain with the towns thereof.

8. **Death of Jeroboam** (1 Kings 14:19, 20; 2 Chron. 13:20). After reigning twenty-two years, Jeroboam slept with his fathers, and Nadab, his son, reigned in his stead.

II. THE REIGN OF NADAB
(1 Kings 15:25-27)

Nadab, the son of Jeroboam, began to reign over Israel in the second year of Asa, king of Judah. He reigned two years, did that which was evil in the sight of the Lord, and was slain by Baasha, of the house of Issachar, at Gibbethon, where he was besieging the Philistines.

III. THE REIGN OF BAASHA

1. **The accession of Baasha** (1 Kings 15:28). Baasha began to reign in the third year of Asa, king of Judah.[1]

2. **Destruction of Jeroboam's house** (1 Kings 15:27-31). Baasha not only slew Nadab, but also all the house of Jeroboam, in fulfillment of the prophecy of Ahijah.

3. **The war between Baasha and Asa** (1 Kings 15:32-34; 2 Chron. 16:1-6). There was war between Baasha and Asa all their days, and Baasha did evil in the sight of the Lord and caused Israel to sin

---
[1] Usher: 954-953 B. C.   Kamphausen: 915-914 B. C.
[2] Usher: 953-930 B. C.   Kamphausen: 914-891 B. C.

THE DIVIDED KINGDOM—ISRAEL

4. **The death of Baasha** (1 Kings 16:6). After reigning over Israel for twenty-four years, Baasha died and was buried at Tirzah, and Elah, his son, took the throne.

IV. THE REIGN OF ELAH
(1 Kings 16:8-14)

Elah began to reign over Israel in the twenty-sixth year of Asa, king of Judah, and reigned two years,[1] when he was slain by Zimri, a captain of his chariots, while he was drunken in the house of Arza, steward of his house in Tirzah.

V. THE REIGN OF ZIMRI
(1 Kings 16:11-20)

The first act of Zimri's reign was the putting to death of all the house of Baasha. When this became known to Israel, who were besieging Gibbethon, they made Omri, captain of the host, king, and he besieged Tirzah. Zimri, seeing that the city was besieged, went into the king's palace and set it on fire, and so died after reigning only seven days.[2]

VI. THE REIGN OF OMRI
(1 Kings 16:21-28)

Omri began to reign over Israel in the thirty-first year of Asa, king of Judah, and reigned twelve years—six years in Tirzah.[3] He bought the hill Samaria from Shemer for two talents of silver,

---
[1] Usher: 930-929 B. C. Kamphausen: 891-890 B. C.
[2] Usher: 929 B. C. Kamphausen: 890 B. C.
[3] Usher: 929-918 B. C. Kamphausen: 890-879 B. C.

built a city upon it and called the name of it Samaria. He was a very wicked man, doing worse than all that were before him. He was buried in Samaria.

VII. THE REIGN OF AHAB

1. **The accession and marriage of Ahab** (1 Kings 16:28-34). Upon the death of Omri, Ahab, his son, took the throne in the thirty-eighth year of Asa, king of Judah.[1] He was even more wicked than his father, and took to wife Jezebel, daughter of Ethbaal, king of the Zidonians, and built an altar and made a grove to the worship of Baal.

2. **The rise of Elijah** (1 Kings 17:1). At this time there arose Elijah the Tishbite, an inhabitant of Gilead, who prophesied to Ahab that there should be no rain or dew upon the land for years, except according to his word.

3. **Elijah flees to Cherith** (1 Kings 17:2-7). By the command of the Lord, Elijah fled to Cherith, where he was fed by the ravens night and morning and drank from the brook.

4. **Elijah goes to Zarephath** (1 Kings 17:8-16). When the brook of Cherith dried up, Elijah went to Zarephath, in Zidon. At the gate of this city he met a widow gathering sticks, whom he asked to fetch him water to drink and a morsel of food to eat. The woman replied that all she had was a handful of meal and a little oil, and that she was gathering sticks to prepare these that she and her son might eat and die. But Elijah assured her that, if she hearkened to him, the meal would not waste nor the

---
[1] Usher: 918-897 B. C.   Kamphausen: 878-857 B. C.

THE DIVIDED KINGDOM—ISRAEL

oil fail during the entire famine. This was fulfilled according to his word.

5. **Elijah raises the widow's son** (1 Kings 17: 17-24). After this, the son of the widow fell very sick, and she inquired of Elijah if he had come to bring her sin to remembrance and to slay her son. At this Elijah demanded the child, and, taking him up into the loft and laying him on his bed, he cried to the Lord and inquired if He had brought this evil upon the widow. He then stretched himself upon the child and said: "O Lord my God, I pray thee, let this child's soul come into him again." The Lord heard the petition and the child revived, and, when he was delivered to his mother, she confessed that the prophet was a man of God.

6. **Elijah meets Ahab** (1 Kings 18: 1-16). The famine continued for three years, and the Lord commanded Elijah to show himself to Ahab, promising him that when he did He would send rain upon the earth. Ahab had a governor over his house, Obadiah by name, a godly man, whom he sent out to find pasturage and water for his horses and mules. As Obadiah was attending to this matter, he met Elijah, who commanded him to return and say: "Behold, Elijah is here." Obadiah reluctantly did this, and Ahab went out to meet him.

7. **Elijah and the prophets of Baal** (1 Kings 18: 17-41). When Ahab met Elijah, he inquired: "Art thou he that troubleth Israel?" Elijah answered that it was not he that troubled Israel, but Ahab and his father's house, who followed after Baalim. He then told Ahab to gather together all Israel, 450 of the prophets of Baal and 400 of the prophets of the

grove upon Mount Carmel. When this was done, Elijah further proposed that he and the prophets of Baal should each take a bullock, cut it in pieces, erect an altar, lay wood upon the altar and the sacrifice upon the wood, and then that each should cry to his God, and that the God who answered with fire should be God. This was agreed to, and the prophets of Baal prepared their sacrifice, but, although they cried from morning until noon, "Baal, hear us," no response came. Then Elijah mocked them, saying: "Cry aloud: for he is a god; either he is talking, or he is pursuing, or he is in a journey, or peradventure he sleepeth, and must be awaked." But, although they cried louder, and cut themselves with knives and lancets, the fire did not fall. When they had failed, Elijah took twelve stones, built an altar and dug a trench around it. On the altar he placed the pieces of the bullock and drenched the whole two times with water. Then, at the time of the evening sacrifice, he called upon the Lord, and fire came down and consumed not only the sacrifice, but also the altar, and licked up the water. Seeing this, the people exclaimed: "The Lord, he is God." And, at Elijah's command, they took the prophets of Baal down to the brook Kishon, where he slew them all. He then commanded Ahab to return, assuring him that there was a sound of an abundance of rain.

8. **Elijah on Carmel** (1 Kings 18:42-46). Ahab departed, and Elijah went up into Mount Carmel, and, casting himself to the ground, put his face between his knees and commanded his servant to go to the summit and look toward the sea. This his servant did, but saw nothing. Elijah then told him

THE DIVIDED KINGDOM—ISRAEL

to repeat it seven times, and on the seventh he came back and told the prophet that a cloud had risen out of the sea the size of a man's hand. Upon hearing this, Elijah commanded his servant to go to Ahab and tell him to prepare his chariot and get down from the mountain that the rain might not stop him. He then girded his loins and ran before Ahab to Jezreel.

9. **Jezebel's threat** (1 Kings 19:1-7). When Ahab told Jezebel what Elijah had done to the prophets of Baal, she became very angry and said: "So let the gods do to me, and more also, if I make not thy life as the life of one of them by to morrow about this time." This threat was carried to Elijah, and he fled to Beer-sheba in Judah, where he left his servant, and from there continued his flight a day's journey into the wilderness, where he sat down under a juniper-tree and requested the Lord to let him die. As he slept, an angel came and, touching him, said, "Arise and eat," and when he arose he saw a cake on the coals and a cruse of water, and he ate and drank and went in the strength of that meat forty days and forty nights.

10. **Elijah at Horeb** (1 Kings 19:8-18). Elijah departed from the wilderness into Mount Horeb, where he lodged in a cave. The Lord appeared to him and inquired what he was doing there. He replied that he had been very jealous for the Lord of hosts, for the children of Israel had forsaken His covenant, broken down His altars, slain His prophets, and he alone was left alive, though they also sought his life. The Lord then commanded Elijah to go out upon the mountain, and, when he had obeyed,

a strong wind rent the mountain, "but the Lord was not in the wind: and after the wind an earthquake; but the Lord was not in the earthquake: and after the earthquake a fire; but the Lord was not in the fire: and after the fire a still small voice." Then the Lord told Elijah that he was jealous with Israel because of what it had done, and commanded him to go to Damascus and anoint Hazael king of Syria, and then to return and anoint Jehu king of Israel, and Elisha as his successor; telling him that those who escaped Hazael, Jehu should slay, and those who escaped Jehu, Elisha should slay; still the Lord told him that there were left in Israel seven thousand men who had not bowed the knee to Baal.

11. **The call of Elisha** (1 Kings 19:19-21). Elijah started as he was bidden and found Elisha, the son of Shaphat, plowing with twelve yoke of oxen. Elijah cast his mantle upon him and he left his oxen and ran after the prophet, crying: "Let me, I pray thee, kiss my father and my mother, and then I will follow thee." To this request the prophet replied: "Go back again: for what have I done to thee?" Then Elisha returned, slew a yoke of oxen, boiled their flesh, gave it to the people to eat, and arose and went after Elijah.

12. **Ahab's first war with Syria** (1 Kings 20:1-22). Ben-hadad, king of Syria, made war with Ahab and besieged Samaria. He sent a messenger to Ahab, who was in the city, telling him that his family and possessions belonged to him. To this Ahab at first agreed. Then Ben-hadad sent him word that on the morrow he should deliver up his wives, children, silver and gold. Upon receiving this

THE DIVIDED KINGDOM—ISRAEL

message, Ahab called the elders of Israel together, who, when they had heard the demands of the Syrian, told Ahab not to hearken nor consent to the proposal. Ahab's refusal was carried to Ben-hadad, who became very wroth and declared that he would destroy the city. Ahab replied to this threat in the following words: "Let not him that girdeth on his harness boast himself as he that putteth it off." At this taunt the Syrian ordered his kings to set themselves in battle array against the city. Ahab was promised victory by a certain prophet, and, sallying forth at the head of 232 princes and seven thousand fighting men, he fell upon the Syrians and routed them with great slaughter, although Ben-hadad himself escaped. Then the prophet came to Ahab again and warned him to strengthen himself, telling him that at the return of the year the Syrians would repeat the invasion.

13. **Ahab's second war with Syria** (1 Kings 20: 23-43). Following his defeat, the servants of Ben-hadad said to him: "Their gods are gods of the hills; therefore they were stronger than we; but let us fight against them in the plain, and surely we shall be stronger than they." Ben-hadad then gathered an army like his first and went against Israel at Aphek. Here, notwithstanding the Israelites were vastly inferior to the Syrians in point of numbers, the army of the Syrians was again defeated with great slaughter, and Ben-hadad, fleeing into the city, girded himself in sackcloth and, coming out to Ahab, pleaded for his life. He promised Ahab that, if he would spare him, he would restore the cities which his father had taken from Ahab's father and make

streets for him in Damascus. Ahab agreed to this and sent him away. Then one of the sons of the prophets came to Ahab and said: "Because thou hast let go out of thy hand a man whom I appointed to utter destruction, therefore thy life shall go for his life, and thy people for his people." These words greatly distressed King Ahab.

14. **Jezebel has Naboth slain** (1 Kings 21:1-16). There was a man of Jezreel, Naboth by name, who owned a vineyard near the palace of Ahab. Ahab coveted the vineyard and offered Naboth another, or its value in money, for it. But Naboth refused to dispose of it, as it was the inheritance of his fathers. Upon this refusal, Ahab went to his palace heavy and displeased, took to his bed and refused to eat. When Jezebel observed his sadness, she inquired the reason, and, when this was told her, she promised Ahab that she would get the vineyard for him. So she wrote letters in the king's name and signed them with his seal, directed to the elders and nobles, instructing them to proclaim a fast and to set Naboth on high among the people. When this was done, she had two of the sons of Belial make the charge against him that he had blasphemed the name of God and of the king. With this, they took him out of the city and stoned him to death, and Ahab took possession of the coveted property.

15. **Elijah announces Ahab's doom** (1 Kings 21: 17-29). The word of the Lord now came to Elijah, and he went to Ahab and declared that for this great sin the Lord would bring evil upon him, cut off his posterity and make his house like the house

of Jeroboam; and also that the dogs should eat Jezebel by the wall of Jezreel. At these words, Ahab rent his clothes, put sackcloth upon his flesh and fasted. The Lord then told Elijah that as Ahab had repented, he would not send the evils pronounced in his days, but in his son's days.

16. **Ahab's third war with Syria** (1 Kings 22:1-40; 2 Chron. 18:1-34). There was peace between Israel and Syria for three years, at the expiration of which time Ahab secured the alliance of Jehoshaphat, king of Judah, so that he might take Ramoth-gilead out of the hands of the Syrians. Before starting out on this expedition, however, Ahab consulted four hundred lying prophets who told him to go up; that the Lord would deliver Ramoth into his hands. Then, by the advice of Jehoshaphat, he consulted Micaiah, the only prophet of the Lord in his domain. But Micaiah, after trying in vain to conceal the real word of the Lord, frankly told him that he saw Israel scattered upon the hills as sheep without a shepherd. This message displeased Ahab, and he had Micaiah shut up in prison until he should return again in peace. The allied kings then went forth to battle, Ahab in disguise, while Jehoshaphat wore his royal robes. In the battle which ensued, Ahab was shot with an arrow between the joints of his harness and Israel was scattered, every man fleeing to his own city and country. The body of Ahab was brought back and was buried at Samaria.

VIII. THE REIGN OF AHAZIAH

1. **The accession of Ahaziah** (1 Kings 22:51). Ahaziah, the son of Ahab, began to reign in the

seventeenth year of Jehoshaphat, king of Judah, and reigned two years over Israel.[1]

2. **The character of Ahaziah** (1 Kings 22:52, 53). He did that which was evil in the sight of the Lord, and walked in the way of his father and mother, worshiping Baal.

3. **The sickness and death of Ahaziah** (2 Kings 1:1-18). During the reign of Ahaziah, Moab rebelled against Israel, and Ahaziah fell through the lattice in his upper chamber in Samaria and injured himself. He then sent messengers to Baal-zebub, god of Ekron, to inquire if he would recover. On the way, these messengers met Elijah, who said: "Is it not because there is not a God in Israel, that ye go to enquire of Baal-zebub the god of Ekron?" He then told them to say to Ahaziah: "Thou shalt not come down from that bed on which thou art gone up, but shalt surely die." When this was told Ahaziah, he sent a captain and fifty men against Elijah, but when these had found the prophet, they were consumed with fire from heaven. Then the king dispatched another captain and fifty with the same fate. Then still another captain and fifty were sent, but as the captain of this fifty pleaded for his life, he and his men were spared. The angel of the Lord then commanded Elijah to go down to Ahaziah and tell him that he should surely die.

IX. THE REIGN OF JEHORAM

1. **The accession of Jehoram** (2 Kings 1:17, 18; 3:1-3). As Ahaziah died without leaving a son, Jehoram, his brother, reigned in his stead. He took

---
[1] Usher: 897-896 B. C.   Kamphausen: 856-855 B. C.

THE DIVIDED KINGDOM—ISRAEL

the throne in the second year of Jehoram, king of Judah.[1] He was a wicked king, but not like his father and his mother, for he put away the image of Baal, although he still walked in the ways of Jeroboam.

2. The translation of Elijah (2 Kings 2:1-18). Elijah went with Elisha from Gilgal and said to him: "Tarry here, I pray thee; for the Lord hath sent me to Beth-el." But Elisha refused to tarry, and they both went to Bethel together. When they were come to that place, the sons of the prophets asked Elisha if he did not know that the Lord would take his master that day, and he replied: "Yea, I know it; hold ye your peace." Then Elijah said to Elisha: "Tarry here, I pray thee; for the Lord hath sent me to Jericho." But Elisha refused again. At Jericho, the sons of the prophets asked Elisha the same question as they had at Bethel. Again Elijah said: "Tarry, I pray thee, here; for the Lord hath sent me to Jordan." But Elisha refused again and went with him. When they came to the Jordan, Elijah rolled his mantle together and smote the waters so that they divided, and the two went over dry-shod. Having reached the other shore, Elijah said to Elisha: "Ask what I shall do for thee, before I be taken away from thee." Elisha replied: "I pray thee, let a double portion of thy spirit be upon me." This Elijah promised, provided Elisha saw him when he was taken away from him. As they went on and talked, there appeared a chariot and horses of fire which separated them, and

---

[1] Usher: 896-884 B. C.   Kamphausen: 854-853 B. C.

Elijah was taken up into heaven by a whirlwind. As Elisha saw him go, he exclaimed, "My father, my father, the chariot of Israel, and the horsemen thereof!" and he saw him no more. Then, picking up Elijah's mantle, he smote the waters of Jordan and went over and met the sons of the prophets at Jericho, who came to meet him and who bowed to the ground, saying: "The spirit of Elijah doth rest upon Elisha." They then, with Elisha's reluctant permission, sent fifty men to seek for Elijah, supposing that the Spirit of God, after taking him up, might have cast him upon some mountain or in some valley. But, after three days' search, they found him not.

3. **Elisha heals the waters** (2 Kings 2:19-22). Some of the men of Jericho came to Elisha and complained that, while the site of the city was pleasant, the water was impure and the ground barren. So, taking a cruse of salt, the prophet cast it into the water and it was cleansed of its impurity.

4. **Irreverent children devoured by bears** (2 Kings 2:23-25). As Elisha was returning from Jericho to Bethel, little children came out of the city and mocked him, saying: "Go up, thou bald head." At which the prophet cursed them in the name of the Lord, and two bears came out of the wood and tore forty-two of them. From Bethel, Elisha went to Carmel and from Carmel he returned to Samaria.

5. **The rebellion of Moab** (2 Kings 3:4-27). Mesha, king of Moab, who was a sheepmaster and who had rendered the king of Israel two hundred thousand sheep with the wool, rebelled against Israel, after the death of Ahab, and Jehoram made an alli-

THE DIVIDED KINGDOM—ISRAEL

ance with Jehoshaphat, king of Judah, and the king of Edom to go against him. When Elisha was consulted, he reproved the alliance, although he promised victory over the Moabites. In the battle that ensued, the Moabites were defeated and Israel beat down their cities, threw stones upon their good land, stopped their wells and felled their trees.

6. Elisha's miracles (2 Kings 4:1-6:7). During the reign of Jehoram, Elisha performed a number of notable miracles:

(1) The wife of one of the sons of the prophets came to him with the complaint that her husband was dead, that she was poverty-stricken and that her creditor had come to take her two sons as bondsmen. Upon inquiry, Elisha discovered that she had nothing but a pot of oil. This oil he miraculously increased so that she had sufficient to pay her debts and redeem her sons.

(2) A certain woman and her husband at Shunem had been very kind to the prophet and his servant, Gehazi, providing them a chamber on their wall whenever they came that way. For this kindness, Elisha promised her a son, although she was childless. When the son was born, he fell sick and died, and his mother went to the prophet with her lament. Then Elisha came into her house, went up into the room where the child lay and, stretching himself twice upon its dead body, restored it to life.

(3) A son of the prophets shred wild gourds into a mess of pottage and his companions ate of it. When they had discovered that the mess was poisonous, they cried: "O thou man of God, there is death in the pot." Upon hearing this, Elisha cast meal

into the pot and no harm came from the pottage.

(4) Again, he fed an hundred men with twenty loaves of barley and full ears of corn in the husk thereof.

(5) Naaman, captain of the host of the king of Syria, was afflicted with leprosy, and, hearing through his Israelitish servant-girl of the power of Elisha, he went down into Israel to visit him. Elisha told him to dip seven times in Jordan, which he reluctantly did, with the result that he was made clean. Naaman offered Elisha a reward, which he refused to take. But Gehazi followed Naaman and received two talents of silver and two changes of raiment, because of which, at the prophet's command, he was stricken with the same disease.

(6) Elisha and the sons of the prophets went to the Jordan to build for themselves a place in which to dwell. As one of them was felling a beam, his axe, which he had borrowed, fell into the stream. This being told Elisha, he cast a stick into the stream and the iron floated upon the water.

7. **Elisha defeats the plans of Ben-hadad** (2 Kings 6:8-23). Ben-hadad, king of Syria, warred against Israel and planned to ambush Jehoram, but his plans were revealed by Elisha. When Ben-hadad heard that it was Elisha who had discovered his plans, and that he was at Dothan, he sent a force to that city to take him. But this force was miraculously stricken with blindness and was led by the prophet himself to Samaria, where their eyes were opened. After saving them from the vengeance of Jehoram and feeding them, Elisha permitted them to return.

8. **The siege and famine of Samaria** (2 Kings 6:

THE DIVIDED KINGDOM—ISRAEL

24-7:20). Ben-hadad again besieged Samaria, and the lack of food was so great that women devoured their children. When Jehoram was told this, he was wroth with Elisha and threatened to take his life. This threat the prophet took calmly and promised the king that the next day there should be plenty of food. There were four lepers who dwelt at the gate of the city, and these determined to go into the camp of the Syrians in search of food. But, entering the camp, they found it deserted, as the Syrians had fled precipitately, believing that the king of Israel had hired the Hittites and Egyptians to fight against them. This being told Jehoram, he doubted and sent out spies, who returned and corroborated the story of the lepers. Then the children of Israel went into the camp and helped themselves to the spoils.

9. **Elisha visits Damascus** (2 Kings 8:7-15). The prophet went to the city of Damascus, and when it was told Ben-hadad, who was sick, that Elisha was in that place, he sent Hazael with presents to inquire if he would recover from his disease. To this inquiry Elisha replied: "Go, say unto him, Thou mayest certainly recover: howbeit the Lord hath shewed me that he shall surely die." Then the prophet began to weep, and when Hazael asked him the reason, he replied that it was because he foresaw that Hazael would yet be king over Syria and that he would burn Israel's cities, slay her young men and destroy her children. Upon hearing this, Hazael went in to the king and told him that he would recover, but, on the morrow, Ben-hadad dipped a cloth in water, placed it on his face and so died, and Hazael reigned in his stead.

10. **Jehoram wars with the Syrians** (2 Kings 8: 28). Jehoram warred with the Syrians in Ramoth-gilead. In this he was joined by Ahaziah, king of Judah. He was wounded in this war.

X. THE REIGN OF JEHU

1. **Jehu anointed king** (2 Kings 9:1-13). Elisha, hearing that Jehoram was wounded, commanded one of the sons of the prophets to go to Ramoth-gilead and anoint Jehu, son of Jehoshaphat, king. This his messenger did, at the same time commanding Jehu to slay both Jehoram and all the house of Ahab.

2. **The destruction of Jehoram and the house of Ahab** (2 Kings 9:14-10:18). When it became known that Jehu had been anointed king, the fact was announced by the blowing of the trumpet, and Jehu, taking a chariot, rode furiously from Ramoth-gilead to Jezreel, where Jehoram was. Jehoram saw him coming, and he and Ahaziah rode out to meet him, whereupon Jehu shot Jehoram through the heart with an arrow so that he died, and, pursuing Ahaziah, he smote him also, but he fled to Megiddo, where he died. As for Jezebel, the mother of Jehoram, she was thrown out of her own window at Jezreel by her own eunuchs at Jehu's command, and was devoured by dogs according to the prophecy of Elijah. Following this, Jehu had all the house of Ahab slain and also forty-two of the princes of Judah, saving only Jehonadab.

3. **The extirpation of Baal-worship** (2 Kings 10: 19-29). The next important event in the career of Jehu was the extirpation of Baal-worship. He said,

THE DIVIDED KINGDOM—ISRAEL

"Ahab served Baal a little; but Jehu shall serve him much," and, sending forth a proclamation of a solemn assembly for Baal, he gathered together all of his priests in their temple, and, surrounding them with eighty of his trusty guards, he slew them all, broke their images and destroyed their house.

4. **The blessing promised** (2 Kings 10:30, 31). Because of his zeal for Him, the Lord promised that four generations of Jehu's descendants should sit upon his throne. Yet Jehu did not entirely depart from the sins of Jeroboam, the son of Nebat.

5. **The decline of Israel** (2 Kings 10:32, 33). But, notwithstanding the power of Jehu, Israel was cut short during his days by the invasion of Hazael the Syrian, who took all of the territory east of the Jordan.

6. **The death of Jehu** (2 Kings 10:35, 36). After reigning twenty-eight years,[1] Jehu died and was buried in Samaria, and his son Jehoahaz reigned in his stead.

XI. THE REIGN OF JEHOAHAZ

1. **The accession of Jehoahaz** (2 Kings 13:1-3). Jehoahaz began to reign over Israel in the twenty-third year of Joash, king of Judah, and reigned seventeen years.[2] He did evil in the sight of the Lord, on account of which Israel was delivered into the hands of Hazael and his son, Ben-hadad.

2. **The repentance of Jehoahaz** (2 Kings 13:4-7). Under these trials, Jehoahaz repented and called upon the Lord, and the Lord heard him and gave Israel

---
[1] Usher: 884-856 B. C.   Kamphausen: 842-815 B. C.
[2] Usher: 856-839 B. C.   Kamphausen: 814-798 B. C.

a savior, so that they went out from under the hand of the Syrians. But Israel did not depart from the sins of the house of Jeroboam.

3. **The death of Jehoahaz** (2 Kings 13:8, 9). Jehoahaz died and was buried in Samaria, and was succeeded by his son Jehoash.

XII. THE REIGN OF JEHOASH

1. **The accession of Jehoash** (2 Kings 13:10, 11). Jehoash began to reign over Israel in the thirty-seventh year of Joash, king of Judah. He reigned sixteen years at Samaria, and did that which was evil in the sight of the Lord.[1]

2. **The illness and death of Elisha** (2 Kings 13: 14-21). After his accession Elisha was taken sick and the king went down and wept over him, saying: "O my father, my father, the chariot of Israel, and the horsemen thereof." Then Elisha told him to shoot an arrow out of the window eastward. When this was done, the prophet exclaimed: "The arrow of the Lord's deliverance, and the arrow of deliverance from Syria: for thou shalt smite the Syrians in Aphek, till thou have consumed them." Elisha then commanded him to take his arrows and smite the ground, which he did three times. At this the prophet was wroth, telling him that he should have smitten the ground five or six times, that then he would have smitten Syria until he had consumed it, whereas he should smite it but thrice. Following this, Elisha died.

3. **The wars of Jehoash** (2 Kings 13:22-25; 14:

---

[1] Usher: 839-823 B. C. Kamphausen: 797-782 B. C.

THE DIVIDED KINGDOM—ISRAEL

8-15). During his reign, Jehoash fought with the Syrians under Ben-hadad and took from them the cities which had been taken from his father. He also fought with Amaziah, king of Judah.

4. **The death of Jehoash** (2 Kings 13:13; 14:16). Jehoash died and was buried at Samaria.

XIII. THE REIGN OF JEROBOAM II.

(2 Kings 14:23-29)

Jeroboam II., the son of Jehoash, succeeded to the throne in the fifteenth year of Amaziah, king of Judah, and reigned forty-one years.[1] He was a wicked king, yet he seems to have possessed some power, for he won back part of the territory taken by the Syrians.

XIV. THE REIGN OF ZACHARIAH

(2 Kings 15:8-12)

Upon the death of Jeroboam II., his son Zachariah succeeded to the throne, in the thirty-eighth year of Azariah, king of Judah. He reigned only six months, when he was slain by Shallum, son of Jabesh.[2]

XV. THE REIGN OF SHALLUM

(2 Kings 15:13-15)

Shallum began to reign in the thirty-ninth year of Azariah and reigned just one month, when he was slain by Menahem, son of Gadi.[3]

---
[1] Usher: 823-772 B. C. Kamphausen: 781-741 B. C.
[2] Usher: 772 B. C. Kamphausen: 741 B. C.
[3] Usher: 772 B. C. Kamphausen: 741 B. C.

XVI. THE REIGN OF MENAHEM

(2 Kings 15: 16-20)

Menahem began to reign in the thirty-ninth year of Azariah and reigned ten years in Samaria.[1] He was a very wicked king. He took the city of Tiphsah and slew all the pregnant women therein. During his reign, Israel was invaded by Pul, king of Assyria, and to him Menahem paid tribute.

XVII. THE REIGN OF PEKAHIAH

(2 Kings 15: 21-26)

When Menahem died, Pekahiah, his son, reigned in his stead. He began to reign in the fiftieth year of Azariah and reigned two years,[2] when he was slain by Pekah, one of his captains.

XVIII. THE REIGN OF PEKAH

(2 Kings 15: 27-31)

Pekah reigned twenty years[3] and did that which was evil in the sight of the Lord. During his reign, Tiglath-pileser invaded his territory and took the inhabitants of the northern part captive to Assyria. Pekah finally met his death at the hands of Hoshea, son of Elah.

XIX. THE REIGN OF HOSHEA

1. **The accession of Hoshea** (2 Kings 17: 1, 2). Hoshea began to reign over Israel at Samaria in the twelfth year of Ahaz, king of Judah, and reigned

---

[1] Usher: 772-762 B. C.   Kamphausen: 740-738 B. C.
[2] Usher: 762-760 B. C.   Kamphausen: 737-736 B. C.
[3] Usher: 760-730 B. C.   Kamphausen: 736-730 B. C.

THE DIVIDED KINGDOM—ISRAEL

nine years.[1] He did that which was evil in the sight of the Lord, but not as the kings before him.

2. **Israel becomes tributary to Assyria** (2 Kings 17:3). During the reign of Hoshea, Shalmaneser, king of Assyria, came against Israel and Hoshea became tributary to him.

3. **The deportation of the ten tribes** (2 Kings 17: 4-41). In the fifth year of Hoshea's reign, Shalmaneser came against Samaria and besieged it three years, when it fell. This was because Hoshea had sent messengers to So, king of Egypt, and had withheld his presents from the king of Assyria. Following the fall of Samaria, the ten tribes were deported to Assyria.

QUESTIONS

Give the causes of the division between Israel and Judah. Give the advantages of the northern kingdom. How many kings ruled over Israel? How many dynasties did they constitute? What was their character? How many of the kings of Israel are mentioned in the Assyrio-Babylonian inscriptions? Name the kings of Israel in their order. Who was the first king to reign over Israel? What form of worship did he institute? Where did he set up idols, and why? What prophecy was uttered against the altar? What prophecy was uttered against Jeroboam? Tell about the conflict between Jeroboam and Abijah. How long did Jeroboam reign? Who succeeded him? How long did Nadab reign? How did Baasha obtain the kingdom? What did he do to the house of Jeroboam? With whom did Baasha carry on war? How long did he reign and where was he buried? How long did Elah reign? Who slew him? How long did Zimri reign? What did he do to the house of Baasha? Who slew Zimri? How long did Omri reign? What city did he build? What was his character? Who was Ahab? Whom did he marry? What prophet began to prophesy under his reign?

---

[1] Usher: 730-721 B. C.   Kamphausen: 730-722 B. C.

THE GIST OF THE BIBLE

What did Elijah do at Zarephath? Tell about the raising of the widow's son. Tell about Elijah's contest with the prophets of Baal. What threat did Jezebel make against Elijah? Where did Elijah flee to get away from Jezebel? What happened there? Tell about the call of Elisha. How many wars did Ahab have with Syria and in how many was he successful? What happened to him in the last? How did Ahab secure the vineyard of Naboth? Who succeeded Ahab? What was his character? What false god did he seek to consult? What did Elijah command Ahaziah's messengers to tell him? Who succeeded Ahaziah? Tell about the translation of Elijah. What miracle did Elisha perform at Jericho? What happened to the children of Bethel, and why? Mention some of the miracles of Elisha. Tell about the siege and famine of Samaria. Who was Jehu? What was his character? What did he do to Jehoram and the house of Ahab? What did he do to Baal-worship? How long did Jehu reign? Under whose reign did Elisha die? What important invasion occurred under the reign of Menahem? What invasion occurred under the reign of Pekah? What monarch invaded Israel under the reign of Hoshea? What city did he besiege? How long did he besiege it? Why did he besiege it? What did he do with the ten tribes?

STUDY XXIII. THE DIVIDED KINGDOM—JUDAH

(1 Kings 12:1-2 Kings 25:30; 2 Chron. 10:1-36:21)

INTRODUCTION

1. **The kings of Judah.** Judah was reigned over by twenty rulers. Of these, six were either good, or fairly good, men.

2. **The advantages of the southern kingdom.** While the southern kingdom did not possess the population, the military power or the fertile soil of the northern kingdom, it had within its bounds the religious and political capital of the nation, and its rulers were the lineal descendants of King David.

3. **Archæological confirmation.** Four kings of Judah are mentioned in the Assyrio-Babylonian inscriptions: Azariah, Ahaz, Hezekiah and Manasseh. We also have an account of the invasion of Judah by Shishak recorded on the walls of Karnak, and the account of the events described in 2 Kings 3 on the Moabite stone which was set up by King Mesha.

4. **The period of the kingdom.** The period of the southern kingdom lay between the years 975 and 586 B. C., Usher's chronology.

I. THE REIGN OF REHOBOAM

1. **The accession of Rehoboam** (1 Kings 14:21; 2 Chron. 12:1). Rehoboam, the son of Solomon, ascended the throne of Judah at the age of forty-

one.[1] His mother was Naamah the Ammonitess. He did that which was evil in the sight of the Lord.

2. **Rehoboam's folly** (1 Kings 12:1-15; 2 Chron. 10:1-11). When Rehoboam ascended the throne, representatives of his people, with Jeroboam at their head, came to him and requested that he lighten the burdens which his father had imposed upon them. Rehoboam asked three days in which to consider this proposition, at the expiration of which time, after listening to his young counselors instead of those who were older, who counseled otherwise, he declared that he would add to the yoke which his father had placed upon the people. This displeased Israel and was the chief cause of the separation.

3. **Rehoboam's apostasy** (1 Kings 14:21-24). Rehoboam forsook God and, under his approval, Judah built high places, images and groves on every high hill and under every green tree. In addition to this, other more sinful and revolting practices were indulged in.

4. **The invasion of Shishak** (1 Kings 14:25-30; 2 Chron. 12:2-12). In the fifth year of Rehoboam's reign, Shishak, king of Egypt, came against Jerusalem and despoiled the Temple of many of its treasures, among them the golden shields which Solomon had made. These were replaced by Rehoboam with shields of brass.

5. **The death of Rehoboam** (1 Kings 14:31; 2 Chron. 12:13-16). After reigning for seventeen years, during which time he was continuously at

---
[1] Usher: 975-958 B. C. Kamphausen: 937-921 B. C.

THE DIVIDED KINGDOM—JUDAH

war with Israel, Rehoboam died and was buried with his fathers.

II. THE REIGN OF ABIJAM

1. **The accession of Abijam** (1 Kings 15:1-3; 2 Chron. 13:1, 2). Abijam, son of Rehoboam ·by Michaiah, began to reign over Judah in the eighteenth year of Jeroboam, king of Israel.[1] He did that which was evil in the sight of the Lord.

2. **The war between Abijam and Jeroboam** (1 Kings 15:6, 7; 2 Chron. 13:3-19). The war which had been begun between Rehoboam and Jeroboam was continued under the reign of Abijam. In the battle at Mount Ephraim, Israel was defeated and fled with great slaughter.

3. **The family of Abijam** (2 Chron. 13:21, 22). Abijam became great and married fourteen wives, by whom he had twenty-two sons and sixteen daughters.

4. **The death of Abijam** (1 Kings 15:8; 2 Chron. 14:1). After reigning three years, Abijam died and was buried in the city of David.

III. THE REIGN OF ASA

1. **The accession of Asa** (1 Kings 15:8-15; 2 Chron. 14:1-8). At the death of Abijam, his son Asa, a wise and good man and one of the best kings that Judah had, began to reign, in the twentieth year of Jeroboam.[2] His mother's name was Maachah.

2. **Asa's victory over Zerah the Ethiopian** (2 Chron. 14:9-15). During the reign of Asa, the Ethiopians

---
[1] Usher: 958-956 B. C.   Kamphausen: 920-918 B. C.
[2] Usher: 956-916 B. C.   Kamphausen: 917-877 B. C.

under Zerah came against Judah. Asa marshaled his forces and met them in the valley of Zephathah. Before going into the battle, he offered the following prayer: "Lord, it is nothing with thee to help, whether with many, or with them that have no power: help us, O Lord our God; for we rest on thee, and in thy name we go against this multitude. O Lord, thou art our God; let not man prevail against thee." In the battle which ensued, the Ethiopians were sorely defeated and were pursued by Asa as far as Gerar, when the children of Judah returned, bringing much spoil with them.

3. **The reforms of Asa** (2 Chron. 15:1-19). Asa began his reign with a number of notable reforms. He took away the altars of the strange gods, broke their images and cut down their groves. Many from the tribes of Ephraim, Manasseh and Simeon, seeing this, joined his standard and, in the third month of his fifteenth year, gathered together in Jerusalem, where they offered seven hundred oxen and seven thousand sheep and entered into a covenant to seek the Lord God of their fathers with all their heart and soul. So zealous was Asa in his service of the Lord that he removed his mother, Maachah,[1] from being queen because she worshiped an idol, and he destroyed her idol by the brook Kidron.

4. **The war between Asa and Baasha** (1 Kings 15:16-22; 2 Chron. 16:1-11). In the thirty-sixth year of Asa's reign, Baasha, king of Israel, came against Judah and built Ramah to prevent further apostasies of his people to Asa. Then Asa made an alliance

---

[1] The terms "father" and "mother" are employed in the sense of "ancestor" in the Bible. Maachah was, in reality, the grandmother of Asa.

THE DIVIDED KINGDOM—JUDAH

with Ben-hadad, king of Syria, to fight with him against Baasha. When Hanani, the seer, heard of this alliance, he rebuked Asa, because he relied upon Ben-hadad in the place of the Lord, telling him that from henceforth he should have wars. This rebuke enraged Asa and he had Hanani shut up in prison. In this war, Ben-hadad took many of the towns of northern Israel, and, as a result, Baasha left off building Ramah.

5. **The illness and death of Asa** (1 Kings 15:23, 24; 2 Chron. 16:12-14). In the thirty-ninth year of his reign, Asa became diseased in his feet, and in the forty-first year died and was buried in his own sepulchre in the city of David.

IV. THE REIGN OF JEHOSHAPHAT

1. **The accession of Jehoshaphat** (1 Kings 22:41, 42; 2 Chron. 17:1). Jehoshaphat, the son of Asa, began to reign in the fourth year of Ahab, king of Israel, and in the thirty-fifth year of his own life.[1]

2. **The revival under Jehoshaphat** (1 Kings 22: 43-49; 2 Chron. 17:6-9). Jehoshaphat carried out the reforms of his father and took away the high places and groves from Judah, and, in the third year of his reign, sent princes, priests and Levites throughout Judah, instructing the people in the law of Moses.

3. **The power of Jehoshaphat** (2 Chron. 17:10-19). So great was the power of Jehoshaphat that the kingdoms round about Judah stood in fear of him, and the Philistines and Arabians paid him tribute. He also built in Judah castles and store-cities, increased

---
[1] Usher: 916-892 B. C. Kamphausen: 876-852 B. C.

the commercial spirit of his people and strengthened his army.

4. **Jehoshaphat's alliance with Ahab** (1 Kings 22:2-40; 2 Chron. 18:1-19:11). Jehoshaphat entered into an alliance with Ahab, king of Israel, to go against Ramoth-gilead, which had been taken from Israel by the king of Syria. The four hundred lying prophets of Israel promised victory, but Micaiah, the true prophet of the Lord, declared defeat. In the battle which ensued, Ahab was slain, but Jehoshaphat escaped and returned to Jerusalem. For this alliance Jehoshaphat was rebuked by Jehu, son of Hanani the seer.

5. **The invasion of Moab and Ammon** (2 Chron. 20:1-34). The Moabites and Ammonites invaded the land of Judah and came to En-gedi. When this was told Jehoshaphat, he proclaimed a fast and gathered all Judah together and besought the Lord for deliverance. This prayer was answered through Jahaziel, a Levite, who assured Jehoshaphat of victory, telling him that Judah would not even have to fight, but that she should simply stand still and see the salvation of the Lord. On the morrow, the army of Jehoshaphat went down into the wilderness of Tekoa, preceded by singers whom Jehoshaphat had appointed to praise the Lord. As the army moved forward, the Lord set ambushments for the Moabites and Ammonites and their allies, the Edomites, and they fell upon one another and slew one another so that, when Jehoshaphat came upon the field, he found it covered with dead bodies. So, gathering up the spoils, he returned to Jerusalem with great joy, and fear came upon all nations round about when

THE DIVIDED KINGDOM—JUDAH

they discovered that the Lord had fought for Judah.

6. The alliance between Jehoshaphat and Ahaziah (1 Kings 22:47-49; 2 Chron. 20:35-37). A commercial alliance was formed between Jehoshaphat and Ahaziah, king of Israel, and they built ships to trade with Tarshish. This alliance was rebuked by Eliezer, son of Dodavah, who declared that, because of it, the Lord had broken Jehoshaphat's works. This prophecy came true and the ships were wrecked.[1]

7. The death of Jehoshaphat (1 Kings 22:50; 2 Chron. 21:1). After reigning over Judah for twenty-five years, Jehoshaphat died and was buried with his fathers in Jerusalem.

V. THE REIGN OF JEHORAM

1. The accession of Jehoram (1 Kings 22:50; 2 Kings 8:16-19; 2 Chron. 21:1-7). Jehoram, the son of Jehoshaphat, was thirty-two years old when he began to reign.[2] He slew all of his brethren with the sword, married Athaliah, the daughter of Ahab, and did evil in the sight of the Lord.

2. The reverses of Jehoram (2 Kings 8:20-23; 2 Chron. 21:8-17). Under the reign of this king there occurred a revolt of the Edomites and the inhabitants of Libnah, and the sacking of Jerusalem by the Philistines and the Arabians, who carried away all the substance found in Jehoram's house, with his wives and children, excepting Jehoahaz, his youngest son.

---

[1] In 1 Kings the record says that Jehoshaphat and Ahaziah did not enter into a commercial partnership; in 2 Chronicles the record says that they did. The explanation is that they did at first form such a partnership, but Jehoshaphat, being reproved by the prophet, would not consent to the proposals of Ahaziah a second time.

[2] Usher: 892-885 B. C. Kamphausen: 851-844 B. C.

3. **Jehoram's disease and death** (2 Kings 8:24; 2 Chron. 21:12-20). So wicked was Jehoram that Elijah sent him a written message declaring that he should be afflicted with an incurable disease of the bowels. He was accordingly afflicted and subsequently died, after reigning eight years, without being lamented. He was buried in Jerusalem, though not in the sepulchre of his fathers.

VI. THE REIGN OF AHAZIAH

1. **The accession of Ahaziah** (2 Kings 8:24-27; 2 Chron. 22:1-4). After the death of Jehoram the inhabitants of Jerusalem made Ahaziah, his son, king in his stead. His mother was Athaliah. He was forty-two years old[1] when he began to reign. With his mother as counselor, he lived a very wicked life.

2. **The alliance of Ahaziah and Jehoram** (2 Kings 8:28; 2 Chron. 22:5). Ahaziah formed an alliance with Jehoram, king of Israel, against Hazael, king of Syria. In the battle which ensued, Jehoram was wounded and returned to Jezreel to be healed.

3. **The death of Ahaziah** (2 Kings 8:29-9:28; 2 Chron. 22:9). After this, Ahaziah went down to Jezreel to visit Jehoram, and while there, with many others of his royal house, was slain by Jehu.

VII. THE REIGN OF ATHALIAH

(2 Kings 11:1-3; 2 Chron. 22:10-23:15)

When Athaliah saw that her son was dead, she slew all of the royal house, excepting Joash, who, with his nurse, was hidden by his aunt in a bed-

---
[1] Usher: 885-884 B. C. Kamphausen: 843 B. C.

chamber. She then took the throne herself and reigned six years.[1] She was a very wicked daughter of Ahab and Jezebel.

VIII. THE REIGN OF JOASH

1. **The accession of Joash** (2 Kings 11:4-12; 2 Chron. 23:1-11). In the seventh year after the death of Ahaziah, Jehoiada the priest, by stratagem, secured the accession of Joash. He made a covenant with the captains of hundreds, the priests, the Levites and the congregation to support the king's seed, and then had the boy brought out and anointed. Joash was seven years of age when he began to reign.[2] He did that which was right in the sight of the Lord all the days of Jehoiada, who took for him two wives.

2. **The execution of Athaliah** (2 Kings 11:13-16; 2 Chron. 23:12-15). When Athaliah heard the sound of the coronation ceremonies, she rent her clothes and cried: "Treason, treason." But, by the command of Jehoiada, she was taken and executed.

3. **The revival of the true worship** (2 Kings 11:17-20; 2 Chron. 23:16-21). Following the accession of Joash, Jehoiada set about reviving the ancient worship. He made Joash and his people enter into a covenant to be the Lord's people. He then broke down the altars of Baal, slew his priest and broke his images. After this, he re-established the temple worship.

4. **The repairing of the Temple** (2 Kings 12:1-

---

[1] Usher: 884-878 B. C. Kamphausen: 842-837 B. C.
[2] Usher: 878-838 B. C. Kamphausen: 836-797 B. C.

16; 2 Chron. 24:1-14). Joash determined to repair the Temple, which had been desecrated by Athaliah's sons. So, gathering together the priests and Levites, he sent them throughout Judah to gather funds for the work. As the Levites did not hasten, Joash complained to Jehoiada and then had a chest placed within the gate of the Temple and made proclamation to the people to bring their money and cast it into the chest. In this way the necessary funds were raised both to repair the Temple and to refurnish it.

5. **The death of Jehoiada** (2 Chron. 24:15, 16). Jehoiada now died and was buried among the kings of Judah because he had done good in Israel both toward God and his house.

6. **The apostasy and pride of the princes of Judah** (2 Chron. 24:17-22). After the death of the faithful Jehoiada, the princes of Judah came before the king and secured his consent to restore the groves and idols. This greatly displeased the Lord, and the Spirit rested upon Zechariah, the son of Jehoiada, who reproved them for their apostasy. For this the princes conspired against him and he was stoned to death.

7. **Judah defeated by the Syrians** (2 Chron. 24: 23, 24). As a punishment for their sins, the Lord sent the Syrians against Judah. This people destroyed her princes and sent spoils back to Damascus.

8. **The death of Joash** (2 Kings 12:19-21; 2 Chron. 24:25-27). After reigning forty years, Joash was slain by his own servants in his bed and was buried among the kings of Judah.

THE DIVIDED KINGDOM—JUDAH

IX. THE REIGN OF AMAZIAH

1. **The accession of Amaziah** (2 Kings 14:1, 2; 2 Chron. 25:1, 2). Amaziah was twenty-five years old when he began to reign.[1] His mother's name was Jehoaddan of Jerusalem. He did that which was right in the sight of the Lord, but not with a perfect heart.

2. **Amaziah's vengeance upon his father's slayers** (2 Chron. 25:3, 4). When his kingdom was fully established, Amaziah slew the servants who had taken his father's life.

3. **Amaziah's war with Edom** (2 Chron. 25:5-16). Amaziah gathered together the army of Judah and, with a large force of mercenaries hired out of Israel, proceeded against Edom. But a man of God came to him, saying: "Let not the army of Israel go with thee: for the Lord is not with Israel, to wit, with all the children of Ephraim." When Amaziah heard this, he sent the children of Ephraim back to their own land, which greatly enraged them, and they fell upon some of the cities of northern Judah, smote three thousand of them and returned with the spoils. In the battle which ensued between Amaziah and Edom, the latter were defeated with great slaughter, but Amaziah carried their gods back with him, made them his gods and offered incense to them, which greatly displeased the Lord.

4. **Amaziah's war with Israel** (2 Kings 14:8-14; 2 Chron. 25:17-25). Amaziah, after his return from fighting Edom, sent a challenge to Jehoash, king of Israel. Jehoash sent a message back advising Ama-

---
[1] Usher: 838-809 B. C.   Kamphausen: 796-778 B. C.

ziah to let him and Israel alone. But Amaziah would not hearken and went against Israel, by whom he was sorely defeated and was taken captive, Jehoash bringing him to Jerusalem, where he broke down the walls, after which he returned to his own land with many spoils.

5. The death of Amaziah (2 Kings 14:18-20; 2 Chron. 25:26-28). A conspiracy was formed against Amaziah in the latter part of his reign and he fled to Lachish, where he was slain. His body was then brought to Jerusalem and he was buried with his fathers. He reigned twenty-nine years.

X. THE REIGN OF UZZIAH (AZARIAH)

1. The accession of Uzziah (2 Kings 15:1-4; 2 Chron. 26:1-5). Uzziah, or Azariah, was sixteen years old when he began to reign.[1] He was the son of Amaziah and Jecholiah, and did that which was right in the sight of the Lord all the days of Zechariah the priest.

2. The wars of Uzziah (2 Chron. 26:6-15). Uzziah had a large army and he strengthened the defenses of Jerusalem. He warred against the Philistines and broke down the walls of Gath, Jabneh and Ashdod. He also warred against the Arabians, and the Ammonites paid him tribute.

3. Uzziah intrudes into the office of the priest (2 Kings 15:5; 2 Chron. 26:16-21). But Uzziah committed sin against God. He went into the Temple and offered incense upon the altar. For this he was reproached by Azariah the priest, which made him

---
[1] Usher: 809-757 B. C. Kamphausen: 777-736 B. C.

THE DIVIDED KINGDOM—JUDAH

exceedingly wroth. But, while he stood with the censer in his hand, he was stricken with leprosy and was driven from the house of the Lord and from his throne, Jotham his son reigning in his stead.

4. **The death of Uzziah** (2 Kings 15:6, 7; 2 Chron. 26:22, 23). After reigning fifty-two years, Uzziah died and was buried with his fathers in the field of burial which belonged to the kings.

XI. THE REIGN OF JOTHAM

1. **The accession of Jotham** (2 Kings 15:32, 33; 2 Chron. 27:1, 2). Jotham, the son of Uzziah, was twenty-five years old when he began to reign.[1] His mother was Jerushah, the daughter of Zadok.

2. **The enterprise of Jotham** (2 Kings 15:34-37; 2 Chron. 27:1-6). Jotham was an upright ruler, although his people were corrupt. He strengthened the defenses of Judah and built cities. He also conquered the Ammonites and from them exacted tribute.

3. **The death of Jotham** (2 Kings 15:38; 2 Chron. 27:7-9). At the time of his death Jotham had reigned sixteen years. He was buried in Jerusalem.

XII. THE REIGN OF AHAZ

1. **The accession of Ahaz** (2 Kings 16:1-4; 2 Chron. 28:1-4). Ahaz, the son of Jotham, was twenty years of age when he began to reign.[2] He did that which was evil in the sight of the Lord and worshiped Baal.

---
[1] Usher: 757-742 B. C. Kamphausen: 750-735 B. C.
[2] Usher: 742-726 B. C. Kamphausen: 734-715 B. C.

2. The wars of Ahaz (2 Kings 16:5-18; 2 Chron. 28:5-25). Because of the wickedness of Ahaz, the Lord delivered him into the hands of the Syrians, who smote him and carried away a multitude of his subjects captive to Damascus. Pekah, the king of Israel, also attacked Judah, slew a multitude and carried a multitude captive to Samaria; but these were sent back to Judah through the intervention of Oded, a prophet of the Lord. The Edomites and Philistines also invaded the land, and Ahaz appealed to Tiglath-pileser, king of Assyria, for help. Ahaz paid the Assyrian king out of the portion of the Temple, but he helped him not. In all of his reverses Ahaz called upon other gods than the God of his fathers.

3. The death of Ahaz (2 Kings 16:19, 20; 2 Chron. 28:26, 27). Ahaz reigned sixteen years and after his death was buried in Jerusalem, though not in the sepulchre of the kings of Judah.

XIII. THE REIGN OF HEZEKIAH

1. The accession of Hezekiah (2 Kings 18:1-3; 2 Chron. 29:1, 2). Hezekiah, son of Ahaz, began to reign at the age of twenty-five.[1] His mother's name was Abijah. He did that which was right in the sight of the Lord.

2. The revival under Hezekiah (2 Kings 18:4-7; 2 Chron. 29:3-31:21). At the very beginning of his reign, Hezekiah set about restoring the worship of his fathers. He opened the doors of the Temple, which Ahaz, his father, had closed, had the priests

---

[1] Usher: 726-697 B. C. Kamphausen: 714-686 B. C.

THE DIVIDED KINGDOM—JUDAH

sanctify themselves, and offered burnt-offerings. He also, at the appointed time, had Judah keep the Passover, and set himself zealously to the work of destroying the idols that were in the land. He also compelled Judah to pay tithes and to walk in the commandments of the Lord.

3. **The invasion of Sennacherib** (2 Kings 18: 13-37; 2 Chron. 32: 1-19). Sennacherib, king of Assyria, entered Palestine and laid siege to Lachish. While engaged in operations against this place, he sent letters to Hezekiah and his people, threatening them with subjugation, boasting of his power and defying the God of Israel.

4. **Judah delivered from Sennacherib** (2 Kings 19: 1-37; 2 Chron. 32: 20-23). When Hezekiah the king, and Isaiah the prophet, heard the blatant words of the emissaries of Sennacherib, they cried unto God, and He heard their prayer and declared that the king of Assyria should not come into the city, shoot an arrow into it nor raise a bank against it, but that he should return by the way that he came. That night the angel of the Lord smote 185,000 of the Assyrians, and Sennacherib returned to Nineveh, where, as he was worshiping in the house of Nisroch, his god, his two sons slew him.

5. **Hezekiah's illness and recovery** (2 Kings 20: 1-11; 2 Chron. 32: 24-26). Hezekiah became very sick, and Isaiah the prophet came into his presence and charged him to set his house in order, telling him that he should die and not live. The king, hearing this, turned his face to the wall and besought the Lord, who told him that He would add fifteen years to his life, and also that He would

THE GIST OF THE BIBLE

deliver him out of the hands of the king of Assyria.

6. **Hezekiah imprudently reveals his wealth to the representatives of Babylon** (2 Kings 20:12-19; 2 Chron. 32:31). Hezekiah recovered from his illness, and Berodach-baladan, son of Baladan, king of Babylon, sent a letter and presents to him congratulating him on his recovery. Hezekiah imprudently showed the bearers the wealth of his house, for which he was rebuked by Isaiah, who told him that the time would come when his possessions and his sons would be carried to Babylon.

7. **The death of Hezekiah** (2 Kings 20:20, 21; 2 Chron. 32:32, 33). Hezekiah reigned twenty-nine years in Jerusalem, at the end of which time he died and was buried with great honor in the chiefest of the sepulchres of the sons of David.

XIV. THE REIGN OF MANASSEH

1. **The accession of Manasseh** (2 Kings 21:1-9; 2 Chron. 33:1-10). Manasseh, son of Hezekiah, was twelve years of age when he began to reign.[1] He was directly the reverse of his father, reinstated the worship of Baal, and refused to hearken to the warnings of the Lord.

2. **The captivity of Manasseh** (2 Chron. 33:11-13). Because of his wickedness the Lord brought upon Manasseh the host of the Assyrians and he was carried to Babylon. But here he called upon the Lord, was delivered and was restored to his throne.

3. **Manasseh returns to the Lord** (2 Chron. 33:

---
[1] Usher: 697-642 B. C.   Kamphausen: 685-641 B. C.

THE DIVIDED KINGDOM—JUDAH

14-19). Following his deliverance, Manasseh took the strange gods out of the house of the Lord and cast them out of the city. He also repaired the altar and offered sacrifices thereon.

4. The death of Manasseh (2 Kings 21:18; 2 Chron. 33:20). Manasseh reigned fifty-five years in Jerusalem and, upon his death, was buried in the garden of his own house.

XV. THE REIGN OF AMON

(2 Kings 21:19-26; 2 Chron. 33:21-25)

Amon, the son of Manasseh, succeeded him. He was twenty-two years of age when he began to reign, and reigned two years,[1] when the people of the land conspired against him and slew him. He was a very wicked king.

XVI. THE REIGN OF JOSIAH

1. The accession of Josiah (2 Kings 22:1, 2; 2 Chron. 34:1, 2). Josiah, son of Amon, was eight years old when he began to reign.[2] He did that which was right in the sight of the Lord.

2. The reformation under Josiah (2 Kings 22:3-23:27; 2 Chron. 34:3-35:19). In Josiah's eighth year he began to seek after the God of David and, later, set himself to the task of purging Judah and Jerusalem. He destroyed the worship of Baal and, in his eighteenth year, repaired the Temple. During this time a copy of the law of Moses was found in the house of the Lord. When this was read to

---
[1] Usher: 642-640 B. C. Kamphausen: 640-639 B. C.
[2] Usher: 640-609 B. C. Kamphausen: 638-608 B. C.

Josiah, he rent his clothes because his fathers had not observed the law. He then sent men to inquire of the Lord concerning the words of the book, and when Huldah the prophetess was appealed to by them, she declared that the Lord would pour out his wrath upon the people because of their sins, but that, as Josiah had humbled himself, the evil would not come in his day. Then Josiah kept the Passover with his people.

3. **The invasion of Pharaoh Necho and the death of Josiah** (2 Kings 23:28-30; 2 Chron. 35:20-27). After Josiah had repaired the Temple, Necho, king of Egypt, came up against Charchemish, and Josiah went out to meet him. Necho sent ambassadors to Josiah assuring him that he had not come against him and urging him to return. But this Josiah refused to do, and in the conflict which ensued he was sorely wounded and was brought to Jerusalem, where he died and where he was buried with great honor. He reigned thirty-one years.

XVII. THE REIGN OF JEHOAHAZ

(2 Kings 23:30-33; 2 Chron. 36:1-3)

Upon the death of Josiah, the people made his son Jehoahaz king. He was twenty-three years of age when he began to reign[1] and reigned only three months, during which he did evil in the sight of the Lord. At the expiration of this period, Pharaoh Necho took him captive to Egypt, where he died.

---

[1] Usher: 609 B. C. Kamphausen: 608 B. C.

THE DIVIDED KINGDOM—JUDAH

XVIII. THE REIGN OF JEHOIAKIM
(2 Kings 23:34-24:5; 2 Chron. 36:4-7)

Jehoahaz being deposed, Necho placed his brother Eliakim upon the throne and changed his name to Jehoiakim. He was twenty-five years of age when he ascended the throne, and reigned eleven years.[1] He did that which was evil, and, after paying tribute to the king of Egypt, he became tributary to the king of Babylon, but, after serving him for three years, he renounced his allegiance and rebelled. Then the Lord sent against him the Syrians, Chaldeans, Moabites and Ammonites. Finally Nebuchadnezzar carried him to Babylon, where he died.

XIX. THE REIGN OF JEHOIACHIN
(2 Kings 24:6-16; 2 Chron. 36:8, 9)

Jehoiachin was eighteen years of age when he began to reign, and he reigned three months.[2] He was a wicked king. During his reign, Nebuchadnezzar came against Jerusalem and took it. He carried the king and his family, with smiths and craftsmen, to Babylon and with them the spoils of the Temple. He then placed Jehoiachin's uncle, Zedekiah, upon the throne.

XX. THE REIGN OF ZEDEKIAH
(2 Kings 24:17-25:7; 2 Chron. 36:11-21)

Zedekiah was twenty-one years of age when he ascended the throne. He reigned eleven years[3] and

---
[1] Usher: 609-598 B. C.   Kamphausen: 607-597 B. C.
[2] Usher: 598-597 B. C.   Kamphausen: 597 B. C.
[3] Usher: 597-586 B. C.   Kamphausen: 596-586 B. C.

did evil in the sight of the Lord. He rebelled against the king of Babylon, because of which that king came against Jerusalem, and, after a siege of more than a year, took it and carried the Jews to Babylon. This king slew Zedekiah's sons before his eyes, and then put out his eyes and bound him with fetters of brass. Nebuchadnezzar also placed Gedaliah as governor over Palestine, but this official was subsequently slain, his slayers fleeing to Egypt.

QUESTIONS

How many rulers did Judah have? How many were good or fairly good? Give their names in their order. Mention the advantages of the southern kingdom. How many of Judah's kings are mentioned in the Assyrio-Babylonian inscriptions so far deciphered? Give the date of the beginning and end of the southern kingdom. Tell about Rehoboam's folly. What kind of a man was Rehoboam? What monarch invaded Judah during his reign? How long did Rehoboam reign? Who succeeded Rehoboam? With whom did Abijam carry on a war? How long did he reign? Who succeeded Abijam? What was his character? Over what foreign monarch did he win a victory? What reforms did Asa undertake? With whom did he make an alliance against Baasha? How was he afflicted? How long did he reign? Who succeeded Asa? What kind of a man was Jehoshaphat? What reforms did he undertake? Tell about Jehoshaphat's power. With whom did he make an alliance? What nations invaded Judah during his reign? With whom did Jehoshaphat make a commercial alliance? How long did Jehoshaphat reign? Who succeeded Jehoshaphat? What was Jehoram's character? How long did he reign? Who succeeded Jehoram? With whom did Ahaziah make an alliance? What happened to Ahaziah? Who was Athaliah? What was her character? What did she do? Who succeeded Athaliah? What was the character of Joash? What happened to Athaliah? What did Joash do? What good man lived during the reign of Joash? How long did Joash reign? Who succeeded Joash? What did

THE DIVIDED KINGDOM—JUDAH

he do to his father's slayers? With what nation did he carry on a war? Tell about his trouble with Israel and the outcome of it. Where was Amaziah slain? Who succeeded Amaziah? How old was Uzziah when he began to reign? With whom did he war? What grave sin did he commit and what happened to him in consequence? How long did Uzziah reign? Who followed Uzziah? What was Jotham's character? Who succeeded Jotham? What was the character of Ahaz? With what nations did Ahaz war? Who followed Ahaz? What was Hezekiah's character? What reform did Hezekiah inaugurate? What foreign monarch invaded Judah during his reign? What did the Lord promise Hezekiah and Isaiah? Tell about Hezekiah's illness and recovery. To whom, and under what circumstances, did Hezekiah imprudently show his wealth? How long did Hezekiah reign? Who succeeded Hezekiah? What was Manasseh's character? Where was Manasseh carried captive, and why? What effect did this have upon Manasseh? Who succeeded Manasseh? What was Amon's character? Who followed Amon? What reform did Josiah inaugurate? What foreign monarch invaded Judah under Josiah's reign? Who succeeded Josiah? How long did Jehoahaz reign? What was his character? What foreign monarch carried him away captive, and where? Who followed Jehoahaz? What was his character? How long did Jehoiakim reign? What finally happened to him? Who succeeded Jehoiakim? How long did Jehoiachin reign? What happened to Jehoiachin? Who was the last king of Judah? How long did Zedekiah reign? Who carried him to Babylon? Who was made governor of Palestine in his place?

STUDY XXIV. THE CAPTIVITIES

(Jeremiah 40-43. Ezekiel. Daniel)

INTRODUCTION

1. **The causes of the captivities.** Primarily, the cause of the Assyrian and Babylonian captivities was sin, the rejection of God and the institution of false worship, with the practice of revolting and offensive rites. Secondarily, the cause was rebellion against the kings of Assyria and Babylonia, Shalmaneser and Nebuchadnezzar.

2. **The period of the captivities.** Samaria fell in the year 721 B. C., and her people were led away captive and have never been restored as a body, although a remnant probably returned with the Jews under Zerubbabel and subsequent leaders. The first of the Jews were taken to Babylon in the year 606 B. C., when the prophetical seventy years began.[1] Jerusalem fell in 587 and the beginning of the return occurred in 536.

3. **The condition of the times.** At the time of the captivity of Israel, Assyria, with its capital at Nineveh on the Tigris River, was the dominant world power. Egypt had fallen before her and Babylon had not yet risen. At the time that the Jews were led away captive, Babylon was the dominant world power, having subdued Assyria and gained the ascendency.

---
[1] Jer. 25:11 and 29:10.

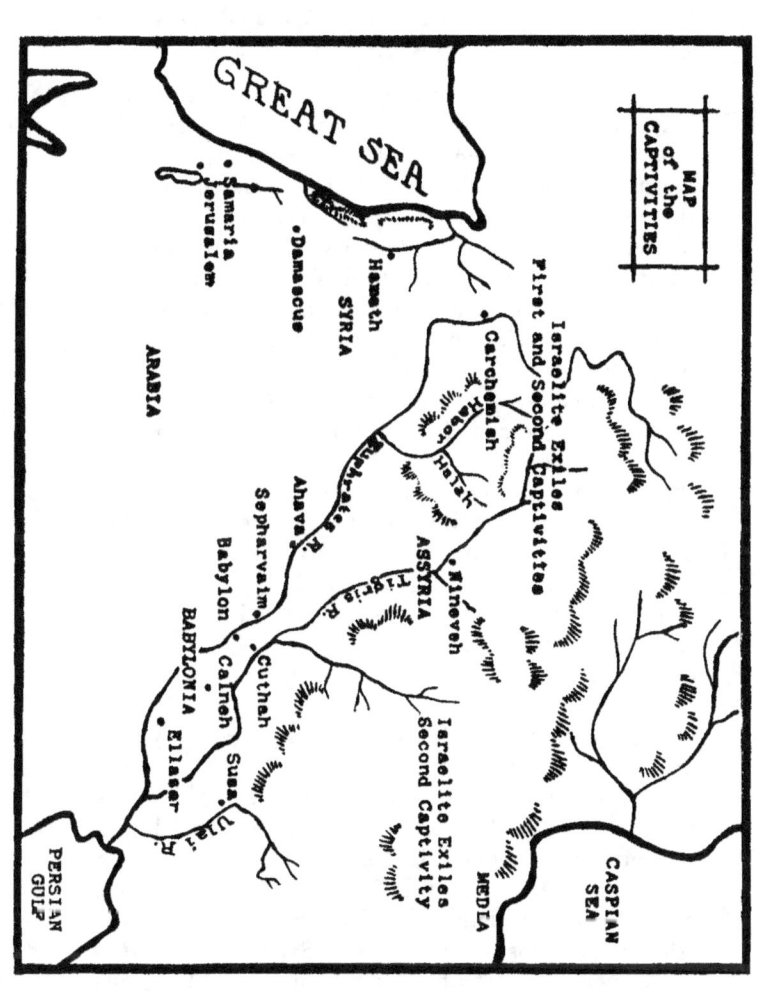

THE GIST OF THE BIBLE

I. THE CAPTIVITY OF THE TEN TRIBES IN ASSYRIA

1. **The Assyrian Empire.** The history of Assyria may be divided into three periods: *First*, from the unknown commencement of the empire to the conquest of Babylon, about 1250 B. C. *Secondly*, from the conquest of Babylon to the accession of Tiglath-pileser II. in 745 B. C. *Thirdly*, from the accession of Tiglath-pileser II. to the fall of Nineveh in 625 B. C. It was during this last period that Assyria came in touch with Israel. The kings who reigned during this period were:

(1) *Tiglath-pileser II.* (745-727 B. C.). This monarch was a bold and successful warrior who conquered Damascus, Samaria, Tyre, the Philistines and the Arabians of the Sinaitic peninsula. He carried away captives from the eastern and northern tribes of Israel and took tribute from Ahaz, king of Judah.

(2) *Shalmaneser IV.* (727-721 B. C.). This king conquered Phœnicia, but was defeated in a naval engagement at Tyre.

(3) *Sargon* (721-705 B. C.). Sargon, who succeeded Shalmaneser IV., took Samaria and carried its people captive to his newly conquered provinces of Media and Gauzanitis.

(4) *Sennacherib* (705-680 B. C.). Sennacherib defeated Merodach-baladan, who had revolted during the latter part of the reign of Sargon, and placed an Assyrian viceroy on the Babylonian throne. He quelled a revolt of the Phœnician cities and extorted tribute from most of the kings of Syria. He defeated the combined forces of the Egyptians and Ethiopians

THE CAPTIVITIES

and came against Jerusalem in the days of Hezekiah, when 185,000 of the flower of his army were destroyed by the angel of death. Upon his return to Nineveh, he was slain by his two sons.

(5) *Esar-haddon* (680-667 B. C.). This king defeated Tirhakah, king of Egypt, and broke up his kingdom into a number of petty states. He also completed the colonization of Samaria with colonists from Babylonia and Persia.

(6) *Assur-banipal* (667-647 B. C.). Under this king, Assyria reached the zenith of its glory. He conquered Egypt, overran Asia Minor and imposed a tribute upon the king of Lydia. He also subdued Armenia, Susiana and many of the Arabian tribes.

(7) *Asshur-emid-ilin* (647-625 B. C.). A number of disasters came under the reign of this king. Assyria was first invaded by the Scythians and then by the Medes and Babylonians under Cyaxares and Nabopolassar, by whom it was overthrown in 625 B. C.

2. **The culture of Assyria.** The Assyrians were an enterprising people. Though in letters and science they were behind both the Chaldeans and Egyptians, they excelled them in the artistic character of their architecture, and their palaces were of extraordinary splendor. Their sculpture, though inferior to the Grecian, was far in advance of the stiff, conventional designs of the Egyptians and displayed grandeur, dignity, boldness and strength. They manufactured transparent glass and even had lenses. They were acquainted with the principle of the arch, and constructed tunnels, aqueducts and conduits. They knew the uses of the pulley, lever and roller. They were

also adepts in the arts of inlaying, overlaying and enameling, and could cut the gems with the greatest skill and finish.

3. **The lands of the captivity of the ten tribes.** The lands to which the ten tribes were deported are given as follows:

> "In the ninth year of Hoshea, the king of Assyria took Samaria, and carried Israel away into Assyria, and placed them in Halah and in Habor by the river of Gozan, and in the cities of the Medes" (2 Kings 17:6).

4. **The successors of Israel.** In the place of the ten tribes, the king of Assyria brought men from Babylon, Cuthah, Ava, Hamath and Sepharvaim, whom he put in the cities of Samaria. But, as these feared Him not, the Lord sent lions among them which slew some of them. Then the children of Israel told the king of Assyria that their successors had been slain because they knew not the manner of the God of the land, and the king of Assyria commanded them to send one of their priests to Samaria to instruct the people. This was done, but, while the people feared the Lord, they continued to serve other gods.

5. **The condition of Israel after her deportation.** With the deportation of Israel, her history practically ends. According to the prophet Hosea, Ephraim had "mixed himself among the people" (Hos. 7:8) and his people were to be "wanderers among the nations" (Hos. 9:17), all of which has been fulfilled in the experiences of the people of the northern kingdom. Since their dispersion, they have been known as "the lost ten tribes," because they have dropped so completely out of sight, and some have tried to find them in the American Indians, others in the Nestorians,

THE CAPTIVITIES

and still others in various European nations. The most reasonable supposition is that they coalesced with the Medes and other adjacent peoples and so became lost to view. Josephus (B. XI., C. 5, p. 2) says of them:

> "The ten tribes are beyond Euphrates till now, and are an immense multitude, and not to be estimated by numbers."

Hosea uttered one prophecy of hope:

> "For the children of Israel shall abide many days without a king, and without a prince, and without a sacrifice, and without an image, and without an ephod, and without teraphim: afterward shall the children of Israel return, and seek the Lord their God, and David their king; and shall fear the Lord and his goodness in the latter days" (Hos. 3:4, 5).

Some have thought that this prophecy was fulfilled in the first return under Zerubbabel; others have declared that it was conditional and will never be fulfilled, while still others insist that it is yet to be fulfilled. The student must decide this question for himself.

II. THE CAPTIVITY OF THE TWO TRIBES IN BABYLON

1. **The Babylonian Empire.** The history of Babylon may be divided into three periods: *First*, from the earliest times to the thirteenth century B. C., when the early Babylonian kingdom was subverted by the Assyrians. *Secondly*, from the thirteenth century to 747 B. C., during which time Babylon was under the dominion of Assyria. *Thirdly*, from 747 B. C., when Nabonassar threw off the Assyrian yoke, to the fall of Babylon in 538 B. C. From 747 to 625

THE GIST OF THE BIBLE

B. C., in which year Nineveh fell, the affairs of the kingdom were in a troubled state. Merodachbaladan, the fifth king, was overthrown by Sargon and was held as a captive for six years, while his throne was occupied by an Assyrian viceroy. But, at the expiration of this time, he escaped and resumed his throne, only to be again deposed by Sennacherib. After this, Esar-haddon completely subjugated Babylon, built a palace and reigned alternately there and at Nineveh. But, in 625 B. C., Nabopolassar, a Babylonian general, taking advantage of the weakened condition of Assyria, which was due to the inroads of the Scythian hordes, allied himself with Cyaxares, king of the Medes, and won Babylonian independence. The kings that followed Nabopolassar are as follows:

(1) *Nebuchadnezzar* (605-561 B. C.). This king, son of Nabopolassar, was one of the greatest monarchs of ancient times. He warred with Phœnicia, the Jews and the Egyptians, and established an empire which extended westward to the Mediterranean Sea.

(2) *Evil-merodach* (561-559 B. C.). Evil-merodach was a very wicked son of Nebuchadnezzar. He was slain by his sister's husband, Nereglissar.

(3) *Nereglissar* (559-555 B. C.). This king was already advanced in years when he ascended the throne, having been an officer in the Babylonian army at the siege of Jerusalem, thirty years before.

(4) *Laborosoarchod* (555 B. C.). This young king was murdered by Nabonidus after reigning only nine months.

(5) *Nabonidus* (555-538 B. C.). Nabonidus associated with him his son Belshazzar, who had com-

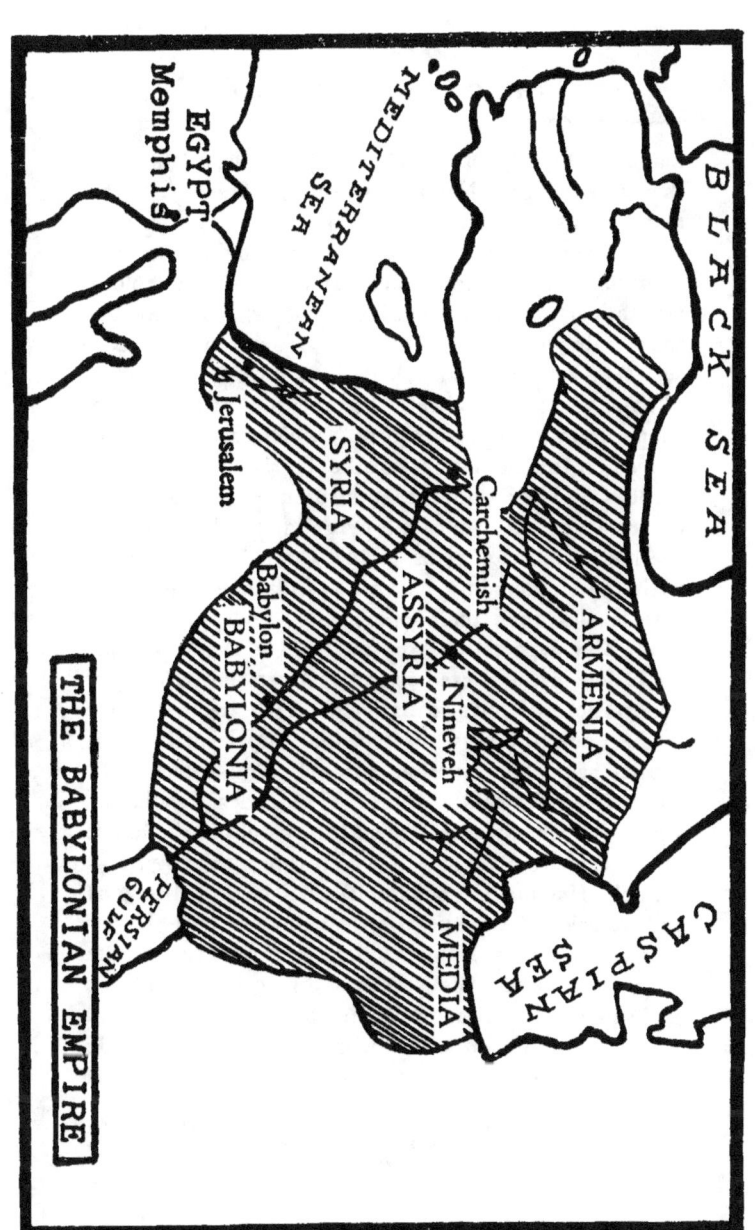

mand of the city of Babylon at the time of its overthrow by Cyrus, Nabonidus himself being in command of his army in Borsippa.

2. **The culture of Babylon.** The Babylonians were astronomers, architects and merchants. Astrology was a part of their religion, and, when Alexander took Babylon in 331 B. C., he found an unbroken series of astronomical calculations covering a period of 1,903 years. They were the inventors of the wedge-shape characters, "cuneiform," which are found inscribed on the monuments of the Tigris and Euphrates Valleys.[1] They built great structures in the shape of terraced and truncated pyramids. They worked the metals and cut gems. They carried on commerce with the surrounding nations. And they made delicate fabrics upon their looms.

3. **The deportations of the Jews.** There is some confusion in the sacred narrative over the number of deportations of Jews to Babylon. Two are mentioned in the Book of Kings, three in that of Jeremiah, while Daniel seems to mention a fourth and earlier one. There were certainly three: (1) Under Jehoiakim, when Nebuchadnezzar carried the vessels of the house of the Lord to Babylon, at which time, probably, also Daniel, Hananiah (Shadrach), Mishael (Meshach) and Azariah (Abed-nego) were taken. (2) Under Jehoiachin, when Nebuchadnezzar carried away the king, his mother, his servants, his princes and his craftsmen and smiths, "all Jerusalem," ten thousand captives, leaving only the poorest sort of the people behind. And (3) under Zedekiah, when the final

---

[1] Dr. A. H. Sayce, "Fresh Light from the Ancient Monuments," p. 21, assigns the invention of these characters to an earlier people, the Accadians.

deportation took place, only a small remnant being left behind under the governorship of Gedaliah.

4. The condition of the captive Jews. The Jews were not carried to Babylon so much as captives as colonists. According to Josephus, they acquired "possessions," and these induced many of them to remain behind even when the edict of Cyrus permitted them to return. It would seem from Jer. 29:4-7 that they had about the same liberties as the other inhabitants of the land, as they were commanded to build houses, plant gardens, take wives and beget children, and also to seek the peace of the city in which they dwelt. We also know that, although they were prohibited from offering sacrifices, they were permitted to assemble in public worship on their sabbaths, at which time their Scriptures were read and commented upon. That some of the captives reached positions of honor is proved by the history of Daniel. Some have claimed that only the poorest of the captives returned under Zerubbabel, Ezra and Nehemiah, the rest being perfectly content to remain in the land of their captivity, which being true, their lot could not have been a hard one.

III. THE HISTORY OF DANIEL

The history of Daniel may be divided into two periods: his history under the reign of the Babylonian kings, and his history under the reign of the Medo-Persian kings.

1. Daniel under the Babylonian kings.

(1) *The captivity of Daniel* (Dan. 1:1-21). In the third year of Jehoiakim, king of Judah, Nebuchadnezzar besieged Jerusalem, overthrew it and carried

some of the people away to Babylon. Among them were Daniel, Hananiah, Mishael and Azariah. These, by the command of Nebuchadnezzar, were taken by Ashpenaz, master of the eunuchs, to be educated in the learning and tongue of the Chaldeans. Being supplied with provisions from the king's table, they refused to eat his meat and to drink his wine, preferring pulse to eat and water to drink. But, after many days had passed, they were brought into the presence of Nebuchadnezzar, who found them superior in every way to their Babylonian companions.

(2) *The dream of Nebuchadnezzar* (Dan. 2:1-49). Nebuchadnezzar had a dream which he forgot and which troubled him. He called in the magicians, soothsayers and astrologers of his realm, but not one could tell him his dream, so Daniel was brought in. In the meantime, in answer to prayer, the Lord had revealed Nebuchadnezzar's forgotten dream to Daniel, and, when he stood before the king, he told him that in his dream he had seen a great and terrible image with head of gold, breast and arms of silver, belly and thighs of brass, legs of iron and feet part of iron and part of clay. He told him, further, that he had seen a stone cut out without hands which smote the image upon the feet, broke them to pieces and then ground the image into chaff. The interpretation that Daniel gave of this dream was that the head of gold represented Nebuchadnezzar; the silver represented a kingdom that should follow his; the brass, a third kingdom, and the iron, a fourth kingdom, after which the kingdom of God, represented by the stone, should be set up. As a reward for his interpretation of this dream, Daniel was made a great man, and Shadrach,

THE CAPTIVITIES

Meshach and Abed-nego were set over the affairs of the province of Babylon.

(3) *Nebuchadnezzar sets up an image of gold* (Dan. 3:1-7). After this, Nebuchadnezzar made a great image of gold and set it up in the plain of Dura, in the province of Babylon, and issued a proclamation that at the sound of music all his subjects should fall down and worship the image which he had set up, saying that whoever refused to do this should be cast into a furnace of fire.

(4) *The three Hebrew children cast into the furnace* (Dan. 3:8-30). But the three Hebrews, Shadrach, Meshach and Abed-nego, refused to worship the image, and, when their enemies discovered this, they went and told the king. Nebuchadnezzar was very wroth, and, calling the three Hebrews, he inquired if they had refused to serve his gods and to worship the image which he had set up. Shadrach, Meshach and Abed-nego replied that they had and that their God would deliver them from the fiery furnace. At this the king commanded them to be cast into the furnace. But, although the furnace was heated seven times hotter than it was wont to be heated, they suffered no harm, and, when Nebuchadnezzar looked in, he saw the form of a fourth which was "like the Son of God." Then the king rose up and delivered Shadrach, Meshach and Abed-nego, and made a decree that any one who should speak a word amiss of the God of the Hebrews should be cut in pieces and his house be made a dunghill.

(5) *Nebuchadnezzar's madness* (Dan. 4:1-37). Nebuchadnezzar had another dream and he called in all the wise men of Babylon, but they could not inter-

pret it. Then he called in Daniel and told him that he had seen a tree growing in the midst of the earth of great height and fair leaves, under which the beasts of the field found shelter, and that he had seen a watcher come down from heaven who commanded that the tree be hewed down, but that the stump be left until seven times had passed over it. Daniel interpreted this dream to mean that Nebuchadnezzar should become mad and should be driven from men until seven times, or years, should pass over him. This interpretation was fulfilled the same hour, and Nebuchadnezzar was driven out as predicted.

(6) *Daniel's first vision under the reign of Belshazzar* (Dan. 7:1-28). In the first year of the reign of Belshazzar, Daniel had a vision in which he saw four great beasts come up out of the sea, diverse one from another. The first was like a lion with eagles' wings; the second was like a bear which raised itself up on one side and had three ribs in its mouth; the third was like a leopard with four wings and four heads, and the fourth was a beast, dreadful, terrible and strong, with iron teeth, and which stamped the residue with its feet. This beast had ten horns, among which came up a little horn which waxed great and rooted up three of the first horns. After this he saw the thrones cast down and the Ancient of days sit, the books opened, the world judged and the everlasting kingdom established. The angelic interpretation of this vision was that the four beasts represented four great kingdoms, the last to be divided into ten kings, or kingdoms, among whom should rise an eleventh who should root up three of the first and who should rule with a high hand until the judg-

THE CAPTIVITIES

ment should sit and his dominion should be consumed and destroyed unto the end. After this the kingdom and dominion and the greatness of the kingdom were to be given to the saints of the Most High.

(7) *Daniel's second vision under the reign of Belshazzar* (Dan. 8:1-27). In the third year of the reign of King Belshazzar, Daniel had another vision, in which he was in the palace of Shushan, province of Elam, by the river Ulai. In this vision he saw a ram with two horns, one higher than the other, which came up last. And the ram pushed westward, northward and southward. He then saw a great he-goat, with a notable horn between his eyes, which came from the west and furiously smote the ram and broke off its two horns. Then he saw that the notable horn was broken, and that in its place there came up four others, out of one of which sprang a fifth, which became great toward the east, the south and the pleasant land. This vision Gabriel explained as follows: The ram with its two horns, represented Medo-Persia; the he-goat represented Grecia; the notable horn, its first king (Alexander); the four horns, the four divisions, or kingdoms, into which Grecia was to be divided (Egypt, Syria, Macedon and Thrace); and the little horn, a power that was afterwards to arise. This latter symbol has been variously applied to Antiochus, Rome, Mohammedanism and to a future antichrist.

(8) *The overthrow of Babylon and death of Belshazzar* (Dan. 5:1-30). Belshazzar, son of Nabonidus, made a great feast in Babylon to a thousand of his lords. During the orgies that followed, there came forth the fingers of a man's hand which wrote upon

the wall the significant words, "MENE, MENE, TEKEL, UPHARSIN." When the wise men of Babylon had failed to translate the writing, Daniel was sent for, and he told the king that it meant, "God hath numbered thy kingdom, and finished it. Thou art weighed in the balances, and art found wanting. Thy kingdom is divided, and given to the Medes and Persians." That same night Belshazzar was slain, and Darius the Mede took the kingdom.

2. **Daniel under the Persian kings.**

(1) *The exaltation of Daniel under Darius* (Dan. 6:1-3). When Darius took the Babylonian throne, he set over the kingdom 120 princes, presided over by three presidents, of whom Daniel was the first.

(2) *Daniel cast into the lions' den* (Dan. 6:4-28). As Daniel was preferred above all the rest, their jealousy was aroused and they sought to find occasion against him. So they went before the king and had him make a decree that any one who should ask a favor of any God or man, save of himself, for thirty days, should be cast into the den of lions. Daniel paid no attention to this decree, but prayed to his God regularly, three times a day, with his windows opened toward Jerusalem. When this was told the king, he was greatly displeased with himself for having made the decree, and set his heart on Daniel to deliver him. But Daniel's enemies declared to the king that the laws of the Medes and Persians could not be changed, so the king commanded and Daniel was cast into the lions' den. So affected was the king that he spent the night in wakefulness and fasting, and early on the morrow went to the den, where he cried with a lamentable voice, and to his surprise he found Daniel

alive. Then the king commanded and Daniel was taken out of the den and his enemies were cast in, and the king made a decree that throughout his dominions men should tremble and fear before the God of Daniel.

(3) *Daniel's first vision under Darius* (Dan. 9:1-27). This vision is commonly known as the "vision of the seventy weeks." With B. C. 457 as starting-point, the "seventy weeks" (heptads), or 490 years, would stretch to A. D. 34, during which period all the things specified (Dan. 9:24) were accomplished. With the same date, which was the seventh year of the reign of Artaxerxes when the commandment was given to restore and to build Jerusalem, as a starting-point, the sixty-nine weeks would stretch to 27 A. D., the time of Christ's baptism, when he became in a true sense the Messiah ("anointed one"). Some have thought that the "one week" (v. 27) was the week of years lying between A. D. 27 and A. D. 34, in the midst of which Christ, by his death, nullified the force of the Jewish law; others detach it from the sixty-nine and give it a place just before the beginning of the millennium. It seems, however, that the "he" of verse 27 is the "prince" of verse 26, which makes it necessary for us to commence this week of years at the beginning of the Roman-Jewish war, 66 A. D., and end it in 73 A. D. In 70 A. D., which would be "the midst of the week," Titus, "the prince," destroyed the Temple, and then for the first time the sacrifice and oblation, according to Josephus,[1] ceased to be offered.

---

[1] Josephus, "Wars," Book VI., Chap. II., p. 1.

THE GIST OF THE BIBLE

(4) *Daniel's second vision under Darius* (Dan. 11: 1-12: 13). This vision remarkably covers the history of the world from the time of Darius to the end of the age.

(5) *Daniel's vision under the reign of Cyrus* (Dan. 10: 1-21). This is known as "the vision of the glory of God." It was given to Daniel in the third year of Cyrus.

QUESTIONS

Give the causes of the captivities. When did Samaria fall? When were the first Jews taken to Babylon? When did Jerusalem fall? Describe the condition of the times. Into how many periods may the history of Assyria be divided? Bound them chronologically. Give, in their order, the names of the kings of Assyria. Give the lands of the captivity of the ten tribes. What people succeeded the ten tribes? What was the condition of Israel after her deportation? Give Hosea's prophecy of hope. Tell how this prophecy has been explained. Into how many periods may the history of Babylon be divided? Bound them chronologically. Give, in their order, the names of the kings of Babylon. Describe the culture of Babylon. How many deportations of Jews were there? What was the condition of the captive Jews? Give the two periods in the history of Daniel. When was he taken captive to Babylon? Give the first dream of Nebuchadnezzar and Daniel's interpretation. Tell about the image which Nebuchadnezzar erected. Tell about the casting of the three Hebrew children into the fiery furnace. Describe Nebuchadnezzar's madness. Give Daniel's first vision under the reign of Belshazzar. Give his second vision. Describe the overthrow of Babylon. Who was Darius? What did he do to Daniel? Tell about Daniel being cast into the lions' den. Describe Daniel's first vision under Darius. Describe his second vision under Darius. What is his vision which was received under the reign of Cyrus called?

STUDY XXV. THE RETURN

(Ezra, Nehemiah, Haggai and Zechariah)

INTRODUCTION

1. **The promise of restoration.** During the captivity, the prophets, Jeremiah and Ezekiel, held out to the Jews the hope of restoration, predicting that they would return to their own land and rebuild the city of Jerusalem. Jeremiah prophesied that this would occur at the end of seventy years.

"For thus saith the Lord, That after seventy years be accomplished at Babylon I will visit you, and perform my good word toward you, in causing you to return to this place" (Jer. 29:10).

2. **The policy of the Persian kings.** The policy of the Persian kings was a reversal of the policy of the kings of Assyria and Babylonia, in that they gave permission to the captive peoples to return to their native lands.

3. **The period of the return.** The period of the return lay between the years 536 and 445 B. C.

4. **The leaders in the return.** The leader of the first company of Jews to return to Palestine was Zerubbabel in 536. He was followed by Ezra in 457, and by Nehemiah in 445 B. C. Zerubbabel was the son of Shealtiel and of the royal house of David.

Ezra was a priest and a scribe. Nehemiah was a prince of Judah.

I. THE RETURN UNDER ZERUBBABEL

1. The decree of Cyrus (Ezra 1:1-4). In the first year of Cyrus he issued the following decree:

> "Thus saith Cyrus king of Persia, The Lord God of heaven hath given me all the kingdoms of the earth; and he hath charged me to build him an house at Jerusalem, which is in Judah. Who is there among you of all his people? his God be with him, and let him go up to Jerusalem, which is in Judah, and build the house of the Lord God of Israel, (he is the God,) which is in Jerusalem. And whosoever remaineth in any place where he sojourneth, let the men of his place help him with silver, and with gold, and with goods, and with beasts, beside the freewill offering for the house of God that is in Jerusalem."

2. The preparations for the return (Ezra 1:5-11). When this decree was issued, there rose up certain of the chief of the fathers of Judah and Benjamin, with the priests and Levites, who determined to return to Jerusalem for the purpose of rebuilding the Temple. Into their hands were placed vessels of silver and gold, with goods, beasts, precious things and freewill offerings. Cyrus also put into the hands of Zerubbabel the vessels which Nebuchadnezzar had taken from the first Temple.

3. The number of those who returned (Ezra 2:1-70). In all, 49,897 people were in the company that left Babylon to go up to the land of Judah. This number included the common people, priests, Levites and the descendants of the servants of Solomon.

4. The altar set up (Ezra 3:1-6). When this company reached the land of their fathers, they dwelt in their respective cities, but, in the seventh month, gathered together at Jerusalem, where Zerubbabel and Jeshua, the high priest, erected the altar and offered burnt-offerings upon the same. They also kept the Feast of Tabernacles.

 5. **The foundation of the Temple laid.** (Ezra 3:7-13). Although the Jews observed the foregoing rites, the foundation of the Temple had not been laid, so they hired masons and carpenters and men of Tyre and Zidon to bring cedar-trees to Joppa from Lebanon according to the grant of Cyrus. And, in the second month of the second year, the foundation was laid amid great rejoicing.

 6. **The help of the Samaritans offered and refused** (Ezra 4:1-16). The Samaritans, learning that the Jews were rebuilding their Temple, came to Zerubbabel and the chief of the fathers and asked permission to join forces with them and help in the work, stating that they worshiped the same God and that they had sacrificed to Him from the days of Esarhaddon. This proposal was indignantly rejected, and the Samaritans, enraged and disappointed, hired counselors at the Persian court and wrote defamatory letters to the reigning monarch, endeavoring to frustrate the plan.

 7. **The decree of Artaxerxes** (Ezra 4: 17-22). When Artaxerxes, who at that time was on the Persian throne, received these false reports from the Samaritans, he issued a decree that the work should cease until he gave further commandment.

 8. **The encouragement of the prophets** (Ezra 4: 23-5: 17). This message was brought to the Jews by the Samaritans Rehum and Shimshai, who made the Jews to cease their work by force and power. But

the prophets Haggai and Zechariah encouraged the people in the name of the Lord and they set themselves to the work again. When Tatnai, the governor, heard this, he and his companions came and inquired who had commanded them to build the house and make up the wall. They replied that King Cyrus had issued a decree permitting them to return to their own land to build their Temple, and that their work was in fulfillment of that decree. These things the governor embodied in a letter which he wrote to Darius and in which he requested the king to ascertain whether or not the story was true.

9. **Cyrus' decree confirmed by Darius** (Ezra 6:1-14). Darius, upon receiving the letter of Tatnai, caused that search be made in the ancient records for this edict. This was done and the decree was found. Then the king wrote Tatnai, instructing him to permit the Jews to continue their work, to render them whatever assistance they needed, and, if any one sought to hinder the work, to pull down his house and, taking the timber, to hang him to the same.

10. **The completion of the Temple and the restoration of the ancient worship** (Ezra 6:15-22). By this new assistance and the encouragement of their prophets, the Jews were greatly strengthened and greatly prospered. The Temple was finally completed on the third day of the month Adar (March), in the sixth year of the reign of Darius. At the dedicatory services, one hundred bullocks, two hundred rams and four hundred lambs were offered, besides twelve he-goats as a sin-offering for all Israel. Following the dedicatory exercises, the people kept the Passover upon the fourteenth day of the first month.

II. THE RETURN UNDER EZRA

1. **The expedition under Ezra** (Ezra 7:1-10). In the seventh rear of the reign of Artaxerxes, Ezra, a scribe, left Babylon with a company to go up to Jerusalem.

2. **The decree of Artaxerxes** (Ezra 7:11-8:14). To Ezra, Artaxerxes gave a letter in which he granted the privilege to those Jews in Babylon, who were so minded, to return to Jerusalem. He also authorized Ezra to collect money and other necessary things to assist in the work at that city, and also gave him power to appoint magistrates and judges to execute the law of Moses.

3. **The gathering and fast at Ahava** (Ezra 8:15-23). Ezra gathered his company together at the river Ahava, where they abode in tents three days. At the expiration of this time, he reviewed the people and found that there were none of the sons of Levi among them, so he sent messengers to Iddo, the chief of the place Casiphia, and requested him to furnish them ministers for the house of God. Iddo sent to Ezra 258 Levites and Nethinims. Then Ezra proclaimed a fast that they might secure the guidance and protection of the Lord on their journey, as he had been ashamed to require of the king a band of soldiers and horsemen.

4. **The arrival at Jerusalem** (Ezra 8:24-36). Having committed into the hands of twelve of the chief of the priests the treasures of the Temple, Ezra and his company set out on the twelfth day of the first month for Jerusalem, and were led on their way by the hand of the Lord, who delivered them from their

enemies. On the fourth day after their arrival in Jerusalem, the treasures for the Temple were weighed and the weights recorded, and all of those who had come up out of captivity offered burnt-offerings unto the Lord. Then Ezra delivered the king's commission unto the king's lieutenants and governors.

5. **The complaint of the princes** (Ezra 9:1-4). After this was done, the princes of the people came to Ezra with the complaint that the people of Israel, the priests and the Levites had not separated themselves from the people of the land, but had intermarried with them and had done according to their abominations. Ezra rent his garments at this information, plucked out his hair and beard and sat astonished until the evening sacrifice.

6. **Ezra's prayer and confession** (Ezra 9:5-15). At the time of the evening sacrifice, Ezra arose from his heaviness and, having rent his garment, fell on his knees before the Lord and confessed the sins of his people Israel.

7. **The people reseparated** (Ezra 10:1-44). As Ezra was praying and weeping before the house of God, a large congregation assembled. When they heard the burden of his prayer, one of them, Shechaniah, son of Jehiel, confessed that the Jews had done wrong in taking strange wives, and proposed that they make a covenant with their God to put away their strange wives and the children that had been born to them. Ezra, at these words, arose and made the congregation swear that they would do according to this suggestion. He then made a proclamation throughout Judah and Jerusalem urging the people to assemble at Jerusalem, and threatening that who-

ever refused to come within three days should forfeit his substance and should separate himself from the congregation of Israel. When the Jews had assembled, Ezra accused them of breaking the law of their God and charged them to put away their strange wives. To this the people replied: "As thou hast said, so must we do." The separation was completed within the following three months.

III. THE RETURN UNDER NEHEMIAH

1. **Nehemiah hears of the distress of the remnant** (Neh. 1:1-3). In the twentieth year of the reign of Artaxerxes, Nehemiah, the son of Hachaliah, was in the palace of Shushan when Hanani and certain others came down from Jerusalem with the tidings that the Jews were in great affliction and reproach and that the wall of the city was broken down and its gates burned with fire.

2. **The prayer of Nehemiah** (Neh. 1:4-11). Nehemiah wept at these sorrowful tidings and fasted certain days, confessing the sins of his people and beseeching the Lord to remember the word which he had commanded Moses, that if his people transgressed His law he would scatter them abroad, but that if they repented He would gather them again.

3. **Nehemiah sent to Jerusalem** (Neh. 2·1-10). In this same year, Nehemiah, who was the king's cup-bearer, offered him wine, but with a sad countenance. Observing this, the king inquired the cause, and when Nehemiah told him that it was due to the low condition of Jerusalem, and begged of him permission to return to the land of his fathers' sepulchres that he might build it up, Artaxerxes granted him the desired

permission and gave him letters to Asaph, the keeper of the king's forest, and to the governors beyond the river.

4. **Nehemiah views the ruined walls** (Neh. 2: 11-16). Nehemiah had been in Jerusalem for three days when he went by night to view the ruined walls. This was done secretly so that neither the nobles, the priests nor the common people might know of it.

5. **The building of the walls** (Neh. 2: 17-3: 32). When Nehemiah saw the dilapidated condition of the city, he encouraged the people to build the wall. With this encouragement, they began again, a certain portion of work being allotted to each family.

6. **The opposition of their enemies** (Neh. 4: 1-6: 14). The enemies of the Jews—Sanballat the Horonite, Tobiah the servant, and Geshem the Arabian—being told that the Jews were rebuilding their walls, ridiculed them and asked: "What do these feeble Jews? will they fortify themselves? will they sacrifice? will they make an end in a day? will they revive the stones out of the heaps of rubbish which are burned?" Nehemiah answered these taunts with a prayer to God to give his enemies for a prey in the land of captivity. The opposition to Nehemiah and his work took various forms. In the first place, as the wall continued to go up, the enemies of Israel conspired to hinder the work, which required that the Jews keep watch both night and day. As the opposition became more bitter, Nehemiah divided the workmen into two bodies, one keeping watch while the other worked. In the second place, some of the Jews became tired and complained that there was so much rubbish that the wall could not be built. In

THE RETURN

the third place, a number complained that while they were spending their time upon the wall, their brethren, who held mortgages upon their lands, were requiring usury, and that, as they were unable to pay this, their sons and daughters were brought into bondage. Nehemiah was exceedingly angry at this last complaint, and, calling the nobles and rulers together, he rebuked them for exacting usury and urged them to remit the excessive interest that they had taken. Then, in order to set an example of unselfishness to the Jews, he lived as the common people and refused to eat the bread of the governor to which he was entitled because of his station. When Sanballat and the other enemies of Israel saw that their sarcasm and threatening had failed, and that the wall was surely being built, they tried by craft to circumvent the plans of Nehemiah. They invited him first to counsel with them in a village in the plains of Ono, but this he refused to do, declaring that he was doing a great work and could not come down. They then wrote him an open letter in which they declared that the report was out that he intended to rebel and become king of the Jews, and that he had appointed prophets to preach at Jerusalem, saying: "There is a king in Judah." This they threatened to carry to the king's ears. But these charges Nehemiah denied and prayed to the Lord to strengthen his hands. Afterwards they hired Shemaiah to decoy Nehemiah into the Temple with the story that his enemies were about to slay him and so cause him to sin that they might have an occasion against him. But here, again, Nehemiah foiled them and refused to go.

7. **The wall finished** (Neh. 6:15-19). The wall of

the city was finally completed in the month Elul (September), provoking the envy and disappointment of the Jews' enemies. Among these was Tobiah the Ammonite, who was on favorable terms with a number of the nobles of Judah, but who wrote Nehemiah letters to put him in fear.

8. **Hanani and Hananiah given charge of Jerusalem** (Neh. 7:1-4). The wall built, Nehemiah gave the city of Jerusalem into the charge of his brother Hanani, and Hananiah, the ruler of the palace, with the command that the gates thereof should not be opened until the sun was hot, and that watches should be appointed. Though the city was large, the inhabitants were comparatively few and the houses were not yet all built.

9. **The census taken** (Neh. 7:5-73). Nehemiah now set about registering the genealogy of the people who had come up out of captivity. This included both the priests and the people, with a record also of their substance and gifts. By this census it was ascertained that the whole number of the people was 42,360, besides 7,337 servants and 245 singing men and singing women.

10. **The law read and explained** (Neh. 8:1-13). All of the people gathered themselves together as one man in the street that was before the water-gate in the city of Jerusalem and requested Ezra, the scribe, to bring out the book of the law of Moses. Ezra did this, and, standing on a pulpit of wood, he read and expounded the law to the people, being assisted in the expounding by others. He then blessed the Lord, and all the people responded "Amen" and worshiped with their faces to the ground.

THE RETURN

11. The Feast of Tabernacles restored (Neh. 8: 14-18). When the children of Israel found in the law that they should dwell in booths in the feast of the seventh month, they prepared booths, and, when the time of the feast came, they dwelt in them seven days, while during this entire time, day by day, Ezra read out of the book of the law.

12. The people fast, repent and confess (Neh. 9: 1-10:39). On the twenty-fourth day of the seventh month the people assembled and with fasting and confession of sin separated themselves, both the priests and the people, from the strangers of the land. They also made a covenant of separation which was sealed by their princes, Levites and priests.

13. The division of the people (Neh. 11:1-12:26). The rulers of the people dwelt at Jerusalem, and the rest of the people cast lots to bring one of every ten to dwell in the city, so that one-tenth dwelt in Jerusalem and nine-tenths dwelt in the other cities.

14. The walls of the city dedicated (Neh. 12:27-43). Nehemiah gathered together the people to dedicate the walls of Jerusalem. He divided the nobles into two companies which he placed at different points upon the wall. These gave thanks unto the Lord and offered sacrifices and rejoiced with joy.

15. The restoration of the Temple order (Neh. 12: 44-47). At this time, treasurers were appointed to receive tithes, and also singers and porters for the Temple.

16. Tobiah cast out of the Temple (Neh. 13:1-14). It was discovered in the law that the Ammonite and the Moabite should not come into the congregation of God, because they had not met Israel with bread and water and had sent Balaam to curse them. When this was ascertained, the people separated from them the mixed multitude. But Eliashib the priest, who had charge of the Temple, had prepared a chamber therein for Tobiah. Nehemiah was at Babylon at this time, but, obtaining leave of the king, he returned to Jerusalem, and, when he had discovered what Eliashib had done, it grieved him sore and he cast out of the chamber all of Tobiah's stuff, after which he commanded that the chamber be cleansed and the vessels of the house of God, with the meat-offering and the frankincense, be brought therein.

17. **The profanation of the sabbath** (Neh. 13:15-22). Nehemiah also saw certain Jews doing divers kinds of work on the sabbath, and men of Tyre, likewise, came into the city with fish and all manner of wares which they sold to the people on that holy day. This greatly incensed Nehemiah, and he complained to the nobles and commanded that the gate should be kept closed throughout the sabbath. He also set watches to see that no burdens were brought into the city. By this the merchants and sellers were forced to lodge without the walls, but Nehemiah went to them and asked them why they lodged there, telling them that if they did so again he would lay hands upon them.

18. **Nehemiah rebukes the intermarriage of the Jews with other races** (Neh. 13:23-31). Nehemiah also saw Jews who had married wives from among the Philistines, Ammonites and Moabites. And the children of some of them spoke half in the language of Ashdod and could not speak the clear speech of Israel. This enraged him and he cursed them, smote

THE RETURN

them, plucked out their hair, and made them swear that they would cease to give their sons heathen wives and their daughters heathen husbands. One of those who were guilty was a son of Joiada, the high priest, who was son-in-law to Sanballat.

QUESTIONS

What hope did the prophets hold out to the captive Jews? How long did Jeremiah predict that the captivity would continue? State the difference between the policy of the Persian kings and that of those of Assyria and Babylonia. Locate the period of the return. Name the leaders of the return. Who was high priest at the time of the return? Give the decree of Cyrus. What preparations were made for the return? How many returned under Zerubbabel? What was the first thing that the Jews did after their return? Tell about the laying of the foundation of the Temple. Who offered assistance? Was it accepted or refused? What did the Samaritans then do? What did Haggai and Zechariah do? How was Cyrus' decree confirmed by Darius? Tell about the completion of the Temple. Who was Ezra? In what year did he return? Give the decree of Artaxerxes. Where did Ezra gather his company and what did they do there? What did they do when they arrived at Jerusalem? What complaint did the princes make? What did Ezra do? Tell about the reseparation of the people. Who was Nehemiah? How did he hear of the distress of the people? What did he do upon receipt of this news? How did he happen to go to Jerusalem? When did he view the ruined walls? What did he urge the people to do? What opposition did he receive? When was the wall finished? How did it make the enemies of Judah feel? Into whose hands did he give the city? Tell about the taking of the census. Tell about the reading and explaining of the law. Tell about the restoration of the Feast of Tabernacles. What did the people do at this time? Tell about the division of the people. How were the walls dedicated? For what were treasurers appointed? Who was cast out of the Temple, and why? How was the sabbath profaned? What sin did Nehemiah rebuke?

STUDY XXVI. THE PROPHETS
INTRODUCTION

1. **The prophets.** The prophets of Israel were not merely *fore*tellers of future events, but were also *forth*tellers of God's will and present conditions. The word "prophet" means, simply, "one who speaks forth," with no intimation as to the nature of the message, whether it be predictive, exhortative or condemnatory.

2. **The early prophets of Israel.** We have already mentioned, or given an account of, several of the earlier prophets of Israel. Of these were Moses, Nathan, Gad, Elijah and Elisha, all of whom are declared to have possessed the prophetic gift. The prophets about whom we are to study in the present lesson lived after the division of the kingdom, and their prophecies are recorded in the Old Testament.

3. **The schools of the prophets.** The schools of the prophets were institutions where divine truth was studied and sacred psalmody was practiced. The first of these schools was founded by Samuel at Ramah. Here he gathered about him a number of men for the purposes mentioned, who lived in huts made of the branches of trees. During the reign of Ahab there were three of these schools comparatively close together—at Bethel, Jericho and Gilgal. Those who attended these schools were known as the "sons of the prophets."

THE PROPHETS

4. The classification of prophecy. The prophecies of the Bible may be classified as follows:

(1) The *literal* and the *symbolical*. A literal prophecy is one that is to be understood according to the primary and natural import of the words in which it is expressed. Examples: Num. 15:21-35; Jer. 25:1-33. A symbolical prophecy is one that is expressed in symbols. Examples: Most of the prophecies of the Books of Daniel and Revelation.

(2) The *discursive* and the *consecutive*. A discursive prophecy presents future events irrespective of the order of their occurrence. Examples: Isaiah and the Minor Prophets. A consecutive prophecy gives future events in the order in which they will transpire. Examples: Daniel and Revelation.

(3) The *conditional* and the *unconditional*. The fulfillment of a conditional prophecy depends upon those to whom it is addressed meeting certain conditions, either stated or implied. Example: Lev. 26:3, 4. An unconditional prophecy is one in which all predictions are absolute in their nature. Example: Num. 14:21.

5. The prophetic groups. The prophets of Israel may be divided into four groups, as follows:

(1) *The prophets of Israel:* Jonah, Amos and Hosea.

(2) *The prophets of Judah:* Isaiah, Joel, Micah, Nahum, Zephaniah, Jeremiah and Habakkuk.

(3) *The prophets of the captivity:* Daniel, Obadiah and Ezekiel.

(4) *The post-exilic prophets:* Haggai, Zechariah and Malachi.

Taken in their chronological order, the prophets are as follows:

I. JONAH
(856-784 B. C.[1])

1. **Who Jonah was** (Jonah 1:1; 2 Kings 14:25). Jonah was the son of Amittai and was born in Gath-hepher. Although no era is assigned to him in his prophecy, he undoubtedly flourished in, or just before, the reign of Jeroboam II. and predicted the conquests, enlargement and prosperity of the Israelite kingdom under that monarch's sway.

2. **Jonah commanded to go to Nineveh** (Jonah 1:1-16). The Lord commanded Jonah to go to Nineveh to preach to the Ninevites. But, instead, he went to Joppa, where he took a ship for Tarshish. On the way a great storm arose and, at Jonah's own suggestion, he was thrown overboard.

3. **Jonah swallowed by a great fish** (Jonah 1:17-2:10). But the Lord prepared a great fish[2] to swallow Jonah, and he was in its belly for three days and three nights. During this time he prayed to the Lord, and the fish vomited him up on dry land.

4. **Jonah receives a second commission** (Jonah 3:1-10). Jonah then received his second commission to go to Nineveh. This time he obeyed, and when he entered that city he cried: "Yet forty days, and Nineveh shall be overthrown." At this the Ninevites repented, and the Lord turned from the evil which he had pronounced against them.

---
[1] In these dates I have followed the "Self-interpreting Bible," Vol. I., p. 37.
[2] This fish was not a "whale," but a fish specially and miraculously "prepared" for that particular occasion.

THE PROPHETS

---

5. **The displeasure of the prophet and the sheltering gourd** (Jonah 4:1-11). Jonah was bitterly displeased with this manifestation of mercy and complained to the Lord. At which the Lord asked: "Doest thou well to be angry?" Jonah then went outside the city and built him a booth, and sat under it until he might see what would become of the city. The Lord prepared a gourd to shadow Jonah, which pleased him exceedingly, whereupon God prepared a worm which smote the gourd and on the morrow it withered. Then God sent a vehement east wind, and it blew upon the head of the prophet and he fainted and wished that he could die. At this God said: "Thou hast had pity on the gourd, for the which thou hast not laboured, neither madest it grow; which came up in a night, and perished in a night: and should not I spare Nineveh, that great city, wherein are more than sixscore thousand persons that cannot discern between their right hand and their left hand; and also much cattle?"

II. AMOS

(810-795 B. C.)

1. **The nativity of Amos** (Amos 1:1; 7:14). Amos was a shepherd and a gatherer of sycamore fruit who lived in Tekoa, a town six miles south of Bethlehem. Although of Judah, he prophesied to the northern kingdom.

2. **The time of his prophecy** (Amos 1·1). The time of Amos' prophecy is said to have been in the days of Uzziah, king of Judah, and Jeroboam II., king of Israel, two years before the earthquake.

3. The subjects of Amos' prophecy. The prophecy of Amos begins with the prediction of certain judgments to fall upon those nations which surrounded Israel. After this he strongly condemns the sins of his own people, warns them of the consequences and predicts their captivity, but ends with a glowing description of the future glory of the Davidic kingdom.

III. HOSEA
(810-725 B. C.)

Nothing is known with certainty of the nativity of the prophet Hosea. It is stated that he prophesied in the days of Uzziah, Jotham, Ahaz and Hezekiah, kings of Judah, and Jeroboam II., king of Israel, hence that he was a contemporary of Amos in Israel and Isaiah and Micah in Judah. He prophesied at a critical time in the history of the northern kingdom. Israel had deeply sinned and the Assyrians were marching to their overthrow. Yet his prophecy is not wholly hopeless and he predicts their final restoration (1:10, 11; 3:4, 5).

IV. ISAIAH
(810-698 B. C.)

1. **The life of Isaiah.** Isaiah, the son of Amoz, prophesied in the days of Uzziah, Jotham, Ahaz and Hezekiah, kings of Judah. He was a married man; had two sons, Shear-jashub and Maher-shalal-hash-baz, and his wife was a prophetess (8:3). His were stirring and critical times, as he lived during the invasions of Tiglath-pileser, Shalmaneser, Sargon and Sennacherib. Some have contended that he lived

into the reign of Manasseh, when, a Hebrew tradition says, he was sawn asunder.

2. The subjects of Isaiah's prophecy. The prophecy of Isaiah opens with this introduction: "The vision of Isaiah the son of Amoz, which he saw concerning Judah and Jerusalem." It contains predictions concerning the Jews, the neighboring nations, the two advents of the Messiah and the glory yet to be revealed in millennial times. Isaiah has been called the "gospel prophet" because of his frequent allusions to Christ (9:6, 7; 11:1-16; 53:1-12, etc.).

3. The integrity of Isaiah. The integrity of Isaiah has been attacked by the critics. Delitzsch, after at first defending the view of the unity of the book, surrendered the prophecies found in Isa. 13:1-14:23; 21:1-10; chapters 24-27; chapters 34 and 35, and stated that they "can not really, as hitherto generally assumed, have been composed by Isaiah." Others declare that the book is simply a complication of fragments and that it bears the marks of many hands. Some of these fragments, they tell us, are genuine, while some others are as recent as the first century B. C. Until these critical difficulties are fully settled, it will be well for the ordinary student to rest on the assumption that the book is wholly the work of Isaiah, the son of Amoz.

V. JOEL

(810-660 B. C.)

But very little is known of this prophet outside of the fact that he was the son of Pethuel. He prophesied to Judah, probably at Jerusalem, although the time of his prophesying is uncertain. He describes a desolating scourge of locusts that was to come upon the land, and which some explain literally and some figuratively; the invasion of hostile armies; the pouring out of the Holy Spirit; the celestial signs and deliverance to follow; the gathering of the nations to judgment, and the restoration of Israel.

VI. MICAH

(758-699 B. C.)

Micah was a native of Moresheth in Gath, and prophesied during the reigns of Jotham, Ahaz and Hezekiah, kings of Judah, and Pekahiah, Pekah and Hoshea, kings of Israel. His prophecy was addressed to both Samaria and Jerusalem, although it chiefly concerned the former. It contains a denunciation of Israel, a promise to the remnant, a prediction of the captivities, the announcement of the coming of the kingdom and the peace to follow, and points out the birthplace of Jesus Christ.

VII. NAHUM

(720-698 B. C.)

Nahum the Elkoshite prophesied in the days of Hezekiah, king of Judah. His prophecy was directed against Nineveh.

VIII. ZEPHANIAH

(640-609 B. C.)

Zephaniah was "the son of Cushi, the son of Gedaliah, the son of Amariah, the son of Hizkiah," and prophesied against Judah and Jerusalem in the days of Josiah, son of Amon. He foretells the coming invasion of Nebuchadnezzar, predicts the judgments that would come upon the neighboring nations, and holds out to his people the hope of restoration.

IX. JEREMIAH

(628-586 B. C.)

1. The account of Jeremiah. Jeremiah was the son of Hilkiah, a priest of Anathoth, in the land of Benjamin. He began to prophesy in the days of the good King Josiah, with whom he was probably on intimate terms. We hear nothing of him during the three months of the reign of Jehoahaz, but in the beginning of the reign of Jehoiakim he prophesied against the city and the land, which drew upon his head the animosity of the priests and prophets to such a degree that he was brought before the civil authorities, and capital punishment would have been inflicted upon him had it not been for the interference of the princes, especially of Ahikam (chap. 26). But, in the fourth year of this king, Jeremiah was commanded to take a roll and to write therein all the words which the Lord had spoken against Israel, Judah and the surrounding nations. When this roll was read to the king, he was greatly displeased, and, cutting it with a penknife, he threw it into the fire. Then Jeremiah was commanded to take another roll and to write in it not only those words which were in the first, but also to add a prediction of the miserable death of Jehioakim (chap. 36). Under Zedekiah, Jeremiah continued to utter warnings, for which he was cast into prison, where he remained until Nebuchadnezzar took the city, when he was released and was shown due consideration by the Babylonian king (39:11, 12). When the greater part of the Jewish people were taken to Babylon, the prophet remained behind with the remnant under Gedaliah, and, after the death of this governor, went with the Jews to Egypt, where he ended his days. The contemporaries of Jeremiah were Zephaniah, Habakkuk, Ezekiel and Daniel.

2. **The contents of Jeremiah's prophecy.** While Jeremiah concerned himself mainly with events and conditions near at hand, as the sins of the people, the Babylonish captivity and the restoration therefrom, we find him occasionally breaking away from these and describing things to transpire in the distant future. He refers particularly to the coming of the Messiah, His kingship and the establishment of the New Covenant.

X. HABAKKUK
(612-598 B. C.)

Of the birth, lineage and life of this prophet we have no certain knowledge. He probably prophesied during the latter years of King Josiah. He emphasizes the thought of the spirituality of God and predicts the time when "the earth shall be filled with the knowledge of the glory of the Lord, as the waters cover the sea."

XI. DANIEL
(606-534 B. C.)

1. **The account of Daniel.** Daniel was probably of royal blood. When but a youth, he was taken to Babylon by Nebuchadnezzar, where he was instructed

in all the learning of that country. By his interpretation of dreams, he gained admittance into the presence of the king and was made ruler over the province of Babylon. When the Persians took the kingdom, Daniel was made the first of three presidents who presided over the affairs of state. Because of his refusal to ask a petition of the king and of his strict adherence to the faith of his fathers, he was cast into a den of lions, from whose mouths he was miraculously saved. He lived to a good old age and to see his people restored to their own land.

2. **The authenticity of Daniel.** Perhaps no book in the entire Bible has met with more severe criticism at the hands of the higher critics than has the Book of Daniel. In the third century A. D., Porphyry the Syrian first attacked it and declared that it was not a production of the man Daniel in Babylon, 607-538 B. C., but of some unknown writer in the Maccabean period, subsequent to 164 B. C. This position was later defended by the infidel Collins in the beginning of the eighteenth century, and has been held by the large body of higher critics ever since. This theory, however, has been fully met and refuted, as have also the strongest of the objections to the authenticity of this book, which have been shown to be founded upon our ignorance of ancient history, our want of a sound exegesis and the perversion of a few passages in the text. In the investigations that have been carried on, the Book of Daniel has in almost every instance certainly come off victor, and many of the accounts and references which have heretofore been considered unhistorical are now accepted without question.

XII. OBADIAH

(588-583 B. C.)

Of this prophet we know but very little, and even the date of his prophecy is uncertain. Some have placed him in the reign of Ahaz, others in the reign of Josiah, and still others during the Babylonian captivity, as here. His prophecy concerns Edom, whose great sin in doing violence to the Jews he describes and whose humiliation and final overthrow he predicts.

XIII. EZEKIEL

(583-562 B. C.)

1. **The account of Ezekiel.** This prophet was the son of Buzi the priest, and, according to tradition, was born in Serera. We first find him with the exiled Jews on the river Chebar in Mesopotamia, where, in the fifth year of the captivity, he received his commission as prophet. He seems to have been a person of considerable importance among the exiles, as there are repeated intimations that the elders consulted him as to what messages God had sent through him. He continued to prophesy for at least twenty-two years, and probably remained with the captives on Chebar throughout his whole life.

2. **The prophecies of Ezekiel.** The unity and genuineness of Ezekiel have never been questioned. His predictions concern the destruction of Jerusalem and the captivity of the Jews, judgments upon various nations and the final restoration of the kingdom and its blessings.

THE PROPHETS

XIV. HAGGAI
(520-518 B. C.)

This prophet prophesied after the return of the Jews from Babylon and in the second year of Darius Hystaspes. His prophecy was to encourage the Jews to prosecute the building of the Temple.

XV. ZECHARIAH
(520-518 B. C.)

Zechariah was the son of Berechiah, the son of Iddo the prophet. He was the contemporary of Haggai, and, like him, sought to encourage the returned Jews in the work of rebuilding the Temple. But he does not alone concern himself with events and conditions near at hand. Here and there we find graphic and glowing descriptions of the coming and reign of the Messiah, with the final victory and rest of Israel.

XVI. MALACHI
(436-420 B. C.)

Malachi, the last of the prophets, prophesied, probably, during the confusion which followed Nehemiah's return to Babylon, after he had led his company of Jews to Jerusalem. The burden of his message is the love of God for Israel, the sins of the priests and the people and the coming of the Lord.

QUESTIONS

Define the term "prophet." Mention the names of some of the early prophets of Israel. About what prophets are we to study in this lesson? What were the schools of the prophets? Who was their founder? Where was the first school founded?

THE GIST OF THE BIBLE

How many existed in the days of Ahab, and where? Define the difference between a literal and symbolical prophecy. Between a conditional and an unconditional prophecy. Between a discursive and a consecutive prophecy. Into how many groups are the prophets of Israel to be divided? Name the prophets of Israel. Name the prophets of Judah. Name the prophets of the captivity. Name the post-exilic prophets. Who was Jonah? To what city did God command him to go? What did Jonah do? What happened to him? Tell about his second commission. Why was Jonah displeased with the Lord? Who was Amos and when did he prophesy? Tell about Hosea. Give an account of Isaiah. What is he sometimes called, and why? What can you say about the integrity of his book? Give an account of Joel. Of Micah. Of Nahum. Of Zephaniah. Of Jeremiah. Of what did Jeremiah prophesy? Tell about Habakkuk. Give an account of Daniel. Who was the first to attack the authenticity of the Book of Daniel? To what date did Porphyry assign this book? What effect has critical investigation had upon its question of authorship? Who was Obadiah? Give an account of Ezekiel. What can you say about the unity and genuineness of this book? To what do the prophecies of Ezekiel relate? Who was Haggai? Who was Zechariah? When did they prophesy? Why did they prophesy? Tell about Malachi.

PART III. INTERBIBLICAL HISTORY

Study XXVII.   The Persian Period.
Study XXVIII. The Grecian Period.
Study XXIX.   The Maccabean Period.
Study XXX.   The Roman Period.

STUDY XXVII. THE PERSIAN PERIOD

INTRODUCTION

1. **The Medo-Persian peoples.** The Medes and Persians were related peoples of the Aryan stock who occupied contiguous territory. The Medes were first mentioned in the Assyrian inscriptions about 820 B. C. They were subsequently subdued by Tiglath-pileser II. and his successors. The legendary history of Persia extends some thousands of years back of the beginning of the Christian era, but it is very much confused, on account of which we can know but little definitely of those early times. For most that we do know we are indebted to the Greek historians Herodotus, Xenophon and Ctesias.

2. **The country of the Medes and Persians.** The country inhabited by the Medes and Persians lies directly east of Assyria and Babylonia. It is a plateau and is called, in the native tongue, Iran.

3. **The period of Persian supremacy.** The period of Persian supremacy lay between the years 538 B. C., the date of the overthrow of Babylon, and 331 B. C., the date of the overthrow of the Persians by Alexander the Great.

I. MEDO-PERSIAN HISTORY

Medo-Persian history naturally falls into two divisions: that under the supremacy of the Medes and that under the supremacy of the Persians.

THE GIST OF THE BIBLE

1. The Median kings.

(1) *Deioces* (740-687 B. C.). In the year 740 B. C. the Medes revolted against the Assyrian power and chose Deioces as their king. This monarch founded his capital at Ecbatana and established a court with a severe ceremonious etiquette. Much that has been written about this king, however, is purely mythical.

(2) *Phraortes* (687-633 B. C.). The first real king of Media was Phraortes, called the son of Deioces. He conquered the Persians and carried his arms into upper Asia. He was killed in a war with Assyria in 633 B. C.

(3) *Cyaxares* (633-593 B. C.). After Phraortes, Cyaxares, his son, ascended the Median throne and continued the Assyrian war to avenge his father's death. He formed an alliance with Nabopolassar, king of Babylon, and with his assistance overthrew Nineveh (625 B. C.). He also overcame the Scythians. Under him the Medes reached the zenith of their glory.

(4) *Astyages* (593-558 B. C.). Upon the death of Cyaxares, Astyages, his son, took the throne. He maintained a peaceful alliance with both Lydia and Babylon. He was the maternal grandfather of Cyrus the Great.

2. The Persian kings.

(1) *Achaemenes*. The first king of Persia was Achæmenes, who was a member of the royal tribe of the Pasargadæ. From him all the subsequent kings of Persia were descended.

(2) *Cyrus* (558-529 B. C.). For the first one hundred years of their history, the Persians were

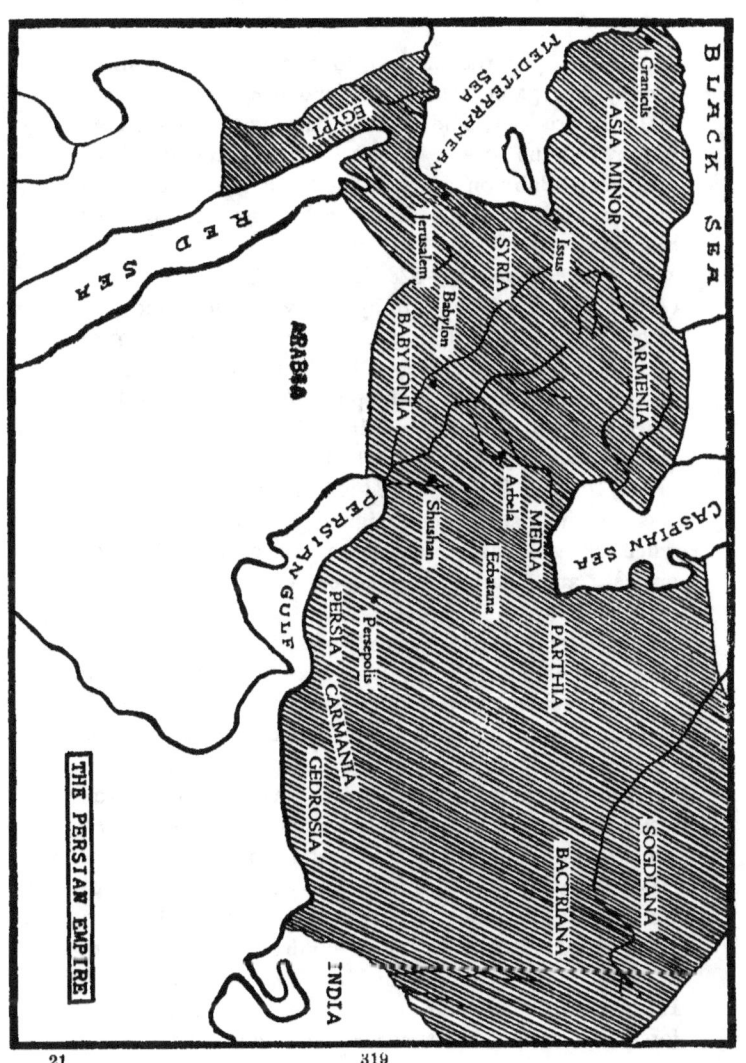

dependent upon the Medes. But in 558 B. C., under Cyrus, they gained their independence, Astyages was made a prisoner, and Persia became the sovereign power. Cyrus was a warrior and conquered Lydia, overthrew Babylon and subdued the Massagetæ. It was in a battle with these barbarians that he lost his life.

(3) *Cambyses* (529-522 B. C.). Cyrus was succeeded by his son Cambyses, who inherited his father's warlike ambition. He first invaded Egypt and subdued that country. He then made an unsuccessful invasion into Ethiopia. After this he hastened home to quell a revolt under Smerdis, but on the way was accidentally killed with his own sword.

(4) *Pseudo-Smerdis* (522-521 B. C.). This king was an impostor who reigned but eight months, when he was slain through a conspiracy of seven princes, and Darius Hystaspes, one of the seven, took the throne.

(5) *Darius Hystaspes* (521-486 B. C.). The first part of the reign of this king was spent in quelling revolts. When these revolts were put down, Darius, to guard against further disturbance, reorganized his kingdom and strengthened his army. He also enhanced the glory of his court. After settling the internal dissensions of his kingdom, Darius turned his attention to foreign conquests. He led an expedition against the Punjab, or "Five Rivers," of western India, and acquired this rich gold tract. With an army of over seven hundred thousand men, he invaded the country of the Scythians in central Europe and defeated them, but was afterwards forced to retire for the want of food and water.

THE PERSIAN PERIOD

Darius was next called to the field to quell a revolt of the Greeks. At first he was successful, but, fired with anger, he determined to punish the Greeks more severely, and, leading a force of one hundred thousand men, he met them upon the field of Marathon (490 B. C.). Here he was signally defeated, and, returning home, died in the year 486 B. C.

(6) *Xerxes I.* (486-465 B. C.). Darius was succeeded by Xerxes I., the Ahasuerus of the Book of Esther. In the second year of his reign he quelled revolts in Egypt and Babylonia, and in the seventh led in his celebrated invasion of Greece. Gathering together an army of 1,700,000 foot soldiers, with 20,000 chariots and camels, 80,000 horse and a fleet of over 4,000 vessels, manned by 517,000 men, he invaded that country. It was during the campaign that ensued that Leonidas so bravely met the Persians at Thermopylæ. Following this battle, the Greeks and Persians met in a number of naval engagements, but no decisive advantage was gained by either side until in the sea-fight off Salamis the Persians were defeated. Xerxes then withdrew to his own land and spent the remainder of his life in indolence and luxury. After reigning twenty years, he was murdered by the captain of his guard.

(7) *Artaxerxes I.* (465-425 B. C.). After the death of Xerxes, his assassin placed upon the throne his youngest son, Artaxerxes Longimanus. This king was first engaged in putting down a revolt in Egypt and in warring with the Athenians, who had assisted that country. In the seventh and twentieth years of his reign, respectively, Ezra and Nehemiah led their

companies of Jews back to Jerusalem. Artaxerxes reigned forty years.

(8) *Xerxes II.* (425 B. C.). This king, the son of Artaxerxes, reigned just forty-five days, when he was assassinated by his half-brother, Sogdianus.

(9) *Sogdianus* (425-424 B. C.). Sogdianus reigned but about six months, when he was deposed and put to death by another half-brother, Ochus.

(10) *Darius II.* (424-405 B. C.). Ochus took the throne and assumed the name of Darius II. During the nineteen years of his reign this king was the mere tool of his wife, Parysatis, a woman noted for her wickedness and cruelty. Under his rule the Egyptians revolted and were successful in regaining their independence, while the Medes failed in a similar attempt. Darius, however, gained one advantage in the recovery of certain Greek cities of Asia Minor.

(11) *Artaxerxes II.* (405-359 B. C.). This king is known as Artaxerxes Mnemon for his wonderful memory. During the latter years of his father's life, his brother, Cyrus, had attempted to gain the throne, so, when Artaxerxes ascended the same, he cast Cyrus into prison. Afterwards, however, the young prince, through the intervention of his mother, was not only released, but was restored to his satrapy. Later he headed a revolt in which he lost his life. The Spartans, by allying themselves with Cyrus, had given great offense to Artaxerxes, so they decided to be the first movers in the war which they knew must certainly ensue. But Artaxerxes formed an alliance with Athens and others of the minor Greek states, and so reduced Sparta to

THE PERSIAN PERIOD

humiliation. After this, with a desire to restore the empire to the greatness that it enjoyed under Darius Hystaspes, Artaxerxes sent an expedition to reduce Egypt, but this expedition failed through the jealousy of the commanding officers. Egypt then retaliated and attempted to take Syria and Phœnicia, but her movements were defeated by management and gold.

(12) *Artaxerxes III.* (359-338 B. C.). At the death of Artaxerxes II., his youngest son, Ochus, assumed the throne under the title of Artaxerxes III. He was a monarch of energy and spirit and attempted to retrieve the fortunes of his failing empire. But he was extremely jealous and suspicious, and one of the first acts to blot his name was the murder of the entire royal race. Having quelled a revolt in Asia Minor, he attempted the subjugation of Egypt, but was defeated. His defeat was the signal for innumerable revolts, and province after province threw off the yoke of his tyranny. But Artaxerxes was more than a match for his enemies and subdued them in the most bloody manner. Having established the peace of his kingdom, he abandoned himself to the pleasures of his palace. He died of poison at the hand of his minister, Bagoas, in the year 338 B. C.

(13) *Arses* (338-336 B. C.). Bagoas not only slew Artaxerxes, but also all of the royal princes, with the exception of the youngest, Arses, whom he placed upon the throne. But, at the expiration of two years, being alarmed by the independent character of the young king, Bagoas added him also to the number of his victims, after which he placed

upon the throne Darius Codomannus, the grandson of Darius II.

(14) *Darius III*. (336-331 B. C.). Darius began his reign by executing the wretch who had bestowed upon him the crown. Distinguished for his personal beauty, he was also noted for the uprightness and benevolence of his character. It was under his reign that Alexander the Great began his conquest of the world, and Darius met his defeat at the hands of this general in the battle of Arbela (331 B. C.). He was assassinated by one of his own satraps, Bessus, who mortally wounded him and left him by the roadside to die.

II. THE CULTURE OF THE PERSIANS

1. **The character of the Persians.** The Persians were a hardy race, brave in war and rude in manners, who abstained from all luxuries of both food and dress. Though not highly intellectual, they were fond of both poetry and art.

2. **The government of the Persians.** The Persian theory of government was an advance over the theories of the other Oriental nations of early times and, though a real imperial dominion, was particularly mild in character.

3. **The architecture of the Persians.** In architectural art the Persians were the pupils of the Assyrians and the Babylonians. However, they did not imitate the architectural designs of their masters, but adapted them in such a way that they became their own. Their great masterpieces of architecture consist of palaces and tombs and belong to a class which stands midway between the massive works of

THE PERSIAN PERIOD

the Egyptian and the Assyrian and the perfect beauty of the Grecian.

4. The literature of the Persians. But few fragments of the literature of the ancient Iranic race have survived. The most important of these is the collection of sacred books called the Zend Avesta, which was compiled by Zoroaster, the great religious teacher of the Persians, probably about the time of Abraham.

5. The religion of the Persians. The religion of the Persians was much purer and nobler than that of the other ancient civilized nations. They were not idolaters, but worshiped a single Supreme Being, called Ormazd, who was looked upon as the great principle of light. Opposed to Ormazd was Ahriman, the principle of darkness. But this pure system of faith was subsequently corrupted with fire-worship, or Magianism, which the Medes had borrowed from the Scythians. The old theory that Cyrus, the first great king of Persia, was a native Persian and a monotheist, which some have derived from certain passages in the Old Testament, will now, however, have to be given up. The inscriptions make it certain that he was both an Elamite and a polytheist. Monotheism was not introduced as the Persian state religion until the reign of Darius, the son of Hystaspes, who was a Zoroastrian.

III. THE BOOK OF ESTHER

The Book of Esther is a history of events that occurred under the reign of the Persian monarch, Xerxes I., or Ahasuerus. It may be outlined as follows:

1. **Vashti deposed** (Esth. 1:1-22). In the third year of King Ahasuerus he made a feast to all the nobles and princes of his dominion and showed to them all of his riches and the honor of his majesty. This feast lasted 180 days, at the expiration of which he gave another to the common people. On the seventh day of this feast, Ahasuerus commanded his servants to bring his wife, Vashti, before him in order that he might show to the people her beauty. But Vashti refused to come, which so enraged the king that he made a decree that she should no more appear before him and that her estate should be given to another better than she.

2. **Esther exalted** (Esth. 2:1-20). But, when the wrath of Ahasuerus was appeased, his heart began to turn again to his deposed queen. So his servants suggested that officers be appointed to gather together the virgins of his realm that he might select one to be queen in Vashti's place. This pleased the king, and his servants set about carrying out his orders. Now, there was in the palace of Shushan a Jew, Mordecai by name, who had brought up a very beautiful niece by the name of Esther. This Jew, when he heard of the king's commands, brought Esther to the officers and placed her in the care of Hegai, the king's keeper of women, instructing her, at the same time, that she should not reveal her nationality. When the twelve months, which had been appointed for the purification of the women, were ended, Esther appeared before the king, who was so impressed with her beauty that he selected her as his queen, in the place of Vashti, and made a feast in her honor.

3. Mordecai saves the life of Ahasuerus (Esth. 2: 21-23). In those days Mordecai discovered a plot against the life of the king in which his chamberlains, Bigthan and Teresh, sought to slay him. The Jew told this plot to Esther, who, in turn, revealed it to the king. An investigation being made, the guilt of these men was proved and they were both hanged on a tree.

4. Haman's plot against the Jews (Esth. 3: 1-15). After this the king promoted Haman the Agagite over all the princes that were with him, and commanded that all of his servants should bow before him. Mordecai refused to do this. When Mordecai's refusal was told Haman, he was full of wrath and laid a plot not only to destroy him, but also all the Jews throughout the entire kingdom. So, in the first month of the twelfth year of Ahasuerus, Haman went to the king and complained that the Jews were different from all the other people and did not keep the king's laws, suggesting at the same time that he order their destruction, and offering for the same the sum of ten thousand talents of silver to be paid into the king's treasury. When the king heard this, he gave Haman his signet-ring, and he called together the king's scribes to write the edict, after which he sealed it with the king's seal and sent it by posts throughout all the provinces.

5. The intervention of Esther (Esth. 4: 1-5: 14). When the Jews were told what Haman had done, there was great mourning among them and many of them lay in sackcloth and ashes. Esther then sent to Mordecai for full information of the plot, and he replied by telling her messenger all that Haman had done and by sending her a copy of the decree. Then Esther set herself to the task of delivering her people. For three days she and the Jews in Shushan[1] fasted, at the end of which time she, dressed in her royal apparel, went in to the king, and, when she had found favor in his eyes, she invited him and Haman to a banquet which she would prepare for them that day. At this banquet, Ahasuerus asked Esther to state her request, promising her that he would grant it if it required one-half of his kingdom. To this the queen replied that, if the king and Haman would come to the banquet on the morrow, she would do as he had said. Haman, upon his return from the feast, called his friends and family together and related to them how he had been advanced above the other servants of the king, and how Esther had invited him alone with the king to sit at her feast. Yet he declared that all this availed him nothing so long as Mordecai sat at the king's gate. His friends then advised him to construct a gallows and to request the king that the Jew be hanged thereon.

6. **The exaltation of Mordecai** (Esth. 6:1-14). That night the king was troubled so that he could not sleep, and he called for the official records to be brought and read before him. In these it was found that Mordecai had saved the king's life from the plot of Bigthan and Teresh. When Ahasuerus discovered this and also that Mordecai had not been rewarded, he inquired: "Who is in the court?" His servants replied: "Haman standeth in the court." He

---
[1] One of the capitals of ancient Persia.

then commanded that he be brought in. This being done, the king said to Haman: "What shall be done unto the man whom the king delighteth to honor?" Haman was greatly pleased with this question, thinking that Ahasuerus had it in mind to honor him, and so replied that he should be clothed in royal apparel, should be set upon the king's horse, should be crowned with the king's crown, and that the horse should be led through the street by one of the most noble princes. Then the king commanded that this be done to Mordecai and that Haman bring him through the street. After this was done, Haman returned to his home greatly humiliated.

7. **The execution of Haman** (Esth. 7: 1-10). At the banquet which Esther had prepared for Ahasuerus and Haman, the king requested Esther to state her petition. The queen answered: "If I have found favor in thy sight, O king, and if it please the king, let my life be given me at my petition, and my people at my request." The king inquired who had sought the destruction of herself and people, and when Esther had replied that it was Haman, Ahasuerus commanded that he be taken and hanged on the same gallows which he had prepared for Mordecai.

8. **The destruction of the Jews' enemies** (Esth. 8: 1-9: 32). After the death of Haman, Mordecai was exalted in his place, and Esther besought the king to annul the edict that he had permitted to be issued. This the king did, and also issued another decree in which he gave the Jews the right to stand for their lives and to destroy all who came against them. Then the Jews smote all their enemies with the sword, after which they rested on the fourteenth

day of the month Adar. This day was ever afterwards kept as the date of the feast of Purim.

9. **Mordecai made prime minister** (Esth. 10: 1-3). After this Mordecai was made prime minister and his fame spread throughout the whole realm of Persia.

QUESTIONS

To what race did the Medes and Persians belong? Give the names of the historians to whom we are indebted for our knowledge of ancient Persia. In what direction from Assyria and Babylonia did the country of the ancient Medes and Persians lie? What is the name of Persia in the native tongue? Bound, chronologically, the period of Persian supremacy. Into what two divisions does Medo-Persian history fall? Give in their order the names of the Median kings. What kings overthrew Nineveh? When did Cyrus the Great reign? What did he permit the Jews to do? Give the name of his son and successor. Under whose reign did Ezra and Nehemiah lead the Jews back to Palestine? What king is identified with Ahasuerus of the Book of Esther? Who was the last king of Persia? By whom was he defeated? Where? When? Describe the character of the Persians. Tell about their government. Their architecture. Give the name that is applied to the collection of their sacred books. Who compiled this collection, and about when? Describe the Persian religion. Was Cyrus a monotheist? Was he a native Persian? When was monotheism introduced as the Persian state religion? Why was Vashti deposed? Who was exalted in her place? Who was Mordecai? What two men conspired against the life of Ahasuerus? Who was Haman? What plot did he lay? What did Esther do? Tell about the exaltation of Mordecai. What became of Haman? What feast commemorates the deliverance of the Jews? What office did Mordecai afterwards fill?

STUDY XXVIII. THE GRECIAN PERIOD

INTRODUCTION

1. **The cultural transition.** With the supremacy of Greece there came a transition in culture, and Greek civilization rapidly supplanted that of the Orient.

2. **Preparation for Christ.** This cultural transition was one of the steps in the world's preparation for the coming of Christ. The Greek language rapidly became the language of commerce and letters and thus prepared the way for the wide dissemination of gospel truth.

3. **The condition of the Jews.** After the death of Alexander, Judea became the bone of contention between the kings of Syria and Egypt, and upon its soil many of the chief battles of these contending powers were fought. Yet the Jews were held in high repute by both powers, and their first kings, Seleucus Nicator and Ptolemy Soter, invited them to their respective realms, where they were generally treated with the greatest kindness and were given the rights of citizenship. Those Jews who took advantage of these offers and settled in Syria and Egypt were known as Hellenists from having come under Hellenic influences and adopting the Hellenic tongue For about the first eighty years of the period of Greek supremacy, Judea was under the dominion of the Ptolemies of Egypt, but it afterwards, through

the conquest of Antiochus the Great, passed under the scepter of the Seleucidæ. The Jews who remained in the home land, although nominally subject either to Egypt or Syria, were governed by their own laws through their high priest and national council. Yet the peace of the country was greatly broken by the almost constant warfare of the two rival kingdoms mentioned and also by the internal contentions over the claims of rival candidates for the office of the high-priesthood. These disturbances had a bad effect upon the people, and they drifted into wickedness and a disregard for religious worship.

4. **The period of Greek supremacy.** This period lay between the decisive victory of Alexander in 331 B. C. and the overthrow of the Ptolemies by Rome in B. C. 30, although, so far as Judea was concerned, it ended with the overthrow of Antiochus by Judas Maccabeus about 165 B. C.

I. GRECIAN HISTORY

1. **The early history of Greece.** The first inhabitants of Greece were the Pelasgi, from whom the country was called Pelasgia. They were followed by the Hellenes, who subdued them and gave their name, Hellas, to the peninsula. Following this conquest, the people were divided into four tribes—the Dorians, Achæans, Æolians and Ionians. These early times are known as the Heroic Age, of whose heroes and heroines later poets and sculptors loved to celebrate the character. The celebrated legend of the siege of Troy belongs to this period.

2. **The rise of Sparta and Athens.** The two most important states of ancient Greece were those of

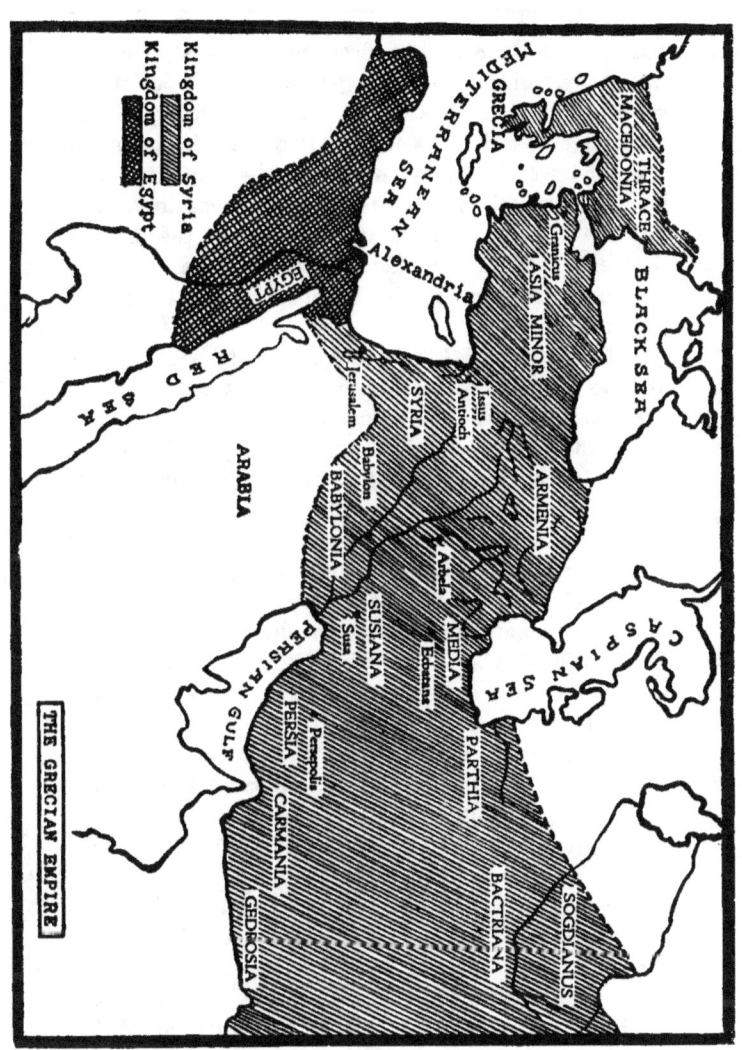

Sparta and Athens. At first, Sparta was a double monarchy, ruled by two kings and a senate of thirty members. About 850 B. C. arose Lycurgus, the celebrated lawgiver, who is noted for his stringent code of laws. By these laws the power of the kings was reduced while that of the people was increased, but his main purpose seems to have been the making of every Spartan a soldier. With him the state did not exist for the individual, but the individual for the state.

The history of Athens begins in the Heroic Age and, as it is followed, presents a greater variety of character and incident than does that of Sparta. At first Athens was ruled by kings, then by archons, and lastly by a council, or board, of nine who were chosen from among the nobles. About 620 B. C., Draco brought out his code of laws, but they were marked with so much cruelty, every crime being punishable with death, that Athens was thrown into a state of anarchy from which she was rescued by Solon (594 B. C.). Though Solon's laws were much more moderate, they were unsatisfactory to many of his contemporaries, and the result was a struggle for power in which Pisistratus, Solon's opponent, was victorious. This dictator ruled mildly and succeeded in transmitting his power to his sons, but the people again becoming dissatisfied, banished his family (510 B. C.), and a noble named Clisthenes assumed the power. Under Clisthenes the people enjoyed a pure democracy, and Athens soon rose to be the leading state of central Greece.

3. **The Persian War.** When Cyrus the Great conquered Lydia, he also came into possession of her

THE GRECIAN PERIOD

dependencies and, among them, of a number of Greek cities in Asia Minor. These cities did not readily submit to Persian rule and, in 500 B. C., revolted, being assisted by their kinsfolk, the Athenians. This drew down upon both the wrath of Darius Hystaspes, with the result that, after he had quelled the revolt in Asia Minor, he turned his attention to Athens. At first, because of several misfortunes, he was forced to retire, but later, with a larger army, he again invaded Greece. At the outset his forces were successful and the Cyclades Islands, with Eretria, on the island of Eubœa, fell before them. But as the Persians advanced on Athens they were met by the Greeks under Miltiades and severely defeated at Marathon in September, 490 B. C. Not being able to continue hostilities, Darius withdrew, and before it was possible for him again to renew the conflict he was cut off by the hand of death (485 B. C.). His son, Xerxes, then took the throne and led a large army into Greece, and met and defeated a small Spartan force, under Leonidas, at Thermopylæ. But, in the sea-fight off Salamis, he met a crushing overthrow and was forced to retire. He left behind him, however, an army under the command of Mardonis, but his army, too, was soon afterwards defeated at Platæa, and this, with the crushing of the remnant of his fleet in a naval engagement at Mycale, Asia Minor, forever put at rest the hopes that the Persian monarchs had of conquering the Greek peoples.

4. **The Peloponnesian War.** During the half-century which followed the battle of Salamis, Athens reached the zenith of her glory and power. This

high state of excellence was largely due to the exertions of Pericles, one of the greatest statesmen that ever lived. For the purpose of protection, the Athenians formed a league with other maritime cities on the Ægean. On the other hand, Sparta exercised a strong influence over the inland states. The friction that was caused brought on what is known in history as the Peloponnesian War, a conflict which, beginning in 431 B. C., lasted twenty-seven years and finally ended with the surrender of Athens. After this, Athens declined in power, and Sparta for a time assumed the ascendency, only to be defeated by the rising power of Thebes. But the glory of Thebes was also of short duration, for she, too, soon fell before the combined forces of the Spartans and Athenians. These struggles exhausted Greece and left her an easy prey to Philip of Macedon.

5. Macedonian supremacy. Although the Macedonians were closely allied to the Greeks in race, they had remained in obscurity while their southern kinsmen were coming to the notice of the world. But, in the middle of the fourth century B. C., the bold and energetic chief, Philip, assumed the government of Macedon and set himself to the task of making it the leading power of Europe. At first he craftily mixed himself in Greek politics and was chosen a member of the great religious council known as the Amphictyonic Council. But, not content with this hidden policy, he came out in the open and, in 358 B. C., began to assert his power, with the result that in twenty years he had made himself master of Greece by the defeat of the combined forces of the Athenians and Thebans at Cheronea (338 B. C.).

THE GRECIAN PERIOD

After this he declared his purpose of uniting all Hellas against Persia, but, before he had time to carry out his plans, he was assassinated by one of his own subjects (336 B. C.). Two things contributed to Philip's success: his invincible military organization and his political tact. Philip was succeeded by his son, Alexander the Great, who was twenty years of age.

6. **The career of Alexander the Great.** No sooner did Alexander ascend the throne than he began to carry out his father's cherished plans of overthrowing Persia. In 334 B. C. he crossed the Hellespont with a small army of thirty-five thousand men and defeated a superior Persian force at Granicus, in Asia Minor. His next engagement was at Issus, near the borders of Cilicia and Syria, where he met Darius Codomannus and was also victorious (333 B. C.). During the next twenty months he reduced Tyre, Gaza and Egypt, and in 331 B. C. plunged into the heart of Persia, where he met Darius at Arbela in Assyria. So decisive was this victory for Alexander that the three capitals of the Persian Empire—Persepolis, Susa and Babylon—surrendered almost without resistance. After this he led his forces into India as far as the river Hyphasis, conquering by the way, when his soldiers refused to go farther, and he returned to Persepolis, where he died at the age of thirty-three (B. C. 323).

7. **Alexander's successors.** Upon Alexander's death, his mighty empire fell to pieces, and in 301 B. C. was divided among his four generals, as follows: Seleucus took Syria and the East; Ptolemy took Egypt; Lysimachus took Thrace, and Cassander

took Macedon. Of these kingdoms, those of Seleucus and Ptolemy were the most important, and almost unceasing warfare was carried on between them until they finally came under the power of Rome. The kings who reigned upon the throne of Egypt at Alexandria and upon the throne of Syria at Antioch were:

EGYPT.

Ptolemy Soter (320-285 B. C.).
Ptolemy Philadelphus (285-247).
Ptolemy Euergetes I. (247-222).
Ptolemy Philopater (222-205).
Ptolemy Epiphanes (205-181).
Ptolemy Philometer (181-146).
Ptolemy Euergetes II. (170-116, jointly with Pt. Philometer till B. C. 146).
Ptolemy Lathrus (116-107).
Ptolemy Alexander and Cleopatra (107-80).
Ptolemy Auletes (80-51, exiled for three years).
Ptolemy Dionysius and Cleopatra (51-30).

SYRIA.

Seleucus Nicator (312-280 B. C.)
Antiochus Soter (280-261).
Antiochus Theos (261-246).
Seleucus Callinicus (246-226).
Seleucus Ceraunus (226-223).
Antiochus the Great (223-187).
Seleucus Philopater (187-175).
Antiochus Epiphanes (175-164).
Antiochus Eupator (164-162).
Demetrius Soter (162-150).
Alexander Balas (150-145).
Demetrius Nicator (145-138).
Antiochus Sidetes (138-128).
Demetrius Nicator (128-125, second reign).
Seleucus V. (murdered at once).
Antiochus Grypus (125-113).
Antiochus Cyzicenus (113-95).
Antiochus Eusebes (95-83).
Tigranes (83-69).
Antiochus Asiaticus (69-65).

II. GRECIAN CULTURE

1. **The character of the Grecian peopie.** The Greeks were of an æsthetic disposition and were intensely patriotic and liberty-loving.

2. **Grecian literature.** Aside from the Hebrew Scriptures, the literature of ancient Greece was the

THE GRECIAN PERIOD

best of antiquity. It was far in advance of that of the Egyptians, Babylonians, Hindoos and Persians in its high tone of thought and sentiment. In Greek literature, poetry preceded prose. The oldest poems are the Iliad and Odyssey, written by Homer, and which are given a date as early as 880 B. C. Following Homer came Hesiod, who wrote two famous books, "Theogany" and "Works and Days." Among the lyric poetry we have the works of Sappho, Alcæus, Anacreon and Pindar. In the age of Pericles the Greek drama was invented, and tragedy attained its highest development at the hands of Æschylus, Sophocles and Euripides. The greatest master of comedy was Aristophanes. The historians were Herodotus, the "Father of History," born in 484 B. C.; Thucydides, Xenophon, Polybius, Diodorus and Plutarch. Of orators there were Pericles, Æschines and Demosthenes, while among the philosophers may be mentioned Thales, Pythagoras, Socrates, Plato and Aristotle.

3. **Grecian art.** The most important works of Grecian architecture were their temples. These were built with columns of three graceful forms or orders, known as the Doric, the Ionic and the Corinthian. Most of these temples were built during the forty or fifty years succeeding the defeat of the Persians at Salamis. The most celebrated temple, following the Ionic order of architecture, was that of Diana at Ephesus, which was 425 feet long by 220 feet wide. The Corinthian order of architecture was most followed in the construction of those temples which were dedicated to Venus, Flora and the Nymphs, while the most famous of the Doric temples

was the Parthenon, "House of the Virgin," dedicated to Athena, at Athens.

4. **The Grecian religion.** The ancient Greeks were polytheists and worshiped a number of gods and goddesses, yet their religious system was far in advance of that of the Egyptians and Babylonians. Their chief gods and goddesses were: Zeus, chief and father of the gods; Poseidon, deity of the sea; Apollo, god of song and music; Artemis, goddess of flocks and the chase; Hephaistos, god of terrestrial fire; Hermes, the messenger of the gods; Ares, god of war; Hera, the wife of Zeus; Athena. goddess of wisdom and war; Hestia, goddess of the hearth; Demeter, goddess of agriculture, and Aphrodite, goddess of love. Besides these, there were a number of lesser deities.

5. **Grecian festivals.** There were four great national festivals: the Olympic, Pythian, Isthmian and Nemean. The first was observed every four years in the plain of Olympia in honor of the god Zeus. The Pythian was observed in the third year of each Olympiad, near Delphi, in honor of Apollo. The Isthmian was kept in honor of Neptune, or Poseidon, on the isthmus of Corinth. And the Nemean was celebrated at the town of Nemea in the Peloponnesus.

6. **The Alexandrian library.** When the Ptolemies began to rule Egypt, they founded their capital at Alexandria, which soon became a great and flourishing city and the center of culture and art. Here was found the celebrated Alexandrian library of five hundred thousand volumes. Here, also, the Hebrew Old Testament was translated into the Greek by a

THE GRECIAN PERIOD

company of learned Alexandrian Jews under the patronage of Ptolemy Philadelphus. This version was begun in 285 B. C. and is known as the Septuagint.

QUESTIONS

What can you say of the cultural transition accompanying the supremacy of Greece? How was this a preparation for Christ? Give the condition of the Jews during the Greek period. Locate the period of Greek supremacy. What were the first inhabitants of Greece called? Who were their successors? Into what four tribes were the ancient inhabitants divided? What is the early age of Grecian history called? What celebrated legend belongs to this period? Name the two most important of the ancient Grecian states. Who was Lycurgus? Tell about his laws. Who was Draco? Tell about his laws. Who was Solon? Who superseded him? Who succeeded Pisistratus? How did the Persians come into possession of Grecian territory? Who was the first Persian king to invade Grecian territory? Where and by whom was he defeated? Give the date of the battle of Marathon. Who was the second Persian king to invade Greece? Whom did he meet at Thermopylæ? Where was he defeated? Give the cause of the Peloponnesian War. When did it begin? How long did it last? Who was victorious? What power afterwards defeated Sparta? What happened to Thebes? What prominent Macedonian arose about this time? What was Philip's ambition? How did he make himself master of Greece? What two things contributed to his success? Who succeeded him? How old was Alexander at this time? Give the names of the first two battles in which he defeated the Persians. What countries did he then reduce? Where and when was the decisive battle fought? After he had conquered Persia, where did Alexander lead his armies? Where did he die? Into how many divisions was Alexander's dominion divided after his death? What were the rulers of Egypt called? What were the rulers of Syria called? Give the character of the Greek peoples. Who was the first poet of Greece? Give the titles of his two works. Who is called the "Father of History"? What were the most important works of Grecian architecture? Give the three orders of Grecian architecture. Were the Greeks monotheists or polytheists? Give the character of their religion compared with that of Egypt and Babylonia. Name some of their gods. Name the four Greek festivals. Where was the greatest library of antiquity founded? How many volumes did it contain? Tell about the translation of the Hebrew Scriptures into the Greek.

STUDY XXIX. THE MACCABEAN PERIOD

(Following Josephus)

INTRODUCTION

1. The Maccabees. The Maccabees were a family of patriots and religious reformers who maintained Jewish independence between the years 167 and 63 B. C. The original term was *Maccabi*, which was probably derived from the Hebrew *makkabah*, "a hammer." The proper name of the family, however, was *Asmonæans*, or *Hasmonæans*.

2. The cause of the Maccabean revolt. The strength of the Jews was greatly weakened by a somewhat protracted contention between rival candidates for the office of the high-priesthood, and Antiochus Epiphanes, king of Syria, taking advantage of this condition, led an expedition against Jerusalem and took possession of it. He pillaged the city, burned the best buildings, desecrated and despoiled the Temple, slew some of the inhabitants and carried others away captive. He also tried to extirpate Jewish worship and to substitute the religion of the Greeks in its place. These acts of violence and sacrilege greatly incensed that part of the population who were devoutly attached to the ancient worship, and led to the revolt of the Jews against the tyranny of the Selucidæan kings. Antiochus was in possession of the city of Jerusalem from 170 to 164 B. C.

I. MATTATHIAS

(168-166 B. C.)

1. **The relations of Mattathias.** Mattathias was a priest of the order of Joarib, who dwelt in the town of Modin, eighteen miles northwest of the city of Jerusalem, of which he was a citizen. He was the father of five sons—John, Simon, Judas, Eleazar and Jonathan.

2. **Mattathias refuses to obey the command of Antiochus.** Antiochus sent officers to Modin for the purpose of erecting an altar to Jupiter Olympus and to compel the Jews to offer sacrifices on the same. This the aged Mattathias, with his family, refused to do, and also slew an apostate Jew who did sacrifice, and Apelles, Antiochus' general, with a number of his soldiers. He then overthrew the idol altar, and, crying out, "If any one be zealous for the laws of his country, and for the worship of God, let him follow me," fled to the mountains.

3. **The Syrians attack the Jews.** Many of the Jews, with their families, followed Mattathias, and when this was told the king's generals, they took all the forces that they had at Jerusalem and followed them. Coming upon them, the generals tried to dissuade them from their rebellious course, but when they discovered that they could not, they attacked them upon their sabbath and slew about one thousand men, besides women and children, because they would not defend themselves upon that day. Following this, Mattathias gathered about him a great army, overthrew the idol altars, slew those Jews who broke the laws, and reinstated the ordinance of

circumcision that had been permitted to relapse under the persecution of the Syrians. He also changed the policy of the Jews so that afterwards they defended themselves even upon their sabbaths.

4. **The death of Mattathias.** At the expiration of one year, Mattathias was taken with a distemper, and, admonishing his sons to live together harmoniously, to observe the ancient customs and to recover their ancient government, he died and was buried, amid the lamentations of his people, at Modin

II. JUDAS MACCABEUS
(166-161 B. C.)

1. **Judas succeeds his father.** Judas, by appointment of Mattathias, succeeded him as the general of the Jewish army and carried on the work of reform with the spirit of his father. He cast his enemies out of the country, put to death those Jews who had broken the ancient law, and purified the land of all the pollutions that were in it.

2. **The victories of Judas.** When Apollonius, commander of the Samaritan forces, learned what Judas had done, he made haste to go against him. In the battle that ensued, Apollonius was defeated and slain. After this, Seron, general of the army of Cœle-syria, led an expedition against Judas and met him at Beth-horon, a village in Judea. But he, too, was defeated and eight hundred of his army were slain. The news of this defeat, coming to the ears of Antiochus, made him very angry, and he gathered together all his army, with many mercenaries, and prepared to invade Judea. But, when the king had

mustered his soldiers, he ascertained that there were not enough funds in his treasury to finance the campaign, so he resolved first to go into Persia to collect the taxes of that country, while the command of his army was given to Lysias, a very able and accomplished general. Lysias divided his forces into three divisions under Ptolemy, Nicanor and Gorgias, but in the campaign which ensued he was severely defeated, as he was also in a second campaign which was carried on the following year.

3. **Judas purges the Temple and restores the ancient worship.** Judas, following these victories, assembled the people together and stated his purpose to go up to Jerusalem and purify the Temple and restore the ancient worship. When this work was accomplished and the Temple worship was once again set in order, the people celebrated the event with a festival which lasted eight days. This festival was ever afterwards known as the Feast of Dedication.

4. **Judas subdues the surrounding nations.** The nations surrounding the Jews became very uneasy at the revival of their power under Judas, and, forming an alliance, attacked the people and destroyed many of them. This moved Judas to action, and, at the head of his army, he successively met and defeated the Idumeans, the sons of Bean and the Ammonites, and then returned into Judea. But no sooner was he off the field than the allies attacked the Jews in Gilead, while the inhabitants of Ptolemais, Tyre and Sidon also formed an alliance against him. So, dividing his army, Judas sent part of it north under his brother Simon to meet the Tyrians and their allies, while he with the remainder went to the defense of

THE MACCABEAN PERIOD

the Jews in Gilead. In both of these campaigns the Jews were victorious.

5. The death of Antiochus Epiphanes. When Antiochus, who was in Persia, heard of the repeated defeats of his armies, and having also failed of obtaining the finances he sought, he fell into a grievous distemper from which he died, bitterly repenting the miseries which he had brought upon the Jewish nation.

6. Antiochus Eupator attacks the Jews. Upon the death of Antiochus Epiphanes, Antiochus Eupator ascended the Syrian throne. He was but a youth, and, through the instigation of apostate Jews from Jerusalem, he collected an army of 120,000 men and, marching into Idumea, besieged the Jews in the city of Bethsura. When Judas, who was besieging the citadel in Jerusalem, learned of the attack on Bethsura, he went to its rescue, but, before the formidable army of Eupator, he was forced to retire, and, re-entering Jerusalem, prepared for a siege. Eupator, with part of his army, followed him, but after a long time was forced to raise the siege and to make peace with the Jews because of the threatened attack of Philip, who was coming against him from Persia. Returning to Antioch, Eupator was finally killed by his own uncle, Demetrius, who took the throne.

7. The persecution of the Jews under Demetrius. Demetrius made peace with Judas, but appointed one of his generals, Nicanor, governor of Judea. Now, Nicanor was of a humane disposition and acted very leniently toward the Jews, especially toward Judas, which provoked the jealousy of the apostate Alcimus, who went to Demetrius with the complaint that Nicanor had ordained Judas to be the king's successor. This greatly enraged Demetrius, and he wrote to Nicanor and demanded that he send the Maccabee a prisoner to Antioch. But Judas discovered the purpose of the governor and fled. A battle was soon afterwards fought at Beth-horon, in which Nicanor was defeated and slain, Judas sending his head and right hand as trophies back to Jerusalem.

8. **The death of Judas Maccabeus.** But the army of Demetrius was still very strong, and Judas retired to Laish with three thousand followers. Here he was attacked with a superior force and was slain. He was buried with great honor at Modin.

III. JONATHAN MACCABEUS

(161-143 B. C.)

1. **Jonathan succeeds Judas.** For sometime after the death of Judas the Jews were without a leader, but finally their oppression became so great that they came to Jonathan and urged him to take command of their army. Jonathan proved to be a worthy successor of his brother Judas.

2. **The invasions of Bacchides.** When Bacchides, the Syrian general, learned that Jonathan had taken command of the Jewish army, he became alarmed and laid a plot to kill him. But Jonathan, hearing of this, fled into the wilderness. Here Bacchides attacked him on the sabbath, presuming that he would not fight on that day. In this battle the Syrians lost two thousand men, but Jonathan escaped by swim-

THE MACCABEAN PERIOD

ming the Jordan. Following this, Bacchides secured all Judea with garrisons and returned to Antioch. The land then had rest for two years, when the apostate Jews again stirred up the anger of Demetrius with their stories, and Bacchides was dispatched a second time to take Jonathan prisoner. Jonathan retired to the city of Bethagla, in the wilderness, which he strongly fortified. Here he was besieged by Bacchides, but, leaving part of his army under Simon to guard the defenses, he made a night sally and attacked the Syrians in the rear. When the Syrian general saw that he was attacked from behind, he was greatly troubled, and determined to raise the siege in as decent a manner as possible. This came to the ears of Jonathan, and he sent ambassadors to Bacchides offering to make a league with him. This offer was accepted, and the Syrians withdrew.

3. **Jonathan made governor by Demetrius.** In the 160th year of the Selucidæ, Alexander, son of Antiochus Epiphanes, revolted against Demetrius, who was out of favor with his people because of his insolent and indolent habits. As a stroke of policy, Demetrius appointed Jonathan governor of Judea and authorized him to raise an army. This Jonathan did, and freed the Jewish captives and restored the city to its former splendor.

4. **Jonathan accepts the offer of Alexander Balas.** But no sooner did Alexander discover what Demetrius had done than he wrote to Jonathan and offered him the high-priesthood if he would assist him. This offer Jonathan accepted and put on the purple robe which Alexander sent him. In the struggle which

ensued, Demetrius was slain, after which Alexander honored Jonathan in a most extraordinary manner and "set him down as the principal of his friends."

5. **The death of Jonathan.** Following this, Jonathan received additional honors from Demetrius, the successor of Alexander, and also from Trypho, Demetrius' successor, but was finally taken captive and slain by the treachery of the latter.

IV. SIMON MACCABEUS

(143-135 B. C.)

1. **Simon becomes leader of his people.** Jonathan was kept a prisoner sometime before his life was taken, and when the Jews heard of it, they were greatly cast down, but Simon, the brother of Jonathan, inspired them with words of encouragement and was received as the general of their army.

2. **Trypho invades Judea.** Simon set at once to strengthen the fortifications of Jerusalem. Hardly was this done, when Trypho left Ptolemais and entered the land, bringing Jonathan with him. Simon went out to meet him, and Trypho proposed that if he would send him one hundred talents of silver and two of Jonathan's sons as hostages, he would permit Jonathan to go free. Fully knowing the treachery of Trypho, the Jews consented to this, but no sooner were the sons of Jonathan and the money in his possession than he broke his word and made ready to attack Jerusalem. This attack was prevented by a snowstorm, and Trypho returned into Cœlesyria, afterwards going into the land of Gilead, where he took Jonathan's life.

THE MACCABEAN PERIOD

3. Simon made high priest. Following the death of Jonathan, Simon was made high priest in his place. He took the cities of Gazara, Joppa and Jamnia and razed to the ground the citadel of Jerusalem, which had been used as a rendezvous by the Jews' enemies. Under him the people were prosperous and happy.

4. Simon makes an alliance with Antiochus Pius. Antiochus Pius, brother of Demetrius, came against Trypho and, after a number of battles, drove him out of upper Syria. Antiochus then sent ambassadors to Simon, proposing an alliance. This proposal Simon readily accepted and sent supplies to him as he was besieging Dora in Phœnicia. During this siege Trypho was taken prisoner and put to death.

5. The injustice and defeat of Antiochus. But Antiochus very soon forgot the kind assistance of Simon and sent an army to invade Judea and seize the Maccabee. When Simon learned that Antiochus had broken the league, he gathered his forces together and stationed them in ambush in the valleys, and so defeated his enemies and turned them back. During the last days of his life he lived in peace and also made a league with the Romans. He was treacherously murdered by his son-in-law, Ptolemy.

V. JOHN HYRCANUS

(135-105 B. C.)

1. John Hyrcanus ejects Ptolemy from the country. The first act of John Hyrcanus, after he had received the high-priesthood, was to drive Ptolemy, his brother-in-law and the slayer of his father, from the country. Ptolemy took refuge with Zeno, the tyrant of the city of Philadelphia.

2. **The invasion of Antiochus Pius.** Antiochus, being very uneasy at the miseries that Simon had brought upon him, invaded Judea in the first year of Hyrcanus and shut the Maccabee up in the city of Jerusalem. However, when the Feast of Tabernacles was at hand, he agreed to a truce of seven days and also sent in, as sacrifices, bulls with gilded horns and all sorts of sweet spices, besides cups of gold and silver. Following this, the two generals entered into an engagement, and Antiochus broke up the siege and departed.

3. **Hyrcanus subdues the surrounding nations.** When Hyrcanus learned of the death of Antiochus, who was slain in a battle with Arsaces, king of Parthia, he led an expedition against the cities of Syria and took Medaba, Samega and neighboring places; also Shechem and Gerizim of the Samaritans. In addition to these, he likewise took Dora and Marissa, cities of the Idumeans, and subdued them, but permitted the inhabitants to remain in their own country upon condition that they would adopt the ordinance of circumcision and observe the law of the Jews; conditions which they gladly accepted.

4. **Hyrcanus makes a league with Rome.** Being desirous of renewing the league of friendship that his father had made with Rome, Hyrcanus sent an embassage to the senate of that country, requesting that the present peace be continued. The Romans considered the epistle and, assenting to the proposition, gave the ambassadors money to pay their expenses home.

THE MACCABEAN PERIOD

5. **Hyrcanus takes Samaria.** At this time Antiochus Grypus and Antiochus Cyzicenus, half-brothers, were contending for the throne of Syria, and Hyrcanus, taking advantage of the weakened condition of that kingdom, attacked Samaria and besieged it. Although they received some assistance from Antiochus Cyzicenus, the Samaritans were forced, after a year's besiegement, to capitulate.

6. **Hyrcanus becomes a Sadducee.** Notwithstanding the highly peaceful and prosperous conditions that prevailed, internal dissensions arose to mar the internal harmony of the Jewish state. Hyrcanus was at first a Pharisee, but he afterwards fell away from the Pharisee party and became a Sadducee. This caused no little envy and strife, and lost for Hyrcanus the popularity of that part of the Jewish people who not only held to the law of Moses, but also to those traditions that had come down from their forefathers. Hyrcanus, however, successfully put an end to this sedition and, unlike his predecessors, died a peaceful and natural death.

VI. ARISTOBULUS I.

(105-104 B. C.)

Aristobulus was the eldest son of John Hyrcanus and was a man of inordinate ambition and murderous disposition. He aspired to change the government into a kingdom, that he might wear the crown. He imprisoned all of his brothers, excepting Antigonus, who for a time he seemed very much attached to, but who afterwards he caused through a plot to be slain. He also shut up his mother in prison, where she was so poorly fed that she starved to death. He added certain provinces of Iturea to Judea and compelled the inhabitants to adopt the Jewish faith. He died in great agony, bitterly repenting his inhuman deeds.

VII. ALEXANDER JANNEUS
(104-78 B. C.)

1. **Alexander Janneus succeeds Aristobulus.** After the death of Aristobulus, Salome (called Alexandra by the Greeks), his wife, released his brethren from prison and made Alexander Janneus king. Alexander began his reign by slaying one of his brethren who aspired to the throne.

2. **Alexander attacks Ptolemais.** Having settled the affairs of his kingdom, Alexander led an expedition against the city of Ptolemais and besieged it. As the two aspirants for the Syrian throne were at war with each other, the only hope of the inhabitants of that place was in Ptolemy Lathyrus, who had been driven from the government of Egypt by his mother, Cleopatra, and who was then in Cyprus. Upon receiving the invitation of the inhabitants of Ptolemais to come to their assistance, Ptolemy took an army of thirty thousand, crossed the sea and, landing upon the Syrian shore, pitched near Ptolemais, at which Alexander raised the siege and retired.

3. **Alexander defeated by Ptolemy.** Alexander then resorted to stratagem, and, while he openly pretended to desire a league of friendship with Ptolemy, he secretly invited Cleopatra to come against him. This becoming known to Ptolemy, he took part of his force and invaded Judea. After taking a number of

cities, he met Alexander at a place called Saphoth, near the Jordan, where he defeated him and routed his army with great slaughter. He then overran the whole country, putting the people to death with the most shocking barbarities.

4. Cleopatra checks the course of Ptolemy. But when Cleopatra learned of the success of her son, she became fearful lest he should come and wrest the government of Egypt from her. So, gathering an army, she marched against him. But Ptolemy evaded her and invaded Egypt, yet he failed of his avowed purpose of taking that country and was subsequently driven out by an army that Cleopatra sent against him.

5. The Jews despise Alexander. Alexander was very unpopular with his own people, and, at a festival which was celebrated in Jerusalem, they pelted him with citrons as he stood by the altar and reviled him with being the son of a captive, which so enraged him that he slew about six thousand of them. He then led expeditions against the Moabites, Gileadites and Arabians, and upon his return desired that his people should desist from their illwill toward him. But they hated him the more, and, when he asked them what he ought to do, they replied "that he ought to kill himself."

6. Alexander's change of fortune. So despicable was Alexander in the eyes of his own countrymen that they invited Demetrius Eucerus to come to their assistance. In the battle which ensued, Alexander was defeated and fled to the mountains, but, as six thousand Jews who had been with Demetrius deserted him and flocked to the standard of Alexander,

Demetrius fled from the country, whereupon these Jews turned upon Alexander, but were severely beaten, after which he returned to Jerusalem, where he barbarously had eight hundred of them crucified. His barbarity won for him the name of "The Thracian" among his people.

7. The death of Alexander Janneus. Alexander at last died from a distemper brought on by hard drinking, after advising his queen, Alexandra, to turn over to the Pharisee party, which he had so bitterly opposed and which had brought so much dishonor upon him.

VII. ALEXANDRA
(78-69 B. C.)

Alexandra did as her husband had counseled her and threw in her fortunes with the Pharisees. She made her eldest son, Hyrcanus, high priest, while Aristobulus, the younger, became the commander of her army. During her entire reign of nine years she showed remarkable ability in the affairs of government, yet she left her own house in such a demoralized condition that after her death it entirely lost the authority.

VIII. ARISTOBULUS II.
(69-63 B. C.)

1. Hyrcanus surrenders to Aristobulus. After the death of Alexandra, Aristobulus made war against his brother Hyrcanus, and defeated him in a battle fought at Jericho. Then Hyrcanus fled to the citadel in Jerusalem, from which he sent messengers to his brother offering to withdraw all claim to the throne

THE MACCABEAN PERIOD

and to retire to private life. This offer was accepted.

2. Hyrcanus makes an alliance with Aretas, king of Arabia. But, through the advice of Antipater the Idumean, Hyrcanus, supposing his life in danger, fled to Aretas, king of Arabia, whom he secured to assist him in deposing Aristobulus upon the condition that he restore to the Arabians the cities which his father had taken. In the struggle that ensued, Hyrcanus was supported by the mass of the people, while the priests alone remained faithful to Aristobulus. Observing this, Aristobulus fled to Jerusalem, where he was besieged by the allied armies.

3. Scaurus raises the siege and Judea becomes a Roman province. At this time Scaurus, the Roman general, was waging war in Syria, and both Hyrcanus and Aristobulus sent ambassadors to him asking for his assistance. Scaurus accepted the offer made by Aristobulus, because he was richer than Hyrcanus, and, raising the siege, ordered Aretas to return home or to be declared the enemy of Rome. After Scaurus had returned to Syria, Aristobulus attacked the combined forces of Hyrcanus and Aretas and defeated them with great slaughter. Later, Pompey took Jerusalem, made Judea a dependency of Syria, appointed Hyrcanus ethnarch and high priest, and carried Aristobulus and his two sons and two daughters captives to Rome (63 B. C.).

QUESTIONS

Who were the Maccabees? Bound, chronologically, the period of Maccabean independence. Give the proper name of this family. How many of the Maccabees were there? Give the name of the only woman who ruled during this period. Give the

THE GIST OF THE BIBLE

cause of the Maccabean revolt. Who was the king of Syria at this time? Who was the first Maccabee? What position did he hold? Where did he live? How many sons did he have? On what day did the Syrians make their first attack? Why did not the Jews defend themselves on that day? Who succeeded Mattathias? Tell about his victories. What did Judas do to the Temple. Tell about the death of Antiochus Epiphanes. Where was Judas Maccabeus slain? Who succeeded Judas Maccabeus? By whom was Jonathan slain? Who succeeded Jonathan? Who murdered Simon? Who was John Hyrcanus? What religious change did Hyrcanus make toward the close of his life? What was the character of Aristobulus? What relation was Alexander Janneus to Aristobulus? With what deposed Egyptian king did Alexander carry on warfare? Give the name of the mother of this king. How did the Jews feel toward Alexander Janneus? How did he die? What advice did he give his queen just before his death? How long did Alexandra reign? What was her character? Give the names of her two sons. What position did Hyrcanus fill? What position did Aristobulus fill? What did the sons do after her death? With what king did Hyrcanus make a league? What Roman general raised the siege of Jerusalem? To what Roman was Jerusalem afterwards surrendered? What did Judea then become? In what year did this occur?

STUDY XXX. THE ROMAN PERIOD
INTRODUCTION

1. **The ancient races of Italy.** The first races (of whom we have any account) to inhabit Italy were the Gauls, Etruscans, Iapygians and Italians proper. The Gauls inhabited the northern part; the Etruscans and Italians, the central part, and the Iapygians, the southern part.

2. **The tradition of the founding of Rome.** Rome is said to have been founded by Romulus in the year 753 B. C. This character, with his twin-brother, Remus, are declared to have been the sons of the god Mars and the vestal Rhea. By the command of the tyrant Amulius, they were exposed in the Tiber, but were suckled by a she-wolf and were fed by a woodpecker till found by a shepherd, Faustulus. When the brothers reached young manhood, they determined to build a city, and, in the quarrel which ensued over its location, Remus was killed and Romulus founded Rome where it now stands.

3. **The Roman period.** The period of Roman history falls between the year 753 B. C., the date of the establishment of the Roman kingdom, and 476 A. D., the date of the overthrow of Rome by Odoacer the Herulian. It naturally falls into three divisions: That of the kingdom (753-510 B. C.), that of the republic (510-27 B. C.) and that of the empire (27 B. C.-476 A. D.).

THE GIST OF THE BIBLE

I. ROMAN HISTORY

1. **Rome as a kingdom.** Tradition gives the names of seven kings who reigned during the first period of Roman history, but great obscurity shrouds the greater part of this epoch.

2. **The contest between the Patricians and the Plebeians.** Roman citizenship was from the earliest times divided into two classes, the Patricians and the Plebeians. To the former belonged all magisterial offices, all the higher degrees of the priesthood and the right of using a family name, while the latter, though free and personally independent, were wholly destitute of political importance. During the reign of the fifth king of Rome, Servius Tullius, called "King of the Commons," the Plebeians were given a share in the government, but under the seventh king, Tarquinius Superbus, an attempt was made to undo this reform, which brought on a civil strife and resulted in the overthrow of the kingdom and the establishment of a republic. The struggle between these two classes continued for nearly four centuries, until 367 B. C., when the Plebeians won the victory and political equality was established.

3. **The early wars of the republic.** During the early years of the republic, wars were carried on with the Etruscans, Sabines and other neighboring nations. In these wars Rome lost a considerable part of her dominion.

4. **The Gaulish invasion.** About the year 390 B. C. the Gauls, under Brennus, pressed southward from northern Italy, defeated the Romans on the Allia and, having burned the city, besieged the

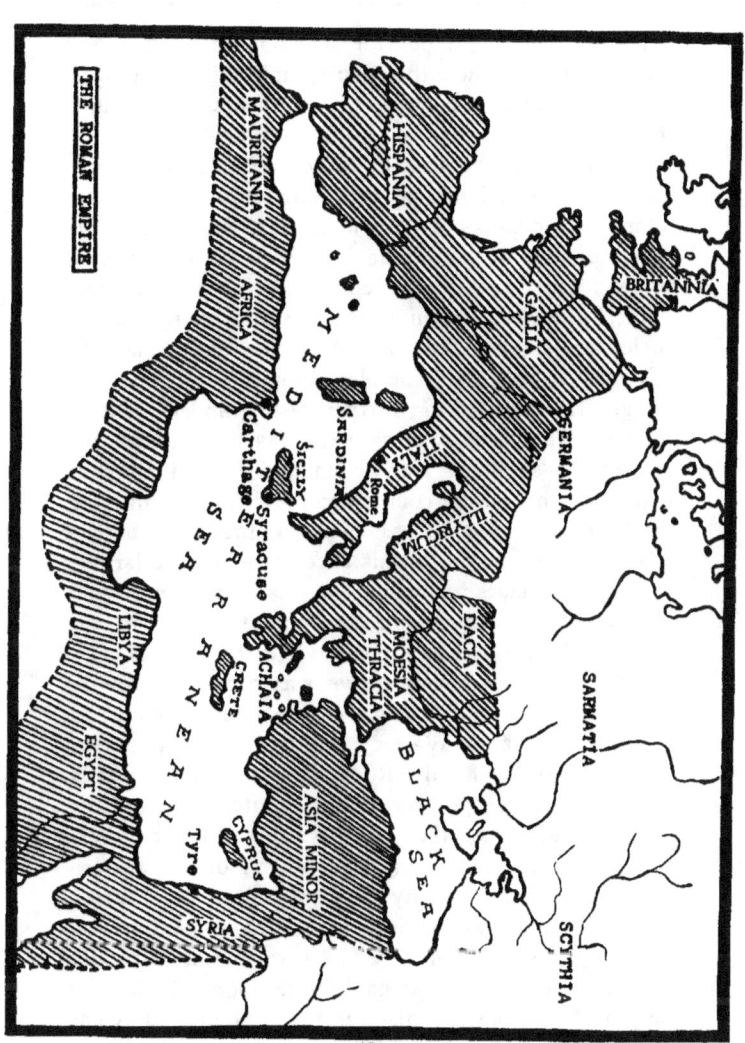

Capitol. This held out for seven months, upon the expiration of which the Gauls, tired of the conflict, agreed to retire upon receipt of a thousand pounds of gold.

5. **Wars of conquest in Italy.** At this time Rome was but a small nation, including only a few townships on the banks of the Tiber. But, with the settlement of her internal strife in 367 B. C., she entered upon a new era, one of conquest. In the struggle which followed, and in which she met on the battlefield the Latins, the Samnites, the Gauls and the Greeks, Rome was completely successful and the stage was cleared for further and grander achievements. The chief of these wars was that against the Greeks of southern Italy, who had invited Pyrrhus over from his native country to repel the "conquering barbarians of the Tiber." In the first two battles Pyrrhus was successful, his success being due largely to the elephants of which he made use and with which the Romans were unacquainted, but in the third and last he was signally defeated (275 B. C.). By 266 B. C. the Roman power was supreme throughout the length and breadth of the Italian peninsula.

6. **The Punic Wars.** Having subjugated the various nations of Italy, Rome now turned her greedy eyes upon those powers whose territory lay outside of the confines of that country. At this time Carthage was the leading maritime power of the western Mediterranean. A body of Campanian mercenaries, called Mamertines, having seized the town of Messana on the Sicilian Straits, were threatened with destruction by the Carthaginians, upon which they appealed to Rome. This was the pretext that Rome

THE ROMAN PERIOD

desired, and brought on the conflict which is known as the First Punic War. It continued for twenty-three years (264-241 B. C.) and ended with victory for the Romans. In the Second Punic War the first commander of the Carthaginians was Hamilcar. He began the campaign by subduing Spain and making it the basis of his operations against the Romans. Falling in battle, Hamilcar was succeeded by his son-in-law, Hasdrubal, and, upon his assassination, he was followed by Hannibal. This commander performed one of the greatest military feats known to history, for, successfully leading his army across the Alps, he poured it down upon the plains of Italy, where he defeated the Romans in battle after battle. It is probable that he would have conquered the entire country had it not been that a young Roman general, Scipio, entered Spain and cut off his reinforcements. Scipio then crossed into Africa and defeated the Carthaginians in so many battles that Hannibal was recalled to defend Carthage, and so ended the Second Punic War. In the Third Punic War, which followed the second after an interval of fifty years, Carthage was taken after a four years' siege and the Carthaginians became the submissive subjects of Rome.

7. **The agrarian struggle.** In the latter half of the second century B. C. the Romans had again become divided into two social classes—the rich and the poor, or the grandees and the paupers. The latter were very much oppressed and suffered untold hardships. This roused the noble young tribune, Tiberius Gracchus, grandson of Scipio Africanus, and he proposed a land law by which the amount of

public land owned by one individual could not be more than five hundred jugera,¹ and provided that the remainder should be divided into small homesteads and distributed among the poorer class. But this measure was strongly opposed by the aristocracy and was vetoed by the colleague of Tiberius, Octavius. Tiberius then secured the expulsion of Octavius by popular vote and the land law was passed by the people B. C. 133. In the meantime, however, Tiberius' year of office expired and he was violently slain by the nobles to prevent his re-election. His death, however, did not render null the law, and the commissioners intrusted with the task set about allotting the lands, although constantly opposed by the aristocracy. After ten years, Caius, the brother of Tiberius, took up the work of reform, but the nobles attacked him and his followers, slew a number of them, and Caius was forced to flee into a wood across the Tiber. Rather than fall into the hands of his enemies, he chose to die there by the hands of a faithful slave.

8. The Mithridatic War. Mithridates, king of Pontus, was a bold and able warrior and an inveterate foe of Rome. He conceived the design of uniting the Asiatic states and Greece into a vast confederacy to check her rising power. To begin with, he caused the massacre of eighty thousand Romans, who dwelt in the cities of Asia Minor, in one day (88 B. C.), after which he invaded Greece. In the struggle which ensued, he was overwhelmingly defeated by Sulla, the Roman commander.

---

¹ A *juger* was a Roman measure of land, 240x120 feet in dimensions.

9. **The struggle between Marius and Sulla.** After the death of the Gracchi, the Romans were divided into two parties, the nobles under the leadership of Sulla and the Commons under the leadership of Marius. When Sulla was given command of the Roman army in the Mithridatic War, the jealousy of Marius was aroused and he succeeded in having the popular party set Sulla aside. But Sulla marched to Rome and compelled Marius to flee to Africa, after which he entered upon his campaign. During his absence, however, Marius returned (86 B. C.) and deluged the city with the blood of his enemies. He then caused himself to be proclaimed consul, but a fortnight later died. Notwithstanding his death, the party of Marius continued in power, and, when Sulla heard of it, he hastily concluded a peace with Mithridates and returned home. Upon reaching Rome, he utterly overthrew the Marians and the city was a second time deluged in blood. He then had himself proclaimed dictator for an unlimited time (81 B. C.), but, after holding this office for three years, he resigned and retired to private life.

10. **The Roman parties.** After the death of Sulla (78 B. C.) the Roman people were divided into four distinct parties—the oligarchical, the aristocratic, the Marian and the military. The oligarchical party was composed of a small number of families, the chiefs of which controlled the senate and thus governed the republic. The aristocratic party was made up of the mass of the senators anxious to obtain the power usurped by a few of their colleagues. The Marians included all those who had been persecuted by Sulla and who were now ambitious of obtaining

power. And the military embraced a number of old Roman officers who were eager for a revolution in order that they might retrieve their squandered fortunes. The leader of the first was the orator Marcus Tullius Cicero, of the second was Crassus, of the third was Julius Cæsar, and of the fourth was Cataline.

11. **The Cataline conspiracy.** Cataline had been one of the ablest of the generals of Sulla. Being defeated for the consulship by Cicero, he became enraged and laid a plot both to kill the orator and burn Rome. This plot was, however, revealed by a woman, and Cicero denounced him with such fiery eloquence that he was forced to flee from the city. In his attempt to reach Gaul he was overtaken and slain in Etruria (62 B. C.).

12. **Julius Cæsar.** From now on the history of Rome is largely interwoven with the history of one man—Julius Cæsar. He was a nephew of Marius, of Patrician birth, but took up the cause of the Commons to serve his own ends. One of his first public acts was the formation of the celebrated "First Triumvirate," in which he, Pompey and Crassus were colleagues. In 59 B. C. he was elected to the consulship, and from 58 to 50 B. C. carried on his celebrated eight campaigns in Gaul. During his absence Crassus was assassinated in Parthia, and this reduced the triumvirate to a duumvirate. For some time there had been a growing coldness between the remaining two, and this developed into an open rupture when Cæsar announced his intentions of running for the consulship. Pompey resented this, and Cæsar crossed the Rubicon (49 B. C.) and soon made himself mas-

THE ROMAN PERIOD

ter of Italy. Pompey retired to the east, where he collected a great army in Thessaly. With this he met Cæsar at Pharsalia (48 B. C.), where he was decisively defeated. He was later assassinated in Egypt. Cæsar next became enamored of Cleopatra, the fascinating queen of Egypt, and became mixed up in the quarrel between her and her brother-husband, Ptolemy. In the struggle that ensued, Cæsar was successful, Ptolemy was slain and Cleopatra was placed upon the throne, but the celebrated library of Alexandria was accidentally destroyed. Following this, Cæsar defeated the Pompeian forces in both Africa and Spain, and by so doing made himself complete master of Rome. He was now given the title of "Imperator" for life and ruled with moderation and good judgment. But, exciting the jealousy of rivals, he was finally assassinated in a plot laid by Caius Cassius and Marcus Junius Brutus (March 15, B. C. 44).

13. **Cæsar's successors.** Immediately following the death of Cæsar, rival claimants arose aspiring to his position. In the war that ensued, Brutus and Cassius, with the republican army, were totally defeated by Antony and Octavius at Philippi (42 B. C.), and both of the defeated generals killed themselves. After this victory the Roman world was divided among three of the victors, as follows: Antony took the east, Octavius the west and Lepidus the province of Africa. But hardly had the division been made when a quarrel arose between Antony and Octavius. Antony had become deeply fascinated with the Egyptian queen, Cleopatra and divorced his own wife, Octavia, sister of Octavius, that he might

marry Cleopatra. This enraged Octavius, and he marched against Antony and severely defeated him in the battle of Actium (31 B. C.). Later, both Antony and Cleopatra committed suicide, and both Rome and Egypt passed into the hands of the Cæsars.

14. **The Roman Empire.** The Roman Empire may be said to date from 27 B. C., when Octavius was saluted with the new and peculiar title of Augustus. The history of Rome as an empire may be divided into two divisions—Rome under paganism and Rome under Christianity. The empire continued a pagan government from 27 B. C. to about 325 A. D., when, under Constantine, the state religion was changed to Christianity. It continued under Christianity from 325 A. D. to its subversion by the Goths under Odoacer in 476 A. D. In the year 395 A. D., upon the death of Theodosius, the Roman Empire was divided between his two sons, Honorius taking the west and Arcadius taking the east. It was the western empire that came to an end in 476 A. D.; the eastern continued down to the fifteenth century, when it was destroyed by the Turks.

II. ROMAN CULTURE

1. **The government of Rome.** As we have seen, Rome passed successively under three forms of government—the kingly, republican and imperial. At the beginning of the latter, when Augustus took the throne, the population of the Roman Empire is estimated as having been one hundred million, fully one-half of whom were slaves, while of the rest only a small proportion enjoyed the privileges of citizenship.

THE ROMAN PERIOD

The various lands and peoples were under military officials called legates, one-half of whom were appointed by Augustus, the other half by the senate. Peace was preserved at home by the *pretorian* cohorts, troops of tried valor under double pay, and throughout the provinces by a standing army of 350,000 men.

2. **Roman morals.** In the beginning of her history, the morals of Rome were pure, but as the centuries slipped by moral sentiment gradually waned until, at the time of Christ, her moral practices beggar description. Vices of all kinds were rampant. Licentiousness was widely spread. Sins that can not be described in plain English were condoned. Murder was common. And infanticide was resorted to by poor parents to get rid of the burden of rearing children. The iniquity of Rome during the reign of the Cæsars was black and deep.

3. **Roman amusements.** The stage, the circus and the arena afforded amusement for the Roman populace. These were employed by the emperors for the purpose of turning the attention of the people from the thought of liberty. On the stage the most vulgar and indecent plays were given. At the circus there were foot-races, horse-races and other feats of strength and skill. But it was in the arena that the Romans found their chief delight. Here hordes of criminals, prisoners of war and slaves fought in the gladiatorial contests with one another or defended themselves against the ravenous beasts that were turned loose upon them. Under Julius Cæsar, at one time, not fewer than 320 pairs of gladiators were compelled to fight. Under Augustus, ten thousand men joined in

these contests, while Trajan (106 A. D.) pitted the same number in these combats after his victories on the Danube. It would seem that Rome at the zenith of her glory was satisfied only with gross licentiousness and the shedding of blood.

4. **Roman religion.** The religion of the Romans was almost identical with that of the Greeks, and they worshiped the same gods, only under different names. These gods and goddesses were Jupiter, Neptune, Pluto, Juno, Mars, Saturn, Apollo, Diana, Mercury, Minerva and Venus. These deities were either deified heroes and heroines, or else they were the personifications of the objects, forces and phenomena of nature. As their worship conduced to the grossest immorality, the educated classes broke away from it and became skeptical, although the lower classes accepted these divinities as *bona-fide* beings.

5. **Roman literature.** Although Rome was pre-eminently a nation of warriors, she had writers who produced literary works of merit. Among her poets may be mentioned the names of Virgil, Horace, Lucretius, Catullus and Ovid, and among her historians, Sallust, Livy and Tacitus. Martial was a writer of epigrams and Juvenal was a bitter satirist. Augustus was a great patron of literary men and artists, as was also his minister, Caius Cilnius Mæcenas, and the interest that they took in literature added to the glories of the "Augustan Age."

6. **Roman art.** The structures of Rome were noted for their solidity and strength as well as their beauty. Although she had been a splendid city before the "Augustan Age," Rome became more splendid under the labors of that emperor. It was

THE ROMAN PERIOD

Augustus' boast that "he found the city brick and left it marble." The walls of Rome were twenty miles in length and were pierced with thirty gates. Her most remarkable structures were the Coliseum, the Capitol with its temples, the Senate-house and the Forum. The Coliseum was an immense amphitheater, with a seating capacity of one hundred thousand spectators. Here is where the gladiatorial contests took place. The Forum was the place of public assembly. It was surrounded with temples, halls of justice and public offices, and was adorned with statues erected in honor of eminent warriors and statesmen. The aqueducts were among the most remarkable of Rome's architectural works. Fully twenty of them were constructed by the emperors and brought pure water from a distance into the city. At the zenith of her glory, Rome is said to have contained 420 temples, five regular theaters, two amphitheaters, seven circuses of vast extent, and sixteen public baths, besides palaces, public halls, columns and porticoes.

QUESTIONS

Name the four ancient races of Italy. Give the tradition of the founding of Rome. In what year was Rome founded? When did Rome finally fall? Locate chronologically the three periods of her history. How many kings reigned in Rome during her first period? Who were the Patricians and the Plebeians? With what nations did Rome fight during the early part of her history? When did the Gauls invade Roman territory? Who was their leader? With what nations did Rome fight in her conquest of Italy? Who was Pyrrhus? In what year was Roman power supreme in the peninsula? What were the Punic Wars? How many of them were there? Who were the commanders of the Carthaginian and Roman forces in the second?

THE GIST OF THE BIBLE

What was the agrarian struggle? Who were the Gracchi? Who won the victory in this struggle? Tell about the Mithridatic War. Tell about the struggle between Sulla and Marius. Into how many parties was Roman citizenship divided after the death of Sulla? Name them and their leaders. Tell about the Cataline conspiracy. Give a brief account of Julius Cæsar. What two men headed the conspiracy which took his life? When was he assassinated? Give the names of his successors. What happened to Cassius and Brutus? What difficulty arose between Antony and Octavius? Where was Antony defeated, and when? What happened, finally, to Antony and Cleopatra? When did the Roman Empire commence? Into what two divisions may we divide the history of the Roman Empire? Give the dates that begin and end each. When was the Roman Empire divided? When did western Rome fall? When did eastern Rome fall? Describe the government of Rome. Tell about the morals of Rome. Describe the amusements of Rome. Give a description of the Roman religion. Tell about Roman literature. What can you say about Roman art?

PART IV. NEW TESTAMENT HISTORY

Study XXXI. The Period of Preparation.
Study XXXII. The Beginnings of Christ's Ministry.
Study XXXIII. The Great Galilean Ministry.
Study XXXIV. The Period of Retirement.
Study XXXV. The Closing of Christ's Ministry.
Study XXXVI. The Last Week.
Study XXXVII. The Resurrection Days.
Study XXXVIII. The Beginnings of the Church.
Study XXXIX. The Life of Paul.
Study XL. The New Testament Writings.

STUDY XXXI. THE PERIOD OF PREPARATION

INTRODUCTION

1. **The pre-existence of Jesus Christ.** The existence of the Son of God did not begin with his birth. He was with the Father in the beginning and was His agent in the creation of the world. This doctrine is plainly taught in John 1:1-14; 17:5; Phil. 2:5-8; Col. 1:16, 17; Heb. 1:2, and many other passages. The incarnation, by which the pre-existent Word became flesh, is one of the great mysteries of the Christian faith.[1]

2. **The Messianic expectation.** The expectation of a Messiah[2] was not alone confined to the Jews, but was also shared by the surrounding pagan nations. Suetonius, the celebrated Roman historian, says: "An

---

[1] "The names Jesus, Christ or Messiah, Only Begotten Son, Son of God, belong to the Founder of the Christian religion, and to none else. They express not a relation existing before the Christian era, but relations which commenced at that time. To understand the relation betwixt the Saviour and his Father, which existed before time, and that relation which began in time is impossible on either of these theories (Trinitarian, Arian and Socinian). There was no Jesus, no Messiah, no Christ, no Son of God, no Only Begotten, before the reign of Augustus Cæsar. The relation that was before the Christian era was not that of a son and a father, terms which always imply disparity; but it was that expressed by John in the sentence under consideration. The relation was that of God and the 'word of God.' This phraseology unfolds a relation quite different from that of a father and a son—a relation perfectly intimate, equal and glorious."
—*Alexander Campbell, in "Christian Baptist," pp. 333, 334.*

[2] The term "Messiah," in the Hebrew, as does also the word "Christ," which is from the Greek *Christos*, means "The Anointed One."

ancient and settled persuasion prevailed throughout the East that the Fates had decreed some one to proceed from Judea who should attain universal empire." And Tacitus, another Roman historian, says: "Many were persuaded that it was contained in the ancient books of their priests that at that very time the East should prevail and that some one should proceed from Judea and possess the dominion."

3. **The time of Christ's birth.** According to our chronology, Jesus was born in the year 1 B. C. But it is now known that this is a mistake and that he was born four years before the beginning of our era. Jamieson, Fausset and Brown, in their "Commentary," say: "As Herod is known to have died in the year of Rome 750, in the fourth year before the commencement of our Christian era, the birth of Christ must be dated four years before the date usually assigned to it." Whether or not He was born on December 25 is a much-discussed question and one upon which we have no certain information.

4. **Palestine in the time of Christ.** In the time of Christ, the population of the Holy Land is estimated to have been about three million, of whom two hundred thousand[1] were found in the city of

---

[1] The population of Palestine, as given, is only conjectural. According to Josephus, there were 2,500,000 Jews assembled at the last Passover just before the city was taken by Titus. Of this number, 1,100,000 perished in the siege, while 347,000 perished in other places. Of the remainder, 97,000 were carried into captivity, while 11,000 more starved through neglect or sullen refusal of food. Making all due allowances for exaggeration, it may not be out of the way very far to put the population of Palestine in the time of Christ at about 3,000,000. For the population of Jerusalem, as given, see Edersheim's "Life and Times of Jesus the Messiah," Vol. I., p. 116, where the author says: "Its population, computed at from 200,000 to 250,000, was enormously swelled by travelers, and by pilgrims during the great festivals."

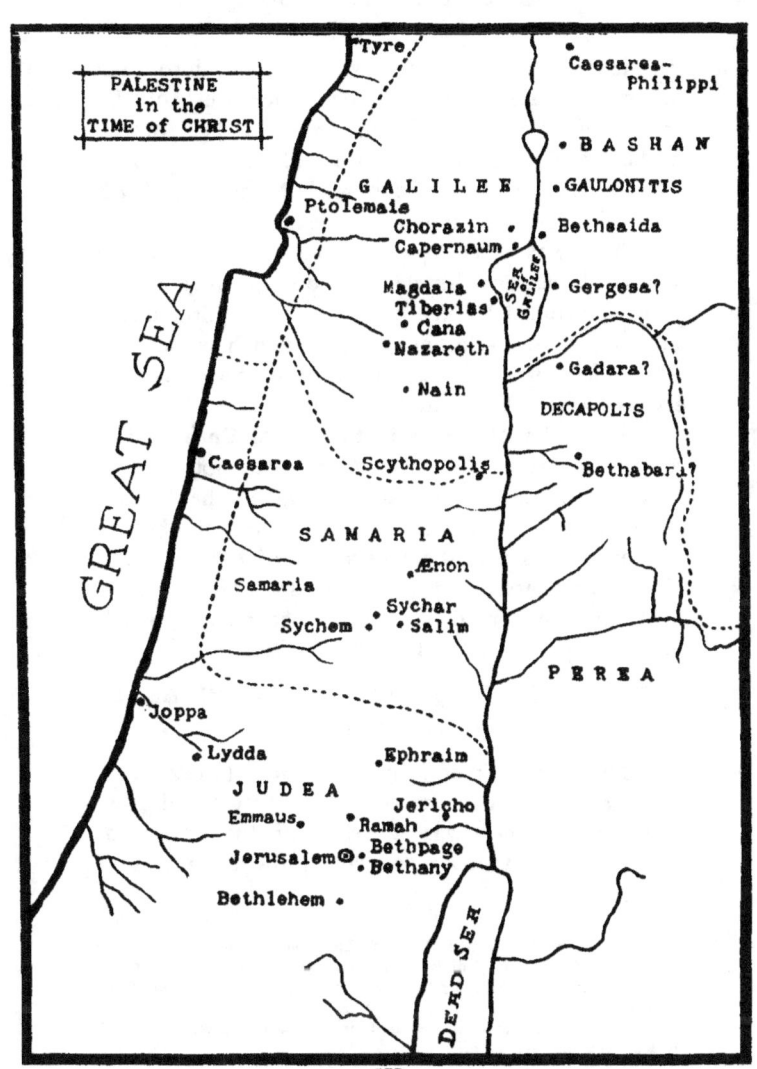

Jerusalem. The territory was divided into five provinces: Judea, Samaria and Galilee west of the Jordan, and Perea and Bashan east of the Jordan. At the birth of Christ this was all under the rule of Herod the Great, an Edomite, but upon his death it was divided into four tetrarchies. One of these tetrarchies was ruled by Archelaus, and comprised Samaria, Judea and Idumea. Another, under Herod Antipas, included Galilee and Perea. A third, under Philip II., took in Bashan. And a fourth, which fell to the lot of Lysanias, comprised the territory between Mount Hor and Damascus.

5. **The order of events in the life of Christ.** The order of events in the life of Christ can not be definitely determined. John alone supplies the history of the first year of His ministry. As for the remainder of His life, the true order of events, probably, is best preserved in the Gospel of Luke, although he omits many important occurrences which must be supplied from the other writers.[1]

I. THE PERIOD OF PREPARATION AS IT CONCERNS JOHN

1. **The parentage of John the Baptist** (Luke 1:5). John the Baptist was the son of Zacharias and Elisabeth. His father was a priest of the course of Abia,[2] and his mother also was of the daughters of Aaron.

---

[1] In the preparation of the "Studies" upon the life of Christ, I have largely followed the general divisions and the order of events as given in "A Harmony of the Gospels," by Dr. J. A. Broadus, to which I acknowledge my indebtedness.

[2] This was the eighth of the twenty-four orders, or courses, into which David divided the priesthood.

THE PERIOD OF PREPARATION

2. **The annunciation of John's birth** (Luke 1:6-25). Zacharias and Elisabeth were both righteous before God, but they were well advanced in years and had no child. As Zacharias was officiating in the Temple, burning incense, the angel Gabriel[1] appeared to him and told him not to fear; that a son should be born to him whom he should call John; that he should drink no wine nor strong drink from his birth,[2] and that he should go before the face of the Lord in the spirit and power of Elijah. Zacharias doubted and demanded a sign, whereupon the angel said that, as a sign, he should be dumb until the child's birth. At these words Zacharias lost the power of speech and did not utter a word until after John was born.

3. **Mary visits Elisabeth** (Luke 1:39-56). In those days Mary went into the hill-country to the city of Judah, where Zacharias and Elisabeth lived, and, entering the house, saluted Elisabeth. When Elisabeth saw Mary, the Spirit of the Lord rested upon her and she exclaimed: "Blessed art thou among women, and blessed is the fruit of thy womb. And whence is this to me, that the mother of my Lord should come to me?" Mary replied to this salutation by declaring that her soul magnified the Lord; that He had looked upon her low estate, and that He had done great things. She abode three months with Elisabeth and then returned to her home.

4. **The birth of John the Baptist** (Luke 1:57-80).

---
[1] In the ordinary traditions, both Jewish and Christian, Gabriel is spoken of as one of the archangels.
[2] John was a Nazarite, the vow of which order is found in Numbers 6.

When the time was fulfilled, John the Baptist was born amidst the rejoicing of Elisabeth's neighbors and kinsfolk. On the eighth day they came to circumcise him and would have called his name Zacharias, but his mother insisted that he be called John. This was objected to as none of her kindred were called by that name, but when by signs his father was asked for a name, he gave the same. Then Zacharias received his speech, was filled with the Holy Spirit and began to prophesy to the astonishment of all present.

5. **The preaching of John the Baptist** (Matt. 3: 1-12; Mark 1:1-8; Luke 3:1-18). In the fifteenth year of the reign of Tiberius Cæsar (probably A. D. 25 or 26), the word of the Lord came to John and he began to preach in the wilderness of Judea the baptism of repentance for the remission of sins, saying that, while he baptized in water, there was to come one after him, mightier than he, who was to baptize with the Holy Spirit and with fire. John was clothed in a garment of camel's hair and his food was locusts[1] and wild honey. Great multitudes flocked to his baptism from Jerusalem and Judea and were baptized of him in Jordan, confessing their sins.[2]

6. **John baptizes Jesus** (Matt. 3:13-17; Mark 1: 9-11; Luke 3:21, 22). Among the multitude who came to John for baptism was Jesus. At first John objected, but when Jesus insisted that it be done to fulfill all righteousness, he consented.

---

[1] The locusts of Palestine were similar to our grasshoppers. Four of the seven or more species were allowed by the Mosaic law to be eaten.

[2] As those who were baptized by John in Jordan confessed their sins, his baptism must have been adult baptism. The so-called baptism of children is a practice unknown to the word of God.

THE PERIOD OF PREPARATION

7. **John's testimony to Jesus** (John 1:19-34; 3: 22-36). After His baptism, Jesus retired into the wilderness of Judea, where He was tempted of the devil for forty days, at the expiration of which time He returned to where John was baptizing. When John saw Him, he exclaimed: "Behold the Lamb of God, which taketh away the sin of the world."

8. **The imprisonment and death of John the Baptist** (Matt. 4:12; 14:1-12; Mark 6:16-29; 9:13; Luke 3:18-20). After this John was put in prison by Herod the tetrarch, at the instigation of Herodias, his brother Philip's wife, because he had said that it was unlawful for Herod to have her. At the celebration of Herod's birthday, Salome, Herodias' daughter, danced before him and so pleased him that he promised to give her whatsoever she should ask, even unto the half of his kingdom. Her mother told her to ask for the head of John the Baptist. Herod was greatly troubled at this request, but was held to his oath and so commanded that John be beheaded. This was done, and the head was brought in a charger to Salome, who took it to her mother. Then John's disciples buried the body and went and told Jesus.[1]

II. THE PERIOD OF PREPARATION AS IT CONCERNS JESUS

1. **The putative parents of Jesus** (Matt. 1:16). The putative parents of Jesus were Joseph, a carpenter, a descendant of David, and Mary, a virgin, a

---
[1] The death of John the Baptist did not occur until after Jesus had begun His ministry, probably just before the third Passover in the same.

daughter of Heli (**Luke 3:23**)[1] and also a descendant of David.

2. **The annunciation to Mary of the birth of Jesus** (Luke 1:26-38). Joseph and Mary lived at Nazareth in Galilee, and it was there announced to the latter by the angel Gabriel that she should miraculously bring forth a son whom she should name Jesus. He was to be called the Son of the Highest, and to Him was to be given the throne of His father David, and He was to reign over the house of Jacob forever, and of His kingdom there was to be no end.

3. **The annunciation to Joseph of the birth of Jesus** (Matt. 1:18-25). When Joseph, the husband of Mary, discovered her condition, he was minded to put her away privately, but an angel of the Lord appeared to him in a dream and said: "Joseph, thou son of David, fear not to take unto thee Mary thy wife: for that which is conceived in her is of the Holy Ghost. And she shall bring forth a son, and thou shalt call his name JESUS: for he shall save his people from their sins."[2]

4. **The birth of Jesus** (Luke 2:1-7). In those days Augustus Cæsar made a decree that the whole world should be enrolled, and Joseph, with his wife Mary, went to Bethlehem, his native city, for that purpose. While there, Jesus was born and was wrapped in swaddling-clothes[3] and was laid in a manger, because there was no room in the inn.

---

[1] In Matthew, Joseph is said to be the son of Jacob, and in Luke, the son of Heli. The latter should probably be rendered "the son-in-law of Heli," which would make this person the father of Mary.

[2] Men have become sons of God in three ways: Adam by creation, Jesus by generation, and the saints by regeneration.

[3] A piece of cloth a few inches broad and several feet long.

THE PERIOD OF PREPARATION

5. **The annunciation to the shepherds of the birth of Jesus** (Luke 2:8-20). There were shepherds in that country keeping watch over their flocks by night, and an angel of the Lord appeared to them who, as they were sore afraid, said: "Fear not: for, behold, I bring you good tidings of great joy, which shall be to all people. For unto you is born this day in the city of David a Saviour, which is Christ the Lord." Then suddenly there appeared with the angel a multitude of the heavenly host, who sang: "Glory to God in the highest, and on earth peace, good will toward men." Going into the city, the shepherds found the babe in the manger and returned glorifying God.

6. **The circumcision and presentation of Jesus** (Luke 2:21-38). On the eighth day, according to the law, Jesus was circumcised, and at the end of forty He was taken to Jerusalem and presented to the Lord in the Temple. Here Simeon, a just and devout man, who waited for the consolation of Israel and who had received the promise that he should not die until he had seen the Lord's Christ, met and blessed Him. And Anna, an aged prophetess of the tribe of Asher, when she had seen Him, also gave thanks and spoke of Him to all them that looked for redemption in Jerusalem.

7. **The visit of the Magi** (Matt. 2:1-12). Wisemen,[1] also, came from the East, guided by a star, inquiring where He could be found who was born

---

[1] These Wise-men, or Magi, were probably of the learned class who studied astrology and kindred sciences. They may have known from the prophecy of Balaam (Num. 24:17) and that of Daniel (Dan. 7:24), that the time was at hand for the Messiah to appear. Whether they came from Mesopotamia, Persia or Arabia is unknown.

King of the Jews. When this came to the ears of Herod, he was greatly troubled and, calling together the chief priests and scribes, he inquired where the Christ should be born. They replied, "In Bethlehem of Judæa." Herod then secretly called the Wise-men to him and told them that, when they had found the child, they should bring him word, that he, too, might come and worship Him. Following the star, the Wise-men were brought to where Jesus lay, but, when they had worshiped Him and had made Him presents of gold, frankincense and myrrh, being warned of God in a dream, they departed into their own country another way.

8. **The flight into Egypt** (Matt. 2:13-18). When the Wise-men had departed, an angel appeared to Joseph and told him to take the young child and His mother and flee into Egypt, as Herod would seek to destroy His life. Joseph did as he was bidden, and, after his departure, Herod slew all the male children of two years old and under, that were within the borders of Bethlehem.

9. **The return to Nazareth** (Matt. 2:19-23; Luke 2:39). After Herod's death, Joseph, by the direction of the angel, took Mary and Jesus and returned to Nazareth of Galilee.

10. **The boyhood visit to Jerusalem** (Luke 2:40-50). The parents of Jesus went to Jerusalem every year to attend the Feast of the Passover. When Jesus was twelve years of age, they went down as was their custom, but, when they returned, He remained behind. After a day's journey, His parents discovered that He was not with them and, turning back, they sought for Him in the city. At the end

THE PERIOD OF PREPARATION

of three days they found Him in the Temple hearing the doctors of the law and answering their questions. His mother reproved Him for his conduct, upon which He asked: "Wist ye not that I must be about my Father's business?"

11. **The eighteen silent years** (Luke 2:52). Of the eighteen silent years that intervened between the visit of Jesus to Jerusalem and his entrance into public life we know but little. This period is covered by these simple words: "And Jesus increased in wisdom and stature, and in favour with God and man."

12. **The baptism of Jesus** (Matt. 3:13-17; Mark 1:9-11; Luke 3:21-23). In the fifteenth year of the reign of Tiberius Cæsar, John the Baptist began his ministry in the wilderness of Judea and multitudes flocked to him to e baptized. Among them was Jesus, who came from ralilee. At first John refused, saying: "I have need t(be baptized of thee, and comest thou to me?" But, as Jesus insisted that it be done to fulfill all righteousness, John baptized Him. When Jesus came up out of the water, the Spirit as a dove descended upon Him and a voice from heaven said: "This is my beloved Son, in whom I am well pleased."

13. **The temptation of Jesus** (Matt. 4:1-11; Mark 1:12, 13; Luke 4:1-13). After his baptism, Jesus was led of the Spirit into the wilderness, where He was tempted of the devil for forty days. The temptation was threefold: to turn stones into bread, the offer of all the kingdoms of the world provided He would worship the devil, and to cast Himself down from the pinnacle of the Temple. In all of these tempta-

tions Jesus repulsed Satan, and, when he had departed, angels came and ministered unto Him.

QUESTIONS

Did the existence of Christ begin with his birth? Give some of the passages in the New Testament which plainly teach Christ's pre-existence. Was the expectation of a Messiah alone confined to the Jews? What can you say about the time of Christ's birth? Do we know for sure that he was born on December 25? Give the population of Palestine in the time of Christ. Give the population of Jerusalem. What great ruler governed Palestine at the birth of Christ? Into how many divisions was his territory divided after his death? What can you say of the order of events in the life of Christ? Give the names of the father and mother of John the Baptist. Tell about the annunciation of his birth to Zacharias. Who visited Elisabeth at this time? Give the circumstances attending the birth of John. In what year did John begin to preach? What did he preach? What did he wear and what did he eat? Who came to be baptized? Give John's testimony to Jesus. Who slew John and why? Give the names of the putative parents of Jesus. What did the angel Gabriel tell Mary? What did an angel of the Lord tell Joseph? Where was Jesus born? Tell about the visit of the shepherds. How old was Jesus when He was circumcised? How old was He when He was presented in the Temple? Give the names of two persons whom he met there. Tell about the visit of the Magi. Where did Joseph and his household flee, and why? To what city did they afterwards return? Where did Jesus go when He was twelve years old? How many years of Christ's life are called silent years, and why? In what year was Christ baptized? Give the circumstances attending His baptism. Tell about Christ's temptation.

STUDY XXXII. THE BEGINNINGS OF CHRIST'S MINISTRY

INTRODUCTION

1. **The date.** This period in the history of our Lord lay, for the most part, probably, within the year 27 A. D. It is known as the "Period of Obscurity" and lasted several months.

2. **The condition of the Jews.** At this time the Jews were restive under the rule of Rome and lived in the expectation of a coming Messiah who should deliver them from their oppressors and should establish an earthly kingdom. Their religion, however, presents many phases: the assumed and outward piety of the Pharisees; the exclusiveness and rigid morality of the Essenes; the infidelity and unbelief, in respect to a future life, on the part of the Sadducees, and the extreme worldliness and indifference to holy things which characterized the Herodians. The popularity of John's startling and revolutionary message is a clear proof that the people generally were becoming tired of these old, effete forms of faith and were ready for the new.

3. **The order of events.** The present study opens with Christ at Bethabara, beyond Jordan, where John was baptizing. From there He goes into Galilee, where, at Cana, He turns the water into wine. Then we find Him going down to Jerusalem to attend the Passover, during which He cleanses the Temple and

converses with Nicodemus. And, after a brief ministry in Judea, He returns again to Galilee, passing through Samaria, where He meets the Samaritan woman at the well of Sychar.

I. CHRIST'S MINISTRY AT BETHABARA

1. **John's testimony to Jesus** (John 1:19-34). After His temptation in the wilderness, Jesus returned to John at Bethabara. The Jews at Jerusalem had sent priests and Levites to the Baptist, asking him who he was. John denied both being the Christ and Elijah, and said: "I am the voice of one crying in the wilderness, Make straight the way of the Lord, as said the prophet Esaias." When asked why he baptized if he were not the Christ, Elijah or one of the prophets, he replied: "I baptize with water: but there standeth one among you, whom ye know not; he it is, who coming after me is preferred before me, whose shoe's latchet I am not worthy to unloose." The next day John saw Jesus coming to him and said: "Behold the Lamb of God, which taketh away the sin of the world."

2. **Jesus calls his first disciples** (John 1:35-51). The day following, John was standing with two of his disciples when Jesus passed by. John said again, "Behold the Lamb of God," and his two disciples left him and followed Jesus. Jesus turned to them and asked: "What seek ye?" They replied: "Rabbi, where dwellest thou?" Jesus answered: "Come and see." And they went with Him and abode that day. One of the two was Andrew, who went, and, finding his brother Simon Peter, said to him: "We have found the Messias." When Jesus saw Peter, He said:

THE BEGINNINGS OF CHRIST'S MINISTRY

"Thou art Simon the son of Jona: thou shalt be called Cephas, which is by interpretation, A stone." The next day Jesus decided to depart into Galilee and, finding Philip, who lived in Bethsaida, the city of Andrew and Peter, He said: "Follow me." Philip went and sought out his brother Nathanael, and said: "We have found him, of whom Moses in the law, and the prophets, did write, Jesus of Nazareth, the son of Joseph." Nathanael asked: "Can there any good thing come out of Nazareth?" Philip replied: "Come and see." When Jesus saw Nathanael coming to Him, He exclaimed: "Behold an Israelite indeed, in whom is no guile!" To which Nathanael answered: "Rabbi, thou art the Son of God; thou art the King of Israel."

II. CHRIST'S FIRST MINISTRY IN GALILEE

1. **The first miracle, at Cana** (John 2:1-11). Returning to Galilee, Jesus, with His mother and His disciples, attended a wedding at Cana. When the wine failed, His mother came to Him, saying, "They have no wine." Jesus replied: "Woman, what have I to do with thee? Mine hour is not yet come." He then commanded the servants to fill six waterpots of stone with water. When they had filled them to the brim, He commanded them to draw out and to bear to the ruler of the feast, who, when he had tasted the liquid, declared it to be good wine.

2. **The first sojourn at Capernaum** (John 2:12). After performing this miracle at Cana, Jesus, with His mother, brethren and disciples, went to Capernaum, where they continued for a short time.

THE GIST OF THE BIBLE

III. CHRIST'S FIRST MINISTRY IN JUDEA

1. **The first cleansing of the Temple** (John 2:13-22). The Passover of the Jews being at hand, Jesus went to Jerusalem to attend it. He found in the Temple those who sold oxen, sheep and doves, and with them the changers of money, and, making a scourge of cords, He drove them out, saying: "Take these things hence; make not my Father's house an house of merchandise." When the Jews required a sign of His authority for doing this, He replied, "Destroy this temple, and in three days I will raise it up," referring to His body and its resurrection.

2. **Jesus and Nicodemus** (John 2:23-3:21). There was in Jerusalem a Pharisee, Nicodemus by name, who had seen the miracles which Jesus performed and who came to Him by night, saying: "Rabbi, we know that thou art a teacher come from God: for no man can do these miracles that thou doest, except God be with him." Jesus replied to him: "Verily, verily, I say unto thee, Except a man be born again, he cannot see the kingdom of God." Nicodemus did not seem to comprehend this statement, so Jesus said further: "Verily, verily, I say unto thee, Except a man be born of water and of the Spirit, he cannot enter into the kingdom of God." The Lord then instructed Nicodemus in the purpose of His mission.

3. **Jesus preaches and baptizes in Judea** (John 3:22-36). Jesus now went into Judea with his disciples, and there he tarried and baptized.[1] At this time John was baptizing at Ænon, near to Salim, because there was much water there. A controversy

---

[1] That is, Jesus baptized through the agency of his disciples.

THE BEGINNINGS OF CHRIST'S MINISTRY

arising between the disciples of John and the Jews over purification, the former came to John, saying: "Rabbi, he that was with thee beyond Jordan, to whom thou barest witness, behold, the same baptizeth, and all men come to him." Then John denied again that he was the Christ, claiming simply that he was His forerunner, and declaring that he must decrease while Christ must increase.

IV. CHRIST'S MINISTRY IN SAMARIA

1. **Christ's reasons for leaving Judea** (Matt. 4:12; Mark 1:14; Luke 4:14; John 4:1-4). When Jesus heard that John had been delivered up and also that the Pharisees had heard that He made and baptized more disciples than John, He went into Galilee, going through Samaria.[1]

2. **Christ and the woman of Samaria** (John 4:5-42). On His way to Galilee, Jesus stopped at Jacob's well, near Sychar. While He tarried, His disciples having gone into the city to buy meat, a woman of Samaria came to the well to draw water and He asked of her a drink. The woman was surprised and asked: "How is it that thou, being a Jew, askest drink of me, which am a woman of Samaria? for the Jews have no dealings with the Samaritans." Jesus answered: "If thou knewest the gift of God, and who it is that saith to thee, Give me to drink; thou wouldest have asked of him, and he would have given thee living water." Then Jesus explained His mission and revealed the woman's sinful life so perfectly that she returned to the city and said to the

---
[1] The usual route for the strict Jew, who despised the Samaritans, was through the Jordan Valley.

people: "Come, see a man, which told me all things that ever I did." The people followed her and, when they had seen Jesus, many of them believed on Him.

3. Jesus' reception in Galilee (John 4:43-45). After two days Jesus departed into Galilee, where he was well received of the people, they having seen the miracles which He had performed at Jerusalem.

QUESTIONS

In what year did the events of this period in the life of Christ occur? What is this period called? Give the condition of the Jews at this time. Give the order of events in this period. Where was John baptizing? What did John deny being? What did he say that he was? What did he call Jesus? Give the names of the first four disciples. Which two are mentioned first? To what city did they all belong? Where was the first miracle in Galilee performed and what was it? At what city in Galilee did Jesus sojourn for a short time? Tell about the first cleansing of the Temple. Tell about the conversation with Nicodemus. Where was John baptizing at this time, and why? Tell about a controversy which arose between his disciples and the Jews. Where did Jesus baptize after the Passover? Why did Jesus leave Judea? Tell about His conversation with the woman of Samaria. How did the Galileans receive Him?

STUDY XXXIII. THE GREAT GALILEAN MINISTRY

INTRODUCTION

1. **The date.** This period probably comprised more than a year in A. D. 27 and 28. It is known as the "Period of Popularity."

2. **Galilee.** Galilee was the northernmost of the three districts of Palestine west of the Jordan. It was divided into Upper and Lower. Upper Galilee was distinctively called "Galilee of the Gentiles" from its having more of a mixed population in which Gentile blood predominated, while Lower Galilee was more distinctively Jewish. The principal city of the first was Cæsarea Philippi; of the second, the principal cities were Tiberias, Chorazin, Nazareth, Nain, Cana, Capernaum and Ptolemais. Josephus represents the Galileans as a turbulent and rebellious people, always ready to revolt against Roman authority. The Sea, or Lake, of Galilee, which plays such an important part in sacred history, is a body of water about twelve miles long by seven wide, which lies very deep among fruitful hills and mountains. Originally, the borders of this lake were well peopled, being covered with towns and villages, but to-day they are almost desolate. The water is very clear and sweet and abounds in various kinds of excellent fish.

3. **The order of events.** This study opens with

Christ in Galilee, at Cana and Nazareth. Rejected at the latter place, He goes to Capernaum, which, during the first part of this period, is the basis of His operations. He then attends the feast at Jerusalem, where He heals a palsied man at the pool of Bethesda. And later He returns to Galilee, but is not so closely confined to Capernaum in His ministrations as at the first.

I. CHRIST'S OPENING WORK IN GALILEE

1. **The general subject of Christ's teaching** (Matt. 4:17; Mark 1:14, 15; Luke 4:14, 15). From the time that Jesus entered Galilee, He preached the gospel of God, saying: "Repent: for the kingdom of heaven is at hand." And His fame spread throughout all the region round about and He was glorified of all.

2. **The healing of the nobleman's son** (John 4:46-54). Jesus came to Cana, and when a certain nobleman of Capernaum, whose son was sick, heard that He was in Galilee, he came to Him and besought Him that He might come down and heal him. The Lord said to him: "Go thy way; thy son liveth." And the nobleman returned to discover that his son had begun to recover at the very hour in which Jesus had spoken to him.

3. **The rejection at Nazareth** (Matt. 4:13-16; Luke 4:16-31). Jesus now returned to Nazareth, where He was brought up, and went into the synagogue on the sabbath day and stood up to read. There was delivered to Him the Book of Isaiah, and He opened it and read: "The Spirit of the Lord is upon me, because he hath anointed me to preach the gospel to

the poor; he hath sent me to heal the brokenhearted, to preach deliverance to the captives, and the recovering of sight to the blind, to set at liberty them that are bruised, to preach the acceptable year of the Lord." Then, closing the book, He sat down and said: "This day is this scripture fulfilled in your ears." And all who heard bore witness to His gracious words until He reproached them for not accepting Him, when they were full of wrath and, leading him out of the city, took Him to the brow of a hill that they might throw Him down headlong; but, passing through the midst of them, He escaped and came to Capernaum.

II. THE GALILEAN MINISTRY WITH CAPERNAUM AS A BASIS

1. **The calling of the fishermen** (Matt. 4:18-22; Mark 1:16-20; Luke 5:1-11). As Jesus was walking by the Sea of Galilee, He saw Simon and Andrew, his brother, casting a net into the sea, for they were fishermen. He said to them: "Follow me, and I will make you fishers of men." So, leaving all, they followed Him. Going farther, He saw James and John, with their father Zebedee, in a boat mending their nets. He called them also, and, leaving the ship and their father, they, too, followed Him.

2. **The healing of a demoniac** (Mark 1:21-28; Luke 4:31-37). While Jesus was preaching in the synagogue at Capernaum, a man with an unclean spirit cried out: "What have w to do with thee, thou Jesus of Nazareth? art thou come to destroy us? I know thee who thou art, the Holy One of God." Jesus rebuked him, saying: "Hold thy peace,

and come out of him." And the unclean spirit, tearing the man, obeyed, to the amazement of all the people. On account of this miracle the fame of Jesus spread throughout all Galilee.

3. The healing of Peter's mother-in-law and others (Matt. 8:14-17; Mark 1:29-34; Luke 4:38-41). Leaving the synagogue, Christ and His disciples went into the house of Simon, where they found his mother-in-law sick of a fever. Taking her by the hand, the Lord lifed her up, and the fever departed and she ministered unto Him. At evening the people brought their sick and those that were possessed of devils to Him, and He healed them.

4. Preaching and healing throughout Galilee (Matt. 4:23-25; Mark 1:35-39; Luke 4:42-44). The next morning Jesus went out into a desert place, and the multitudes followed Him and would have detained Him, but He said that He must go and preach the good tidings of the kingdom to other cities. So, leaving Capernaum, He preached in the synagogues of Galilee.

5. The healing of a leper (Matt. 8:2-4; Mark 1:40-45; Luke 5:12-16). At one of the cities where Jesus preached, a leper came and, kneeling before Him, said: "Lord, if thou wilt, thou canst make me clean." Jesus, stretching forth His hand, said: "I will; be thou clean." And straightway the leprosy departed, and, charging the man to tell no one, but to go and offer the gift required by the law of Moses, the Lord sent him away. But, when the man went out, he published his healing abroad, and great multitudes flocked to Jesus to hear Him preach and to be healed of their infirmities.

THE GREAT GALILEAN MINISTRY

6. **The healing of a paralytic** (Matt. 9:2-8; Mark 2:1-12; Luke 5:17-26). Jesus now returned to Capernaum and, when it was noised abroad that He was in the place, great multitudes gathered together and He spake the word of the Lord to them. Then they brought a man who was sick of the palsy and, uncovering the roof, let him down where Jesus was. When the Lord saw him, He exclaimed: "Son, be of good cheer; thy sins be forgiven thee." At this certain of the scribes murmured, saying: "This man blasphemeth." But Jesus, knowing their thoughts, said: "Wherefore think ye evil in your hearts? For whether is easier, to say, Thy sins be forgiven thee; or to say, Arise, and walk? But that ye may know that the Son of man hath power on earth to forgive sins, (then saith he to the sick of the palsy,) Arise, take up thy bed,[1] and go unto thine house." And the sick man arose and did as he was commanded.

7. **The calling of Matthew** (Matt. 9:9-13; Mark 2:13-17; Luke 5:27-32). As Jesus went by the seat of custom He saw Matthew, or Levi, and said: "Follow me." Matthew arose and followed Him, and they went into his house and sat down to eat. The Pharisees, observing this, said to His disciples: "He eateth and drinketh with publicans and sinners." Jesus, hearing their complaint, said: "They that are whole have no need of a physician, but they that are sick."

8. **The discourse on fasting** (Matt. 9:14-17; Mark 2:18-22; Luke 5:33-39). The disciples of John came to Jesus, saying: "Why do we and the Pharisees fast

---
[1] This bed was nothing but a mat that could be easily rolled up and carried away.

oft, but thy disciples fast not?" Jesus replied: "Can the children of the bridechamber mourn, as long as the bridegroom is with them? but the days will come, when the bridegroom shall be taken from them, and then shall they fast."

9. **The raising of Jairus' daughter** (Matt. 9:18-26; Mark 5:22-43; Luke 8:41-56). While Jesus was in Capernaum, a ruler of the synagogue, Jairus by name, came to Him and said: "My little daughter lieth at the point of death: I pray thee, come and lay thy hands on her, that she may be healed; and she shall live." As Jesus went with him, a woman, who had an issue of blood for twelve years, touched the hem of His garment and was healed. Entering Jairus' house, Jesus found the people mourning, for the child was dead, but He said to them: "Give place: for the maid is not dead, but sleepeth." At this the people laughed Him to scorn, but, taking the maid's hand, He said: "Damsel, I say unto thee, Arise." And immediately she arose and walked, and those that looked on her were greatly astonished.

10. **Two blind men healed** (Matt. 9:27-34). As Jesus was leaving the home of Jairus, two blind men followed Him, crying: "Thou son of David, have mercy on us." Jesus said to them: "Believe ye that I am able to do this?" And they said: "Yea, Lord." Then, touching their eyes, He said: "According to your faith be it unto you." And, charging them to tell no man, He sent them away. But they spread His fame abroad throughout the land, and, as He went forth, they brought to Him a dumb man, possessed of a devil. When the devil was cast out, the multitudes marveled and said: "It was never so seen

THE GREAT GALILEAN MINISTRY

in Israel." But the Pharisees said: "By the prince of devils casteth he out devils."[1]

III. CHRIST'S ATTENDANCE AT THE FEAST AT JERUSALEM

1. **The healing at the pool of Bethesda** (John 5: 1-47). There was a feast[2] of the Jews, probably the Passover, and Jesus went to Jerusalem to attend it. In that city there was a pool called Bethesda, and when Jesus came He found that it was surrounded with a great multitude of the sick, lame and blind who were waiting for an angel to trouble the waters in order that they might step in and be healed. Among them was a man who had been afflicted with the palsy for thirty-eight years, to whom Jesus said: "Wilt thou be made whole?" The man replied: "Sir, I have no man, when the water is troubled, to put me into the pool: but while I am coming, another steppeth down before me." Then Jesus said: "Rise, take up thy bed, and walk." And immediately the man was made whole. Because Jesus performed this miracle on the sabbath the Jews sought to kill Him.

2. **The disciples pluck ears of grain upon the sabbath** (Matt. 12:1-8; Mark 2:23-28; Luke 6:1-5).[3] As Jesus was going through the cornfields on the sabbath day, His disciples were an hungred and, plucking the ears of corn,[4] began to eat. The Pharisees observed this and said to Him: "Behold, why

---

[1] The sin against the Holy Spirit consists in attributing the works of the Lord, which He did by the power of the Spirit, to the power of the devil.
[2] This feast was probably a Passover.
[3] This event probably occurred on His return to Galilee.
[4] Probably heads of wheat or barley.

do they on the sabbath day that which is not lawful?" Jesus answered: "Have ye never read what David did, when he had need, and was an hungred, he, and they that were with him? How he went into the house of God in the days of Abiathar the high priest, and did eat the shewbread, which is not lawful to eat but for the priests, and gave also to them which were with him?" And He said further to them: "The sabbath was made for man, and not man for the sabbath: therefore the Son of man is Lord also of the sabbath."

3. **The healing of the withered hand upon the sabbath** (Matt. 12:9-14; Mark 3:1-6; Luke 6:6-11). Jesus went into the synagogue on the sabbath and found a man there with a withered hand. The scribes and Pharisees watched Him to see whether He would heal on the sabbath day, and, knowing their thoughts, He said to the man: "Rise up, and stand forth in the midst." When the man had done this, Jesus said to the scribes and Pharisees: "Is it lawful on the sabbath days to do good, or to do evil? to save life, or to destroy it?" And, turning to the man, He said: "Stretch forth thy hand." The man did as he was commanded, and his hand was restored. Jesus' enemies were filled with madness at this miracle and sought what they might do to Him.

IV. THE LATTER PART OF THE GREAT GALILEAN MINISTRY

1. **Jesus preaches by the Sea of Galilee** (Matt. 12:15-21; Mark 3:7-12). Jesus and His disciples went down to the Sea of Galilee, and a great multitude from all parts of the country followed Him, so

THE GREAT GALILEAN MINISTRY

that it was necessary for Him to enter a little boat and push out from the land, where He taught the people.

2. **The choosing of the twelve** (Mark 3: 13-19; Luke 6: 12-16). After this He went into a mountain, and, when His disciples followed Him, He chose twelve to be with Him and whom He might send out to preach and to have authority to cast out devils. The names of the twelve, as given by Mark, are: Peter, James, John, Andrew, Philip, Bartholomew, Matthew, Thomas, James the son of Alphæus, Thaddæus, Simon the Canaanite and Judas Iscariot.[1]

3. **The Sermon on the Mount** (Matt. 5-7; Luke 6: 17-49). Seeing the multitude, Jesus went again into the mountain, where He delivered His celebrated Sermon on the Mount to His disciples. This sermon fills the place in the present dispensation that the Ten Commandments filled in the dispensation of the law.

4. **The healing of the centurion's servant** (Matt. 8: 1, 5-13; Luke 7: 1-10). As the Lord entered into Capernaum a certain centurion[2] met Him who told Him that his servant lay grievously sick of the palsy. Jesus offered to go and heal him, but the centurion objected and said: "Lord, I am not worthy that thou shouldest come under my roof: but speak the word only, and my servant shall be healed." At this Jesus said to those who followed Him: "Verily I say unto you, I have not found so great faith, no,

---

[1] The names of the apostles are given in Matthew 10, Mark 3, Luke 6 and Acts 1. It was common at that time for men to have more than one name, hence the seeming discrepancy in this respect which appears among these lists.

[2] A centurion was a commander of one hundred men.

not in Israel." He then said to the centurion: "Go thy way; and as thou hast believed, so be it done unto thee." And his servant was healed that very hour.

5. **The raising of the widow's son** (Luke 7:11-17). The day following, Jesus went into the city of Nain, and as He came near to the gate, a dead man was being carried out, the only son of a widow. When Jesus saw the mother, He said to her, "Weep not," and, touching the bier, He said to the dead: "Young man, I say unto thee, Arise." And at His command, the young man sat up and began to speak and was delivered to his mother.

6. **The message from John the Baptist** (Matt. 11: 2-30; Luke 7:18-35). John, who was in prison, heard of the works of Jesus and sent his disciples to Him, inquiring: "Art thou he that should come? or look we for another?" The Lord answered: "Go your way, and tell John what things ye have seen and heard; how that the blind see, the lame walk, the lepers are cleansed, the deaf hear, the dead are raised, to the poor the gospel is preached." When the disciples of John had gone their way, Jesus declared that "among those that are born of women there is not a greater prophet than John the Baptist: but he that is least in the kingdom of God is greater than he."

7. **The anointing of Jesus' feet by a woman that is a sinner** (Luke 7:36-50).[1] One of the Pharisees invited Jesus to dine with him, and, as He sat at meat, a woman of the place who was a sinner came

---
[1] This anointing in Galilee must be kept distinct from the anointing in Bethany one year later at the house of Simon the leper.

THE GREAT GALILEAN MINISTRY

in, and, weeping, wet His feet with her tears and wiped them with the hair of her head, after which she kissed them and anointed them with ointment. Now, when the Pharisee saw what the woman did, he said to himself: "This man, if he were a prophet, would have known who and what manner of woman this is that toucheth him: for she is a sinner." Jesus, perceiving his thoughts, replied to him in the parable of the debtors and, turning to the woman, said, "Thy sins are forgiven," and, "Thy faith hath saved thee; go in peace."

8. **The lakeside parables** (Matt. 13:1-53; Mark 4:1-34; Luke 8:4-15). Jesus went down by the sea, and, as the multitudes pressed Him, He went into a ship and, sitting down, taught them in parables. These parables were the following: The Sower, the Wheat and the Tares, the Mustard Seed, the Leaven in the Meal, the Hidden Treasure, the Pearl of Great Price and the Drag-net.

9. **The stilling of the tempest** (Matt. 8:18, 23-27; Mark 4:35-41; Luke 8:22-25). After delivering these parables to the multitude, Jesus said to His disciples: "Let us pass over unto the other side." So, sending the people away, they launched forth. As they sailed, He fell asleep and a great storm arose. In great fear His disciples came and awoke Him, saying: "Master, master, we perish." Then Jesus arose, rebuked the wind, the storm ceased and there was a great calm.

10. **The healing of the Gadarene demoniacs** (Matt. 8:28-34; Mark 5:1-20; Luke 8:26-39). When Jesus and His disciples came to the other side of the sea, in the country of Gadara, there met them two men

possessed with demons, who dwelt among the tombs and who were so fierce that no man could pass that way. Jesus rebuked the demons and they went into a herd of swine, which ran violently down a steep place and perished in the sea.

11. **The second rejection at Nazareth** (Matt. 9:1; 13:54-58; Mark 5:21; 6:1-6; Luke 8:40). After this, Jesus returned to Galilee and went into His own city, Nazareth. Going into the synagogue on the sabbath day, He taught the people and many were astonished, saying: "Is not this the carpenter's son? is not his mother called Mary? and his brethren, James, and Joses, and Simon, and Judas? And his sisters, are they not all with us?" But He could not do many mighty works because of their unbelief and so departed, saying: "A prophet is not without honour, save in his own country."

12. **Preaching throughout Galilee** (Matt. 9:35-38; Mark 6:6). Leaving Nazareth, Jesus went about all the cities and villages, teaching in the synagogues, preaching that the kingdom of heaven was at hand and healing all manner of diseases. But, when He saw the multitude, scattered as sheep without a shepherd, He had compassion on them and said to His disciples: "The harvest truly is plenteous, but the labourers are few. Pray ye therefore the Lord of the harvest, that he will send forth labourers into his harvest."

13. **The twelve sent out** (Matt. 10:1-42; Mark 6:7-13; Luke 9:1-6). Then Jesus called to Him His twelve disciples, and, giving them authority over unclean spirits and to heal all manner of diseases, He sent them forth, saying: "Go not into the way of the

THE GREAT GALILEAN MINISTRY

Gentiles, and into any city of the Samaritans enter ye not: but go rather to the lost sheep of the house of Israel. And as ye go, preach, saying, The kingdom of heaven is at hand." The disciples departed and did as they were commanded.

14. Herod Antipas supposes Christ to be John the Baptist resurrected (Matt. 14:1, 2; Mark 6:14, 15; Luke 9:7-9). When Herod the tetrarch heard what Jesus did, he said: "This is John the Baptist; he is risen from the dead; and therefore mighty works do shew forth themselves in him." But others said that He was Elijah, while still others declared that He was one of the prophets.

QUESTIONS

Give the date of the great Galilean ministry. Give a description of Galilee. Give the order of events during this period. What was the general subject of Christ's teaching in Galilee? Tell about the healing of the nobleman's son. Give the circumstances of His first rejection at Nazareth. To what city did He go? What fishermen did he call by the seaside? Did Jesus confine Himself to Capernaum in His ministrations? Name five miracles that He performed at Capernaum during the time that He made that city the basis of His ministry in Galilee. What was the occupation of Matthew, or Levi? Why did not Christ's disciples fast? Where did Jesus go to attend a certain feast? Give the name of a pool in that place and tell about the miracle performed there. How did Jesus excuse His disciples for plucking grain upon the sabbath? Near what sea did Jesus often preach? Where did Christ choose twelve special disciples and what were their names? To whom was the celebrated Sermon on the Mount delivered? What does it take the place of under the New Covenant? Tell about the healing of the centurion's servant. At what city did He raise a widow's son? What message did Christ receive from John the Baptist? Tell about the anointing of Jesus at the house of a Pharisee. Name the lakeside parables. Tell about the stilling of the tempest. In what country did Christ drive the demons out of two demoniacs and what became of them? Tell about the second rejection at Nazareth. In what condition did Christ find the people of Galilee? What authority did He give to the twelve when He sent them out? Whom did Herod Antipas suppose Him to be, and why?

STUDY XXXIV. THE PERIOD OF RETIREMENT

INTRODUCTION

1. **The date.** This period covers six months, probably from spring to autumn, A. D. 29 (or 28). It is called the "Period of Opposition."

2. **The reason of Christ's retirement from Galilee.** Christ evidently withdrew from Galilee out of fear of Herod Antipas, who had slain John the Baptist. Notice that he largely keeps out of the territory of Herod, which includes Galilee and Perea, and spends the greater part of this period in the tetrarchate of Philip, which was Bashan. Philip was a better man than Herod, and also had no occasion to fear the popularity of Jesus.

3. **The order of events.** During this period we find our Lord making four withdrawals from, and as many returns to, Galilee. First, we find him withdrawing across the Sea of Galilee, where He feeds the five thousand. Secondly, He goes into the region of Tyre and Sidon, where He heals the daughter of the Syro-Phœnician woman. Next, He goes into Decapolis, where a number of important events take place. And, lastly, He goes into Bashan, after which He returns to Galilee and, later, goes to Jerusalem, where he attends the Feast of the Tabernacles.

THE GIST OF THE BIBLE

I. THE RETIREMENT ACROSS THE SEA OF GALILEE

1. **The return of the twelve** (Mark 6:30, 31; Luke 9:10). The apostles that Jesus had sent out now returned and told Him all the things which they had both taught and done.

2. **The feeding of the five thousand** (Matt. 14:13-21; Mark 6:30-44; Luke 9:10-17; John 6:1-14). Immediately following the return of the twelve, Jesus went with them into a desert place beyond the Sea of Galilee which belonged to the city of Bethsaida. But the multitude followed Him there, and at evening His disciples urged Him to send them away, but He said to them: "Give ye them to eat." His disciples replied: "We have no more but five loaves and two fishes; except we should go and buy meat for all this people." Hearing this, Jesus made the multitude to sit down, and, taking the loaves and fishes, blessed them and distributed them to the people. After they had eaten and were filled, there were taken up twelve basketfuls of the fragments.

3. **Jesus walks on the water** (Matt. 14:22-36; Mark 6:45-56; John 6:15-21). When the five thousand had been fed, Jesus constrained His disciples to enter a ship and cross the sea to Bethsaida. This they attempted to do, but when the ship was in the midst of the sea, a great storm arose and, in the fourth watch, Jesus came walking upon the water. The disciples were greatly troubled when they observed Him, supposing that it was a spirit, but He said to them: "Be of good cheer; it is I; be

THE PERIOD OF RETIREMENT

not afraid." Peter then attempted to go to Him, but his faith failed him and he sank, crying: "Lord, save me." Immediately Jesus stretched forth His hand and caught him and said: "O thou of little faith, wherefore didst thou doubt?" The wind ceased when they reached the ship.

4. Jesus teaches in the synagogue at Capernaum (John 6:22-71). The next day, the multitude, seeing that Jesus did not enter the ship with His disciples, entered boats themselves and came to Capernaum, seeking Him. When they had found Him, they asked: "Rabbi, when camest thou hither?" Jesus replied: "Verily, verily, I say unto you, Ye seek me, not because ye saw the miracles, but because ye did eat of the loaves, and were filled." He then delivered to them His celebrated sermon on the Bread of Life, saying: "Labour not for the meat which perisheth, but for that meat which endureth unto everlasting life."

5. Jesus is reproached by emissaries from Jerusalem for disregarding tradition (Matt. 15:1-20; Mark 7:1-23; John 7:1). Certain Pharisees and scribes came to Jesus from Jerusalem, complaining that His disciples transgressed the traditions of the elders by eating bread with unwashed hands. Jesus answered by accusing them of hypocrisy and declaring that they had made the law of God void by their traditions. After this occurrence, His disciples came and told Him that the Pharisees were offended at what He had said. The Lord replied: "Every plant, which my heavenly Father hath not planted, shall be rooted up. Let them alone: they be blind leaders of the blind. And if the blind lead the blind, both shall fall into the ditch."

II. THE RETIREMENT INTO THE REGION OF TYRE AND SIDON

1. **The healing of the daughter of the Syro-Phœnician woman** (Matt. 15:21-28; Mark 7:24-30). Jesus now withdrew into the territory of Tyre and Sidon, and a Canaanitish woman came to Him and cried: "Have mercy on me, O Lord, thou son of David; my daughter is grievously vexed with a devil." His disciples urged Him to send her away, but He answered them: "I am not sent but unto the lost sheep of the house of Israel." The woman was importunate and came and worshiped Him, saying: "Lord, help me." Jesus answered her: "It is not meet to take the children's bread, and cast it to dogs." The woman replied: "Truth, Lord: yet the dogs eat of the crumbs which fall from their masters' table." At this, Jesus was moved with compassion toward her and said: "O woman, great is thy faith: be it unto thee even as thou wilt." And her daughter was healed that very hour.

III. THE RETIREMENT INTO DECAPOLIS

1. **Jesus heals the multitude** (Matt. 15:29-31; Mark 7:31-37). Jesus returned to the Sea of Galilee again, and, going through the country of Decapolis, He healed many that were lame, blind, dumb and maimed, so that the multitude wondered and glorified God.

2. **Jesus feeds the four thousand** (Matt. 15:32-38; Mark 8:1-9). Jesus called to Him His disciples and told them that He had compassion on the multitude because they had continued with Him for three

THE PERIOD OF RETIREMENT

days without food, and that He would not send them away hungry, lest they should faint by the way. His disciples in astonishment replied: "Whence should we have so much bread in the wilderness, as to fill so great a multitude?" Jesus asked how many loaves they had, and they answered: "Seven, and a few small fishes." He then commanded the multitude to sit down, and, taking the loaves and fishes, He broke them and gave them to His disciples and they to the multitude, who ate and were filled. When the hunger of all had been satisfied, there were taken up seven basketfuls of fragments.

3. **Jesus returns to Galilee and warns His disciples against the doctrines of the Pharisees and Sadducees** (Matt. 15:39-16:12; Mark 8:10-21). Jesus and His disciples now crossed the sea and came into the vicinity of Magdala and Dalmanutha, where certain Pharisees and Sadducees came to Him and demanded a sign from heaven. Jesus replied by saying: "A wicked and adulterous generation seeketh after a sign; and there shall no sign be given unto it, but the sign of the prophet Jonas." When His disciples came to Him, He said to them: "Take heed and beware of the leaven of the Pharisees and Sadducees." At first the disciples thought that He referred to literal bread, but when He had explained Himself, they understood that He meant the teachings of the Pharisees and Sadducees.

IV. THE RETIREMENT INTO BASHAN

1. **Jesus heals a blind man at Bethsaida** (Mark 8:22-26). Jesus and His disciples now came to Bethsaida. Here a blind man was brought to Him

THE GIST OF THE BIBLE

to be healed. When He had spit on his eyes and had laid His hands upon him, He asked him if he saw anything. The man replied: "I see men; for I behold them as trees, walking." Then Jesus again laid His hands upon his eyes and his eyesight was fully restored.

2. **Peter's confession at Cæsarea Philippi** (Matt. 16:13-20; Mark 8:27-30; Luke 9:18-21). Leaving Bethsaida, Jesus and His disciples went into the vicinity of Cæsarea Philippi. Here he asked those who were with Him, whom men said that He was. They replied that some said that He was John the Baptist; others, Elias, and still others, one of the prophets. Then Jesus said to them: "But whom say ye that I am?" Peter answered: "Thou art the Christ, the Son of the living God." Jesus replied: "Blessed art thou, Simon Bar-jona: for flesh and blood hath not revealed it unto thee, but my Father which is in heaven. And I say also unto thee, That thou art Peter, and upon this rock[1] I will build my church; and the gates of hell shall not prevail against it. And I will give unto thee the keys of the kingdom of heaven: and whatsoever thou shalt bind on

---

[1] This rock is not Peter, but Christ, as is proved by the gender of the original Greek word for "Peter" and that for "rock." This is brought out in the following literal translation: "And I say also unto thee, That thou art a *he*-rock, and upon this *she*-rock I will build my church; and the gates of hell shall not prevail against it." St. Augustine, the father of Christian theology, says: "The Church does not fall, because it is founded on the rock from which Peter received his name. For the rock is not called after Peter, but Peter is so called after the rock: just as Christ is not so denominated after the Christian, but the Christian after Christ; for it is on this account our Lord declares, 'On this rock I will build my church,' because Peter had said: 'Thou art the Christ, the Son of the living God.' On this rock which thou hast confessed, he declares, 'I will build my church;' for Christ was the rock on whose foundation Peter himself was built."

THE PERIOD OF RETIREMENT

earth shall be bound in heaven: and whatsoever thou shalt loose on earth shall be loosed in heaven." Then He charged His disciples that they should tell no man that He was the Christ.

3. **Jesus foretells His death and resurrection** (Matt. 16:21-28; Mark 8:31-38; 9:1; Luke 9:22-27). From this time Jesus began to teach His disciples that He must go to Jerusalem, suffer many things at the hands of the officials, be killed and be raised up the third day. At this Peter began to rebuke Him, saying that these things should never come upon Him. But Jesus, turning to him, said: "Get thee behind me, Satan: for thou savourest not the things that be of God, but those that be of men." The Lord then proceeded to give the test of discipleship, and ended by saying that there were some standing there who should not taste of death till they saw Him coming in His kingdom.

4. **The transfiguration** (Matt. 17:1-13; Mark 9:2-13; Luke 9:28-36). More than six days after this, Jesus took Peter, James and John and went into a high mountain, probably Hermon, where He was transfigured before them. There appeared with Him two men, Moses and Elias, talking with Him, and a voice out of heaven said: "This is my beloved Son, in whom I am well pleased; hear ye him." The disciples were greatly frightened, but Jesus came and touched them and commanded them to tell no man the vision until after His resurrection.

5. **The disciples fail to heal a demoniac boy** (Matt. 17:14-20; Mark 9:14-29; Luke 9:37-43). Jesus and His three disciples, upon their return from the mount, found a great multitude of people gathered

about the disciples who had been left behind. When the Lord asked the cause of the gathering, one of the multitude came to Him and said that he had brought his demoniac son to Him and that the disciples had not been able to heal him. Jesus said to him: "All things are possible to him that believeth." At which the man cried out: "I believe; help thou mine unbelief." Jesus then rebuked the spirit and it came out of the child. The disciples inquired why they had not been able to cast the spirit out, and He replied: "This kind can come forth by nothing, but by prayer and fasting."

6. **Jesus returns to Galilee and again foretells His death and resurrection** (Matt. 17:22, 23; Mark 9:30-32; Luke 9:43-45). Jesus now left the territory of Philip and re-entered Galilee secretly, telling His disciples again of His approaching death.

7. **Jesus pays the half-shekel for the Temple** (Matt. 17:24-27). Jesus and His disciples came to Capernaum, and those who collected funds for the Temple came to Peter and asked him if his Master did not pay His half-shekel. Peter answered in the affirmative, and Jesus told him to go to the sea, cast in a hook and that the first fish he should catch would have in its mouth a shekel, which he was to turn over to the collectors for himself and his Lord.

8. **The contention of the twelve as to who should be greatest in the kingdom** (Matt. 18:1-14; Mark 9:33-50; Luke 9:46-50). While Jesus and His disciples were at Capernaum, there arose a contention among them as to who should be greatest in the kingdom. Jesus, taking a little child, set him by His side and said: "Whosoever shall receive this

THE PERIOD OF RETIREMENT

child in my name receiveth me: and whosoever shall receive me receiveth him that sent me: for he that is least among you all, the same shall be great."

9. **The right treatment of a sinning brother** (Matt. 18: 15-35). After this occurrence, Jesus taught His disciples that if a brother sinned against one of them, he was to go and tell him his fault privately; and, if he would not hear him, he was to take with him one or two more; and if he would not hear them, he was to tell it to the church; and if he refused to hear the church, he was to become unto him as a Gentile and a publican. Then Peter came to Him and asked: "Lord, how oft shall my brother sin against me, and I forgive him? till seven times?" And Jesus answered: "Until seventy times seven." As illustrative of this teaching, our Lord spoke the parable of the Unmerciful Debtor.

10. **The sacrifices that the followers of Christ must make** (Matt. 8: 19-22; Luke 9: 57-62). One of the scribes came to Jesus and said: "Master, I will follow thee whithersoever thou goest." Jesus replied: "The foxes have holes, and the birds of the air have nests; but the Son of man hath not where to lay his head."

11. **Jesus' unbelieving brethren urge Him to go into Judea** (John 7: 2-9). The Feast of Tabernacles was near at hand, and the brethren of Jesus who did not believe on Him urged Him to go into Judea that He might prove His claims to the world. But Jesus refused to do this, telling them that His time had not yet come.

12. **Jesus goes to Jerusalem secretly through Samaria** (Luke 9: 51-56; John 7: 10). But, after His

THE GIST OF THE BIBLE

brethren had departed for the feast, Jesus also went, not publicly, but secretly, through Samaria.

QUESTIONS

Give the general outline of this study. In what year did the events of this study probably occur? What is this period sometimes called? Why did Jesus retire so often from Galilee? Contrast the characters of Herod and Philip. Tell about the return of the twelve. Give the miracle of the feeding of the five thousand. Give the account of Christ walking on the water. What reason did Jesus assign for the multitude following Him? Of what did certain Pharisees and scribes from Jerusalem accuse Him? Tell about the healing of the Syro-phœnician girl. Give the miracle of the feeding of the four thousand and contrast it with the miracle of the feeding of the five thousand. What term did Christ apply to the doctrines of the Pharisees and Sadducees? Describe the healing of the blind man at Bethsaida. Tell about Peter's confession at Cæsarea Philippi. Did Jesus foreknow His suffering, death and resurrection? Tell about the controversy that He had with Peter over these things. In what mountain was Christ transfigured before his disciples? Give the account. What had the disciples, who had been left behind, failed to do? Did Jesus pay His Temple tax? How did He do it? Over what did the twelve contend and how did Jesus settle the contention? How did Christ say we should treat an offending brother? How many times should we forgive him? Where did Christ's brethren urge Him to go? Did they believe in His claims?

STUDY XXXV. THE CLOSING OF CHRIST'S MINISTRY

INTRODUCTION

1. **The date.** This period in the life of our Lord lay, probably, between the autumn of 29 and the spring of 30 A. D., or it may have been a year earlier.

2. **The order of events.** This study opens with Jesus at Jerusalem at the Feast of Tabernacles. After this He preaches in that city and its vicinity, and performs a number of miracles. He next crosses the Jordan into Perea, but soon returns again to the regions west of the Jordan. Later, He goes again into Perea, after which He turns his face finally in the direction of Jerusalem.

I. CERTAIN EVENTS AT JERUSALEM AND IN ITS VICINITY

1. **Jesus attends the Feast of Tabernacles** (John 7: 11-53). Leaving Galilee, Jesus came to Jerusalem to attend the Feast of Tabernacles, and taught in the Temple to the amazement of the Jews. On the last great day of the feast, He cried: "If any man thirst, let him come unto me, and drink. He that believeth on me, as the scripture hath said, out of his belly shall flow rivers of living waters." This caused a division among the people, some saying that He was a prophet; others, that He was the Christ. When the officers went to the chief priests and

Pharisees, the latter inquired why they had not brought Him, and they replied: "Never man spake as this man."

2. **An adulteress is brought before Jesus**[1] (John 8:1-11). Jesus went out and spent the night in the Mount of Olives, but in the morning returned into the city, when an adulterous woman was brought before Him. Her persecutors said: "Master, this woman was taken in adultery, in the very act. Now Moses in the law commanded us, that such should be stoned: but what sayest thou?" Jesus, stooping down, wrote upon the ground and said: "He that is without sin among you, let him first cast a stone at her." At these words, the woman's accusers went out, one by one, after which Jesus dismissed the woman by saying: "Go, and sin no more."

3. **Jesus declares His divine Sonship and pre-existence** (John 8:12-59). Jesus now spake again to the people, declaring that He was the light of the world and that He existed before Abraham. The latter assertion greatly angered the Jews and they took up stones to stone Him.

4. **Jesus heals a man born blind** (John 9:1-41). As Jesus and His disciples passed by, He saw a man who had been blind from his birth. His disciples asked Him if the blindness of this man was due to his own sin or to that of his parents. The Lord replied: "Neither hath this man sinned, nor his parents: but that the works of God should be made manifest in him." And, saying this, He spat on the

---

[1] This account is probably not a part of the inspired record. It is doubtless a true story of our Lord that has come down from early times, probably drawn from the collection of Papias, about 140 A. D.

THE CLOSING OF CHRIST'S MINISTRY

ground, and, making clay of the spittle, anointed the eyes of the blind man, and commanded him to go and wash in the pool of Siloam.¹ Which, having done, he received his sight.

5. **The parables of the Sheepfold** (John 10:1-21). After this miracle, Jesus spoke two parables on the sheepfold, in one of which He declared Himself to be the Good Shepherd, and in the other, the Door of the sheep.

6. **The mission of the seventy** (Luke 10:1-24). Jesus appointed seventy of His disciples, as He had appointed the twelve, and sent them out, two and two, into the surrounding country to preach the gospel and heal the sick. When the seventy returned, they said: "Even the devils are subject unto us through thy name."

7. **The parable of the Good Samaritan** (Luke 10:25-37). A certain lawyer came to Jesus and tempted Him, saying: "Master, what shall I do to inherit eternal life?" Jesus answered: "What is written in the law? how readest thou?" The lawyer replied: "Thou shalt love the Lord thy God with all thy heart, and with all thy soul, and with all thy strength, and with all thy mind; and thy neighbour as thyself." Then Jesus said: "Thou hast answered right: this do, and thou shalt live." But the lawyer, anxious to justify himself, inquired: "And who is my neighbour?" To which Jesus replied by speaking the parable of the Good Samaritan.

8. **Jesus visits Martha and Mary** (Luke 10:38-

---

¹ A pool in Jerusalem which is 53 feet long, 18 feet broad and 19 feet deep, though it is never filled, the water passing through it at a depth of three or four feet. A descent of steps leads to the water.

42). Jesus came to Bethany, where lived Martha and Mary. When He had been received into their house, Mary sat at His feet and listened to His words, but Martha was burdened with the serving. Coming to the Lord, she inquired: "Lord, dost thou not care that my sister hath left me to serve alone? bid her therefore that she help me." Jesus answered: "Martha, Martha, thou art careful and troubled about many things: but one thing is needful: and Mary hath chosen that good part, which shall not be taken away from her."

9. **Jesus teaches His disciples to pray** (Luke 11: 1-13). As Jesus was praying in a certain place, His disciples came to Him with the request: "Lord, teach us to pray, as John also taught his disciples." Jesus then taught them what is commonly called the Lord's Prayer. As further illustrative of the principle and power of prayer, the Lord spoke His parables of the Importunate Friend and Fatherhood.

10. **Jesus is accused of being in league with Beelzebub** (Luke 11:14-36). Jesus cast out a dumb devil and the people wondered, some saying that it was by Beelzebub that He cast out devils, while others demanded a sign from heaven. The Lord replied: "And if I by Beelzebub cast out devils, by whom do your sons cast them out? therefore shall they be your judges. But if I with the finger of God cast out devils, no doubt the kingdom of God is come upon you."

11. **Jesus breakfasts with a Pharisee** (Luke 11: 37-54). While Jesus was speaking, a Pharisee requested that He should dine with him. He accepted the invitation, but sat down with unwashed hands.

THE CLOSING OF CHRIST'S MINISTRY

The Pharisee marveled at this, and our Lord said: "Now do ye Pharisees make clean the outside of the cup and the platter; but your inward part is full of ravening and wickedness." For these and other words which He spake, the scribes and Pharisees sought to provoke Him that He might say something by which He might be convicted.

12. **Jesus preaches to His disciples on various subjects** (Luke 12:1-59). During this discussion, a great multitude gathered together, and, turning to His disciples, Jesus warned them of the doctrine of the Pharisees and spoke the parables of the Rich Fool, the Watchful Servant and the Wise Steward.

13. **Jesus heals on the sabbath—Parables of the Mustard Seed and Leaven** (Luke 13:10-21). As Jesus was teaching upon the sabbath in the synagogue, a woman, who had been afflicted with an infirmity for eighteen years, came before Him, to whom Jesus said, "Woman, thou art loosed from thine infirmity," and, having laid His hands upon her, He healed her. The ruler of the synagogue was very indignant at this and exclaimed: "There are six days in which men ought to work: in them therefore come and be healed, and not on the sabbath day." Jesus replied: "Thou hypocrite, doth not each one of you on the sabbath loose his ox or his ass from the stall, and lead him away to watering? And ought not this woman, being a daughter of Abraham, whom Satan hath bound, lo, these eighteen years, be loosed from this bond on the sabbath day?" When He had said these words, His adversaries were all confounded and the people rejoiced.

14. **Jesus retires into Perea** (John 10:22-42). The

Jews now sought to take Jesus, but He escaped out of their hands and went into Perea beyond Jordan, where John at first baptized, and there He abode.

II. CHRIST'S FIRST MINISTRY IN PEREA

1. **Teachings in Perea** (Luke 13:22-35). Jesus went on His way through the cities and villages, teaching and journeying toward Jerusalem. As He went, a certain man said unto Him: "Lord, are there few that be saved?" Jesus answered: "Strive to enter in at the strait gate: for many, I say unto you, will seek to enter in, and shall not be able." The same day, certain of the Pharisees came to Him, saying: "Get thee out, and depart hence: for Herod will kill thee." Jesus said to them: "Behold, I cast out devils, and I do cures to day and to morrow, and the third day I shall be perfected. Nevertheless I must walk to day, and to morrow, and the day following: for it cannot be that a prophet perish out of Jerusalem."

2. **Jesus heals on the sabbath and speaks the parables of the Ambitious Guest and the Great Supper** (Luke 14:1-24). Jesus went into the house of one of the chief Pharisees to eat bread upon the sabbath, and a certain man came before Him who was afflicted with the dropsy. Turning to the lawyers and Pharisees, Jesus asked: "Is it lawful to heal on the sabbath day?" But they made no answer and He healed the man. Following this miracle, our Lord spoke the parables of the Ambitious Guest and the Great Supper.

3. **The five great Perean parables** (Luke 15:1-16:31). The five great parables which Jesus spoke

THE CLOSING OF CHRIST'S MINISTRY

at this time are called the Lost Sheep, the Lost Coin, the Lost Son, the Unrighteous Steward and the Rich Man and Lazarus. The first three were directed against the scribes and Pharisees, who had said: "This man receiveth sinners, and eateth with them." The fourth was delivered to His disciples, and the fifth, again, to the Pharisees.

III. CHRIST RETURNS TO THE COUNTRY WEST OF THE JORDAN

1. **The raising of Lazarus** (John 11:1-46). While Jesus was in Perea, Lazarus, the brother of Martha and Mary of Bethany, was taken ill and his sisters sent to Him, saying: "Lord, behold, he whom thou lovest is sick." After two days, against the advice of His disciples, Jesus returned to Bethany, to find that Lazarus was dead. As He neared the place, Martha ran to meet Him and said: "Lord, if thou hadst been here, my brother had not died." Jesus said to her: "Thy brother shall rise again." Martha replied: "I know that he shall rise again in the resurrection at the last day." Then Jesus said to her: "I am the resurrection, and the life: he that believeth in me, though he were dead, yet shall he live: and whosoever liveth and believeth in me shall never die." When Jesus saw Mary and her friends weeping, He also wept, and, groaning within Himself, went to the grave. After the stone had been removed, He cried with a loud voice: "Lazarus, come forth." And he that was dead came forth, bound in his grave-clothes, and, at the command of Jesus, was unbound and was permitted to go.

2. **Jesus escapes to Ephraim** (John 11:47-57).

Many of the Jews believed on Jesus because of the things which He did. When this was told the Pharisees, they, with Caiaphas the high priest, laid a plot to kill Him, and He fled to the city of Ephraim, between Jerusalem and Jericho.

3. **Jesus discourses on His second coming** (Luke 17:11-37). As Jesus was passing through Samaria and Galilee, on His way to Jerusalem, He was met in a certain village by ten lepers, who cried: "Jesus, Master, have mercy on us." Jesus cleansed them and commanded them to go and show themselves to the priests. Only one of the ten returned to thank Him, and he was a Samaritan. The Pharisees demanded that He tell them when the kingdom of God should come. He replied: "The kingdom of God cometh not with observation: neither shall they say, Lo here! or, lo there! for, behold, the kingdom of God is within you." He then spoke of His second coming, likening it to the coming of the flood and the coming of the destruction upon Sodom.

4. **The parables of the Unjust Judge and the Pharisee and Publican** (Luke 18:1-14). The Lord now spoke the parables of the Unjust Judge and the Pharisee and Publican.

IV. CHRIST'S SECOND MINISTRY IN PEREA

1. **Teachings concerning divorce** (Matt. 19:1-12; Mark 10:1-12). The Pharisees tempted Jesus with the question: "Is it lawful for a man to put away his wife for every cause?" Jesus answered this question by saying that in the beginning God made them male and female, because of which a man should cleave to his wife and the two should be

THE CLOSING OF CHRIST'S MINISTRY

one flesh. He further declared that Moses suffered them to put away their wives because of the hardness of their hearts, while He also declared that for only one sin was this permissible.

2. **Jesus blesses little children** (Matt. 19:13-15; Mark 10:13-16; Luke 18:15-17). There were brought unto Jesus little children that He might touch them, but His disciples rebuked Him, and He said: "Suffer little children to come unto me, and forbid them not: for of such is the kingdom of heaven."

3. **The rich young ruler** (Matt. 19:16-20:16; Mark 10:17-31; Luke 18:18-30). A certain young ruler came to Jesus and inquired what he should do to inherit eternal life. Christ answered that he should keep the commandments. He replied that all these he had kept from his youth up. Then Jesus told him to sell all that he had and give to the poor. At these words, the young man went away sorrowful, for he was very rich.

4. **Jesus again foretells His death and resurrection** (Matt. 20:17-19; Mark 10:32-34; Luke 18:31-34). Jesus and His disciples now started back to Jerusalem, and on the way he taught them, saying: "Behold, we go up to Jerusalem; and the Son of man shall be betrayed unto the chief priests and unto the scribes, and they shall condemn him to death, and shall deliver him to the Gentiles to mock, and to scourge, and to crucify him: and the third day he shall rise again."

5. **The selfish ambition of the sons of Zebedee rebuked** (Matt. 20:20-28; Mark 10:35-45). The mother of James and John, with her sons, came to Jesus and requested that they might sit, the one

on His right hand and the other on His left, in His kingdom. Jesus asked them if they were able to drink the cup that He was to drink and to be baptized with the baptism with which He was to be baptized. They replied that they were. Then Jesus answered that this was indeed true, but to sit on His right hand and His left was not His to give, but that it would be given to those for whom it was prepared by His Father.

V. CHRIST'S FINAL RETURN TO JUDEA

1. **Blind Bartimæus receives his sight** (Matt. 20: 29-34; Mark 10: 46-52; Luke 18: 35-43). When Jesus and His disciples came to Jericho on their return to Jerusalem, they met two blind men sitting by the wayside begging, who cried out: "Have mercy on us, O Lord, thou son of David." Jesus asked what they desired of Him, and they replied that He should open their eyes. Moved with compassion, He touched their eyes and they received their sight. The name of one of these blind men was Bartimæus.

2. **Jesus visits Zacchæus** (Luke 19: 1-27). As Jesus was passing through Jericho, Zacchæus, a rich publican who was small of stature, climbed into a sycamore tree that he might see Him. When the Lord saw Zacchæus, He said: "Zacchæus, make haste, and come down; for to day I must abide at thy house." Zacchæus, coming down, received Him joyfully and said: "Behold, Lord, the half of my goods I give to the poor; and if I have taken any thing from any man by false accusation, I restore him fourfold." To which Jesus replied: "This day is salvation come to this house, forsomuch as he also

THE CLOSING OF CHRIST'S MINISTRY

is a son of Abraham." He then spoke the parable of the Pounds.

3. **Jesus comes to Bethany** (John 11:55-12:1; 12:9-11). The Lord now came to Bethany, where He spent the sabbath with Lazarus and his sisters. Because many of the Jews believed on Jesus through Lazarus, the chief priests sought to put him to death.

QUESTIONS

Give the general outline of this study. When did the events of this study probably occur? At the opening of this period, what feast did Jesus attend, and where? What different opinions did the people have of Jesus? What kind of a woman was brought before Jesus and what did He say to her accusers and herself? Before whom did Jesus say that He existed? Tell about the healing of the man born blind. Give, in substance, the two parables of the Sheepfold. How many disciples did Jesus send out at this time, and what for? What did they say when they returned? How did Jesus come to speak the parable of the Good Samaritan? Whom did Jesus visit at Bethany and what occurred? What prayer did Jesus teach His disciples to pray? With whom was Jesus accused of being in league? How did He answer the accusation? What occurred when Jesus ate with unwashed hands at the house of a prominent Pharisee? Of whose doctrines did Jesus warn His disciples? Into what country did Jesus retire? What warning did the Pharisees give Jesus in Perea? Name the five great Perean parables and tell to whom they were spoken. Tell about the raising of Lazarus. To what place did Jesus escape after the raising of Lazarus? To what did Jesus compare His second coming? What did Jesus teach concerning divorce? Tell about Him blessing little children. Tell about the rich young ruler coming to Jesus. What did Jesus say concerning His approaching death and resurrection? How did Jesus answer the selfish request of the two sons of Zebedee? What man was healed of blindness at Jericho? Give the circumstances. What rich publican did Jesus meet at Jericho and what occurred? Where did Jesus go from Jericho?

STUDY XXXVI. THE LAST WEEK

INTRODUCTION

1. **The date.** The events of this study probably occurred in the spring of A. D. 30, or they may have occurred in the spring of A. D. 29.

2. **The place.** Jerusalem and its environs. The Mount of Olives lay just east of the city proper. Calvary lay just north. Bethany was a town or village lying about two miles southeast. And Gethsemane was a garden just over the brook Kidron and at the foot of the Mount of Olives.

3. **Crucifixion.** Crucifixion was the most degrading, inhuman and painful of all the ancient forms of punishment. It was practiced by the Romans in the case of slaves and such as were guilty of rebellion or highway robbery. Though the agony was most excruciating, the victim sometimes lived for many hours.

I. SUNDAY—THE DAY OF TRIUMPH

1. **The triumphal entry** (Matt. 21:1-9; Mark 11:1-10; Luke 19:35-38; John 12:12-19). The day following the visit at Bethany, the Lord rode into Jerusalem upon the colt of an ass, and the people, who had assembled to keep the Passover, went forth to meet Him, waving palm branches and crying: "Hosanna: Blessed is the King of Israel that cometh in the name of the Lord." This popu-

larity raised the jealousy of the Pharisees, and they said: "Perceive ye how ye prevail nothing? behold, the world is gone after him."

II. MONDAY—THE DAY OF AUTHORITY

1. **The cursing of the fig-tree** (Matt. 21:18, 19; Mark 11:12-14). On the morrow, as Jesus and the twelve were coming from Bethany, He was hungry, and, seeing a fig-tree, He came to it, but found no fruit. He then cursed it and said: "No man eat fruit of thee hereafter for ever." And His disciples heard it.

2. **The second cleansing of the Temple** (Matt. 21:12, 13; Mark 11:15-18; Luke 19:45-48). After He had entered the city, Jesus went into the Temple and again cast out those who bought and sold, and overturned the tables of the money-changers, saying: "It is written, My house shall be called the house of prayer; but ye have made it a den of thieves."

3. **The Gentiles seek Jesus** (John 12:20-50). There were certain Greeks in the city who had come to worship at the feast. These came to Philip of Bethsaida, saying: "Sir, we would see Jesus." Philip and Andrew then came and told Jesus, who replied: "The hour is come, that the Son of man should be glorified. Verily, verily, I say unto you, Except a corn of wheat fall into the ground and die, it abideth alone: but if it die, it bringeth forth much fruit."

III. TUESDAY—THE DAY OF CONTROVERSY

1. **The lesson from the withered fig-tree** (Matt. 21:19-22; Mark 11:19-25; Luke 21:37, 38). The same evening, Jesus and His disciples passed out of

the city, but the following morning re-entered it. As they passed by the fig-tree which the Lord had cursed, they observed that it was dried up from the roots. Peter called Jesus' attention to this, saying: "Master, behold, the fig tree which thou cursedst is withered away." The Master replied: "Have faith in God. For verily I say unto you, That whosoever shall say unto this mountain, Be thou removed, and be thou cast into the sea; and shall not doubt in his heart, but shall believe that those things which he saith shall come to pass; he shall have whatsoever he saith."

2. **Christ's authority questioned** (Matt. 21:23-27; Mark 11:27-33; Luke 20:1-8). The chief priests and elders now came to Jesus and asked: "By what authority doest thou these things? and who gave thee this authority?" Jesus answered them by asking: "The baptism of John, whence was it? from heaven, or of men?" Then they reasoned among themselves that if they said from heaven, he would say, "Why did ye not then believe him?" and if they said, "Of men," the people would oppose them because they believed that John was a prophet; so they replied: "We cannot tell." To which Jesus said: "Neither tell I you by what authority I do these things."

3. **The three warning parables** (Matt. 21:28-22:14; Mark 12:1-12; Luke 20:9-16). At this time the Lord spoke three warning parables: the parable of the Two Sons, the parable of the Vineyard and the parable of the Marriage Feast.

4. **The three hostile questions and the question of Jesus** (Matt. 22:15-46; Mark 12:13-40; Luke 20:

THE LAST WEEK

19-47). The following hostile questions were now asked of Jesus:

(1) *The question of the Pharisees and Herodians.* The Pharisees took counsel how they might entangle Him and so sent their disciples, with the Herodians, to ask Him: "Is it lawful to give tribute unto Cæsar, or not?" Jesus answered: "Render therefore unto Cæsar the things that are Cæsar's; and unto God the things that are God's."

(2) *The question of the Sadducees.* The same day the Sadducees came to Him with the question: "There were with us seven brethren: and the first, when he had married a wife, deceased, and, having no issue, left his wife unto his brother: likewise the second also, and the third, unto the seventh. And last of all the woman died also. Therefore in the resurrection whose wife shall she be of the seven? for they all had her." Jesus replied: "Ye do err, not knowing the scriptures, nor the power of God. For in the resurrection they neither marry, nor are given in marriage, but are as the angels of God in heaven."

(3) *The question of the Pharisees.* When the Pharisees heard that the Sadducees had been put to silence, they gathered together, and one of them, a lawyer, asked: "Master, which is the great commandment in the law?" The Lord answered: "Thou shalt love the Lord thy God with all thy heart, and with all thy soul, and with all thy mind. This is the first and great commandment. And the second is like unto it, Thou shalt love thy neighbor as thyself. On these two commandments hang all the law and the prophets."

(4) *The question of Jesus.* The Lord now turned

upon His questioners and asked: "What think ye of Christ? whose son is he?" They replied: "The son of David." Then Jesus said: "How then doth David in spirit call him Lord, saying, The Lord said unto my Lord, Sit thou on my right hand, till I make thine enemies thy footstool? If David then called him Lord, how is he his son?" At this question, they were all confounded.

5. Jesus discourses against the scribes and Pharisees (Matt. 23:1-39; Mark 12:38-40; Luke 20:45-47). Jesus then discoursed to the multitude and His disciples against the scribes and Pharisees, condemning their hypocrisy and pride and pronouncing a woe upon them. He closed His discourse with His memorable lament over Jerusalem: "O Jerusalem, Jerusalem, thou that killest the prophets, and stonest them which are sent unto thee, how often would I have gathered thy children together, even as a hen gathereth her chickens under her wings, and ye would not! Behold, your house is left unto you desolate. For I say unto you, Ye shall not see me henceforth, till ye shall say, Blessed is he that cometh in the name of the Lord."

6. The widow's two mites (Mark 12:41-44; Luke 21:1-4). As Jesus looked up, He saw the people casting their money into the treasury. Among them was a certain poor widow who threw in two mites, which were all that she had. Jesus said to His disciples: "Verily I say unto you, That this poor widow hath cast more in than all they which have cast into the treasury: for all they did cast in of their abundance; but she of her want did cast in all that she had, even all her living."

7. **Christ's great prophecy** (Matt. 24:1-51; Mark 13:1-37; Luke 21:5-36). As Jesus was going out of the Temple, He said to His disciples: "Verily I say unto you, There shall not be left here one stone upon another, that shall not be thrown down." He then went with His disciples into the Mount of Olives, where He delivered to them His last and greatest prophecy. In this prophecy He predicted that false Christs and false prophets should arise, that wars should come, that scourges should sweep over the earth, that persecutions should fall upon His followers, that the Jews should be led away captive into all nations, that the world should be evangelized, that certain physical signs should precede His second advent, and that, following all these things, He should come to judge the world.

8. **The three great Olivet parables** (Matt. 25:1-46). As illustrative of His second coming and attendant events, the Lord spoke three parables on the Mount of Olives, as follows: The Ten Virgins, the Absent Nobleman and the Sheep and Goats.

9. **The conspiracy against Jesus** (Matt. 26:1-5; Mark 14:1, 2; Luke 22:1, 2). The chief priests and scribes now sought how they might kill Jesus, but they said: "Not during the feast, lest a tumult arise among the people."

IV. WEDNESDAY—THE DAY OF RETIREMENT

1. **Mary anoints Jesus at Bethany** (Matt. 26:6-13; Mark 14:3-9; John 12:2-8).[1] Jesus now went to

---
[1] John would seem to place this event before the opening of the Passion Week; the Synoptics, Matthew and Mark, give it as we have it here.

Bethany, where they made a feast for Him at the house of Simon the leper. At this feast Mary took a pound of ointment of pure nard, very precious, and, anointing the Saviour's feet, wiped them with her hair; and the house was filled with the perfume of the ointment. Judas Iscariot complained of this and said: "Why was this waste of the ointment made? For it might have been sold for more than three hundred pence,[1] and have been given to the poor." But Jesus said: "Let her alone; why trouble ye her? she hath wrought a good work on me. For ye have the poor with you always, and whensoever ye will ye may do them good: but me ye have not always. She hath done what she could: she is come aforehand to anoint my body to the burying."

2. **Judas offers to betray Jesus** (Matt. 26:14-16; Mark 14:10, 11; Luke 22:3-6). Judas was greatly offended at this, and, Satan entering his heart, he went to the chief priests and captains and offered to betray Jesus into their hands. For this they were glad and covenanted with him for thirty pieces of silver.

V. THURSDAY—THE DAY OF FELLOW-SHIP

1. **Preparation for the Passover** (Matt. 26:17-19; Mark 14:12-16; Luke 22:7-13). On the first day of unleavened bread the disciples came to Jesus inquiring where they should go that they might make ready to eat the Passover. Jesus sent Peter and John into the city, telling them that they should meet a man bearing a pitcher of water, that they

---
[1] Between nine and ten pounds sterling.

THE LAST WEEK

should follow him, and that they should say to the man of the house which they should enter: "The Master saith unto thee, Where is the guestchamber, where I shall eat the passover with my disciples?" The man of the house was then to show them a large upper room, where they were to make ready. The two disciples departed and made ready for the feast.

2. **The strife among the disciples** (Luke 22: 14-16, 24-30). When the hour was come, Jesus sat down with His disciples to eat the Passover, and there arose a contention among them as to who was to be accounted the greatest. Jesus settled the controversy by saying: "The kings of the Gentiles exercise lordship over them; and they that exercise authority upon them are called benefactors. But ye shall not be so: but he that is greatest among you, let him be as the younger; and he that is chief, as he that doth serve."

3. **Jesus washes His disciples' feet** (John 13: 1-20). During supper, Jesus arose, and, laying aside His garments, took a towel and girded Himself, and proceeded to wash His disciples' feet. When He came to Peter, that disciple objected, saying: "Thou shalt never wash my feet." To which Jesus replied: "If I wash thee not, thou hast no part with me." Then Peter answered: "Lord, not my feet only, but also my hands and my head." The Lord then said: "If I then, your Lord and Master, have washed your feet; ye also ought to wash one another's feet."[1]

---

[1] This was not an ordinance to be perpetuated, but a simple custom practiced by the people of that day, and enjoined by our Lord upon the apostles, and the apostles alone. There is no record that it was ever observed as an ordinance under the new covenant.

THE GIST OF THE BIBLE

4. **Jesus foretells His betrayal by Judas** (Matt. 26:21-25; Mark 14:18-21; Luke 22:21-23; John 13:21-35). As Jesus and His disciples were eating, the Lord said: "Verily I say unto you, that one of you shall betray me." At these words they were all sorrowful, and each asked: "Lord, is it I?" Jesus answered: "He that dippeth his hand with me in the dish, the same shall betray me." Then Judas inquired: "Master, is it I?" And the Lord said unto him: "Thou hast said."

5. **Jesus foretells His denial by Peter** (Matt. 26:31-35; Mark 14:27-31; Luke 22:31-38; John 13:36-38). The Lord declared further that all of His disciples should be offended because of Him that night. But Peter objected, saying: "Though all men shall be offended because of thee, yet will I never be offended." Jesus replied: "Verily I say unto thee, That this night, before the cock crow, thou shalt deny me thrice."

6. **Jesus institutes the Lord's Supper** (Matt. 26:26-29; Mark 14:22-25; Luke 22:17-20). As they were eating, Jesus instituted the memorial of His death by taking bread and breaking it, saying, "Take, eat; this is my body," and also by taking the cup, saying: "Drink ye all of it; for this is my blood of the new testament, which is shed for many for the remission of sins."[1]

---
[1] The ordinance of the Lord's Supper must be divorced from those superstitions that have been grafted on it by the Roman Catholic Church. The bread and wine are not the very flesh and blood of the Lord, but are simple emblems of the same. The demand that we take the statements, "This is my body" and "This is my blood," literally, is absurd from the fact that Christ's body had not yet been broken nor his blood shed. Our Lord is not present at the communion service, but absent, as will be seen from 1 Cor. 11:26.

7. Christ's farewell discourse to His disciples (John 14-17). Following the instituting of the Lord's Supper, Jesus delivered to His disciples His farewell discourse, in which He told them that He was going to prepare a place for them, but that He would come again, and promised them another Comforter who was to abide with them for the age and who was to teach them all things, bring all things to their remembrance whatsoever He had said to them, and to guide them into all truth.[1]

VI. FRIDAY—THE DAY OF SUFFERING

1. The agony in Gethsemane (Matt. 26:36-46; Mark 14:32-42; Luke 22:39-46; John 18:1). When the feast was ended and Jesus and His disciples had sung a hymn, they went out and came to the garden of Gethsemane, which lay at the foot of the Mount of Olives. Leaving His disciples, excepting Peter, James and John, whom He took with Him, the Lord went a short distance away to pray. But He began to be exceedingly sorrowful, and so, leaving the three, He went still farther, where He fell upon His face and prayed: "O my Father, if it be possible, let this cup pass away from me: nevertheless, not as I will, but as thou wilt." He then returned, and, finding His disciples asleep, He said to Peter: "Could ye not watch with me one hour? Watch and pray, that ye enter not into temptation." Again He went away and prayed, and again returned to find His disciples asleep. Still yet a third time did He retire to pray, but when He returned, He said: "Arise, let

---
[1] The apostles, and they alone, were guided into all truth. This does not apply to the Church in general.

us be going: behold, he that betrayeth me is at hand."

2. **The betrayal of Jesus** (Matt. 26:47-56; Mark 14:43-52; Luke 22:47-53; John 18:2-12). While Jesus was yet speaking, Judas appeared with an armed force and, kissing the Lord, exclaimed: "Hail, Rabbi." The officers of the Jews then seized Him and bound Him, but Simon Peter, drawing a sword, smote the servant of the high priest and cut off his ear. Jesus said to Peter: "Put up the sword into the sheath: the cup which the Father hath given me, shall I not drink it?" And touching the servant's ear, He healed it. Then all of the disciples left Him and fled, and He was led away.

3. **The trial of Jesus** (Matt. 26:57-27:32; Mark 14:53-15:19; Luke 22:54-23:25; John 18:12-19:16).

(1) *Before Annas.* Jesus was first led to Annas, the father-in-law of Caiaphas and ex-high priest, who, after he had examined Him in regard to His teachings, sent Him bound to Caiaphas.

(2) *Before Caiaphas.* Here certain Jews bore false witness against Him, saying: "We heard him say, I will destroy this temple that is made with hands, and in three days I will build another made without hands." Then the high priest said to Jesus: "Answerest thou nothing?" But He held His peace, and the high priest asked again: "Art thou the Christ?" To which He said: "I am: and ye shall see the Son of man sitting on the right hand of power, and coming in the clouds of heaven." The high priest, at this, rent his clothes, exclaiming: "What need we any further witnesses? Ye have heard the blasphemy: what think ye?" They an-

THE LAST WEEK

swered: "He is worthy of death." And, spitting upon Him and smiting Him, His accusers said: "Prophesy unto us, thou Christ, Who is he that struck thee?"

(3) *Peter's denial.* When Jesus was led before Caiaphas, Peter followed afar off and, entering the court, sat down with the officers at a fire. One of the maids of the high priest saw him and accused him of being with Jesus, which accusation Peter denied three times, cursing and swearing the last time. Then the cock crew and the Lord turned and looked upon Peter, and he remembered what He had said unto him.

(4) *Before the Sanhedrin.* When it was day, the assembly led Jesus before the Sanhedrin, who, when they had examined Him and had decided that He was guilty of blasphemy, sent him to Pontius Pilate.

(5) *The suicide of Judas.* Judas, when he saw that Jesus was condemned, repented and brought the thirty pieces of silver and cast them down before the chief priests and elders, saying: "I have sinned in that I have betrayed innocent blood." But they said: "What is that to us? see thou to it." Then Judas went out and hanged himself,[1] and the priests took the money and with it bought the potter's field to bury strangers in.

(6) *Christ's first appearance before Pilate.* The Jews then brought Jesus before Pontius Pilate and demanded that he judge Him. This Pilate reluctantly did, but when he had heard His claims to Kingship, he went out to the Jews and said: "I find in him no fault at all." At this they were much enraged

---
[1] This information is supplemented, but not necessarily contradicted, by Acts 1: 18.

and said: "He stirreth up the people, teaching throughout all Judæa, and beginning from Galilee even unto this place."

(7) *Jesus sent to Herod Antipas.* When Pilate heard that Jesus was a Galilean, he sent Him to Herod, tetrarch of Galilee. Herod was pleased to see Jesus, as His fame had already reached him and he was desirous of seeing some miracle performed by Him. But when he questioned Him, Jesus did not answer a word, and, as the chief priests and scribes vehemently accused Him, he had Him clothed in gorgeous apparel and sent Him back to Pilate.

(8) *Christ's second appearance before Pilate.* Jesus was now a second time brought before Pilate, who, when he had questioned Him, went out and declared to the Jews that he found no fault in Him. But the people cried: "Away with this man, and release unto us Barabbas," "Crucify him, crucify him." Then Pilate scourged Jesus and, washing his hands, said: "I am innocent of the blood of this righteous man; see ye to it." After which he delivered Him to the Jews, who platted a crown of thorns and put it upon His head, arrayed Him in a purple garment and mocked Him.

4. **The crucifixion of Jesus** (Matt. 27:31-56; Mark 15:20-41; Luke 23:26-49; John 19:16-30). The Jews now led Jesus away to be crucified. On the way He stumbled under the weight of the cross which He bore, and it was placed upon the shoulder of Simon of Cyrene. A multitude of people and of the women followed, lamenting, and the Lord, turning to them, said: "Daughters of Jerusalem, weep

not for me, but weep for yourselves, and for your children. For, behold, the days are coming, in the which they shall say, Blessed are the barren, and the wombs that never bare, and the paps which never gave suck." When the company came to Calvary, they crucified Jesus between two thieves, one on the right hand and the other on the left, and a superscription was placed over His head, which read: "THIS IS THE KING OF THE JEWS." One of the thieves railed at Him, saying: "If thou be Christ, save thyself and us." But the other condemned him and, turning to the Lord, said: "Lord, remember me when thou comest into thy kingdom." To which the Lord replied: "Verily I say unto thee, To day shalt thou be with me in paradise." After which He said, "Father, into thy hands I commend my spirit," and expired. Attending the death of Jesus were many notable signs: the rocks were rent, the earth quaked, the veil of the Temple was rent and the graves were opened, so that many of the bodies of the saints which slept, arose after His resurrection and appeared to many in the Holy City. The centurion in command greatly feared, saying: "Truly this was the Son of God."

5. **The entombment** (Matt. 27:57-61; Mark 15:42-47; Luke 23:50-56; John 19:38-42). When evening was come, Joseph of Arimathæa, a just and righteous man, and Nicodemus, who had come to see Jesus by night, with the permission of Pilate, took the body of the Lord down from the cross, wound it in a linen cloth with spices, and laid it in a tomb hewn out of a rock and in which man had never before lain.

VII. SATURDAY—THE DAY OF REST AND SORROW

1. **The watch at the tomb** (Matt. 27:62-66). On the day following the day of the preparation, the chief priests and Pharisees came to Pilate and said: "Sir, we remember that that deceiver said, while he was yet alive, After three days I will rise again. Command therefore that the sepulchre be made sure until the third day, lest his disciples come by night, and steal him away, and say unto the people, He is risen from the dead: so the last error shall be worse than the first." Pilate replied: "Ye have a watch: go your way, make it as sure as you can." So they departed and sealed the mouth of the sepulchre and set a watch about it.

2. **The resting of the women** (Luke 23:56). After the burial of our Lord, the women who were with Him, returning, prepared spices and ointments and rested the sabbath day according to the commandment.

QUESTIONS

Give the probable date of the events of this study. Locate the points of interest and importance in this study. What can you say of crucifixion as a mode of punishment? From what village did Jesus go into Jerusalem upon the day of His triumphal entry? What did the people say when He entered the city? What three events occurred on Monday, the Day of Authority? What events occurred on Tuesday, the Day of Controversy? Who questioned Christ's authority and how did He answer them? Name the three warning parables. What three classes of people tried to entrap Jesus with their questions? Give the question of the Herodians. Of the Sadducees. Of the Pharisees. What question did Christ propound? Give the lament of Jesus over Jerusalem. Tell about the widow's gift. Give the substance of

THE LAST WEEK

Christ's last prophecy. Name the three Olivet parables. Who conspired against Jesus? Where did Jesus go upon Wednesday, the Day of Retirement, and what occurred there? Who offered to betray Christ, and how much did he receive? Mention, in their order, the events which occurred upon Thursday, the Day of Fellowship. Tell about the preparation for the Passover. Over what did the disciples contend, and how did Jesus silence them? Tell about Jesus washing His disciples' feet. Did Jesus foretell the betrayal by Judas and the denial by Peter? Give the circumstances in each case. Describe the institution of the Lord's Supper. Give the substance of Christ's farewell address to His disciples. Give, in their order, the events that occurred on Friday, the Day of Suffering. In what garden did Jesus pray? Tell about the betrayal of Jesus. Give the successive steps in the trial of Jesus. Describe the crucifixion of Christ. Tell about the entombment of Jesus. Why was a watch placed over Christ's tomb? Upon what day did the women rest, and why?

STUDY XXXVII. THE RESURRECTION DAYS

INTRODUCTION

1. **The date.** Probably in the spring of A. D. 30, or in A. D. 29. Jesus was raised on the first day of the week, which we now celebrate, not by divine precept, but by apostolic example.

2. **The resurrection of Jesus Christ a literal occurrence.** The Scriptures plainly teach that it was the literal grave body of Jesus that came forth from the tomb, and any other explanation of the mystery is wholly subversive of divine truth.

3. **The importance of Christ's resurrection.** Paul says: "If Christ be not risen, then is our preaching vain, and your faith is also vain. Yea, and we are found false witnesses of God; because we have testified of God that he raised up Christ: whom he raised not up, if so be that the dead rise not. For if the dead rise not, then is not Christ raised: and if Christ be not raised, your faith is vain; ye are yet in your sins. Then they also which are fallen asleep in Christ are perished" (1 Cor. 15:14-18).

I. THE EVENTS OF THE RESURRECTION DAY

1. **The resurrection of Jesus Christ** (Matt. 28:2-4). Early in the morning, on the first day of the week, there was an earthquake, and an angel of the

THE RESURRECTION DAYS

Lord descended from heaven, rolled away the stone from the door of the sepulchre and sat upon it, and Jesus Christ arose triumphant from the dead. For fear of the angel, the watchers did quake and became as dead men.

2. **The angelic announcement of Christ's resurrection** (Matt. 28:1-8; Mark 16:1-8; Luke 24:1-8; John 20:1-10). After the sabbath, but while it was yet dark upon the first day of the week, came Mary Magdalene and Mary the mother of James and Salome, with spices, to anoint the body of Jesus. But they found the stone rolled away from the door of the sepulchre, and, when they entered, they saw a young man, arrayed in a white robe, sitting on the right side of the tomb and who said: "Be not affrighted: Ye seek Jesus of Nazareth, which was crucified: he is risen; he is not here: behold the place where they laid him. But go your way, tell his disciples and Peter that he goeth before you into Galilee: there shall ye see him, as he said unto you." Then Mary Magdalene ran and, meeting Peter and John, said: "They have taken away the Lord out of the sepulchre, and we know not where they have laid him." When these disciples had come to the place where Jesus had lain, and had stooped down and had looked in, but had not found the body of Jesus, they returned to their homes.

3. **Jesus appears to the women** (Matt. 28:9, 10; Mark 16:9-11; Luke 24:9-11; John 20:11-18). After the departure of Peter and John, Mary Magdalene was standing by the tomb weeping. Here Jesus appeared to her, but at first she did not recognize Him. When He had revealed Himself, He said:

"Touch me not; for I am not yet ascended to my Father: but go to my brethren, and say unto them, I ascend unto my Father, and your Father; and to my God, and your God." Jesus also appeared to the other women who came and took hold of His feet and worshiped Him. Then the women went and told the disciples that they had seen Jesus, but they did not believe.

4. **The report of the guard** (Matt. 28:11-15). Some of the watch went into the city and told the chief priests all of the things that had occurred. Then the chief priests gave them money and told them to report that Jesus' disciples had come by night and had stolen Him away. This they did, and this was the common report among the Jews at that time.

5. **Jesus appears to Cephas and to two disciples on the way to Emmaus** (1 Cor. 15:5; Mark 16:12, 13; Luke 24:13-35). Jesus next appeared to Cephas and then to two disciples on their way to Emmaus. As the two were proceeding on their way, they were talking of the things that had recently occurred, when Jesus Himself drew near and joined them, but they did not recognize Him. He said to them: "What manner of communications are these that ye have one to another, as ye walk, and are sad?" They replied by telling Him of the crucifixion and of the report of the women that He had been raised from the dead. Then He said: "O fools, and slow of heart to believe all that the prophets have spoken: ought not Christ to have suffered these things, and to enter into his glory?" They then constrained Him to tarry with them, and while at meat He revealed

THE RESURRECTION DAYS

Himself and vanished out of their sight, after which they returned to Jerusalem and told the eleven and them that were with them that they had seen the Christ.

6. **Jesus appears to the disciples, excepting Thomas** (Mark 16:14; Luke 24:36-43; John 20:19-25). In the evening of the first day of the week, when the doors were shut because the disciples were afraid of the Jews, Jesus appeared to them as they sat at meat, saying, "Peace be unto you." He then showed them His hands and His feet, saying, "A spirit hath not flesh and bones as ye see me have," after which He breathed upon them and said: "Receive ye the Holy Ghost: whose soever sins ye remit, they are remitted unto them; and whose soever sins ye retain, they are retained." When Thomas, who had been absent, returned and heard the things that were told him, he refused to believe.

II. THE EVENTS AFTER THE RESURRECTION DAY

1. **Jesus appears to the disciples, including Thomas** (John 20:26-31; 1 Cor. 15:5). One week after, the disciples, with Thomas, were together behind closed doors, and Jesus appeared to them and said: "Peace be unto you." He then commanded Thomas to feel the nail-prints in His hands and the spear-wound in His side, which Thomas did and exclaimed: "My Lord and my God." Jesus then said to him: "Thomas, because thou hast seen me, thou hast believed: blessed are they that have not seen, and yet have believed."

2. **Jesus appears to seven disciples beside the Sea**

of Galilee (John 21). Jesus next appeared to seven of His disciples beside the Sea of Galilee. They had gone fishing, but, though they had fished all night, they had caught nothing. In the morning Jesus stood upon the shore and said: "Children, have ye any meat?" They answered: "No." He then said: "Cast the net on the right side of the ship, and ye shall find." This they did, with the result that they were not able to draw it for the multitude of fish. The disciples now recognized Jesus, and Peter, drawing about him his fisher's coat, leaped into the sea, while the other disciples followed him in their boats, drawing the net with them. When they reached the shore, they found a fire of coals and fish laid thereon with bread. Jesus said to them: "Bring of the fish which ye have now caught." And Simon brought one hundred and fifty and three. When they had dined, Jesus said to Simon: "Simon, son of Jonas, lovest thou me more than these?" Simon replied: "Yea, Lord; thou knowest that I love thee." And Jesus answered: "Feed my lambs." Again Jesus asked the same question, and, when He had received the same answer, He replied: "Feed my sheep." Still a third time was the same question asked and the same answer given. And Jesus replied for the last time: "Feed my sheep."

3. **Jesus appears to five hundred and commissions His apostles upon a mountain in Galilee** (1 Cor. 15:6; Matt. 28:16-20; Mark 16:15-18). Jesus now appeared to about five hundred brethren at once, probably upon a mountain in Galilee, where He gave the Great Commission to His apostles and committed to them the power to perform signs and miracles.

THE RESURRECTION DAYS

4. Jesus appears to James and then to all of the disciples (1 Cor. 15:7; Luke 24:44-49; Acts 1:3-8). After this Jesus appeared to James and then to all of the apostles, demonstrating His resurrection by many infallible proofs and teaching them the things concerning the kingdom of God. He said: "John indeed baptized with water; but ye shall be baptized with the Holy Ghost not many days hence." When asked if He would at that time restore the kingdom to Israel, He replied: "It is not for you to know the times or the seasons, which the Father hath put in his own power. But ye shall receive power, after that the Holy Ghost is come upon you: and ye shall be witnesses unto me both in Jerusalem, and in Judæa, and in Samaria, and unto the uttermost part of the earth."

5. The ascension (Mark 16:19, 20; Luke 24:50-53; Acts 1:9-12). After these things, Jesus led His disciples out of Jerusalem toward Bethany, where he was parted from them and was received into heaven. While they looked, two men, clothed in white apparel, stood by them, who said: "Ye men of Galilee, why stand ye gazing up into heaven? this same Jesus, which is taken up from you into heaven, shall so come in like manner as ye have seen him go into heaven." The disciples then returned to Jerusalem

QUESTIONS

In what year did the events of this study probably occur? What do the Scriptures teach in regard to the resurrection of Jesus? Tell what Paul says about the importance of Christ's resurrection. Describe the resurrection of Jesus Christ. Give the angelic announcement of the resurrection. To whom did

Jesus first appear? What explanation did the guard invent of the absence of the body of Jesus from the tomb? Tell about the appearance of Jesus to the two disciples on the way to Emmaus. Where did Jesus appear to ten of His disciples on the evening of the resurrection day and what did He say to them? What occurred one week later? Give the circumstances of Christ's appearance to the seven disciples at the Sea of Galilee. Where was the Great Commission given, and how many brethren are supposed to have been there? Give an account of the last appearance of Jesus just prior to His ascension. Describe the ascension.

STUDY XXXVIII. THE BEGINNINGS OF THE CHURCH

(Acts 1:12-12:25)

INTRODUCTION

1. **The meaning of the term "church."** The term "church" is translated from the Greek *ecclesia*, which means "an assembly of people, convoked by public proclamation."

2. **The change of dispensation.** The death of Jesus Christ upon the cross marked the ending of the Mosaic and the beginning of the Christian dispensation. The change that occurred involved the abrogation of the Mosaic law, the annulment of the covenant with Israel as a nation and the offer of salvation to the Gentiles upon the same terms that it was offered to the Jews. This is made plain from 2 Cor. 3:6-18; Eph. 2:14-18; Col. 2:14-17; Heb. 9:14, 15, and other Scriptures.

3. **The mission and work of the Holy Spirit.** Our Lord declared that the mission of the Holy Spirit was to "reprove the world of sin, and of righteousness, and of judgment" (John 16:8). Before the day of Pentecost the Holy Spirit manifested Himself only occasionally and to a certain class (Heb. 1:1; 2 Pet. 1:21), but at Pentecost He came to all flesh (Joel 2:28, 29; Acts 2:16, 17) and to abide unto the end of the age. At Pentecost, and through the

apostolical period, He manifested Himself supernaturally, in prophecies, tongues and supernatural knowledge, but, these special spiritual gifts ceasing when the purpose for which they were designed had been fulfilled (1 Cor. 13:8-13), He has operated since in the various functions of His office only and wholly through the Word (John 6:63; 17:17; Rom. 1:16; Heb. 4:12; Jas. 1:18, etc.).

4. **The period covered.** The period covered in the present study extended from the ascension of our Lord, about 30 A. D., to the first missionary journey of the apostle Paul, about 48 A. D.

I. THE CHURCH AT JERUSALEM

1. **The ten days' waiting** (Acts 1:12-14). After the ascension the disciples returned to Jerusalem, where they abode in an upper chamber and where they continued with one accord in prayer and supplication with the women, and Mary the mother of Jesus, and His brethren.

2. **The choosing of Matthew** (Acts 1:15-26). At this time Peter stood up in the midst of the disciples, of whom there were 120, and declared that one of their number should be selected to take the place in the apostleship which Judas Iscariot had lost by transgression. They then selected two, Joseph called Barsabas, who was surnamed Justus, and Matthias; and when they had prayed, they cast their lots, and Matthias was chosen.

3. **The outpouring of the Holy Spirit** (Acts 2:1-13). When the day of Pentecost was fully come, the disciples were all with one accord in one place. Suddenly there came a sound as of a mighty rushing

THE BEGINNINGS OF THE CHURCH

wind which filled all the house where they were sitting.¹ Cloven tongues of fire also sat upon each, and they spoke in other tongues as the Spirit gave them utterance. There were dwelling in Jerusalem devout Jews out of many nations, who were greatly amazed at what they saw and heard, some inquiring what these things meant, others mocking, saying that the disciples were filled with new wine.

4. **Peter's first discourse** (Acts 2:14-41). But Peter, with the eleven, stood up and declared that the things which were occurring were but the fulfillment of the prophecy of Joel, and, further, that Jesus of Nazareth was the Christ, the seed of David, whom God had raised up to sit on His throne. At these words the multitude were convicted and cried out: "Men and brethren, what shall we do?" Peter replied: "Repent, and be baptized every one of you in the name of Jesus Christ for the remission of sins, and ye shall receive the gift of the Holy Ghost." Then those that gladly received the word were baptized, and there were added unto the disciples about three thousand souls.²

5. **The first church** (Acts 2:42-47). These continued steadfastly in the apostles' doctrine and fellowship, and in breaking of bread and in prayers. They also sold their possessions and divided with

---

¹ Their baptism with the Holy Spirit did not consist in the pouring out of the same upon them, but in their submersion in it when it "filled all the house where they were sitting."

² It has been offered as an objection to immersion that the three thousand could not have been immersed in one day, hence that they must have been baptized by some other "mode." The fallacy of this argument will be seen at once when it is discovered that there were ample means for such immersion in the great number of pools in Jerusalem and within its vicinity, and an ample force to perform the rite in the 120 disciples who were present in that city upon this particular day of Pentecost.

one another. Many wonders and signs were performed by the apostles, and the Lord added daily to the church such as were being saved.[1]

6. **The first apostolic miracle** (Acts 3:1-11). Peter and John went into the Temple at the ninth hour, which was the hour of prayer. There they found, lying at the Beautiful Gate, a man who was lame from his birth and who asked alms of them. Peter, looking upon him, said: "Silver and gold have I none; but such as I have give I thee: In the name of Jesus Christ of Nazareth rise up and walk." And the man, with Peter's help, arose and walked and went into the Temple, leaping and praising God.

7. **Peter's second discourse** (Acts 3:12-26). This miracle excited the wonder of the people and they gathered around Peter, who again declared unto them that Jesus whom they slew was the very Christ and that He had been raised from the dead, and further demanded that they repent and turn that their sins might be blotted out, so that times of refreshing might come from the presence of the Lord, and He might send Jesus the second time to consummate the restitution of all things.

8. **The first persecution** (Acts 4:1-22). When the Sadducees learned that the apostles were preaching the resurrection, they were much displeased, and arrested them, and put them in prison until the following day. On the morrow they were brought before the Sanhedrin, who asked: "By what power,

---

[1] Pentecost marks the beginning of the Christian Church. Everything that was done prior to this time was merely preparatory to that grand event in which were accomplished the promises of God.

or by what name, have ye done this?" Then Peter, filled with the Holy Ghost, declared that it was through the power of the risen Christ that the lame man was enabled to walk, and, further, that Jesus was the stone whom the builders had rejected and that it was through His name, and His name alone, that salvation could be obtained. When the Sanhedrin perceived that Peter and John were unlearned and ignorant men, they marveled, and, charging them that they should no more preach in the name of Jesus, let them go.

9. **The second filling with the Holy Spirit** (Acts 4: 23-37). Peter and John now returned to their own company and reported what the chief priests and elders had said to them. When the disciples heard them, they raised their voices in praise to God, and the place was shaken, and they were all filled with the Holy Spirit and spoke the word of the Lord with boldness. The multitude of them that believed were of one heart and of one soul, and brought their possessions and laid them at the feet of the apostles, who distributed them to those who were in need.[1]

10. **The sin of Ananias and Sapphira** (Acts 5: 1-16). But there was a certain man named Ananias who, with his wife, Sapphira, sold a possession, but kept back part of the price and only brought a portion to lay at the apostles' feet. Then Peter said to Ananias: "Ananias, why hath Satan filled thine

---
[1] Some have argued from this that Christian communism should be practiced to-day. But this was only a temporary arrangement for that particular day and time, and was not practiced afterwards, as is shown by the teachings of the remainder of the Acts of the Apostles and the Epistles. In none of the later New Testament writings does such a practice appear.

heart to lie to the Holy Ghost,' and to keep back part of the price of the land? Whiles it remained, was it not thine own? and after it was sold, was it not in thine own power? why hast thou conceived this thing in thine heart? thou hast not lied unto men, but unto God." At these words Ananias fell down dead, and the young men wound him up, carried him out and buried him. About three hours afterwards Sapphira came in, and, when she had confessed the sin, she, too, fell down dead and was buried by the side of her husband. Because of this judgment upon Ananias and Sapphira, fear came upon all the church, and by the hands of the apostles many signs and wonders were wrought among the people, and many who were afflicted were healed of their diseases.

11. **The second persecution** (Acts 5: 17-42). Indignant at the popularity of the apostles with the people, the high priests and the Sadducees arrested them and put them in the common prison. But, in the night, the angel of the Lord opened the prison doors and said: "Go, stand and speak in the temple to the people all the words of this life." On the morrow, when the officers discovered that their prisoners had escaped, they went in search of them, and, finding them in the Temple, brought them again before the council, who inquired: "Did not we straitly command you that ye should not teach in this name? and, behold, ye have filled Jerusalem with your doctrine, and intend to bring this man's blood upon us." Then Peter and the other apostles

---

[1] As the Holy Spirit can be lied to, it is evident that He is a personality, and not simply an influence.

THE BEGINNINGS OF THE CHURCH

answered that they ought to obey God rather than man, and declared again the resurrection and exaltation of Jesus Christ. When the council had heard these words, Gamaliel, a Pharisee and doctor of the law, urged caution in dealing with the apostles, saying that if what they did was through the counsel of men, it could be overthrown, but if it was of God, it could not be overthrown. So, calling the apostles, the council beat them and let them go, admonishing them to cease speaking in the name of Jesus. The apostles departed, rejoicing that they were worthy to suffer shame for Christ, but refrained not from preaching Him in the Temple and in every house.

12. **The first deacons** (Acts 6:1-7). The number of the disciples increased, and the Greeks complained against the Hebrews because their widows were neglected in the daily ministrations. Then the twelve called the church together and commanded them to look out from among them seven men of good report and full of the Holy Ghost and wisdom who should be given charge over this matter. Those chosen were Stephen, a man full of faith and the Holy Spirit, Philip, Prochorus, Nicanor, Timon, Parmenas and Nicolas, a proselyte of Antioch. These they set before the apostles, who, when they had prayed, laid their hands upon them.

13. **The arrest and stoning of Stephen** (Acts 6:8-7:60). Stephen was a man of faith and power and did great wonders and miracles among the people, by which he stirred up the enmity of certain opponents of the Christian faith. These had him arrested, and, when he was brought before the coun-

cil, they charged that he had declared that Jesus would destroy that place and would change the customs which Moses had delivered to the people. When Stephen was permitted to speak for himself, he declared how God had delivered the fathers and ended by scathingly denouncing his persecutors for the crucifixion of Jesus Christ. Enraged at his boldness, they took Stephen out of the city and, laying their clothes at the feet of a young man whose name was Saul, stoned him to death.

II. THE CHURCH OUTSIDE OF JERUSALEM

1. **The scattering of the church** (Acts 8:1-4). By the persecution which followed the stoning of Stephen the church at Jerusalem was scattered abroad throughout Judea and Samaria, except the apostles. And they that were scattered abroad went everywhere preaching the word.

2. **The conversion of the Samaritans** (Acts 8:5-25). Philip, one of the seven deacons, went down to Samaria, where he preached Christ unto the people and performed many miracles. As a result, many, both men and women, believed and were baptized, among them Simon the sorcerer. Now, when the apostles at Jerusalem heard that Samaria had received the word, they sent unto them Peter and John, who, when they were come, prayed for them and laid their hands upon them that they might receive the Holy Spirit, for as yet He had fallen upon none of them. Simon, seeing that the Holy Spirit was given by the laying on of hands, offered the apostles money for the power, but Peter condemned him, saying: "Thy money perish with thee, because

THE BEGINNINGS OF THE CHURCH

thou hast thought that the gift of God may be purchased with money." When Simon saw that he had sinned against God in his request, he besought the apostles to pray that none of the things of which they had spoken might come upon him. After the apostles had testified and preached the word of the Lord, they returned to Jerusalem.

3. **The conversion of the eunuch** (Acts 8:26-40). Being commanded by an angel, Philip went toward the south on the road that led from Jerusalem to Gaza, where he met a man of Ethiopia, a eunuch of great authority under Candace, queen of that country. This man had been at Jerusalem to worship, and, as he was returning in his chariot, he was reading Isaiah the prophet. The Spirit said to Philip: "Go near, and join thyself to this chariot." Philip did as he was directed, and asked: "Understandest thou what thou readest?" The eunuch answered: "How can I, except some man should guide me?" Then Philip began and taught unto him Jesus, and, as they went on their way, they came to a certain water and the eunuch said: "See, here is water; what doth hinder me to be baptized?" Philip answered: "If thou believest with all thine heart, thou mayest." And he said: "I believe that Jesus Christ is the Son of God." Then Philip took him down into the water and baptized him,[1] and he went on his way rejoicing.

4. **The conversion of Saul of Tarsus** (Acts 9:1-19). The next event of importance in the history of the church was the conversion of Saul of Tarsus.

---
[1] The going down into the water of both Philip and the eunuch was wholly unnecessary unless baptism is immersion.

5. **The healing of Æneas** (Acts 9:32-35). Peter went down to the saints who dwelt at Lydda and found there a man named Æneas, who had been sick of the palsy for eight years. To him Peter said: "Jesus Christ maketh thee whole: arise, and make thy bed." And immediately he arose, and all that dwelt at Lydda and Saron were converted to the faith.

6. **Tabitha raised from the dead** (Acts 9:36-43). There was dwelling at Joppa a certain disciple named Tabitha (also called Dorcas), a woman of good works, and she died. As Lydda was near to Joppa, the disciples sent two men to Peter, requesting him to come to them. When he was come, they took him into an upper chamber, where he found the widows weeping and showing the garments which Tabitha had made. But, putting them out, Peter turned to the body and said: "Tabitha, arise." And she opened her eyes and sat up. After this miracle, Peter tarried many days with Simon the tanner.

7. **The conversion of Cornelius and his household** (Acts 10:1-48). There was a certain centurion by the name of Cornelius who lived in Cæsarea and who was a devout man and one who feared God. Cornelius had a vision in which he was commanded to send men to Joppa and to call for one Simon Peter, who would tell him what he ought to do. On the day following, Peter went upon the housetop to pray, and, when he hungered, a sheet was let down from heaven in which were all manner of four-footed beasts of the earth and wild beasts and creeping things and fowls of the air, and a voice from heaven said: "Rise, Peter; kill, and eat." But Peter ob-

THE BEGINNINGS OF THE CHURCH

jected, saying: "Not so, Lord; for I have never eaten anything that is common or unclean." To which the voice replied: "What God hath cleansed, that call not thou common." While Peter doubted as to the meaning of this vision, the messengers from Cornelius came to him and stated their mission, and he received them into the house. On the morrow, he returned with them to Cæsarea, where he met Cornelius, who explained to him his vision. Then Peter preached Jesus to him and his house, declaring His Messiahship and His resurrection. While he was speaking, the Holy Spirit fell upon them, and they spoke in tongues and magnified God to the astonishment of the Jewish believers who were with Peter.[1] Then Peter said: "Can any man forbid water, that these should be baptized, which have received the Holy Ghost as well as we?" And he commanded them to be baptized in the name of the Lord.

8. Peter vindicates his ministry to the Gentiles (Acts 11:1-18). Following this, Peter returned to Jerusalem, and, when the apostles and brethren met him, they contended with him because he had eaten with the uncircumcised. Then Peter related to them his vision and gave an account of the outpouring of the Holy Spirit upon Cornelius and his household. When they heard these things, they glorified God, saying: "Then hath God also to the Gentiles granted repentance unto life."

9. **The founding of the church at Antioch** (Acts 11:19-30). Some of those who were scattered

---
[1] The baptism with the Holy Spirit of the household of Cornelius was not for a blessing to them, but was an evidentiary sign to Peter and those who were with him that God had accepted the Gentiles.

abroad in the persecution, which arose at the time of the stoning of Stephen, were men of Cyprus and Cyrene, who, when they were come to Antioch, preached the word to the Greeks of that city. As a result, a great number believed and turned to the Lord. When this came to the ears of the church at Jerusalem, they sent Barnabas to Antioch, who, when he was come, exhorted the disciples that they should cleave to the Lord. Then, departing, Barnabas went to Tarsus in search of Saul, whom, having found, he brought back to Antioch with him. For one whole year they taught the people and assembled with the disciples, who were called Christians first in that city. In those days certain prophets came from Jerusalem to Antioch, among them Agabus, who predicted that there should be a famine throughout the whole world. This determined the disciples to send relief to their brethren in Judea, which they did by the hands of Barnabas and Saul.

10. **The arrest and deliverance of Peter** (Acts 12: 1-19). About this time Herod stretched forth his hand against the church, slew James, the brother of John, with the sword and, because it pleased the Jews, had Peter shut up in prison. But prayer was made for him without ceasing in the church, and the night before Herod would have brought him forth, and while he was sleeping between two soldiers, an angel of the Lord appeared to him, commanded him to rise and gird himself, smote the chains from off his hands and told him to follow him. This Peter did, and, after the angel had led him through the iron gate which led into the city. he departed from Peter. Peter then came to the

THE BEGINNINGS OF THE CHURCH

house of Mary, the mother of John, surnamed Mark, and knocked at the door. A damsel, named Rhoda, came to the door, who, when she heard his voice, did not open the door, but, with gladness, ran and told those within that Peter stood without. When they saw him they were astonished, but, after he had declared how the Lord had brought him out of the prison, he departed to another place. On the morrow, when Herod sought for Peter and he could not be found, he commanded that the keepers should be put to death. And, leaving Judea, he went to Cæsarea, where he abode.

11. **The death of Herod** (Acts 12:20-25). Herod became much displeased with the inhabitants of Tyre and Sidon, but, when they came to make peace with him, he sat upon his throne and delivered an oration to them. At this the people shouted: "It is the voice of a god, and not of a man." And an angel of the Lord smote him and he was eaten by worms and gave up the ghost. But the word of God grew and multiplied, and Barnabas and Saul returned from Jerusalem, when they had fulfilled their ministry, bringing with them John, whose surname was Mark.

QUESTIONS

Give the general outline of this study. What is the meaning of the term "church"? Describe the change of dispensations. Give the mission and work of the Holy Spirit. How much time is covered in this study? How long did the disciples wait at Jerusalem before they received the baptism of the Holy Spirit? Who was chosen to succeed Judas Iscariot in the apostleship? Describe the outpouring of the Holy Spirit on the day of Pentecost. Give the substance of Peter's first discourse. Give the characteristics of the first church. Describe the first apostolic

THE GIST OF THE BIBLE

miracle. Give the occasion and substance of Peter's second discourse. Tell about the first persecution. Describe the second outpouring of the Holy Spirit. Give the sin and fate of Ananias and Sapphira. Tell about the second persecution. Give the circumstances of the choosing of the first deacons. Tell about the arrest and stoning of Stephen. Tell about the scattering of the church. Who first preached the word at Samaria? What apostles followed him from Jerusalem? Tell about the conversion of the eunuch. What young man was converted about this time? Describe the conversion of the household of Cornelius. How did the disciples at Jerusalem feel toward Peter because of his associations with the Gentiles at Cæsarea? Describe the founding of the church at Antioch. Give the account of the arrest and deliverance of Peter. Tell about the death of Herod.

STUDY XXXIX. THE LIFE OF PAUL

(Acts 7:58-28:31)

INTRODUCTION

1. **The Roman Empire.** When Augustus Cæsar took the throne at the age of thirty-six, the Roman Empire comprised one hundred million inhabitants and a territory in southern and central Europe, western Asia and northern Africa twenty-seven hundren miles long and with an average breadth of one thousand miles. This territory was divided into twenty-seven provinces. The following emperors reigned after Augustus and until A. D. 70: Tiberius (14 A. D.), Caligula (37), Claudius I. (41), Nero (54), Galba (68), Otho (69) and Vitellius (69).

2. **The heathen religions.** The heathen religions with which Paul came in contact were polytheistic. Those of Greece and Rome were similar and, in some respects, identical. In both countries twelve great gods, with a multitude of lesser divinities, were worshiped. These gods were the prototypes of man with his powers magnified. They were described as gigantic of size, swift of foot, strong of body and limb, treacherous and deceitful in character, amorous in their relations and sometimes violent in their passions. Zeus, or Jupiter, who presided in their councils, was supposed to have his throne on Mt. Olympus. When Rome conquered a people, their

divinities were besought to take up their abode within the Imperial City and their images were placed in the Pantheon. Rome was hostile to Christianity only because the faith of Christ was intolerant of other faiths.

3. **The conditions conducive to the spread of the gospel.**

(1) *One great government.* This insured peace and a facility of travel.

(2) *One great language.* This language was a simplified form of the Greek and was the language of commerce and social intercourse.

(3) *The spread of monotheism.* Wherever the Jews went, in their spread throughout the civilized world after their return from Babylon, they carried with them the doctrine of one God. This, with its related doctrines, formed a firm foundation upon which the apostles could build.

4. **The companions of Paul.** On his first missionary journey, Paul had, as companions, Barnabas and John Mark. On his second, Silas, Timothy, Luke and Aquila and Priscilla. And, on his third, probably Titus, Luke, Gaius, Aristarchus, Secundus, Timothy, Tychicus and Trophimus. Among those who were associated with Paul at Rome were Tychicus, Epaphras, Luke and Timothy.

5. **Chronological data.** The conversion of Paul occurred, probably, in A. D. 36 or 37. His first missionary tour occurred in 48 and 49; his second missionary tour, 51-54; his third, 54-58; his imprisonment at Cæsarea, 58-60; his first imprisonment at Rome, 61-63; his second imprisonment at Rome, probably 67 and 68.

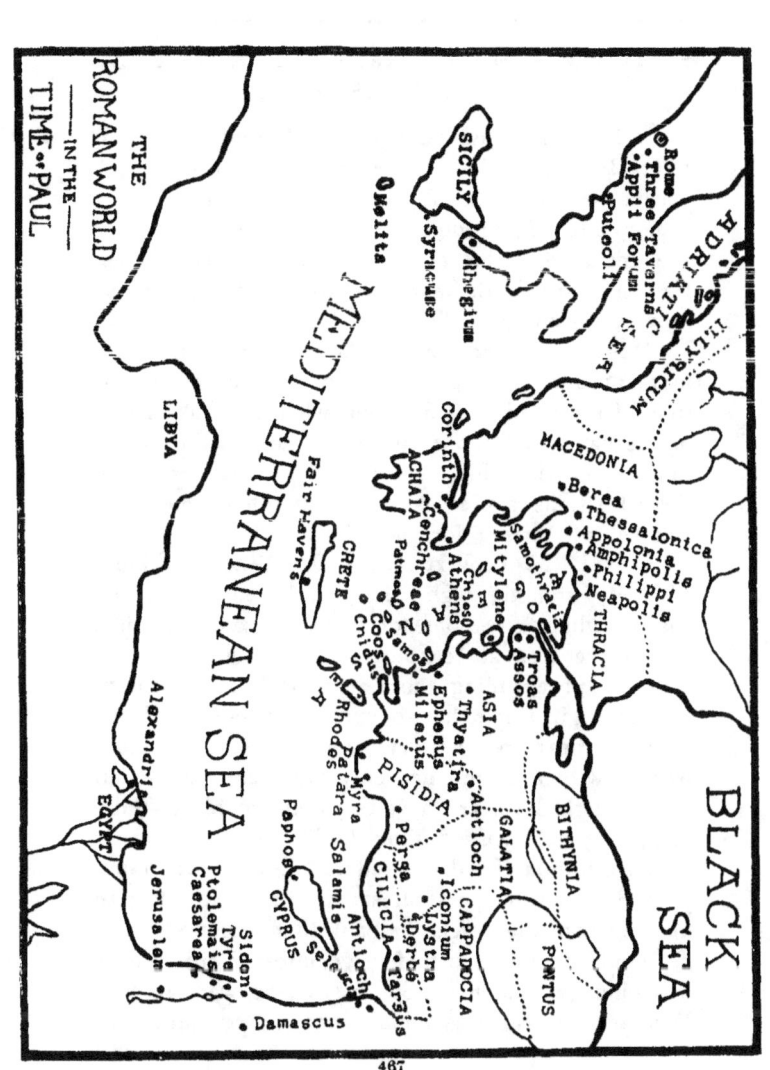

I. THE BIRTH AND EARLY LIFE OF SAUL OF TARSUS

1. **The birth and advantages of Saul of Tarsus** (Acts 22:3; Phil. 3:5). Saul, afterwards called Paul, was a Jew, born in Tarsus, a city of Cilicia, Asia Minor, but was brought up in Jerusalem, where he was educated at the feet of the great Jewish teacher, Gamaliel. By birth he was a Roman citizen and by religious training a Pharisee.

2. **Saul the persecutor** (Acts 7:58-8:3). Saul first appeared as a persecutor of the church at the time of the stoning of Stephen, when he took charge of the clothes of those who took part in the execution. Following this, he was active in the arrest of the Christians at Jerusalem, casting both men and women into prison for their faith.

3. **Saul the convert** (Acts 9:1-19). Receiving authority from the high priest, Saul went to Damascus, to which city some of the Christians who had been persecuted at Jerusalem had fled, for the purpose of apprehending those who believed in Christ, that he might bring them bound to Jerusalem. When he came near to Damascus, he was suddenly confronted with a bright, heavenly light, and, as he fell to the earth, he heard a voice saying to him: "Saul, Saul, why persecutest thou me?" Saul answered: "Who art thou, Lord?" And the Lord said: "I am Jesus whom thou persecutest: it is hard for thee to kick against the pricks." Saul then inquired what he should do and was told to go into the city, where it should be told him. So, arising, he was led into Damascus, for he was blind, where he continued for

THE LIFE OF PAUL

three days without food or drink. At the expiration of this time, Ananias, one of the disciples in that city, by the direction of the Lord came to where Saul was, and, putting his hands upon him, said: "Brother Saul, the Lord, even Jesus, that appeared unto thee in the way as thou camest, hath sent me, that thou mightest receive thy sight, and be filled with the Holy Ghost." And immediately he received his sight and was baptized, after which he continued certain days with the disciples at Damascus.

4. Saul the Christian.

(1) *At Damascus* (Acts 9:20-22). Saul straightway preached Christ in the synagogue, to the amazement of the people, and confounded the Jews with the proof of His divinity.

(2) *In Arabia* (Acts 9:23; Gal. 1:18). The "many days" of Acts are probably the "three years" of Galatians, during a part of which time, at least, Saul was in Arabia.

(3) *At Jerusalem* (Acts 9:24-29). Saul evidently returned to Damascus, where the Jews took counsel to kill him. But the disciples let him down from the wall in a basket and he fled to Jerusalem. Here he found the Christians afraid of him until Barnabas had declared unto them the fact and circumstances of his conversion.

(4) *At Tarsus* (Acts 9:30). From Jerusalem, Saul went to his old home in Tarsus by way of Cæsarea.

(5) *At Antioch and Jerusalem* (Acts 11:25-30; 12:25). After a time Barnabas came to Tarsus seeking Saul, and, finding him, returned with him to Antioch, where for one whole year they assembled with the church and taught the people. During this

time there came to Antioch from Jerusalem prophets who predicted a great famine in the land during the reign of Claudius Cæsar. Hearing this, the disciples sent relief to their brethren in Judea by the hands of Barnabas and Saul.

(6) *The return to Antioch* (Acts 12:25). Having fulfilled their ministry at Jerusalem, Barnabas and Saul returned to Antioch, bringing with them John whose surname was Mark.

II. PAUL'S FIRST MISSIONARY JOURNEY

1. **Barnabas and Saul commissioned** (Acts 13:1-3). While Barnabas and Saul tarried at Antioch, the Holy Spirit said: "Separate me Barnabas and Saul for the work whereunto I have called them." So, when the church had fasted and prayed, they laid their hands upon them and sent them away.

2. **The opposition of Elymas, the sorcerer, at Paphos** (Acts 13:3-12). Departing from Antioch, the apostles, accompanied by John Mark, went through Seleucia and sailed for Cyprus, where, in Salamis, they preached the word in the synagogues of the Jews. At Paphos, where they also preached the word, the deputy of the country, Sergius Paulus, believed. But there was in that place a certain sorcerer, Bar-jesus, or Elymas, by name, who sought to turn away the deputy from the faith. For his opposition Elymas was stricken by Paul, through the power of the Holy Spirit, with blindness, that he might not see the sun for a season. Then, leaving Paphos, the apostles went to Perga in Pamphylia, where John Mark left them and returned to Jerusalem.

3. **Paul preaches in the synagogue at Antioch of Pisidia** (Acts 13:13-52). From Perga the apostles departed to Antioch of Pisidia. Here Paul, upon the sabbath, by the invitation of the ruler of the synagogue, preached Christ and His resurrection to the Jews, declaring that through Him all that believe are justified from all things from which they could not be justified by the law of Moses. When, on the next sabbath, the multitude came together to hear Paul and Barnabas, the Jews were filled with envy and spoke against the things which Paul had declared. Then Paul and Barnabas boldly said: "It was necessary that the word of God should first have been spoken to you: but seeing ye put it from you, and judge yourselves unworthy of everlasting life, lo, we turn to the Gentiles." At this the Jews stirred up the devout women and chief men and expelled the apostles out of the city. So, Paul and Barnabas, shaking the dust off their feet against them, came to Iconium.

4. **Paul and Barnabas at Iconium** (Acts 14:1-7). At Iconium the apostles preached the gospel in the synagogue and performed a number of signs and wonders through which many believed. But those who did not believe attempted to assault the apostles and they fled to Lystra and Derbe.

5. **The healing of an impotent man at Lystra** (Acts 14:6-18). When Paul and Barnabas came to Lystra, they found an impotent man whom Paul healed of his infirmity. The people, beholding the miracle, cried, "The gods are come down to us in the likeness of men," and they called Barnabas, Jupiter, and Paul, Mercurius, because he was the

chief speaker. The priest of Jupiter also brought oxen and garlands to the gates and would have sacrificed with the people. But, when Paul and Barnabas heard it, they rent their clothes and, running in among the people, declared that they were men of like passions with their would-be worshipers, and that they should turn from their vanities unto the true God. Yet, even with these explanations, could they scarcely restrain the people from sacrificing unto them. Following this, however, certain Jews from Antioch and Iconium coming to Lystra and inciting the people, Paul was stoned and was drawn out of the city for dead.

6. **The return to Antioch** (Acts 14: 20-28). Leaving Lystra, the apostles went to Derbe, where they taught many, following which they returned again to Lystra, Iconium and Antioch of Pisidia, confirming the disciples and exhorting them to continue in the faith. They also ordained elders in every church and commended them to the Lord on whom they believed. After this they passed through Pisidia and Pamphylia and came again to Antioch in Syria, where they abode with the disciples a long time.

7. **The council at Jerusalem** (Acts 15: 1-35). Certain Christian Jews had come down to Antioch from Jerusalem, declaring that, unless a man was circumcised according to the law of Moses, he could not be saved. After much discussion, Paul and Barnabas, with others, were sent to Jerusalem to consult the apostles and elders on this matter. Passing through Phœnicia and Samaria, where they declared the conversion of the Gentiles, the apostles came to Jerusalem. Here they consulted the apostles and elders,

and it was decided that no greater burden should be laid upon the Gentile converts than that they should abstain from meats offered to idols, from blood, from things strangled and from fornication. With this decision, Paul and Barnabas returned to Antioch, where they read it to the church and where it caused rejoicing among those who believed.

III. PAUL'S SECOND MISSIONARY JOURNEY

1. **Paul and Barnabas separate** (Acts 15:36-41). Some days later, Paul suggested to Barnabas that they visit the brethren in the cities where they had preached the word. Barnabas was favorable, but insisted that they take John Mark, to which Paul was opposed, as John had deserted them in Pamphylia. So strong was the contention that the two separated, and Barnabas, taking John, sailed for Cyprus, while Paul, taking Silas, went through Syria and Cilicia, confirming the churches.

2. **Timothy joins Paul and Silas** (Acts 16:1-5). Coming to Derbe and Lystra, Paul and Silas found a certain disciple, Timotheus by name, a man of good report among the brethren at Lystra and Iconium. The mother of Timotheus was a Jewess, but his father was a Greek, because of which, as a matter of policy, Paul had him circumcised, after which he joined Paul and Silas on their journey.

3. **Paul's Macedonian vision** (Acts 16:6-12). Passing through Phrygia, Galatia and Mysia, Paul and his companions came to Troas, where the apostle had a vision in which he saw a man of Macedonia, who said: "Come over into Macedonia, and help

us." Immediately, Paul, with Silas, Timothy and Luke, who joined them here, started for that country. Leaving Troas, they passed through Samothracia and Neapolis and came to Philippi, one of the chief cities of Macedonia.

4. Paul and Silas at Philippi.

(1) *The conversion of Lydia* (Acts 16:13-15). On the sabbath, Paul and his companions went down to a river-side, where prayer was wont to be made, and spoke to the women who resorted there. Among them was Lydia, a seller of purple of the city of Thyatira, who believed the things spoken by Paul and was baptized with her household.

(2) *The conversion of the jailor* (Acts 16:16-40). As they were going to the place of prayer, they were met by a certain damsel who was possessed with a spirit of divination and who brought her masters much gain by soothsaying. Paul cast the evil spirit out of her, which so enraged her masters that they had him and Silas thrown into prison. But at midnight they prayed and sang praises, and the place was shaken with an earthquake and their bands were loosed. The keeper, at this, supposing that his prisoners had escaped, drew his sword and would have killed himself, but Paul cried: "Do thyself no harm: for we are all here." And, calling for a light, he sprang in where Paul and Silas were and, bringing them out, inquired: "Sirs, what must I do to be saved?" Paul replied: "Believe on the Lord Jesus Christ, and thou shalt be saved, and thy house." And, when he had spoken the word of the Lord to the jailor and his household, they washed his stripes and were baptized. On the morrow, when the

magistrates learned that Paul and Silas were Romans, they released them and urged them to depart from the city.

5. **The founding of the church at Thessalonica** (Acts 17:1-10). From Philippi, Paul and those who were with him came to Thessalonica, passing through Amphipolis and Apollonia. Here there was a synagogue of the Jews, and Paul, as was his custom, reasoned with them for three sabbath days, as a result of which some of them, with a multitude of devout Greeks and chief women, believed. But the Jews, who did not believe, incited a riot, and Paul and Silas were sent by the brethren to Berea.

6. **Paul and Silas at Berea** (Acts 17:10-14). Now the Bereans were more noble than the Thessalonians, and readily received the word and searched the Scriptures daily to discover whether the things taught by Paul were so. Therefore many, both Jews and Greeks, believed. But, when this came to the knowledge of the Jews at Thessalonica, they came down to Berea and stirred up the people, and Paul was immediately sent away by the brethren, though Silas and Timothy remained there still.

7. **Paul at Athens** (Acts 17:15-34). Paul now came to Athens, where his spirit was stirred when he saw the idolatry of the city. Therefore, he disputed with the Jews in their synagogues and with certain philosophers of the Epicureans and Stoics who brought him to Mars' hill, where they demanded that he give them further information concerning the doctrine of which he spoke. It was here that Paul preached his celebrated discourse on "THE UNKNOWN GOD," declaring that He had made of one

blood all nations and that He would eventually judge the world through Jesus Christ. When Paul spoke of the resurrection, some mocked, while others believed, among them Dionysius the Areopagite, and a woman named Damaris.

8. **Paul at Corinth.**

(1) *The founding of the Corinthian church* (Acts 18:1-11). At Corinth, to which city Paul came from Athens, the apostle found a Jew, Aquila, and his wife Priscilla, with whom he abode and followed with them the occupation of tentmaking. Here Silas and Timothy joined him, and here he reasoned in the synagogue every sabbath, persuading both Jew and Greek. Among these were Crispus, the chief ruler of the synagogue, and his house, who believed and were baptized.

(2) *The Jews' fruitless appeal to Gallio* (Acts 18:12-17). At this time Gallio was the deputy of Achaia, and the Jews brought Paul before him. But, when Gallio discovered that the charge pertained to their law, he drove them from the judgment-seat, and the Greeks took Sosthenes, the chief ruler of the synagogue, and beat him.

9. **Paul returns to Antioch** (Acts 18:18-23). After continuing in Corinth for one year and six months, Paul returned to Antioch through Ephesus and Cæsarea, bringing with him Aquila and Priscilla. At Cenchrea he shaved his head and made a vow.

IV. PAUL'S THIRD MISSIONARY JOURNEY

1. **The extent and purpose of Paul's third missionary journey** (Acts 18:23). After Paul had spent some time at Antioch, he departed again and went

over the countries of Galatia and Phrygia, strengthening the disciples.

2. **Apollos at Ephesus** (Acts 18:24-28). A certain Jew by the name of Apollos, born at Alexandria, who was eloquent and learned in the Scriptures, came to Ephesus, where he taught diligently the things of the Lord. But, as he knew only the baptism of John, he was taken by Aquila and Priscilla, who expounded to him the way of the Lord more perfectly. And when he left Ephesus to go into Achaia, the brethren gave him letters, exhorting the disciples to receive him, whom, when he had come, he helped much, for he mightily convinced the Jews that Jesus was the Christ.

3. **Paul at Ephesus.**

(1) *The conversion of certain of John's disciples* (Acts 19:1-7). While Apollos was at Corinth, Paul came to Ephesus and, finding certain disciples, inquired: "Have ye received the Holy Ghost since ye believed?" They replied: "We have not so much as heard whether there be any Holy Ghost." Then Paul said: "Unto what then were ye baptized?" And they said: "Unto John's baptism." To which Paul answered: "John verily baptized with the baptism of repentance, saying unto the people that they should believe on him which should come after him, that is, on Christ Jesus." When they heard this, they were baptized in the name of the Lord Jesus, and when Paul had laid his hands upon them, the Holy Ghost came on them, and they spoke with tongues and prophesied. In all, there were twelve men.

(2) *Paul disputes with certain opponents* (Acts 19: 8-10). For three months Paul preached in the syna-

gogue, but, meeting with opposition, he separated the disciples and disputed daily in the school of one Tyrannus. This continued for two years, so that all in Asia, both Jew and Greek, heard the word of the Lord.

(3) *Paul performs certain miracles* (Acts 19:11-22). At Ephesus Paul performed a number of miracles, because of which many believed. Certain vagabond Jews attempted to imitate these miracles through the name of Christ, but failed. At the close of his work here, Paul purposed that, after he had passed through Macedonia and Achaia and had returned to Jerusalem, he would visit Rome.

(4) *The Ephesian silversmiths oppose Paul* (Acts 19:23-41). The silversmiths of Ephesus, who made shrines for Diana and other divinities, became enraged at Paul because he had converted the people from their idolatry and so had cut down the sale of images, and, raising a riot, dragged Gaius and Aristarchus, two of Paul's companions, into the theater. Paul determined to go to their rescue, but was prevented by the disciples and certain friends. The tumult was finally quieted by the town clerk, who advised the people that, if they had a grievance against any man, to take the matter to law.

4. **Paul's return trip to Jerusalem.**

(1) *Paul goes through Macedonia and Greece* (Acts 20:1-3). After the tumult, Paul embraced the disciples and departed for Macedonia, later going into Greece, where he abode three months. At the expiration of this time, he purposed to sail for Syria, but, learning that the Jews were lying in wait for him, he determined to return through Macedonia.

THE LIFE OF PAUL

(2) *The stop at Troas* (Acts 20:4-12). After the days of unleavened bread, Paul and Luke sailed from Philippi, and in five days came to Troas, where they found Sopater, Aristarchus, Secundus, Gaius, Timotheus, Tychicus and Trophimus awaiting them. It was at Troas that the young man, Eutychus, falling asleep while Paul was preaching, fell from the third loft and was taken up dead, and Paul brought him back to life.

(3) *From Troas to Miletus* (Acts 20:13-16). From Troas Paul went by foot to Assos, where he met his companions who had come by sea. From Assos the company sailed to Mitylene, then to Chios, then to Samos, then came to Trogyllium and, finally, to Miletus.

(4) *Paul and the Ephesian elders* (Acts 20:17-38). From Miletus Paul sent to Ephesus and called to him the elders of the church, and, after recounting his experiences among them and charging them to take heed to the flock over which the Holy Ghost had made them overseers, he kneeled down and prayed with them all. And they all wept and fell on his neck and kissed him, sorrowing for the words which he spake and that they should see his face no more.

(5) *From Miletus to Tyre* (Acts 21:1-6). From Miletus Paul and his companions sailed to Coos, then to Rhodes, then to Patara, then to Cyprus and, finally, to Tyre in Phœnicia.

(6) *From Tyre to Cæsarea* (Acts 21:7-14). At Tyre Paul found certain disciples, with whom he tarried seven days and who declared through the Spirit that he should not go to Jerusalem. So, leav-

ing Tyre, he passed through Ptolemais and came to Cæsarea, where he entered the house of Philip the evangelist and abode with him. While he tarried with Philip, a certain prophet, Agabus by name, came down from Judea and declared that the Jews at Jerusalem would bind him and deliver him to the Gentiles. To which Paul replied: "I am ready not to be bound only, but also to die at Jerusalem for the name of the Lord Jesus."

(7) *From Cæsarea to Jerusalem* (Acts 21:14, 15). When Paul could not be deterred, the company made ready and went up to Jerusalem.

V. PAUL'S ARREST, IMPRISONMENTS AND DEATH

1. **Paul at Jerusalem** (Acts 21:16, 17). Paul was received of the brethren at Jerusalem with gladness, and lodged with Mnason, an old disciple of Cyprus.

2. **Paul takes a Jewish vow** (Acts 21:18-26). The day following, Paul went to see James, and, when he had recounted the things which God had done through him among the Gentiles, James and those who were with him glorified God. But, as the Jews had reported that he had taught the Jewish converts to forsake the law of Moses, they urged him, with four others who were of that purpose, to purify himself, shave his head, take a Jewish vow and offer a sacrifice.

3. **The arrest of Paul** (Acts 21:27-34). When the seven days of his vow were almost ended, the Jews from Asia, seeing Paul in the Temple, raised a tumult, charging that he taught the people against the law and that he had polluted the Temple by

bringing Greeks into it. And, drawing him out, they beat him and delivered him to the chief captain, who bound him with two chains and ordered that he be carried into the castle.

4. **Paul defends himself before the people** (Acts 21:35-22:29). When they came to the castle stairs, Paul demanded that he be permitted to speak to the people, which was granted. So, in the Hebrew tongue, he addressed the multitude, declaring the facts of his high birth, his persecution of the church, his conversion and his commission to preach the gospel. But, when the people heard him, they cried out against him, and the chief captain commanded that he be brought into the castle. As they were binding him with thongs, Paul inquired: "Is it lawful for you to scourge a man that is a Roman, and uncondemned?" When the chief captain learned that Paul was a Roman citizen, he feared greatly.

5. **Paul is brought before the Sanhedrin** (Acts 22:30-23:10). On the morrow the chief captain called the chief priests and the council together and brought Paul before them. But, when he attempted to speak in his own defense, Ananias, the high priest, commanded those who stood near to smite him in the mouth, at which Paul said: "God shall smite thee, thou whited wall: for sittest thou to judge me after the law, and commandest me to be smitten contrary to the law?" But, when he was told that it was the high priest, he apologized, saying: "I wist not, brethren, that he was the high priest: for it is written, Thou shalt not speak evil of the ruler of thy people." When Paul spoke of the resurrection, there was a division in the council, the Pharisees

supporting Paul and the Sadducees opposing him. The contention became so strong that, for fear of violence to Paul, it became necessary for the chief captain to take him by force from among them and bring him into the castle.

6. **Paul imprisoned in the castle** (Acts 23:11-22). The night following, the Lord stood by Paul and said: "Be of good cheer, Paul: for as thou hast testified of me in Jerusalem, so must thou bear witness also at Rome." When it was day, certain Jews to the number of forty banded themselves together and took an oath that they would neither eat nor drink until they had killed Paul. This plot was revealed to Paul and the chief captain by Paul's sister's son.

7. **Paul sent to Cæsarea.**

(1) *The journey to Cæsarea* (Acts 23:23-35). After the discovery of the plot to kill Paul, the chief captain called two centurions and commanded them to take two hundred soldiers, seventy horsemen and two hundred spearmen, and depart with Paul at the third hour of the night to Felix, the governor, at Cæsarea. With this company the chief captain also sent a letter explaining to Felix the trouble that Paul had had with the Jews. Then the soldiers took Paul by night to Antipatris and, on the morrow, returned to the castle, leaving him to continue his journey with the horsemen. Upon arriving at Cæsarea, Paul was confined in Herod's judgment-hall.

(2) *Paul before Felix* (Acts 24:1-26). After five days Ananias, the high priest, with the Jewish elders and a certain orator named Tertullus, came down from Jerusalem to appear against Paul. Tertullus

THE LIFE OF PAUL

began by flattering Felix and ended by declaring that Paul was a pestilent fellow, a mover of sedition among the Jews, a ringleader of the sect of the Nazarenes and a profaner of the Temple. At the conclusion of Tertullus' address, the governor beckoned Paul and he replied in his own behalf, denying the charges made against him, declaring his belief in a resurrection both of the just and the unjust, and explaining his conduct in the Temple at the time of his arrest. When Felix heard Paul's defense, he deferred his decision until he could hear the statement of Lysias, the chief captain, and, giving Paul into the hands of the centurion, he commanded that he should have his liberty. After certain days, Felix and his wife Drusilla, who was a Jewess, called for Paul, but when he reasoned of righteousness, temperance and judgment to come, Felix trembled.

(3) *The silent two years at Cæsarea* (Acts 24:27). For two years Paul remained at Cæsarea, at the expiration of which time Porcius Festus succeeded Felix as governor.

(4) *Paul before Festus* (Acts 25:1-12). When Festus became governor, he went from Cæsarea to Jerusalem, where the Jews desired that he should send Paul. But Festus refused to do this, and, upon his return to Cæsarea, commanded that Paul should be brought before him. As Paul stood in his presence, the Jews made many untruthful complaints against him and, when he had answered these, Festus, willing to do the Jews a favor, asked: "Wilt thou go up to Jerusalem, and there be judged of these things before me?" To which Paul replied: "I appeal

unto Cæsar." Then said Festus: "Unto Cæsar shalt thou go."

(5) *Paul before Agrippa* (Acts 25:13-26:32). After certain days, Agrippa the king, with his wife Bernice, came to Cæsarea to visit Festus. And, when Festus had explained to Agrippa the case of Paul, the king desired to hear him, and on the morrow, at Festus' command, Paul was brought forth. Then Agrippa said: "Thou art permitted to speak for thyself." And Paul, stretching forth his hand, expressed his satisfaction at being permitted to make his defense before the king, and declared the facts of his birth, persecution of the church, conversion and ministry. At which Festus cried: "Paul, thou art beside thyself; much learning doth make thee mad." But Paul replied: "I am not mad, most noble Festus; but speak forth the words of truth and soberness." After Paul had made his defense, those who heard declared that he had done nothing worthy of death or bonds and that he might have been set at liberty had he not appealed to Cæsar.

8. **Paul sent to Rome.**

(1) *The voyage and shipwreck* (Acts 27:1-44). When it was determined that Paul should be sent to Rome, he was delivered to a centurion of Augustus' band, named Julius. Accompanied by Aristarchus and Luke, they set sail. When they came near to Crete, a great storm arose and the ship was wrecked, the ship's company saving themselves by swimming or on boards and broken pieces of the ship. The soldiers would have killed the prisoners to prevent them escaping, but the centurion, willing to save Paul, kept them from their purpose. During

the storm Paul encouraged the company, and declared that not one life should be lost, which proved true, for the entire number was saved.

(2) *Paul bitten by a viper on Melita* (Acts 28: 1-6). The land to which the company escaped was the island of Melita. As it was intensely cold and rainy, the barbarous inhabitants of the island kindled a fire for the comfort of the company. As Paul took up a bundle of sticks, a viper fastened itself upon his hand. Seeing this, the barbarians exclaimed: "No doubt this man is a murderer, whom, though he hath escaped the sea, yet vengeance suffereth not to live." But, when they saw no harm come to him, they changed their minds and declared that he was a god.

(3) *Paul performs a number of miracles on Melita* (Acts 28: 7-10). Among the miracles performed by Paul upon the island of Melita was the healing of the father of Publius, the chief man of the island, who was afflicted with bloody flux. Many others, also, were healed of their diseases.

(4) *The completion of the journey* (Acts 28: 11-15). After spending three months upon the island of Melita, Paul and his companions departed in a ship of Alexandria for Syracuse, where they tarried three days. From Syracuse they sailed to Rhegium, and from thence to Puteoli, from which place, after seven days, they came to Rome.

9. **The career of Paul at Rome.**

(1) *Paul's first Roman imprisonment* (Acts 28: 16-31). When Paul and his companions came to Rome, he was delivered by the centurion to the captain of the guard and was permitted to live by himself with

a soldier. For two whole years, in his own hired house, he received all who came to him, and preached the kingdom of God and the things concerning Jesus Christ to all, both Jew and Gentile, no one forbidding him.

(2) *Paul's second Roman imprisonment and death.* It has been much disputed whether Paul endured two distinct imprisonments at Rome between A. D. 61 and 68, or only one. The tradition from Clement and Eusebius favors two, with a year or more of liberty between. But, howsoever this may be, it is the unanimous testimony of tradition that he eventually sealed his testimony with his blood and that he was beheaded at Rome in the year 68 A. D.

QUESTIONS

Give the population and extent of the Roman Empire in the time of Augustus Cæsar. Name the emperors who reigned after Augustus and until A. D. 70. What was the character of the heathen religions with which Paul came in contact? How many great gods were worshiped in Greece and Rome? Why did Rome oppose Christianity? Give the conditions conducive to the spread of the gospel. Name Paul's companions on his first missionary tour. On his second. On his third. At Rome. Give the probable date of Paul's conversion. Of his first missionary tour. Of his second. Of his third. Of his imprisonment at Cæsarea. Of his first imprisonment at Rome. Of his second imprisonment at Rome. Where was Paul born and where was he raised? What was he politically? What was he religiously? What event marks the beginning of Paul's persecution of the church? Tell about Paul's conversion. Give an account of the movements of Paul from his conversion to his first missionary tour. Where did Paul and Barnabas start from on their first missionary tour? What opposition did they meet at Paphos? How were Paul and Barnabas received by the Jews at Antioch of Pisidia? Tell about the healing of the impotent man at Lystra and the effect it had upon

THE LIFE OF PAUL

the people. To what city did Paul and Barnabas finally return? Describe the council at Jerusalem. Why did Paul and Barnabas part company? Whom did Paul select as his companion in the place of Barnabas on his second missionary tour? Who joined Paul and Silas at Lystra, and what can you say of him? Describe the vision that Paul had at Troas. Give two events that occurred at Philippi. Tell about the founding of the church at Thessalonica. What was the difference between the Jews of Berea and those of Thessalonica? Tell about Paul's visit to Athens. Give two events that happened at Corinth. Where did Paul go at the close of his second missionary tour and whom did he take with him? Give the extent and purpose of Paul's third missionary tour. Who, at this time, preached the Word at Ephesus? Give the things that occurred at Ephesus under Paul's ministrations. Give the points touched by Paul on his return from his third missionary tour. How did the Jews at Jerusalem feel toward Paul? Did Paul know that they hated him? With whom did Paul lodge at Jerusalem? Tell about Paul's visit to James, and tell what James advised him to do. Why did James advise this? Upon what charge was Paul arrested at Jerusalem? Where was Paul taken immediately after his arrest? Give his defense before the people. What caused the chief captain to fear Paul? Before what council was Paul first brought and what happened there? What plot was laid against Paul's life and who revealed it? When the plot was discovered, where was Paul sent? Who accompanied him? To whom was Paul sent at Cæsarea? What office did Felix hold? Tell about Paul's trial before Felix. How many years was Paul in Cæsarea? Who succeeded Felix as governor? Tell about Paul's appearance before Festus. What position did Agrippa fill? Tell about Paul's appearance before Agrippa. Where was Paul sent from Cæsarea, and why? Where was he shipwrecked? What happened to him on Melita? What miracles did he perform on Melita? Give the points touched in the completion of the journey. How many imprisonments is Paul supposed to have suffered at Rome? How was he treated at Rome? How does tradition say he died?

STUDY XL. THE NEW TESTAMENT WRITINGS

INTRODUCTION

1. **The New Testament.** This title is applied to that collection of sacred and inspired books which were written by the apostles or their associates after the ascension of our Lord and within the first century of the Christian era.

2. **The canon of the New Testament.** By the term "canon" we mean a rule of faith and practice. The twenty-seven books of the New Testament are accepted as such by all Catholics and the majority of Protestants. Some, however, would reduce the number of New Testament books by rejecting such as Hebrews, James,[1] 2 Peter and Revelation, the genuineness of which they either question or deny.

3. **The text of the New Testament.** The text of the New Testament comes down to us in no less than 2,080 manuscripts, of which eighty-three are *uncials* and 1,997 are *cursives*.[2] The uncial manuscripts are those which were written in capitals and which date from the fourth to the tenth century; the cursive manuscripts are those which were written in a running hand and which date from the tenth century to the invention of printing from movable

---
[1] Martin Luther called the Epistle of James an "epistle of straw."
[2] For a good description of these manuscripts, see "The Text and Canon of the New Testament," by McGarvey.

THE NEW TESTAMENT WRITINGS

type about the middle of the fifteenth. Among these different manuscripts there exist thousands of different readings which have perplexed the casual and uninformed student, but to those who have given their close attention to this matter, these discrepancies possess but little force. Prof. J. W. McGarvey says:

> The various readings consist mainly in differences of Greek orthography; in the form of words not affecting the essential meaning; in the insertion or omission of words not essential to the sense; in the use of one synonym for another; and in the transposition of words whose order in the sentence is immaterial. It is obvious that such variations, however numerous, leave the text uncorrupted as regards its thoughts. An essay might be written in English, with almost every word misspelt and every sentence ungrammatical, which would still express its meaning as clearly as the most accurate and elegant composition. The writings of "Josh Billings" are as clear as those of Addison. It is only, then, in the one-thousandth part of the New Testament, or the part in which the variations affect the meaning, that the text has undergone corruption worthy of any serious inquiry.—*The Text and the Canon of the New Testament*, p. 14.

On the same point Dr. Philip Schaff says:

> This multitude of various readings of the Greek text need not puzzle or alarm any Christian. It is the natural result of the great wealth of our documentary resources; it is a testimony to the immense impotrance of the New Testament; it does not affect, but it rather insures, the integrity of the text; and it is a useful stimulus to study.
>
> Only about 400 of the 100,000 or 150,000 variations materially affect the sense. Of these, again, not more than about fifty are really important for some reason or other; and even of these fifty not one affects an article of faith or a precept of duty which is not abundantly sustained by other and undoubted passages, or by the whole tenor of Scripture teaching. The *Textus Receptus* of Stephens, Beza and Elzevir, and of our English version, teach

THE GIST OF THE BIBLE

precisely the same Christianity as the uncial text of the Sinaitic and Vatican manuscripts, the oldest versions, and the Anglo-American Revision.—*Companion to the New Testament,* p. 177.

4. **The textual critics.** Those who have sought to restore the orginal text to its uncorrupted form are known as textual, or lower, critics in distinction to the so-called higher critics. Among them may be mentioned such scholars as Richard Bentley, J. A. Bengel, J. J. Wetstein, J. J. Griesbach, Charles Lachman, Constantine Tischendorf, S. P. Tregelles, B. F. Westcott and F. J. A. Hort.

5. **The writers of the New Testament.** The writers of the books of the New Testament were mostly unlearned men, and as such were wholly incapable of producing such a work independent of divine help. In number there were eight, named as follows: Matthew, John, Paul, James, Peter, Mark, Luke and Jude. Of these, the first five were apostles; the other three, companions of the apostles.

I. THE FOUR GOSPELS

1. **Matthew.** The author of this book was a Galilean Jew who had been a receiver of customs under the Roman Government. He is also called Levi (Mark 2:14), which was probably his original Hebrew name, while Matthew was his assumed Roman name. The date of this book has been much discussed, but there is little reason for discrediting the traditional date of 37 A. D. It is known certainly to have been written before the destruction of Jerusalem, for it contains an unfulfilled prophecy of that event (24:1-28). Whether or not it was originally written in Hebrew is a debated question. If it was,

THE NEW TESTAMENT WRITINGS

it is certain that it was translated into Greek during the first century.

2. **Mark.** Mark was the son of a pious woman in Jerusalem and the intimate friend of the apostle Peter (Acts 12:12; 1 Pet. 5:13). He was also the friend and companion of Paul until a misunderstanding between that apostle and Barnabas respecting him produced a separation (Acts 15:36-41). According to the earliest testimony, Mark wrote his Gospel at Rome, under the personal superintendence of the apostle Peter and for the instruction of Roman converts from paganism. The date of this Gospel has been variously fixed between A. D. 57 and 63. The uncontradicted testimony of antiquity is that the author spent the latter part of his life in Alexandria, Egypt, as an overseer of the churches there.

3. **Luke.** Luke was probably a Gentile by birth and was a physician by profession (Col. 4:11, 14). He was a citizen of Antioch and was familiar with Greek literature, as is evidenced by the structure of his Gospel and the Book of Acts. His Gospel was written sometime between A. D. 63 and 68. We find him mentioned in Acts as the companion of Paul, and it is said that, after the latter's death, he preached the gospel in Italy, Dalmatia, Macedonia and Bithynia until an advanced age, when he suffered martyrdom.

4. **John.** This Gospel was written by the beloved disciple, who was the son of Zebedee and Salome, probably people of some social distinction, and the brother of James. He was born in Bethsaida of Galilee, the home of Andrew and Peter, and was by occupation a fisherman. At first he was a

disciple of the Baptist, but he left him to follow Jesus, of whom he afterwards became an apostle. He was four or five years younger than the Lord. After the crucifixion he remained at Jerusalem until the death of Jesus' mother and the imprisonment of Paul, when he removed to Ephesus, about 65 A. D., and took charge of that important church. Later he was banished to the island called Patmos. His Gospel was written sometime between A. D. 85 and 90.

II. THE ACTS OF THE APOSTLES

The Acts of the Apostles was written by the evangelist Luke, and is to the apostles what the four Gospels are to the Lord. It covers the history of the church from the ascension of Jesus Christ to the first imprisonment of the apostle Paul, or from 30 to about 63 A. D. Probably written about A. D. 64, at Rome.

III. THE SPECIAL EPISTLES

The special Epistles were written by the apostle Paul and may be classified as follows:

1. The Epistles written during the second missionary journey, 51-54 A. D.—1 Thessalonians and 2 Thessalonians.

2. The Epistles written during the third missionary journey, 54-58 A. D.—1 Corinthians, 2 Corinthians, Galatians and Romans.

3. The Epistles written during the first imprisonment, 61-63 A. D.—Philippians, Colossians, Philemon and Ephesians.

4. The Epistles written during Paul's closing

THE NEW TESTAMENT WRITINGS

years, after 63 A. D.—1 Timothy, 2 Timothy and Titus.

Considered in their chronological order, the special Epistles are as follows:

1. **1 Thessalonians.** Thessalonica was the principal city of Macedonia and was visited by Paul and Silas during the second missionary journey. This first Epistle was written at Corinth, probably late in 52 A. D., and was for the purpose of comforting the Thessalonian Christians in trial and to encourage them to walk according to their profession and to take comfort in the hope of Christ's second coming and the resurrection of the dead.

2. **2 Thessalonians.** The second Epistle to the Thessalonians was also probably written at Corinth and early in the year 53 A. D. The Thessalonians seem to have imbibed the notion, probably from Paul's first Epistle, that the day of the Lord was near at hand and had neglected to labor. This Epistle was written to relieve their minds of this erroneous expectation and to inform them that a great apostasy must first come before the Son of man would appear in his glory.

3. **1 Corinthians.** This Epistle was written at Ephesus about 57 A. D. Having heard through the household of Chloe that there were in that church certain divisions and moral disorders, Paul wrote to overcome the spirit of schism and immorality that prevailed. In the fifteenth chapter he gives an extended account of the resurrection of the dead.

4. **2 Corinthians.** Paul wrote his second Epistle to the Corinthians probably at Philippi and early in 58 A. D. In it he expresses his joy that the

Corinthians had taken heed to the admonitions given in his first Epistle and defends his own calling and work.

5. **Galatians.** The Epistle to the Galatians was probably written at Corinth in 58 A. D. Its purpose was to preserve the fickle Galatians, who were not of Grecian, but of Gaulish, descent, from the teachings of the Judaizing missionaries from Palestine.

6. **Romans.** Paul's Epistle to the Romans was written at Corinth in A. D. 58. As he was about to visit the city of Rome, he announced beforehand the doctrines that he would personally deliver there. The theme of this Epistle is justification by faith and not by the deeds of law.

7. **Philippians.** The date of this Epistle was 62 A. D., and the place where it was written, Rome. Its theme is Christian experience, and in it Christ is brought before the Christian as his life, his pattern, his object and his strength.

8. **Colossians.** Colossians was written at Rome in 63 A. D. Like a number more of Paul's Epistles, it was written in defense of the true faith against the Judaizers.

9. **Philemon.** Written at the same time and in the same place as Colossians. Onesimus, a slave of Philemon, a Christian of Colosse, had robbed his master and had fled to Rome, where he had been converted to the Christian faith through Paul. The occasion of this Epistle was to urge Philemon to receive favorably his former slave again.

10. **Ephesians.** Written at the same time and place as Colossians and Philemon and sent to Ephesus by the same messenger that bore them. In it

Paul emphasizes the doctrine of the unity of the church, representing it as the body of Christ.

11. **1 Timothy.** This Epistle was probably written in Macedonia and shortly after Paul's release from his first imprisonment in 66 A. D. It contains certain admonitions to Timothy regarding his work as a minister of Jesus Christ.

12. **Titus.** Date and place the same as 1 Timothy. It contains a number of admonitions to Titus similar to those given to Timothy.

13. **2 Timothy.** This Epistle was written by Paul shortly before his martyrdom. In it he speaks of the coming apostasy and warns Timothy to continue in the things which he had learned and had been assured of.

IV. THE GENERAL EPISTLES

1. **Hebrews.** The author of this Epistle is unknown, though it is probably the production of Paul; at least, the point of view is Pauline. However, some have ascribed it to Barnabas and others to Silas or Apollos. The date is also unknown, except that it was written before the destruction of Jerusalem. This is inferred from chap. 10:11, and other circumstances. Its purpose was to show that the law was fulfilled in Christ.

2. **James.** The author of this Epistle was James "the just," one of the "pillars" of the church at Jerusalem (Gal. 2:9). He was extremely austere and legalistic. The date of this Epistle is unknown, but probably very early. Tradition says that James suffered martyrdom in 62 A. D.

3. **1 Peter.** This Epistle was probably written

in 60 A. D. Just where it was written is uncertain. If we understand "Babylon" of chap. 5:13 literally, it must have been written on the site of that city on the Euphrates; if we understand it figuratively, it may have been at Rome. Roman Catholics, almost universally, take the latter view. Special emphasis is laid in it on the atonement.

4. **2 Peter.** Probably written in 66 A. D. This Epistle has many things in common with 2 Timothy. As in the latter, Paul is anticipating his death, so, also, in this Peter is anticipating his. In this Epistle Christian virtue is extolled; the Scriptures are exalted; the church is warned against apostate teachers, and those addressed are taught to keep in memory the coming of the Lord and attending events.

5. **The Three Epistles of John.** They were all probably written in 90 A. D. They are the most intimate of the inspired writings.

6. **Jude.** Written by Jude, the brother of James, and about 66 A. D. The theme is earnestly contending for the true faith. The great apostasy is treated as having already commenced.

V. THE BOOK OF REVELATION

The author of this book was John, and the place, the island of Patmos. There is much dispute over the date, some ascribing it to the reign of Nero in 67 or 68, and others to 96 or 97, after the death of Domitian. The book abounds in symbols which have not been uniformly interpreted and applied. In reference to the Book of Revelation, there are three schools of interpretation: the præterist, the historical and the futurist. Those of the first find a fulfillment

THE NEW TESTAMENT WRITINGS

of most of the symbols within the first three or four centuries of the Christian era. Those of the historical school contend that these symbols stand for events and conditions that were to occur and arise during the whole period of time between the ascension of Christ and the final consummation, while the futurists contend that the book, excepting the first three chapters, is yet to be fulfilled. The Roman Catholics have largely held to the first view; the reformers, to the second, while the third has been strongly advocated by the English literalists and many American premillennialists.

QUESTIONS

Define the New Testament. What do we mean by the term "canon"? Give the names of the New Testament books that are rejected by some. Give the difference between an uncial and a cursive manuscript. How many manuscripts, in all, have we of the New Testament? What can you say of the different readings among these manuscripts? Give the substance of the passage from McGarvey. Give the substance of the passage from Schaff. What is the difference between a Textual Critic and a Higher Critic? Name some of the Lower Critics. How many New Testament writers have we? How many of them were apostles? Name them. Give an account of Matthew. Of Mark. Of Luke. Of John. Of Acts. Of 1 Thessalonians. Of 2 Thessalonians. Of 1 Corinthians. Of 2 Corinthians. Of Galatians. Of Romans. Of Philippians. Of Colossians. Of Philemon. Of Ephesians. Of 1 Timothy. Of Titus. Of 2 Timothy. Of Hebrews. Of James. Of 1 Peter. Of 2 Peter. Of the Epistles of John. Of Jude. Of Revelation. Classify the Epistles of the apostle Paul.

www.ingramcontent.com/pod-product-compliance
Lightning Source LLC
Chambersburg PA
CBHW071135300426
44113CB00009B/977